The Murder of Adolf Hitler

*The Truth about the Bodies
in the
Berlin Bunker*

The Murder
of Adolf Hitler

The Truth about the Bodies in the Berlin Bunker

Hugh Thomas

St. Martin's Press ☙ New York

Library of Congress Cataloging-in-Publication Data

Thomas, W. Hugh (Walter Hugh).
    The murder of Adolf Hitler : the truth about the bodies in the
Berlin bunker / by Hugh Thomas.
        p.   cm.
    ISBN 0-312-14018-5
    1. Hitler, Adolf, 1889–1945—Death and burial.   2. Braun,
Eva—Death and burial.   3. Heads of state—Germany—Biography.
4. Hitler, Adolf, 1889–1945—Friends and associates.   I. Title.
DD247.H5T498   1996
943.086'092—dc20   95-26160
                                                           CIP

First published in Great Britain by Fourth Estate

First U.S. Edition: April 1996
10   9   8   7   6   5   4   3   2   1

Contents

—

Hitler's Bunker in the Reich Chancellery

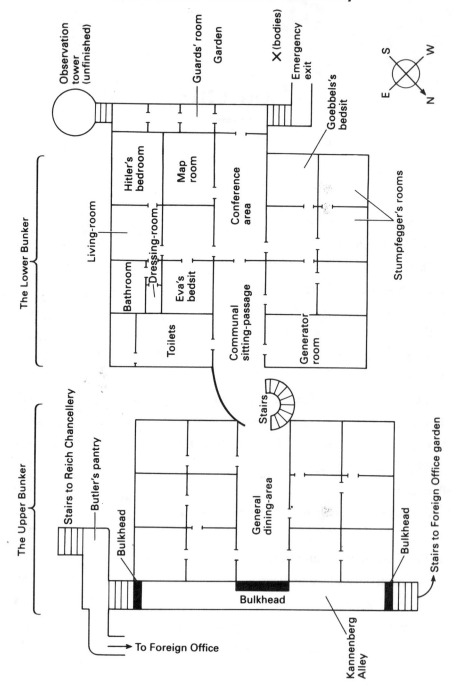

Acknowledgements

I must acknowledge the following: Käthe Heusermann, dental assistant to Adolf Hitler's dentist, Colonel John McCowan, the British intelligence officer who broke into the Bunker and the late Albert Speer, Hitler's armaments minister, for their time and cooperation.

An especial debt is due to Professor R. F. Sognnaes, whose diligent preparatory work clarified many issues and to the diverse opinions of several other forensic odontologists ably marshalled by Dr Lester Luntz.

I would like to thank Dr Mike Wysocki of Cardiff University Archaeology Department and Dr Tony Busuttil, Regius Professor of Forensic Medicine at the University of Edinburgh for the benefit of their particular expertise concerning the effects of combustion on the human skeleton.

Thanks are also due to Dr Sheila Dowling of Guy's Hospital Toxicology Laboratories and Dr Bernard Charnley of the University of Wales for their advice.

Nevertheless, I must emphasise that the forensic conclusions reached are entirely my own, for which I bear sole responsibility.

Central to the understanding of the key issues in this book has been the evaluation of the newly discovered La Técnica Archives in Asunción, Paraguay, and of the Russian State Archive material, comprising the six folios and skull fragments said to be those of Adolf Hitler and Eva Braun. Access to this material was far from straightforward. Especial thanks are due to those who assisted in obtaining the necessary documentation and its translation. Their quite understandable reluctance to be named makes this acknowledgement necessarily incomplete.

Further extraordinary assistance came from Ms Andrea Machain, formerly of BBC World Service Latin American Section and from Dr Andrew

Nickson of the University of Birmingham, as well as Mr Kripalov and his associates at *Isvestia*.

Lastly a word of thanks to my publishers, especially Clive Priddle for his encouragement and Bob Davenport for his excellent editing.

Hugh Thomas
October 1994

Introduction

The deaths of Adolf Hitler, his wife Eva Braun and his personal secretary Martin Bormann might seem like little more than a historical footnote. By the end of 1944 the outcome of the war in Europe was not in doubt: the German Army was evidently in disarray, having suffered huge losses as the Soviet Armies squeezed it from the east and the British and Americans from the south and west.

But throughout Hitler's period in office the cult of personality centred on the body and mind of the Führer had been assiduously cultivated, most particularly by Joseph Goebbels's propaganda ministry. A deliberate attempt had been made to create a new mythology, a new ideology to inspire and unite the German *Volk*. Even in the final days of the war the need to perpetuate the heroic image of Hitler and, by association, his entourage remained acute. Defeat may have been inevitable, but it had to be faced gloriously, so that future generations might admire the military dignity and fortitude of the father of the nation. He would be seen to have faced the final act of the drama as the complete soldier: a leader who bade a dignified farewell to his immediate staff before decisively and calmly ending his own life in order to deny the enemy the ultimate satisfaction of his capture. In himself he would *never* be defeated.

But this is the mythology talking: the truth was rather different.

The evidence produced in this book reveals a quite different scenario. The evidence is drawn from eyewitness testimonies, many here collated for the first time, and from forensic and other medical data, much of which is hitherto unpublished.

As the book deals with the subject of forensic fraud, it contains all the essential technical data necessary to establish identity, and to understand the exact nature of the methods used in its concealment.

The old adage 'the devil is in the detail' was never more applicable, for these crucial new facts completely destroy all our previous concepts of these 'deaths'. As a result, the story of what really happened in Hitler's Bunker in Berlin in April and May 1945 can now be ascertained for the very first time.

History at present records Hitler as having committed suicide by a totally unique method, which, even though derided by forensic scientists, has for half a century been accepted by historians almost without demur. The Führer allegedly bit a cyanide capsule and shot himself at one and the same time! But neither cyanide nor a bullet was the real cause of death of the corpse identified as 'Hitler'.

The new data, along with separate unpublished British and Soviet testimony about the Bunker, also allow a re-enactment of the events as they must have occurred in 1945, based this time not on the stories of witnesses concealing their part in the events but on fact. So that that data can be considered complete, Hitler's true medical and mental status, highly relevant to the final days, is discussed in full.

Was Hitler the supreme military commander abandoned by defeatist, craven generals in the last days of the war in Europe? Again the facts fly in the face of the myths: Hitler was isolated by mental and physical decrepitude. The Bunker in Berlin was equally defective: a poor communications centre, its telephone lines running through the central Berlin exchange, with inadequate water, sewerage, ventilation and power, it was an inexplicable choice as a last redoubt for an active military commander. It was, in effect, a squalid foxhole in which to hide a commander-in-chief who, in person, could have commanded neither the respect nor the obedience of his troops. That Adolf Hitler was neglected with deliberate hostility by his SS valet, and even, in the last few days, by the SS guards, runs counter to the mythology of a glorious Twilight of the Gods with which neo-Nazi ideology currently threatens historical truth.

Just as the image of the final citadel was deliberately falsified, so were the many legends of its escapees. The most celebrated of these was Martin Bormann, the announcement of whose death could scarcely have been more greatly exaggerated. Forensic science and detailed analysis of the testimonies of witnesses from a number of agencies, including the CIA and the security services of Argentina and Paraguay, enable a firm conclusion to be drawn about one of the abiding mysteries of the postwar period: did Bormann survive and, if so, how did he and where was he? The Bormann story, starting with his break-out from the Bunker in May

1945, is here seen to its certain end, the hitherto contradictory pieces now brought coherently together.

The nineteenth-century German historian Leopold von Ranke exhorted historians to search for facts and desist from opinions. As the twentieth century draws to a close, and as the fiftieth anniversary of the end of the Second World War approaches, it is a sad reflection that we have hitherto been supplied with a paucity of facts and an abundance of spurious rhetoric about events at the end of the war from historians too ready to defend existing accounts and too reluctant to hunt for truth among the blood and bones.

When there were no relevant facts to relate, von Ranke's contemporary the Prussian military strategist Count Helmuth von Moltke wisely claimed to be proficiently 'silent in seven languages'. Such men are exceptional.

The Murder of Adolf Hitler

*The Truth about the Bodies
in the
Berlin Bunker*

1

Hitler – the Myth
and the Man

The dramatic re-emergence of neo-Nazism and fascism in its European cradle has refocused attention on Adolf Hitler and the SS state.

Hitler has come to be endowed with an almost surreal aura. The perception of Hitler as an individual has become wreathed in the postwar guilt of a German intelligentsia still trying to come to terms with what happened during the Holocaust. Their tortured deliberations have created a more than suitable word for their agonising: *Vergangenheitsbewältigung* – 'overcoming the past'. As a direct consequence, Hitler's image has been distorted, his magnetic qualities being magnified out of all proportion to help diminish the intellectuals' own culpability and expunge their guilt.

Even seemingly sane, eminent historians engaged in rationalising the subject of Hitler – a subject they very obviously find heinous – nevertheless engage in eulogy over what they see as the extraordinary clarity of his vision, in terms such as 'Oh what a mind'.[1]

Others join in a chorus of apologia which presents Hitler as mainly the victim of circumstances – a man born before his time, whose ideas were unfortunately distorted by his overzealous followers; a man struck down by a strange, indefinable illness, his physical and mental functions grossly impaired, poisoned by his doctors. They imply by default that, had Hitler not been so afflicted – or misunderstood – his true genius would have led to an altogether different outcome for Europe and the world, not to the saga of the Bunker.

It is possible to strip away the milieu from the man. The first and most obvious extension of Hitler's persona was his audience, the German people, the mores and attitudes of whom he managed to influence so disastrously. These attitudes were the product of both circumstances and geography.

1

The term *Reich* means empire. It was a word deliberately chosen at the founding of the German state in 1871 at Versailles. Even then there was an ominous uncertainty about the borders of this Reich.

In August 1841 on the small island of Heligoland, Hoffman von Fallersleben wrote what was to become the basis of the German national anthem:

> *From the Maas to the Memel,*
> *From the Etsch to the Belt,*
> Deutschland über alles.

The Maas is in Holland, and the Memel (Nemunas) in Lithuania. The Etsch is in the Italian South Tyrol. Only the Belt lies in present-day German territory, in Schleswig-Holstein.

Von Fallersleben, writing at a time when Germany was split into thirty-nine states, was in fact describing the geography of the Germanic races. There were ethnic Germans in Russia, Poland, along the Baltic, and down through Czechoslovakia and Hungary and even in Romania and Croatia. Little wonder that the word *Heimat*, or homeland, had such an emotive appeal. Awareness of their own origins was kindled in the thirteenth century with the development of the German language. The song '*Ich habe lande vil gesehen*' – 'I have seen many lands' – by Walther von der Vogelweide (*c.* 1170–1230) exemplified the spread of national awareness.

Along with the development of the language came the growth of Germanic legends such as the *Nibelungenlied*, the work of an anonymous thirteenth-century cleric. Mythology became part of the soul. The word *Volk* – meaning people, nation or race – evoked the very origins of the Germanic races and culture and became coated with a similar mysticism. After it had been hijacked by Hitler, postwar Germans became so sensitive to the word that it became widely replaced by *Gesellschaft* (society).

So Hitler was born into a society whose people were unusually readily roused by emotional references to their *Volksgeist* – their Germanic soul. Hitler was not the first to appeal to their sense of a lost empire that never was: many before him had espoused the same ever-popular sentiments. After the defeat of the Prussians at Jena in 1806, the Berlin academic Johann Gottlieb Fichte used to transfix his audiences with his orations on their divine duty towards the Germanic peoples.

This is not to say that other great civilisations did not suffer their own similar maladies – reflection on the embarrassing words of 'Rule Britannia' should make that clear – but, instead of subjugate masses in far-flung lands, the Germans had seams of Germanic culture running through a phantom empire across an all too contiguous Europe. Tardy in achieving nationhood, their nationalism relatively untried, their temptation to dream and their temptation to act were both latent and potent.

Bismarck's creation of a German nation-state capable of competing with its neighbours had been achieved without sacrificing or even limiting the previous aristocratic/monarchical order. He paid only lip-service to democracy, and the result was a state with a fatal flaw – the incapacity to deal with populist movements such as fascism when they did occur; a state, moreover, replete with advancement by sycophancy.[2]

A state tailor-made to be run by Bismarck would also suit the needs of anyone successful in seizing the trappings of power. Once Hitler had gained power, the state was virtually tailor-made for Nazism: very few alterations were required.

The flaw in the state and the flaw in the character of the German proletariat of the time were aggravated by an additional factor – the purposeful orchestration of the phenomenon of mass hysteria by the man who made the phenomenon of Hitler available to the people, the man who marketed Hitler: Joseph Goebbels.

In its wilder forms, mass hysteria falls into the category of 'collective psychoses', phenomena that have plagued European culture for centuries, merging human excesses with the very mythology that sometimes encouraged the excesses themselves.

In 1832, the psychiatrist J. C. F. Hecker was one of the first to pinpoint the effect that the shared mass psychology of a huge crowd can have on the crowd's individual members, who become capable in such circumstances of behaving totally differently to how they would do normally.[3] Part of the phenomenon is the need to feel superior, the need to belong to something quite exceptional, the need for exclusivity. Even the Nazis, with their ideas of Aryan supremacy, fell far short of the exclusivity of previous times, as evidenced by the ritualistic behaviour of the Palmatites of the Middle Ages, who used to touch their umbilicuses with their heads to see the glory of the divinity (a physical contortion whose necessary achievement severely restricted membership). When Goebbels sold Hitler to a frenzied audience at torchlit rallies, the SS silver flashes, the sound of jackboots in unison and the orchestrated chants all became part of Hitler's mystique.

Hitler's rise as an actor was in no small part due to the siting of the stage. But in dealing with his demise we are dealing with the actor not the stage, the man and not the myth.

3

Fortunately it is possible to come to some very specific conclusions about Hitler's physical and mental status which not only provide the necessary context for his final actions in the Bunker but also help to dispel the clouds of nostalgia for the 'good times' that his myth is supposed to represent.

Hitler's Physical State

There is very little doubt that in the 1940s Hitler was suffering from a type of Parkinson's disease, even though his symptoms were not entirely characteristic of the main variety of this disease. From around late 1942 his degeneration was quite rapid; most cases, mercifully, take far longer to progress.

Parkinson's disease is a common disease of the nervous system. Under the names 'shaking palsy' and 'paralysis agitans', it was first described in 1817 by the English surgeon James Parkinson, who gave the following definition:

> Involuntary tremulous motion, with lessened muscular power in parts not in action and even when supported; with a propensity to bend the trunk forward, and to pass from a walking into a running pace, the senses and intellect being unimpaired.

We now know considerably more than Parkinson himself, and the more we know the greater is the awareness of the complexity of the disease. For example, we now know that about a third of severe cases eventually exhibit a dementia of insidious origin, and about a half suffer from depression. We also know that many other conditions can mimic Parkinson's disease, although in its fully developed form Parkinson's disease cannot be mistaken for any other – the stooped posture, the stiffness and slowness of movement, the fixity of facial expression, and the rhythmic tremor of the limbs which subsides on active voluntary movement or complete relaxation are quite characteristic. Even though the face becomes staring and immobile, there are often discernible tremors in the eyelids when closed. The voice often becomes monotonous very early on in the disease, and noticeably weaker. There is also a most noticeable absence of the little spontaneous movements of postural adjustment that are so characteristic of a normal individual and which give the individual his outward 'character'. Lacking this essential body language the patient becomes zombie-like. There is no paralysis – even though that is implied by the original name – but the weakness, stiffness and slowness may effectively simulate such a condition, rendering the patient helpless and in need of constant attention.

Characteristically the disease starts in middle or late life, and at first it affects one side more than the other. The patient often learns to mask tremors by such tricks as putting his hands in his pockets. Patients differ greatly in the degree of rigidity in the trunk and spine (so-called axial rigidity), as opposed to the limbs, and in the degree of trembling.

We cannot examine Hitler in the same way as we can examine living patients, but we can assess the evidence of many newsreels and photographs. We also have the testimony both of his physicians and of those who knew him well and, though not medically trained, recorded their shock at his physical degeneration.

Towards the end of the war, German newsreels showing Hitler were allowed to be shot only from certain angles and were severely limited in their scope. Both he and Goebbels were only too aware of how evidence of the Führer's growing incapacity would damage the Hitler myth. There is an especial paucity of newsreel coverage of the final weeks of his existence in the Berlin Bunker. Nevertheless, the axial rigidity, the stooping, the difficulty in walking, the slowness, the problems with co-ordination, the staring mask of a face, the fixed peering eyes, the hand fixed in his pocket are obvious, and all tell their neurological tale – even though Hitler had been physically cleaned up and psyched up for the camera.[4] In fact he must have been markedly worse in his everyday Bunker existence, for it is a well-known aspect of the disease that patients when upset emotionally or very excited can suddenly perform complex movements far more efficiently and quickly than usual, surprising their carers or companions.

The testimony of non-medical witnesses is so exact and comprehensive that it almost betters that of Hitler's doctors. The historian Joachim Fest quotes an elderly staff officer, long acquainted with Hitler, who recorded these impressions during the Führer's last few weeks:

Physically he presented a dreadful sight, he dragged himself about painfully and clumsily – throwing his torso forward and dragging his legs after him from his living-room to the conference room of the Bunker. He had lost his sense of balance – if he were detained on the brief journey (75–100 ft), he had to sit down on one of the benches that had been placed along either wall for this purpose, or

5

else cling to the person he was talking to. His eyes were bloodshot and, although all the documents intended for him were typed out in letters three times ordinary size on special 'Führer typewriters', he could only read them with the aid of a magnifying glass. Saliva frequently dripped from the corners of his mouth.[5]

Hitler's secretaries reported that in 1944–5:

Whenever Hitler took his glasses into his left hand during the daily report, they clinked against the desk top as his hand shook. His lips were dry and covered in crumbs, his clothing stained with food.[6]

The Gestapo official Werner Best, visiting Hitler at the Wolf's Lair in July 1944, found him 'stooping so low he seemed to bow'.[7] By 28 December 1944, as noted by General Johannes Blaskowitz, Hitler's left shoulder was markedly drooping, and his left hand was swollen with disuse. Yet under moments of acute stress Hitler could still use this hand, as is evidenced by the photograph showing Hitler shaking Mussolini with his left hand, just after the explosion of the July 1944 bomb plot had temporarily damaged his right hand. Not that it needed damaging much, for in functional terms this was also suspect: his signature became so unreadable that from December 1944 a civil servant was called upon to forge it.[8]

The armaments minister Albert Speer recalled that on one occasion he saw Hitler trying to draw on a wall map. His pencil started what was obviously intended to be a straight line and ended up precipitously on the lower right-hand margin. Speer's description fits exactly the tendency of people with Parkinson's to overshoot in such a fashion.[9]

It was his opinion that Hitler was quite incapable of signing anything – a fact that worried Speer inordinately at the time, as he suspected that the Hitler signature had become nothing but a front to cover the machinations of Martin Bormann, the head of the Party Chancery and Hitler's personal secretary.

Luftwaffe general Albert Zoller stated that 'Hitler used to stand up with difficulty, with shaking legs and quivering hand',[10] and Admiral Heinz Assmann noticed that 'Hitler's handclasp was weak and soft – all his movements were those of a senile man.'[11]

Fest cites several testimonies that by early 1945 the Führer was exhibiting weakening memory and showed an inability to concentrate, mainly lying in a seeming torpor of exhaustion as witnessed by several of his secretaries.[12] Nevertheless, witness after witness stressed that they thought that Hitler was not insane as such – though if they had come to that conclusion at the time then they surely should have asked themselves why they allowed themselves to be led by someone whose sanity was even in question.

Several witnesses recalled that Hitler used to lean his left leg against a table to prevent it shaking, and that he used to grasp his shaking left arm with his right hand, keeping it close to his body.

Significantly, in view of later events, even by March 1944 the testimonies described Hitler's having to be guided into a sitting position at his desk, having great difficulty in sitting on the couch in his room, and having to have his feet lifted up on to the couch whenever he wanted to lie down. His left leg shook uncontrollably when fully recumbent. Speer recalled that the benches that were placed around the Bunker were built at Hitler's mid-thigh level, because Hitler's valet, Heinz Linge, complained about the strain of having to lift Hitler's dead weight upwards to his feet from a lower position.[13]

Speer regarded it as Linge's responsibility to see that Hitler's clothes were free from food stains and soiling – which they most evidently were not – and he recalled his anger that 'Of all Hitler's devoted servants Linge was the one who should have been most proud to do the most, and did the least. The Führer's condition was disgraceful, and no one gave a damn.'[14]

Captain Peter Hartmann was a young guard who had been involved in Hitler's security for long enough to have a very good knowledge of the Führer's habits and appearance. Even though a lay opinion, his comments are pertinent, though the ageing process that he observed may have been due either to rapidly progressive Parkinsonism or to premature ageing itself:

We all knew the man was only fifty-five, and those of us who had known him in the earlier years before the war, when he was a human dynamo often bursting with restless energy, noted, from about 1942 on, that he seemed to be ageing at least five full years for every calendar year. Near the very end, on the day he celebrated his last birthday [20 April 1945], he seemed closer to seventy than fifty-six. He looked what I would call physically *senile*. The man was living on nerves, dubious medicaments, and driving will power.[15]

If Hitler's physical deterioration was apparent to his followers, it was staggeringly obvious to his physicians.

Professor Werner Haase, a tall, ill-looking, thin, silver-haired figure, was a surgeon who had been the Reich Chancellery private physician in 1933, and by virtue of his seniority he had been called in to help look after Hitler in the last few weeks in the Bunker. Haase was appalled at Hitler's condition, but we only have his diagnosis second-hand, through the testimony of Professor Ernst-Günther Schenk, who had an operating theatre in the cellar of the Reich Chancellery, next to the Bunker. Haase apparently diagnosed Parkinson's disease – a diagnosis with which Schenk apparently fully agreed, even though he had only seen Hitler properly on 30 April 1945, when, standing a metre away from his Führer, he regarded the pathetic patient in front of him with a clinician's eye:

I knew of course that this was Adolf Hitler and no *Doppelgänger*. Hatless, he was still wearing the familiar, once spotless pearl grey tunic with green shirt and black trousers, the simple uniform he had donned on the first day of the war. He wore his golden party badge and his World War One Iron Cross on his left breast pocket. But the human being buried in these sloppy, food-stained clothes had completely withdrawn into himself. I was still standing erect, on a kind of concrete step above him. As I glanced down, I could see Hitler's hunched spine, the curved shoulders that seemed to twitch and tremble. Somehow his head seemed withdrawn into his shoulders, turtlelike. He struck me as an agonised Atlas with a mountain on his back. All of these thoughts must have raced through my mind in thirty seconds or so, not more. The pause came because Hitler seemed hardly able to shuffle the two paces forward to greet us.

His eyes, although he was looking directly at me, did not seem to be focusing. They were like wet pale-blue porcelain, glazed, actually more grey than blue. They were filmy, like the skin of a soft ripe grape. The whites were bloodshot. I could detect no expression on his vapid, immobile face. Drooping black sacks under his eyes betrayed loss of sleep, although Hitler was not the only one suffering from this Bunker malaise.

Today [in the 1970s] I can see him there still, although the whole scene lasted only about four, maybe five, minutes. Deep folded lines ran down his rather large pulpy nose to the corners of his mouth. His mouth was set firmly, his lips nervously pressing each other. The cold-fish, flapping gesture with which he shook my hand was listless. It was really only a jerky reflex, although it was meant to be amiable enough. As he mumbled his thanks, perfunctorily, I was at a loss to make any coherent reply. He then apologised for having summoned us at such a late hour. I must have uttered something trivial, probably '*Dankeschön, mein Führer*.'

I was profoundly shocked, and reacted, I suppose, as any doctor would have, not without sympathy. And yet it was far too late, in more ways than one, for any mortal doctor. At fifty-six the Führer was a palsied, physical wreck, his face puckered now like a mask, all yellow and grey. The man, I am sure, was senile.[16]

Perhaps Schenk's most cogent remark about this episode was: 'Now I knew that there could never be a Saint Helena for Adolf Hitler . . . This ruined hulk of a man had, at the very most, one, two, maybe three years to live. He must have sensed this, as the mortally stricken often do.'[17]

From the evidence available, it is clear that Hitler's physical degeneration had been very noticeable in the last two years of the war. His pathetic physical condition was inescapably evident; his difficulty in communicating was profound. The overall impression must have been as mind-numbing as Schenk described. Yet, although totally and obviously incapable, Hitler remained in power – but in an isolation absolutely essential if his condition was not to be realised.

There were, however, those such as Göring and Himmler who not only joked about Hitler's incapacity but, as in the case of Himmler, actively sought advantage from the Führer's ill health.

Quack Medicine

Himmler had, very early on, asked his own physicians, Dr Karl Brandt and Professor Karl Gebhardt, about the true nature of Hitler's disease. Hitler clearly had an obsession with syphilis – almost an entire chapter of *Mein Kampf* is devoted to the subject – and when, in the early 1930s, he began to be seen by Dr Theodor Morell, a so-called venereal specialist, whose Kurfürstendamm office walls were covered not with diplomas or qualifications but with the signed photographs of his clients – film actors and others who had benefited from his treatment – Himmler became more than interested.

His first enquiries revealed that Hitler's mother had had two stillbirths, suggestive to a medical mind that there might be a question of congenital syphilis. Such syphilis sometimes leaves physical stigmata, though none were observable in Hitler – not that that satisfied Himmler's curiosity. When Hitler began to show evidence of a neurological disorder – stiffness in walking and getting up; shaking – Himmler's interest was rekindled, and he now made enquiries about Hitler's early life as a vagrant in Vienna, where his none too exemplary behaviour might have exposed him to the risk of catching syphilis through liaisons with prostitutes etc. Himmler's investigators also managed to get at the results of Dr Morell's 1936 blood tests on Hitler, especially the serological tests for previous syphilitic infection. These blood tests were now to become the basis for all subsequent rumour and intrigue.

Congenital syphilis may give rise to disease in the adult life of a person who has inherited it, but the resulting symptoms are characteristic and readily recognisable. There is no evidence that Hitler exhibited such symptoms. Active syphilis, acquired directly by sexual intercourse, was, however, a very real concern for all Hitler's physicians and had to be ruled out as far as possible in reaching a diagnosis of the Führer's illness.

Before the advent of the sulphonamide antibacterial drugs – in the 1930s and 1940s – and the antibiotic era, such active syphilis ran its course, sometimes ameliorated by treatment with antimony compounds and the like, but more often than not subsiding to leave scarring on the genitalia and a terrible legacy – the much later onset of what was termed 'general paralysis of the insane'. If Hitler had caught active (non-congenital) syphilis in his youth and early adulthood in Vienna, then some twenty years later – around the early 1930s – he qualified to become a victim of the late symptoms of the disease.

Nowadays, very few people, including physicians and neurologists, have any idea of the diversity of neurological syndromes that can be exhibited when syphilis affects the nervous system. However, there remain many excellent descriptions of the resulting diagnostic chaos, in particular the testimony of old physicians of note who had treated such cases. Not without cause is it said that syphilis is the great mimicker of neurological disease, the joker in the diagnostic pack. Physicians of the 1940s were taught to 'think of this, think of that, then think of syphilis'.

It must be explained that a blood test that is positive for syphilis need not mean that the disease is progressing: a positive result will be obtained even if syphilis has been diagnosed and successfully arrested previously. A person who is going to get general paralysis of the insane may have had positive blood tests for decades beforehand without suffering any symptoms whatsoever.

Nowadays Hitler's case would be treated as primarily one of Parkinson's even if the results of a syphilis test had proved positive – there being no reason why both conditions cannot coexist. No reason – may I quickly add – other than political. For to go mad from venereal disease would be politically quite unacceptable – even for the Führer. Himmler and others were well aware of that, and the blood tests were a potent weapon in the power struggle in the Reich.

Although the actual results of Hitler's 1936 tests have never surfaced, we can guess that the tests were positive from the repeated references that Himmler was to make to them, and from his threats to publicise the results. Morell's records, when they became available in 1981, proved to be incomplete.

According to the US National Archives record of the testimony given to the Americans in 1945 by Dr Brandt – who had treated Hitler as well as Himmler – Morell was 'a businessman and not a doctor'. His alert financial brain never bothered with the niceties of truth or clinical diagnosis. As most quacks do, he played on the phobias and fears of his patients. As Brandt explained, Morell set up business agreements with his chosen colleagues, and always asked for two sets of results from the laboratories or colleagues to whom he had referred his famous patient – denoted always as 'Patient A'. One set gave the actual results; the other, as Morell himself used to admit, were for him to show the patient if necessary.[18]

When Hitler first attended Dr Morell it was as a patient of a venereal specialist, and for the blood tests for syphilis to have been performed at that time was no more than routine. Indeed Morell never gave up a chance of performing them on all of his patients. It is, however, of interest to note that the only blood test results for Hitler found in Morell's diaries are dated 5 January 1940. These purport to come from the Medical Diagnostic Institute in Berlin, on the Schiffbauerdamm – the VD clinic near the dockside. They record that Dr Schmidt Burbach found the blood of Patient A to have shown negative Wassermann and Kahn reactions – suggesting that the patient did *not* have syphilis.

But why would these tests have been performed at that time? For it is obvious from Morell's own diaries that Hitler was exhibiting nothing whatsoever to indicate that such tests were even remotely necessary. Moreover, these tests – which at that time in the Führer's career carried a definite political stigma – need hardly have been carried out when the earlier results were already available, for a patient who has once tested positive will more or less permanently continue to test positive, even after treatment.

11

As Hitler was not displaying any noticeable symptoms of neurological disorder at that time, the tests cannot have been intended for elimination purposes in making a diagnosis. Indeed, Morell was to prove such a dreadful physician that it was not until 15 April 1945 that he realised that the Führer was suffering from advanced Parkinson's disease.[19] There is therefore every reason to be extremely suspicious of the 1940 test results allegedly found in Morell's papers.

But back in 1945, for Dr Erwin Giesing, Professor Werner Haase and Dr Hans Karl von Hasselbach, Hitler's medical advisers, belatedly grappling with the complexities of his atypical Parkinson's disease, syphilis had to be excluded. But here the physicians faced a quandary. Although Himmler had been able to get hold of the results of Morell's blood tests, they could not. Nor could they raise the delicate question of the Führer's possible syphilis without very good reason.

Dr Theodor Morell was a degenerate figure who revolted the American doctors who questioned him after his capture at the end of the war. He was grossly overweight – over 500 kg – and so fat that when he sat down on a chair with a straight back he would become instantly breathless as his massive abdomen obstructed his diaphragm.

His standard of cleanliness was noted by both Americans and Germans alike to be appalling, his filthy shirt collar and lewdly stained clothing being obvious to the most casual observer. Speer, who subjected himself to a consultation with Morell to please Hitler, recalled him leaving trails of half-eaten food after him in his surgery in the Kurfürstendamm, and picking up and eating a sandwich in an unwashed rubber-gloved hand before disappearing back into his consulting-room.[20]

His speech was indecipherable. He used to mumble and wheeze his advice, and was so out of breath the whole time that he was unable to spend more than a couple of hours at the Berghof, Hitler's mountain retreat, claiming that the lack of air at that altitude was killing him. An assistant had to look after his interests there.

Morell was totally obsessed with money. He owned a company in Budapest which produced a drug called 'Ultraseptyl', which he used to ladle out whenever Hitler had a sore throat or there was the slightest possibility of his catching a cold. He also owned factories producing so-called vitamin chocolate and 'Russia lice powder'. The German health and safety investigators tested the latter and reported on its effectiveness: 'After being incubated with the lice powder for twenty-four hours the lice crawled out in rollicking spirits!'[21]

In his postwar testimony to the same American investigative team that interviewed Morell, Brandt explained that it had been he who had first told Morell about penicillin. Morell had thought this was phenacetin (a painkiller), but quickly realising his mistake, he got a 100,000-mark grant from Hitler to try to produce the antibiotic. When, at Brandt's insistence the final product was tested, it was found to be sterile cane sugar.[22] Nevertheless, Morell told the Americans that it was he who had invented penicillin, but the formula had been stolen from him by British secret service agents.

Morell's influence over the Führer was almost certainly initially established because of his professed expertise in venereal disease, and Hitler might well have preferred to be treated by someone of Morell's character rather than by someone of a superior intellect, given his distrust of intellectuals and his marked preference for peasant values.

Morell furthered his influence by ameliorating Hitler's allegedly 'gastric' symptomatology in 1936. There was, in fact, absolutely no evidence that Hitler suffered from any such disorder; nor was any adequate investigation made by Morell. Again, it is highly likely that Hitler simply preferred the magical hocus-pocus doled out by Morell to the more scientific opinions of properly qualified specialists.

One of the more obvious reasons for this may have been Morell's cosseting of what he himself termed Hitler's 'hysteria', there being no better patient possible for a quack than such a hysteric. In Hitler, Morell found a patient whose hypochondria extended to constantly checking his own pulse rate and avidly reading the previous medical reports on his health. The exact nature of Hitler's tendency to hysteria will be dealt with later, but it is obvious from Morell's recorded observations on Hitler that he thought the tremors that became discernible by March 1943 were purely the result of hysteria and not worthy of investigation.[23]

Examination of the electrocardiograms taken on Hitler from 1941 onwards and of the correspondence between Morell and a Dr A. Weber, at the so-called Balneological University Institute at Bad Nauheim, shows how Morell used fellow quacks to ensure Hitler continued as a rabid hypochondriac. Although there were excellent cardiological clinics in Berlin, Morell chose to have the ECGs performed, inexpertly, often without standardisation, and have them sent to this glorified swimming-pool and massage parlour to be interpreted to his needs. The actual ECG traces in US archives show not the 'rapidly progressive heart failure – or coronary sclerosis' diagnosed by Morell but only the mild changes caused by a slight diminution in blood supply to the heart muscle, typical of ageing patients (though often associated with Parkinson's disease) which in itself would be no cause for great concern.

Similarly many of the results of so-called 'tests of glandular function' carried out on Hitler at Morell's request were totally meaningless.

Morell increased his control over Hitler's psyche by the simple expedient of insisting that he be the first (other than the valet) to see the Führer in the mornings when he awoke – later and later. He also fed Hitler's phobias and hypochondria with daily injections of one form or another. Hitler became addicted not so much to the strange mixture of concoctions he was given but to being injected – Göring was sarcastically to call Morell the 'Reich's Injection Master'. Hitler's other medical advisers were to hear alarming snippets about these multiple injections – not least the total lack of cleanliness with which they were administered, and the unlabelled nature of the ampoules – but they were totally unaware of what was being injected.

Morell also played on Hitler's already existing fetish with faecal manual evacuation and self-administered calomel enemas. Hitler had suffered from increasing constipation, and in May 1943 Morell himself in his records commented upon 'Constipation and colossal flatulence on a scale I have seldom before witnessed.'[24]

In 1936 Morell had ousted the ineffectual, but at least sound, Dr Brandt, who two years earlier had been appointed surgeon to Hitler at the tender age of twenty-three. Brandt, just having qualified, was a total novice (and so Hitler probably felt he could more easily dominate him), but he was a novice with the common sense to realise that he had hardly any training, and he immediately advised that he have two 'deputies' – Haase and von Hasselbach.

For two years Hitler was properly cared for, but when Morell took over he insisted that no other physician be employed to give Hitler advice, and he refused Brandt access both to his patient and to the notes which he made on Hitler's progress. Examination of these notes reveals a total ignorance of medicine, a total lack of proper investigative procedures, and an intellect reciprocal to his girth.

Brandt was to remain excluded until the July 1944 bomb attempt on Hitler's life, when one of the surgeons urgently called to attend the Führer was Dr Erwin Giesing, a very capable ENT surgeon with considerable experience of medicine and surgery. (He was to later impress his American inquisitors with his intelligence.) Giesing was horrified to observe Hitler's general condition – enlarged lymph glands in the neck and an awful dirty-greyish pallor, as well as senility – which was far more worrying than the perforated eardrums that he had been called to treat. He shared his concerns with Brandt, who, having found an authoritative ally with a reputation, then informed von Hasselbach of the deterioration in Hitler's condition and the totally inappropriate quackery which was aggravating it. Giesing had found a drawer full of pills – mainly the atropine and strychnine anti-flatulence pills that Linge, the valet, now admitted to giving Hitler on demand – and in all Hitler was receiving some seventy-seven different preparations.

Brandt and Giesing were advised to approach Hitler directly, and found allies among Hitler's adjutants, who now had the courage to berate Morell for allowing the Führer to deteriorate. Linge, however, remained firmly behind Morell, well aware of his own culpability in ladling out the medication.

Hitler met the critics of Morell with stony silence, but the issue escalated to others. Sensing Hitler's mood, Bormann rapidly sided with Morell, and Himmler was also asked for his advice. The political infighting continued throughout September and October, but it proved to be one-sided: Hitler's faith in Morell was apparently unshakeable and the doctor's opponents were routed.

Throughout this period Morell remained firmly in charge, steadfastly refusing to allow Giesing, his main critic, access to his records. On 27 September 1944 Giesing was also refused further access to the Führer (although he continued to advise Brandt).

Hitler became worse, developing a transitory jaundice and stomach cramps. As those were not adequately investigated, we are unable belatedly to make a proper judgement as to whether Hitler was suffering from infective hepatitis or a gall-stone obstruction. From the repeated comments about the stools 'now being brown', and references to upper abdominal tenderness, it is likely, however, that Hitler was suffering from a stone in the common bile duct, eventually being fortunate enough to pass this stone on his own. Morell thought that the gall bladder might be affected with 'nervous worry'.[25]

Morell's treatment was as impressive as his diagnosis: inhalation of oxygen, camomile-tea enemas, followed by 'liver-extract injections', vitamins, 'calcium' and 'Septo-Iodine' (a medication supposedly giving respiratory relief), Tonophospan (yet another supposed tonic) and an injection of the supposed virility-enhancer Testoviron, which was presumably for Eva's benefit.

Despite such treatment the jaundice subsided, but not Bormann's opportunism. Brandt was first sacked and then hounded – branded as a traitor by Bormann, who drew attention to Brandt having moved his family to relative safety, away from the advancing Soviets. It took Himmler to intervene and save Brandt from execution. Von Hasselbach was also effectively removed – as a result of his allegedly having been indiscreet about Morell's competence in the company of some of Hitler's adjutants.

There has been much speculation about Himmler's playing a sinister role in this medical intrigue. Almost all the suppositions that have been made result from several historians' all too liberal interpretation of remarks made by Himmler's deputy, Walter Schellenberg, as the war drew to a close and subsequently to his Allied inquisitors. Schellenberg seemed quite convinced that Hitler would be poisoned at the appropriate moment. But Himmler had had nothing to do with Morell's initial appointment, which had been suggested by Hitler's photographer, Heinrich Hoffmann. Neither had Professor Gebhardt, Himmler's own SS doctor, anything to do with Morell or with Hitler's treatment.

When asked for advice on the issues raised by Brandt and Giesing, Himmler had turned to Gebhardt. The result was the appointment on 31 October 1944 of Dr Ludwig Stumpfegger, a 190 cm orthopaedic SS surgeon, to replace Dr Brandt.

There is no reason to suppose anything sinister about Stumpfegger's appointment, other than the fact that he very quickly established a rapport with Morell, who was allowed to continue his influence unabated.

When Morell begged to leave Berlin, in advance of the Soviet assault, it was Stumpfegger and Haase who took over responsibility for Hitler's health. Left in the Bunker in their charge was a prematurely aged, grossly weakened, stooped, uncontrollably shaking, partially paralysed, impotent insomniac. A food-stained, urine-soiled caricature, incapable of writing his own signature, barely capable of reading a wall map even with his glasses; a man whose unfocused visual world was further blurred with the pain from the light itself. A man often melancholic, sometimes barely able to mutter his wishes, but still paradoxically capable of vindictively raging and ranting in increasingly vulgar language against his hatreds and phobias from earlier years. A Führer whose obvious physical state was cynically tolerated to the extent that he be allowed to lie in a torpor for a couple of days like a Nile crocodile, isolated from outside circumstances or understanding, cynically manipulated, his mumblings readily interpreted, his signature forged by the opportunistic sycophants who had consolidated their power as Hitler's physical weakness was now accompanied by evidence of a worsening mental disorder.

2

The Mind of Adolf Hitler

When the nerves break down, there is nothing left but to admit that one can't handle the situation and shoot one's self.[1]

If one hadn't a family to bequeath one's house to, the best thing would be to be burnt in it with all its contents – a magnificent funeral pyre.[2]

We shall never capitulate, we may drag a world with us, a world in flames.[3]

We will leave no one alive to triumph over Germany.[4]

These quotations have often been used as evidence of Hitler's intent – even his need – to commit suicide. In isolation they sound fine enough, but to forget the context in which they were uttered is, effectively, to misunderstand them. They speak the language of noble Nazi nihilism – death or glory, no compromise or concession. They are parroted to add a lustre of mythological intensity to events in the Bunker. But this lustre was, in reality, entirely absent.

In the same way, in eulogy after eulogy, trite monologue after trite monologue, Goebbels continued to the bitter end to emulate, better and propagate the heady nonsense of his Führer, while, as we shall see, attempting to make arrangements for his own salvation.

Inside the Bunker, all sentiment was to degenerate into dribbling nostalgia and latent hysteria. The test pilot Hanna Reitsch gave a tearfully defiant testimonial to the loyalty of the Bunker personnel: according to her, she left them on 29 April in full accord that they were going to commit a glorious mass suicide. Instead, self-preservation dictated the reality – the mass exodus that actually occurred.

In the intervening half-century the image of Nazism and of Hitler himself has been totally revised. He has been declared a military genius even by the British military strategist Basil Liddell Hart, and has even been called a social reformer and a misunderstood visionary, hardly responsible for the unfortunate if nevertheless marginal excesses of his followers that led to the 'grossly overstated' Holocaust. Other historians, such as Hans Dietrich Rötter, have helped 'reevaluate' Hitler's personality in the belief that it was destroyed by illness and outside pressure.[5]

But historians have, as yet, failed properly to *evaluate*, let alone re-evaluate, the most important phenomenon of the twentieth century. Before entering the twilight world of the Bunker and grappling with the reality of forensic evidence, it is essential to understand the psyche of the man around whom the Bunker was constructed.

The Hitler of the Historians

No study of Hitler's psyche has been written by a historian with any clinical experience or knowledge of what is regarded as normal or indeed legally certifiable. Most analyses have embarrassed followed the guidance of theorists of the Freudian or neo-Freudian schools, and, with few exceptions, the net result has been an unhelpful mishmash of meaningless descriptions.

British historians, in particular, have almost entirely failed to address the problem. Instead they have tried to produce so-called commonsensical statements about Hitler's state of mind. Unfortunately common sense does not compensate for a lack of knowledge of a subject outside their remit.

As far as A. J. P. Taylor was concerned, Hitler was really a normal person, a traditional German leader who was 'no more wicked or unscrupulous than any other contemporary statesman' and whose ideas were 'commonplace'. For Taylor, Hitler's most striking characteristic was 'his patience'.[6]

Hugh Trevor-Roper seems to have thought that Hitler was essentially normal but evil – a bloodthirsty tyrant. He had very little time for the excesses of the Germanic character that had allowed such a tyrant to emerge. He criticised what he saw as the German tendency to indulge in 'cloudy German rhetoric', 'gaseous metaphysics' and 'Nordic nonsense'.[7] This may be justified criticism of a nation that, having lost its self-esteem in 1918, sought verbally to redress the balance, but such behaviour has been none too uncommon throughout history – or among historians.

Alan Bullock is yet another commonsensical British historian who found Hitler's strange behaviour 'offensive' both to his reasoning and to his historical training.[8]

Nor have the Germans themselves been more enlightening. A late German authority on Hitler, Professor Percy Ernst Schramm, displayed some confusion about the responsibilities of his own speciality of history. Being unable to cope with the grossness of the abnormalities displayed by his subject, he came to the remarkably convenient conclusion that psychiatry and psychology were of no use in determining whether Hitler was sane or insane.[9]

In his otherwise monumental works on Hitler, Karl Dietrich Bracher came to the conclusion that it was 'pointless to speculate' about Hitler's mental status.[10] This is another example of a layman completely failing to understand the nature of a personality disorder, trying to explain Hitler's behaviour in the rational terms of mental normality without any concept of the lack of emotional depth and the vagaries that personality disorders can display.

It is obvious that the case of Hitler exposes the limitations of the traditional historical method. Although the historians already cited have loftily declined to address the issue of Hitler's mental state, historians of lesser calibre seem to have readily accepted all the more lurid father-hating, oral, anal and other fantasies of Freudianism in order to explain his motives.

But Hitler is too important a phenomenon to leave unexplained, and the explanation need not be couched in nonsensical terms.

Hitler's Youth

Hitler did not come from a socially deprived background, as is sometimes alleged, but from the lower middle classes. Even if his background had been deprived, however, this would not explain his personality. Nevertheless, much has been made about a passage in *Mein Kampf* in which Hitler describes scenes of an estranged, brutalised wife greeting a drunkard of a husband in front of the children:

When he finally comes home . . . drunk and brutal, but always without a last cent or penny, then God have mercy on the scenes which follow. I witnessed all of this personally in hundreds of scenes and at the beginning with both disgust and indignation.[11]

When one remembers the paucity of friendships made by the youthful Hitler – he had scarcely one intimate friend – it is difficult to envisage where he had come across such happenings if not at home.

Hitler continued with a remarkable forecast of what was to come:

The other things the little fellow hears at home do not tend to further his respect for his surroundings. Not a single good shred is left for [his perception of] humanity, not a single institution is left unattacked [respected]; starting with the teacher, up to the head of State, be it religion, or morality as such, be it the State or society, no matter which, everything is pulled down in the nastiest manner into the filth of a depraved mentality.[12]

All of this may have been no more than sympathy-invoking rhetoric. Fortunately, most children from such homes don't end up as monsters. Hitler's upbringing may well have coloured his attitude towards the world, but if such violence did indeed occur it played a minor part in the make-up of his personality.

Much has also been made of the adverse effects of Hitler's supposedly having only one testicle. However, the only evidence that this was the case comes from the Soviet post-mortem on the corpse identified as Hitler's. Since there are several uncertainties about the identification of that corpse, it seems reckless to base any study of Hitler's psychological make-up on this 'fact' alone. In any case, most youths who end up with one testicle have absolutely no manifest psychological trauma because of this, other than occasional embarrassment. No otherwise normal child would exhibit any effects as a result of such a defect.

Nevertheless, the Americans who interviewed Hitler's doctors after the war were fascinated to learn that he had been very reluctant to let anyone see his genitalia, and even the 'venereologist' Dr Morell claimed not to have any knowledge of his Führer below the waist. Later Dr von Hasselbach was to say that 'Hitler had an extreme disinclination to let people see his body. Probably his manservant Emil Maurice could give information as to whether his sexual organs were deformed – he dropped hints when we were in captivity together.'[13]

20

The only possible relevant factor that can be discerned from a study of his youth which may possibly have played a significant part in Hitler's later obsessive anti-Semitism was the question of Hitler himself being possibly a quarter Jewish.

The only evidence of his early anti-Semitism comes from an unpublished memoir of his Vienna room-mate August Kubizek, preserved in the Upper Austrian Archives at Linz. This tells us that Hitler joined an anti-Semitic society in April 1908.[14] The rumour that spread about Hitler's possible Jewish parenthood followed claims by, among others, the industrialist and author Fritz Thyssen and the historian Hans Jürgen Köhler that Austrian chancellor Dollfuss had ordered Austrian police to investigate whether or not Hitler's father, Alois, was an illegitimate son of Baron Rothschild, at whose house it was claimed Alois's mother had been employed.[15] It was alleged that Hitler had ordered Dollfuss's assassination in 1934 in order to obtain a document supporting these rumours that Dollfuss had threatened to reveal. There is, however, nothing but circumstantial evidence for this.

Nevertheless the attitude of society in both Austria and Bavaria, the cradle of Hitler's rise to power, was violently anti-Jew, and to be born Jewish would have been the death-knell for anyone with political aspirations. Even the possibility of truth in the rumours would have been devastating to the young Hitler and to his envisaged career. (Witness the fierce controversy about the background of the Russian leader Vladimir Zhirinovsky.)

There is in fact evidence that not only did General William O'Donovan of the American Office of Strategic Services regard such rumours as serious enough to warrant setting up his own investigation, but that Hitler's rivals were also busily enquiring along the same lines. It is one of history's great ironies that while O'Donovan's investigation was in progress so was an investigation launched by Heinrich Himmler. On his behalf, Gottlob Berger commissioned the first of several Gestapo reports which have now at last surfaced. These reports are dated 1935, 1938, 1941, 1942, 1943 and 1944, illustrating the continued relevance of this subject in the jockeying for power in the Third Reich.[16]

Hitler's upbringing therefore reveals only one possible source of anxiety that may have influenced his adult behaviour: the fear of being Jewish. This fear was pragmatic: to be Jewish would be to be disbarred from a career in politics. There is no evidence that he was otherwise traumatised by anti-Semitism, and it cannot be offered as an explanation of Hitler's character.

Hitler's Behaviour

We can best get an insight into Hitler's personality from the testimonies of those who knew him at various later stages of his career. The problem with these testimonies is that they are often written both with the advantage of hindsight and by people who have every reason to tailor their version of events to excuse their own actions. Even the supposedly reasoned and sane armaments minister Albert Speer covered his own ambition with references to his reason having been overwhelmed by the supposed magnetism of the Führer. He denied categorically, though unconvincingly, that the Führer would have proved less mesmeric without the power to confer advancement which so evidently underlay Speer's sycophantic approaches.[17]

Speer did, however, give a first-hand, very important account of how extraordinarily loutish and juvenile was Hitler's everyday speech. It was almost like the ranting of a schoolboy. Unformed sentences and explosive threats were almost always along the very same lines, and the repetitive nature of the words used was very obvious. 'I'll smash him', 'I'll fix him', 'I'll personally put a bullet through his head', 'I'll club him down' were his customary phrases to gentle along conversation about any adversary, but apparently only in retrospect did Speer find such sentiments 'over the top and irrational'. When things were going well, Hitler's speech was characterised by words and phrases showing his fortitude and resolution – 'absolutely', 'unshakeable', 'iron perseverance' etc. – always emphasised with a gesture.[18]

Speer also noticed that Hitler seemed devoid of relaxed natural small talk in the presence of men: 'Looking back on it now, it was *the* feature that made most of his acquaintances uneasy. I suppose I knew it was odd, I knew he was weird – I just didn't want to admit it to myself.'

The testimonies of those who knew Hitler early on and whose opinions were recorded at that time are also unfortunately skewed, for the very reason why they were prepared to criticise or comment on Hitler at that stage was because they had fallen out with him or had fallen foul of his ambitions. Nevertheless the early testimony of Hitler's Nazi rivals Ernst Röhm and Otto Strasser, and of the usurped foreign press chief Putzi Hanfstängl, remain invaluable, especially given the scarcity of other rational criticism.

According to both Röhm and Strasser, Hitler was so averse to criticism that he would walk out of meetings where his viewpoint was challenged. It was noticeable that he hated meeting with industrialists, who had the self-assurance that long association with money brings – a self-assurance which ran counter to Hitler's need to take centre stage. Strasser claimed that this was due to Hitler's lack of aplomb and confidence: he hated to be in the position where he was not a seeming expert in the topic under discussion. Furthermore, he was painfully aware of his lack of education and his modest social background. He constantly disparaged intellectualism throughout his life, condemning 'Overeducated people, stuffed with knowledge and intellect, but bare of any sound instincts'.[19]

This attitude became so perverse that his advisers learned not to be too forward with their erudition. The quality of those advisers who were tolerated fell accordingly. Those who remained would hear Hitler's usual opinion of 'these impudent rascals who always know everything better than anybody else' and, even more pointedly, that 'The intellect has grown autocratic, and has become a disease of life.'[20]

Hitler was more impressed with obvious cleverness which brought instant reward. In the 1920s one man with such obvious talent so impressed Hitler that he took lessons from him in public speaking. The man, named Hanussen, was also an astrologer and fortune-teller – in short, a con-man. According to Strasser, he taught Hitler the importance of theatrical staging in political meetings, so as to gain the maximum effect. He also advocated evoking the mysticism necessary to capture the Germanic soul.[21]

It is difficult for an adult, non-Germanic audience to listen to tapes of 'Hitler Talks' without marvelling at the effect that these speeches had on the audience of his day. The truly odd mixture of High German phrases with an Austrian accent later became known as *Knödlige Sprache*, or dumpling-speak.[22] The sentences were badly constructed, the speeches were long and extremely repetitive, making them painful to read, yet they had a remarkable effect on the Germanic recipients. To an incredulous outside world, whose cynical reporters reported the phenomenon in terse, baffled sentences, it was inexplicable. *Newsweek* reported that 'Women faint, when, with face purpled and contorted with effort, he blows forth.' According to the journalist Janet Flanner, 'His oratory used to wilt his collar, unglue his forelock, glaze his eyes – he was like a man hypnotized, repeating himself in a frenzy.'[23] The billing, the staging, the attitude of the audience – only too willing to hear what they really wanted to hear most; only too prepared to enter into mass hysteria – explain most of the phenomenon, but not all. The other factor was Hitler's air of 'difference'.

According to the East Prussian industrialist and politician Hermann Rauschning, 'Anyone who has seen this man [Hitler] face to face, has met his uncertain gaze, without depth or warmth, from eyes that seem hard and remote, and has then seen that gaze go rigid, will have certainly experienced the uncanny feeling that that man is strange, that man is not normal.'[24] And an adjutant Gerhard Boldt, recalled a few months before the end 'an indescribable flickering stare in his eyes that is at the same time shocking and completely unnatural'.[25] Even Hitler himself was to recall that people thought he was abnormal – 'They always said I was crazy.'[26]

'Difference' was something that Mussolini also exemplified; in his case it was transmitted through an absurd posturing and strutting, combined with theatrical head gestures which threatened to dislocate his neck but which emphasised arguably his favourite physical attribute – his chin.

Hitler lacked the jutting chin, and by comparison seemed less comical than Mussolini. Nevertheless, the newsreels of the time show his tremendous, absurd self-awareness – scarcely a natural bearing. The shoulders were always squared and brought forward by tightening of his pectoral muscles; his chest was thrust forward; his arms were held in front of him, with inwardly rotated forearms – a stance which, especially when in his raincoat, evokes a waiting flasher. Many of his movements were ridiculously, pompously, out of place. Often when he walked and postured he had the swagger of a Mickey Rooney. Yet the audience loved it – they interpreted it as decisiveness. Even so, there appear moments of physical uncertainty – awareness that he might not be cutting such a grand figure after all. Both in the very early newsreels and in the increasingly rare later film coverage the uncertainty is easily discernible in his body language – his changes of stance and the uncertain positioning of his arms, his palms facing forward in a feminine way – though there is always the glare noted by Rauschning.

This glare would have caused most physicians to regard him with a good deal of unease, for, as Rauschning said, it was strange – not normal. The occasions when the glare was most in evidence, according to Speer, were when Hitler used to be at his most recriminatory, and most explosive. Speer also noted that Hitler's speech would suffer, and Speer thought that he could gauge the degree of uncertainty from this: 'Hitler would often begin a sentence three or four times, repeatedly breaking off and then starting out again with almost the same words, especially when he was angry or embittered.'[27] Nevertheless:

He was expert at making agonisingly repetitive and long-winded monologues seem somehow vivid. None of us dared interrupt or prompt, and woe betide anyone stupid enough to do so. In retrospect I suppose it was we – his private audience, who he knew were waiting upon his every word – who wanted his utterances to be great when I think they were sometimes plainly confused.[28]

Hitler's glare was used by Goebbels in numerous carefully staged photographs to spread the notion that the Führer was all-seeing, that he could look piercingly through into the soul. The photos had to be used sparingly, for, whereas Rauschning found Hitler's eyes merely lacking in sparkle and animation, there are many newsreels which show a truly baleful glare. At its most obvious, this was associated with characteristic limitations in the head movements – almost as if Hitler suffered from a slipped disc in his neck – his head held slightly forward, the glare directed somewhat upwards. Even allowing for a consciously melodramatic stance, this is the body language of paranoia – a body language commonly found in schizophrenia and associated psychopathic states, but very rarely in entirely normal individuals.

Very early on, in the 1930s, we hear that Hitler had an opinion of himself which, when expressed publicly with seemingly total conviction, was in itself possibly abnormal. Martin Fuchs reported that Hitler asked the Austrian politician Kurt von Schuschnigg at Berchtesgaden, 'Do you realise that you are in the presence of the greatest German of all time?'[29] And Hitler was to inform Rauschning that 'I do not need your endorsement to convince me of my historical greatness.'[30]

Hitler by this time already thought of himself as a Messianic cleanser, a furious Jesus engaged in a Mission Immortal. His planned mausoleum, befitting such a great emperor, was no more grandiose than the tombs of the pharaohs – it was just a little on the unusual side in a Europe not yet prepared for such resplendence. Such a concept of historical immortality would just seem part of the baggage of mythology were it not that it emanated from Hitler himself and was modestly put forward as his honest, considered opinion.

Most people who espouse such convictions, running contrary to the reality perceived by their fellows, have been quickly put away in large, purpose-built hospitals to save them from their own delusions. But this wasn't a true delusion: it was more a form of extraordinarily positive thinking, encouraged by the euphoria of power. Had he won the war, such ideas might well have been made concrete, at whatever cost. In Nazi Germany every grandiose utterance by the Führer was met not with stony silence or awkward embarrassment but with acclaim, accord and even adoration. It would have been very confusing for even the most steadfast schizophrenic – though, as we shall see, Hitler didn't actually qualify for that epithet – but with very little effort he was getting greatness thrust upon him by sycophancy.

Once established as a leader with a court of sycophants, his reaction to opposition was a tirade which seemed to convulse his whole being with a quite extraordinary violence. It terrified both the target and the onlookers, who were fearful of being tainted by association with the offending presence. It had the effect of ensuring that opposition was hastily quashed, and that those who dared to give offence were denied further access.

Rauschning thought this phenomenon to be a ploy – 'a technique by which he would throw his entire entourage into confusion by well-timed fits of rage and thus make them more submissive'.[31]

Karl von Wiegand reported that there was a tacit understanding among Hitler's staff: 'For God's sake don't excite the Führer – which means do not tell him bad news.'[32] The contention that the rage was often contrived is supported by the fact that earlier in Hitler's career – before he was surrounded by sycophants – the rages were rare.

In extremely difficult situations Hitler was reported as offering to commit suicide; but these reports have to be regarded with caution, as unfortunately the offers were not accepted. The first recorded was in 1923 at the Hanfstängl home after the failure of the putsch in which he attempted to seize control of the Bavarian government; the second was during his subsequent term in Landsberg prison. The threat was supposedly repeated after the strange death of his niece Geli in 1930, and again in 1932 in response to Strasser's attempts to split the Party. In 1933 he threatened to commit suicide if not appointed chancellor, and in 1936 a hysterical outburst included a threat to do so if the occupation of the Rhineland failed.

Such immature, oft-repeated gestures are customarily attention-seeking, and any accompanying physical attempts are almost invariably unsuccessful. Quite often such emotional volatility is accompanied in early life by hysterical paralysis or similar episodes, and in Hitler's case there does seem to be a badly recorded episode of transient blindness,[33] but not enough is known about the episode for it definitely to be attributed to latent hysteria.

Of equal interest are Hitler's bouts of depression, which have been cited by Reinhold Hanisch, a vagabond with whom he once lived – 'I have never ever seen such helpless letting down in distress'[34] – but the descriptions are lacking in clarity and clinical data, as are the suppositions of Hans Mend about Hitler's alleged episodes of depression during their First World War service together.[35]

The reason why these episodes of depression interest psychiatrists so much is because a diagnosis of depression can signify a schizo-affective state, a type of depression associated with schizophrenia. There are many types of depression, and one of the most frustrating aspects of Hitler's life – confronting both historians and psychiatrists – is that, even now, very little is known about Hitler in the so-called silent period of his late teens and early twenties, when he could well have suffered from more than just depression without too many people giving a damn.

Hitler's whereabouts in Vienna and in Munich during his formative period are now known – but very little else about him then, except that he was indolent, seemingly aimless, and lived first on a small inheritance and then, when that ran out, on his wits. We do know that he was extremely sensitive about anyone knowing too much about his past – so much so that historians such as Joachim Fest now claim substantive evidence that in 1938 Hitler had Reinhold Hanisch tracked down and murdered, as he obviously knew too much.[36]

In the 1950s documents became available which revealed another unknown aspect of Hitler's youth. It is evident that he was a draft-dodger, being sought by the police for evading the call-up for the First World War. He left Vienna and deliberately registered in Munich as stateless, in order to evade capture, before eventually deciding to enlist. Had he been caught and arrested, his future career could never have blossomed. Later, in *Mein Kampf*, Hitler falsified the date of his departure from Vienna; in fact he left the city in the spring of 1913, not 1912 as he claimed. In March 1938 he himself engaged in a desperate unsuccessful search for these documents.

It seems that Hitler might have had much to be depressed about in his youth, but for that depression to have become discernible to several of his contemporaries, as they claimed after the war, does suggest some degree of abnormality, something more than just moroseness. All that can be said with any degree of certainty is that for a young man in his early twenties to suffer from discernible depression is in itself abnormal – possibly the harbinger of more serious mental illness.

There are other aspects of Hitler's character which have fascinated psychiatrists and have received by far the most attention, especially in the popular press.

The first is Hitler's sexuality. This issue bears little or no relevance to his normality. Schizophrenics and psychopaths seem to procreate without discernible difficulty, and as there is still no general consensus on what is and what is not sexually normal there would seem to be little to be gained by surmise about Hitler's sexual proclivities in the almost total absence of any first-hand evidence. All the tales of his homosexual inclinations that have been produced to date are entirely hearsay, and a hearsay employed by his detractors.

Nevertheless we do know that there was a distinct lack of warmth in Hitler's relationship with men, and it became very noticeable towards the last few months of his existence that he enjoyed and preferred the company of women – his secretaries, his cook and Eva Braun.

We also know that the relationship with Eva Braun was as close as Eva's distinct lack of intellect and childish schoolgirl behaviour allowed, but that in their three years – certainly since 1943 – Hitler's physical impotence frustrated this to some extent, as Speer claimed he was told by Eva herself.[37]

But before reaching any conclusion about Hitler's psyche *before* he entered the Berlin Bunker in the final phase, we need to consider the fact that for most of his career he showed considerable single-mindedness and perseverance.

Despite many testimonies as to his occasional tortured irresolution and apathetic states – Röhm claimed that Hitler's worst problem was procrastination: 'Usually he solves at the last minute a problem that has become intolerable and dangerous only because he vacillates'[38] – there is no question that he was an effective, resolute leader who achieved some remarkable results. Was this as a result of his 'psychopathic' brilliance at spotting weakness in other European leaders? He himself boasted of his utter ruthlessness in this regard: 'I have not come into this world to make men better, but to make use of their weaknesses'[39] – almost the perceived credo of psychopathia.

There are sufficient testimonies to his remarkable recall of military data to put his mental ability for things that interested him into a class well above the norm. The late Basil Liddell Hart, one of the greatest British military strategists and historians, paid Hitler the compliment of calling him possibly one of the greatest military strategists of all time. I am hardly in a position to argue with Liddell Hart, but I have spent hours discussing with his son Adrian the exact nature of his father's appreciation of Hitler.

One fact that emerges out of these discussions – a fact also substantiated by Speer and others – is that until about 1941 Hitler would let others talk, listen, and then procrastinate for indeterminate periods during which he often held himself open to other counsels. Only when he was satisfied would he then act decisively. The genius that Basil Liddell Hart extolled was an informed genius – little wonder that Hitler's strategies worked.

According to Speer, this attitude changed progressively and markedly as the war progressed – especially as the news from the Russian front became highly embarrassing.

This change was due first to Hitler's refusal to hear any news which ran counter to his aura of perceived infallibility. Less than a week before General Friedrich von Paulus was to surrender outside Stalingrad on 31 January 1943, Hitler held a conference at which he deliberated at length about the construction of a suitably large stadium in Nuremberg in which to hold the Victory-over-Russia celebrations.

Second, the change was due to his increasing irritability when corrected or crossed – an irritability which began to have disastrous results for his commanders at the front as he became surrounded by sycophants who told him only what he wanted to know.

What Adrian Liddell Hart was referring to was Hitler's performance before he became ill-informed, before he lost touch with reality let alone military strategy; before he became the prisoner of the results of his own megalomania – but, it must be added, a prisoner too of his embarrassment at his own physical state, which certainly accentuated his isolation. Hitler's decisions – taken too late, too hastily, without adequate consultation – were to cease to be a true reflection of his mental agility and so allow very few conclusions of value to be drawn about any possible mental degeneration.

We must conclude that, since the exact state of Hitler's mental abilities cannot be accurately determined at the end of the war, it is impossible to diagnose any mental degeneration. Even though it may be tempting to contrast the bombastic, seemingly sure Hitler of 1940 with the vacillating end product, it would be a comparison of circumstances as much as of the man.

Where does that leave us in determining the mental state of the Führer before the final days? Did he show characteristics that enable a *psychiatric* diagnosis?

Hitler's Psychiatric State

The term 'psychiatry' was probably first coined by Johann Christian Reil (1759–1813). Confronted with people that were *odd*, he proposed a new form of treatment whereby the doctor used his intellect and 'psyche' (the

Greek word for soul) as a therapeutic agent. Similar developments were made in France by Philippe Pinel and in England by William Tuke, but they named their treatments 'Moral Treatment'. Little wonder that the term 'psychiatry' seemed less censorious and caught on more readily.

Over two centuries, clinicians worldwide were eventually able to classify various recognisable disease patterns, and to divide the mentally ill broadly into *neurotics* – those with the capacity to harm themselves – and *psychotics* – those with the capacity to harm others. Each recognisable syndrome within these broad groups is characterised by specific behavioural patterns.

So what of Hitler? First it is important to dispel the thought that he was a true schizophrenic.

Schizophrenia is the heartland of psychiatry – its real *raison d'être* – for it can prove more destructive to society as a whole than even the ravages of cancer. It was first recognised as a clinical entity in the Hindu Ayur Veda as long ago as 1400 BC, and was again described by the writings of the Cappodocian physician Arataeus in the first century AD. However, the first unambiguous descriptions come from only the end of the eighteenth century, and it was another hundred years before it was identified with total clarity. That was achieved by Professor Emil Kraepelin in Munich, in the fifth edition of his 1896 *Lehrbuch*. In 1911 the Swiss psychiatrist Eugen Bleuler invented the actual term 'Schizophrenia', or 'split mind'.

The next important breakthrough in Germany in the 1940s was a classification (the Schneider classification) which gave the minimal criteria necessary to classify a case as being one of true schizophrenia – the quandary having previously been the wide variability not only of symptoms but of their interpretation, recording and importance. Schneider identified first-rank symptoms that he considered it essential for the patient to exhibit in order to qualify for a diagnosis of schizophrenia. These included auditory hallucinations and acts that the patient thought he was carrying out under external control, as well as thoughts that he believed came into his head from outside sources, and sensations that he believed he was experiencing because of outside interference. This classification became the cornerstone of German psychiatry.

In America an almost identical set of rules was first brought in as the St Louis Criteria, and was subsequently updated, in 1980, by a computerised system from the American Psychiatric Association – the so-called DSM system, based on the *Diagnostic and Statistical Manual of Mental Disorders*. As far as schizophrenia was concerned, the Americans considered that the disease had also to start before the age of forty-five and be present for periods of at least six months, otherwise the condition was classified as a 'schizophreniform disorder'.

Hitler never claimed to be guided by voices, other than on one occasion when God mistakenly told him to get out of a foxhole in the First World War – a foxhole blown up immediately after he got out. But such a story was just a story and no more, and Hitler apparently made no other such claims.

The speech of such schizophrenics exhibits a distinctive, immature pattern. There have been justified criticisms of Hitler's own speech patterns (which, as I have recorded, were even noticed by Speer), making the point that some of his speech exhibited the so-called 'primitive' form associated with schizophrenia, in which, apart from numerous grammatical errors (the psychologist Erik Erikson pointed out that Hitler feminised German neuter nouns, for example),[40] there are fewer subordinate clauses than the norm. However, the newer linguistic concepts such as cohesion, lexical density and dysfluency have not, as far as I am aware, been properly applied to any such analysis of Hitler's speech patterns, and furthermore, such primitive speech pattern is also typical of other disorders, and not just characteristic of schizophrenia alone.

Hitler was *not* a schizophrenic. Nor did he justify diagnosis as having a schizophreniform disorder. But some accounts have tried to label Hitler as exhibiting a 'schizo-affective state'. (The 'affect' is the mood of a patient, which can swing from severe depression at one extreme to mania at the other.) Their authors point to his allegedly suffering from manifest depression, and regard his untoward statements of grandeur as evidence of mania. These accounts have not been written by qualified psychiatrists or clinicians but by laymen using terminology which they had picked up, and unfortunately their use of such terminology is totally inappropriate.

The term 'schizo-affective disorder' was first popularised by the American J. Kasanin, in 1933, and became widely used for the simple reason that many patients exhibiting odd behaviour were also subject to depression or mania. Kasanin made the diagnosis of schizo-affective disorder partly by exclusion: 'A case exhibiting marked and prolonged mood swings or severe depression or mania alone, which did *not* exhibit definite schizophrenia, but did suffer from delusional episodes or hallucinations for a period of at least two weeks, without having any reason to suspect any other organic factor.'[41] It must be concluded that Hitler exhibited no evidence of any such behaviour.

I have already mentioned Hitler's defensive and self-important postures on film. The combination of delusions of persecution and self-importance is characteristic of paranoia. This does not, however, mean that Hitler was a paranoic, nor does it mean that Hitler was a paranoid schizophrenic.

If their paranoia is stable and not progressive, paranoid schizophrenics can quite often exist for many years without ever showing evidence of psychosis – that is, without ever hearing voices or receiving untoward instructions or sensations, or otherwise losing touch with reality. But paranoia is also a symptom of several other disorders. Paranoics are tense and insecure, and find it difficult to form close relationships – being what is termed 'socially incompetent'; being habitually self-centred and thus reacting badly to criticism. Although Hitler exhibited paranoia, this was only one of *several* facets of his disordered personality.

How, then, can this disordered personality be classified?

Most people are only aware of one all-embracing term – a term continually applied to Hitler – *psychopath*. But, although many of his actions were psychopathic, his behaviour does not warrant such a diagnosis in psychiatric terms.

The original conceptions of this mental affliction still ring true. Pinel, well over a century ago, called it *'Manie sans delire'*, E. P. Trelat *'La folie lucide'*, whereas J. C. Pritchard in 1835 called it 'moral insanity'. It can encompass a wide spectrum of activity springing from a seeming failure to act responsibly or to have any conscience about doing evil.

The psychopath is often of above-average intelligence and highly manipulative and convincing. He seeks out human weakness – the main weakness that a psychopath perceives being that of morality itself. His lack of such a restraining factor often gives him a tremendous – one could even say 'political' – advantage. But, even in a cut-throat world where politicians, bankers and many others could be said to ignore morality, the conduct of a truly psychopathic individual is still exceptional. Nevertheless the term is a nightmare for the legal profession, which has sought in vain to define a baseline moral code against which to measure such amoral behaviour.

Why, it may be asked, need we look further to explain Hitler's personality? Indeed, Hitler was in many ways the psychopath personified – bolstered by an audience that he didn't really have to try too hard to deceive. And yet true psychopaths only very rarely show the persistence and perseverance with which Hitler pursued his goal, and, mainly for that reason, Hitler can only be said to have displayed psychopathic *traits*. In fact he displayed several other characteristics which allow us to come closer to a diagnosis.

Hitler's Personality Disorder

There are as many definitions of personality as there are psychiatrists, but it is a subject which causes the lay person far less difficulty.

An aggressive psychopath needs no introduction to any cinema audience. A histrionic type – obviously indulging in egoism, exhibitionism and florid displays of affection or excitability – he is also easily recognisable by the populace at large. Less obvious are the so-called 'sociopaths' of today's world, although Hervey Cleckley in his publication *The Mask of Sanity*[42] gave us an insight into their ruthless and irresponsible amorality concealed by a façade of normality.

It has recently become clear that there are other types of disorder, and an enormous amount of literature has appeared about these in the last twenty years, corroborating the work originally done in 1940 by Paul Hoch and Philip Polatin. These are the so-called 'personality disorders' – the 'borderline states' and the 'schizotypal disorder'.

A word of caution is necessary, for a diagnosis of personality disorder should not be made lightly, and both these states can often themselves merge with psychopathia. But it may be useful to know that the term 'borderline' refers to the border between psychosis and normality. 'Borderline' patients are characterised by lassitude and boredom, depression, and inappropriate, sudden, intense bursts of anger.

The schizotypal disorder is often said to be found among the relatives of schizophrenics.[43] The appearance and body language of these individuals with schizotypal disorder, as well as their overactive suspiciousness and strange habits, give warning signals that they are 'odd'. Their characteristics are also said to include odd speech – digressive, overelaborate, sometimes vague – inadequate rapport in face-to-face interaction, undue sensitivity to real or imagined criticism, and a marked tendency to superstitiousness. Although work is continuing into this disorder, these are at present the discernible *overt* behavioural patterns necessary for diagnosis.

Hitler had recognisable characteristics shared by both borderline personality and schizotypal disorder – in fact these groups overlap considerably – but it is the opinion of all the psychiatric professionals that I have consulted that Hitler displayed a personality disorder at present identifiable as most likely that of borderline schizophrenia. However, there is strong suppositive evidence for this being of a schizotypal origin. The characteristic overt behavioural pattern may be belatedly recognised by the layman. The reason that Hitler *seemed* so odd was because he *was* odd!

To read the index of any of the postwar memoirs about Hitler written by his collaborators such as Speer is to read a list of the character traits exhibited by such a personality disorder – even though the authors apparently didn't notice them at the time.

The Pressures on Hitler's Mind

Hans Dietrich Rötter's claim that Hitler's physical illness destroyed his personality, while untrue, nevertheless has an element of reality. For there is thought to be a 25 to 30 per cent mental retardation associated with Parkinsonism of his degree, though drugs such as Leva-dopa (unavailable to the Führer at that time) are said to ameliorate this. This retardation normally takes the form of depression, but undoubtedly it would also adversely affect cognitive function – or, in lay terms, his Parkinson's disease would indeed take away Hitler's mental edge.

If we can believe his collaborators' testimony, Hitler's personality defects were discernible long before he was taking any of Dr Morell's concoctions. But were Morell's medications to play any part in his mental disorder? What were the mental effects of the massive amounts of strychnine and atropine contained in the handfuls of anti-flatulence pills that Morell and also Bormann encouraged Hitler to take?

It is known that Hitler took up to ten pills at least three times a day, to counter his excessive body odour and severe flatulence. Speer told me that even in the early 1930s at Obersalzberg, in Bavaria, he dreaded Hitler taking off his coat to be in his shirtsleeves on a hot summer's day – the stench was overwhelming. Being unaware that excessive sweating (or hyperhidrosis) is a medical condition, Speer had attributed the problem to the Führer's incorrigible uncleanliness – a subject which was strictly taboo. Gregor and Otto Strasser, among the founders of the Nazi Party, were to have no such inhibitions about the subject – deploring Hitler's peasant habits, and calling Hitler's living-quarters in the early days a 'pit'.[44] The Nazi stalwart Kurt Ludecke also described Hitler's disorderliness and slovenliness in detail, terming it an Austrian *Schlamperei* or mess.[45] Goebbels was yet another who had described Hitler's HQ in the early 1930s as a pigsty.

Again, according to two independent sources on differing sides of the political spectrum, Speer and Basil Liddell Hart (who had visited Hitler), everyone who had anything to do with the Führer was aware of his propensity to pass wind copiously and noiselessly, even during official functions in Berlin in the early 1930s.

Whereas the strychnine in the anti-flatulence pills would have had very little effect – being only a mild stimulant even in the doses taken by Hitler (despite being the rat poison of the sixteenth century) – the atropine could certainly not be discounted. Atropine has a decided delaying effect on the passage of food through the intestines, making the passage of wind slower (but even quieter). It also has an anti-tremor effect, which might have been discernible to the Führer and have added to his liking for the tablets. We know that from its other pharmacological actions atropine also may have adversely affected his memory, and may have increased his irritability and restlessness. It was not, however, taken in doses large enough to cause hallucinations, nor disorientation.

To add to his misery, Hitler became a devotee of atropine eye-drops, which he found improved his vision – again indicating the extent of his neurological disease, for by mid-1944 he was using a magnifying-glass to read the wall maps, his visual acuity being grossly impaired. He used three or four atropine drops at a time, sometimes every half-hour, with the result that they would cause both photophobia (aversion to light) and intense headaches on exposure to light. This is another physical explanation of his reluctance to venture out into daylight.

Along with these tablets Hitler was given methyl-amphetamine as a stimulant, combined with caffeine and a certain amount of cocaine. The dosage of the pills that he took didn't seem to be regulated to any set format, and the available testimony is inadequate to work out exactly how much was taken of what and hence come to any meaningful conclusions. It is known that delusional states are known to be caused by overdosage with amphetamines, but there is no evidence that Hitler exhibited any such syndrome.

However, chronic fatigue, irritability, anxiety and depression, along with a marked sleep disorder would very likely result from such medication. Indeed, many observers noted the progressive increase in Hitler's irritability from 1942 onwards, and he was given a variety of tablets and injections to combat his insomnia – resulting in an enforced, disordered and bizarre pattern of existence. His twilight world reached its zenith in the Bunker, when the only pattern discernible in Hitler's behaviour was the fact that he held meetings in between the American daytime bombings and the British night-time blitz.

This all added to the immense mental strains under which Hitler lived in the last few months of his existence – strains which would adversely affect anyone, personality disorder or not.

First, even though cocooned from reality, he was only too aware of impending retribution – he is recorded as showing acute anxiety about being put on display and humiliated by the Soviets if he were to fall into their hands alive.[46]

In addition to this, he was increasingly aware and fearful that his magnetic effect on the German people had declined almost totally since the war had begun to go badly for Germany. This itself indicates that the magnetism which had previously affected audiences was indeed mass hysteria – a wish to hear expounded their cherished inner thoughts about their superiority, rather than any innate quality of the Führer. Speer has recorded that 'His relationship with the people changed – their enthusiasm and capacity to respond to him had faded and his magnetic power over them seemed likewise to have fled.'[47] Speer thought that this was the sole reason why Hitler had ceased all public speaking. But Hitler was also equally aware of his growing physical incapacity and of the effect that public awareness of this would have on his grip on the Reich.

From the testimony of Speer about remarks by Eva Braun and the supposed injections of pulverised bulls' testicles in grape sugar and of extracts of prostate and seminal vesicles, we know that Hitler was also inordinately concerned about the effect of his impotence – a worry dating back to the mid-1930s. If we are to believe Speer, Hitler had already despairingly instructed Eva Braun that she had better look to someone else for sexual gratification – even as early as 1938 – but the situation still concerned Hitler, and the 'hormonal' treatment continued until the last few months of the war.

It is highly likely, however, that these 'hormonal' injections were in fact pure grape sugar, containing none of the rubbish claimed, as the reactions to 'foreign' proteins would probably have been noticeably severe. It is possible to induce a condition known as amyloidosis by such methods, but, despite this in effect causing premature ageing, there is no evidence to show that this syndrome was induced in Hitler. (A number of British notables, including Sir Stafford Cripps, also received similar injections of assorted rubbish such as monkeys' adrenals and thyroids, from quacks in Germany.)

The mental staleness of life cloistered in the Bunker was bound to affect everyone adversely, but it affected Hitler possibly less than it affected his entourage. He had the consolation of being cocooned from reality – of being protected and used by the trio of Martin Bormann, the publicist Robert Ley and the Nazi Party secretary Hans Heinrich Lammers; of still being the constant centre of attention. It had become noticeable that he had long ago ceased to hold consultations with the General Staff. Gone were the days when he would scan four or five vast maps in such company and impress them with his tactical grasp. This withdrawal from reality was certainly one of Hitler's choosing – an avoidance of unpleasant facts – and that again is a characteristic both of psychopathia and of a personality disorder.

The result was that, despite the urgency of the German position, much time was wasted in hanging around in banal activity waiting for the Führer to surface or to be in a fit enough state to take decisions. It had been bad enough for Speer in the early 1930s, when he had called such an equally impossible situation at Obersalzberg 'The Mountain Disease' – hanging around, bored to tears, with nothing to do. But as the reality of retribution approached, stabbing through the fluffy rhetoric and rosy nostalgia of his protectors, a Hitler whose personality disorder was by now as obvious as his physical state had to be forced into making a choice about his own survival.

What were the chances of Hitler committing suicide? Reports that Hitler in the last few weeks of Bunker existence stated his intentions to kill himself are of absolutely no value, as they were made by suspect, posturing individuals, all telling a tale to their personal advantage. Speer was allegedly asked for advice about suicide by an uncertain Führer,[48] possibly indicating that Hitler was undecided until near the last; yet Speer's written testimony presents Hitler as decidedly resolved:

> I shall not fight personally – there is a chance that I would fall into the hands of the Russians. I don't want the enemy to disgrace my body so I have given orders that I be cremated. Fräulein Braun wants to depart this life with me, and I'll shoot Blondi [Hitler's Alsatian] beforehand. Believe me, Speer, it is easy for me to end my life. A brief moment and I am free of everything – liberated from this painful existence.[49]

Those around him, especially Goebbels, were extolling the virtues of mass suicide – pointing out the supposed popularity of this procedure among Roman legionaries – but for some reason this course of action didn't gain the popularity it deserved. Hitler himself apparently never gave this serious consideration.

The relevance of having a proper diagnosis of Hitler's mental condition is that it gives psychiatrists a chance to make a more realistic assessment of the possibility that he would commit suicide, or indeed pretend to commit suicide so as to evoke sympathy – the so-called parasuicide attempt. It is difficult to quantify, but it can be said that histrionic rhetoric about committing suicide is extremely common among those with schizo-typal borderline personality disorders, parasuicide attempts are less so, and genuine suicide attempts are much rarer. Even so, the incidence of such attempts is several times higher than the norm.

When all the fears of retribution and the strains of his unreal twilight existence are added, it must be admitted that the chances that Hitler would commit suicide are not inconsiderable – but still far less than probable. Nevertheless, the situation was compounded by the fact that in the Bunker there were several others who each had a specific vested interest in Hitler's suicide.

The importance of such a suicide had preoccupied both the Allies and the Soviets, neither of whom wished to allow the realisation of a sentiment first expressed by Hitler to Rauschning in the early 1930s: 'Yes, in the hour of supreme peril I must sacrifice myself for the people.'[50] The last thing that the Allies or Soviets wanted was the establishing of a myth of such self-sacrifice which would take generations to eradicate.

Indeed General William O'Donovan, the head of the American OSS, had realised the importance of ascertaining Hitler's likely fate before the war had even started, having realised that Hitler was a more serious phenonemon than the 'crazy paperhanger' depicted in the popular cartoons. In 1943 O'Donovan approached one of America's leading psychiatrists, Dr Walter Langer, to head a team of experts to compile a secret report on Hitler's psyche, his ambitions, his weaknesses and his eventual probable fate. 'Keep it brief and make it readable to the layman', were his very necessary guidelines.

Langer set three research assistants to combing public records in New York, and he had access to the vast resources of the American State Department, with its contacts in Austria and Germany. He questioned Princess von Hohenlohe, a 'groupie' of the Nazis, in a detention camp in Texas, Otto Strasser in exile in Montreal, and many others. The background material for his report was so detailed that it contained 1,100 pages of single-spaced typescript paper, and became known as the 'Hitler Source Book'.

In this remarkable and prescient report, Langer honestly acknowledged that there would prove to be understandable deficiencies in his research, and warned about the likelihood of incorrect conclusions. But, as it turned out, Langer's report was to be the prime and first example of the devastatingly accurate use of medical psychiatric expertise in warfare. Its subsequently being virtually ignored by historians is a lasting indictment of their failure to grasp the significance of such techniques in political life.

The conclusions that concern us relate to Part VI of the report: 'Hitler – his Probable Behavior in the Future'.

Langer felt that Hitler was unlikely to become discernibly insane, although he showed 'many characteristics that border on the schizophrenic'.[51] (From his own immense psychiatric clinical experience, Langer came to the same diagnosis of schizotypal personality disorder before the syndrome had been clarified.)

He felt certain that 'His [Hitler's] public appearances will become less and less, for . . . is unable to face a critical audience.'[52]

Langer felt there was a distinct risk that Hitler's nightmares would 'drive him closer to a nervous collapse'.[53]

He also felt that Hitler would do his utmost not to fall into enemy hands, but felt that it was unlikely that the German military would revolt and seize Hitler, as this would 'puncture the myth of the loved and invincible leader'[54] – a myth required by Hitler and the people.

Last of all, he predicted that Hitler might well commit suicide: 'This is the most plausible outcome. Not only has he threatened to commit suicide, but . . . he could undoubtedly screw himself up into the superman character and perform the deed.'[55]

Langer felt that it would not be a simple suicide – Hitler 'has much too much of the dramatic for that, and since immortality is one of his dominant motives we can imagine that he would stage the most dramatic and effective death scene he could possibly think of . . . He might even engage some other fanatic to do the final killing at his orders.'[56]

It is obvious that Dr Langer's analysis led him to believe that, given the inexorable circumstances of looming defeat and humiliation, Hitler would *probably* commit suicide. Now, we witness the divergent opinions of psychiatric groups separated by half a century of knowledge and differing experience. Possibly, not probably, would be the present-day assessment. The difference is arguably only a matter of degree.

It is high time to try to end the conjecture. Time to examine a more than distinctly odd man in a twilight zone where he expressed banalities and irrelevances in a low, monotonous, repetitive monologue. Time to assess the military and political effects of his failing mental grasp; to witness his isolation, his neglect by shabby ill-disciplined guards; to witness the extent to which he and the Third Reich parted from reality in the Bunker which Speer was to call 'The Isle of the Departed'.[57]

3

Overture to *Götterdämmerung*

In 1945, Berlin, the capital of Nazi Germany, was increasingly menaced by Soviet, American and British armies, its capture inevitable. The only uncertainty seemed to be about which force would finally face down Hitler in his Bunker.

In fact it was to be the Soviet armies that eventually accomplished this task – but for political as much as military reasons, as we shall see. It was evident that Berlin would play a central strategic role in the postwar settlement, and it was the politics of the postwar world, with new alliances and new fears, that was to determine the city's fate.

Berlin, as much as any other issue in the course of the Second World War, demonstrated that the ties that apparently bound the so-called Allies were strangely friable. Aside from the battle against the Nazis, the Soviet, British and American objectives were in stark opposition to one another.

Pettiness, Naïvety and Confusion among the Allies

The seeds of confusion, mistrust and conflict between the Allies had been sown long before the war. Britain's interests in its empire – especially in the Middle East – were threatened by the burgeoning financial power of the USA. America came into the war in Europe out of self-interest, and for no other reason. Churchill, delighted to have the Americans on board, nevertheless had bitterly to witness his nation being put into hock for American support long before the Normandy landings.

Churchill's worries about Soviet aims were tempered by his uncertainty about the future of Europe, let alone the Empire, once American financial power was unleashed; but he saw the gigantic American war machine as

41

the only buffer to Soviet expansion. He thought that the increasingly belligerent and seemingly hysterical Soviet tone and demands augured ill for the whole of Eastern Europe, with potentially dire consequences for the West, but there is evidence that on this issue he failed to convince not only Roosevelt, who seemed desperately unconcerned, but even his close colleagues and members of the War Cabinet.

Examination of his papers and the official Eden–Churchill correspondence show that Anthony Eden, the British foreign secretary, was somewhat flattered by Stalin's personal attention and as early as 1942 urged Churchill to agree *immediately* to Stalin's suggestion that the Soviet Union's 1941 frontier should continue to be recognised after the war. Churchill's angry reply shows that he felt that this would be to reward Stalin's aggression towards Poland, while the Soviet Union had been in alliance with Germany in 1939.[1]

The remarkable personal effect that Stalin seemed to have had on Eden – an effect which has hitherto been neglected – may perhaps be judged by Eden's feeling it necessary to act as devil's advocate and reply that 'For Stalin, recognition of these frontiers is an acid test of our sincerity.'[2]

Although defence of Polish sovereignty had been the nominal reason for Britain's declaration of war, Eden was now quite prepared to sacrifice Poland to its fate without too much discussion: he felt Poland was 'a special case which should be explored';[3] he failed to see how discussion of its frontiers was sufficiently important to delay moving forward in full accord with the Soviet war effort. When the issue came to the War Cabinet, he was surprisingly supported by Beaverbrook, the minister of supply, who felt that Stalin should be appeased to show appreciation of the Soviets' commitment.

The American State Department was furious that an alliance was even being considered between the Soviet Union and Britain. To the State Department the question was not the details of any agreement but the very necessity for one.

Even though the final Soviet–British agreement was watered down because of American pressure, its existence was proof that the Soviets had succeeded in splitting the Allies. Churchill was now to show that the true reason for his concern about Poland was not entirely altruistic: he was also concerned to keep the USA out of the eastern Mediterranean, the route to Britain's Middle East oil interests.

The extent of the deviousness is best seen by studying the memoirs of the American Secretary of State Cordell Hull, and not by examination of those scant scraps of apologia the *Documents on British Foreign Policy*. Not that Cordell Hull's memoirs were themselves anything but one long denial of his part in the shadier events of those years. But that is why they are so very useful, for in their moral rectitude they successfully manage to besmirch the other side – in this case Perfidious Albion.

In the second volume of his 1948 *Memoirs*, Hull deals with the shock that America had in May 1944, after Soviet foreign minister Andrei Gromyko had visited him on 1 April to reassure the USA that Soviet intentions in Poland conformed to what had already been agreed with the British – to regain the territory the Soviet Union had previously seized in 1939. Furthermore, as the Soviets advanced in Romania, their intentions were to eventually repossess only Bessarabia, previously part of the Russian Empire (from 1812 till the end of the First World War) but never part of the Soviet Empire. This, as Hull realised, would give the Soviets a fingerhold on the border of Czechoslovakia.

At the same time, Hull was to learn from his embassies elsewhere that there was talk of another secret agreement between Britain and the Soviets, designed to exclude the Americans from the sphere of Mediterranean influence.

On 1 May further speculation was rendered unnecessary when the British ambassador in Washington, Lord Halifax, asked him outright how the American government would feel about 'An agreement between the British and the Russians whereby Russia would have a controlling influence over Rumania and Britain over Greece'.[4]

When Hull replied that this would be totally unacceptable, Churchill sent a telegram to Roosevelt, on 31 May, arguing strongly in its favour. It seemed the same kind of agreement was to apply to Yugoslavia, and the Soviets were to have Bulgaria. The telegram further revealed that it was the *British* government that had suggested the idea to Russian ambassador Gousev.

The British Foreign Office did not help allay suspicions when, under pressure, it lied stupidly and unnecessarily about the Eden–Gousev meeting of 5 May, claiming that the documented meeting had in fact been only a chance exchange of remarks. The Soviet aide-memoire sent to Cordell Hull on 1 July by Gromyko disclosed the *full* proposals. The Americans reluctantly agreed to only a three-month agreement excluding the USA from the Balkans – purely to preserve the damaged façade of Anglo-American trust.

British intentions were further brought into question, and the façade shattered, when Churchill and Eden visited Moscow in October 1944 to see Stalin and extend the agreement further – even fatuously specifying the degrees of financial influence that Britain should retain in the Balkans, where its pre-war investment had been so high.

American embassies now poured secret reports into Washington. From Ankara and Moscow, the Americans were to learn that Britain and the Soviets were to share Yugoslavia 50/50, whereas Britain would retain a 20 per cent share in Romania, Hungary and Bulgaria. This Soviet assumption of power in the Balkans and British persistence in pursuing their own interests were to have a considerable effect on American attitudes before the final battle for Berlin.

In February 1945 Churchill, Roosevelt and Stalin met at Yalta to discuss the political problems of postwar Europe. This Yalta conference was to prove so disastrous that Cordell Hull was to later emphasise three times in his memoirs his total lack of any culpability. He stressed that he had resigned beforehand – he was in ill health – and he was *never* consulted by Roosevelt.

Roosevelt, himself also in ill health, was determined to show that he could handle Stalin better than Churchill. It was to be with the Americans, not the British, that Stalin would have to deal. It was, as he explained to Lord Halifax, 'only a matter of presentation'.[5] Stalin gratefully came away with the present of Europe as far as the Elbe.

No one, even today, seems to have realised how ill Roosevelt was, nor how ineffectual at the time; his fractious behaviour masked his inability to concentrate. Churchill's description of Roosevelt at Yalta could have been written by a physician, so accurately does it portray a man having those transient symptoms that precede a full-blown stroke or collapse:

> On the other hand I am sorry to say that I was rather shocked at the President. He did not look well and was rather shaky. I know he's never a master of detail, but I got the impression that most of the time he really didn't know what it was all about. And whenever he was called upon to preside over any meeting he failed to make any attempt to grip it or guide it, and sat generally speechless, or, if he made any intervention it was generally completely irrelevant. It really was rather disturbing.[6]

Whatever Churchill claimed later to have made of the proceedings, he should have shown some irascibility of his own and stopped the débâcle. Instead, he was dragged along with the moment, later declaring portentously that although Neville Chamberlain had been wrong to believe he could trust Hitler, he did not think that he, Churchill, was wrong about Stalin.

Cerebral arteriosclerosis does not get better, and Roosevelt's illness left an undeclared gap in Allied command and cohesion. Stalin drove straight through it. On 23 March 1945 Roosevelt looked at the glum reports of Averell Harriman, his ambassador in Moscow. 'Averell is right,' he said. 'We can't do business with Stalin. He has broken every one of the promises he made at Yalta.'[7]

Meanwhile Churchill looked uneasily at the Soviet advance across Poland, and the fate of that country, where the free elections promised at Yalta were signally not occurring. Telephoning Roosevelt, he suggested the Western Allies take Berlin: 'I deem it highly important that we should shake hands with the Russians as far to the East as possible.'[8]

Yet, despite this perception, on 3 April Churchill, Roosevelt and Stalin entered into the 'Milepost' agreement, whereby a near bankrupt Britain was immediately to supply the Soviet Union with 1,000 fighter aircraft, 300 tanks, 240,000 tons of aviation fuel and 24,000 tons of rubber, in addition to which the USA was to deliver 3,000 planes, 3,000 tanks, 9,000 jeeps, 16,000 weapon-carriers and 41,000 trucks. This was at a time when there was plenty of evidence that the Soviets were actually selling off to other countries the equipment they had already received; when, further-more, it was clear that, as Churchill had told Roosevelt, the war in Europe would probably last only another month.[9]

The fact that, in essence, they were about to arm the Soviet Army that they were about to be facing across the Elbe cannot have lessened the unease of the Western Allies – an unease which became acute as the suddenness of their own advance through southern Germany made it possible for them to envisage that they themselves could capture not only Berlin but also Prague, and even Vienna. In view of this obvious realis-ation, there is a surprising lack of documentation about the discussions that Churchill and Roosevelt had about the true war aims of both sides. The distrust that Churchill's actions over the Balkans had engendered, and for which he had refused to apologise when given this option by Roosevelt, may have contributed greatly to the failure of these two states-men to collaborate and define their essential aims. Another feature con-tributing to the lack of accord at this momentous time was Roosevelt's very dubious state of health: the USA was virtually leaderless, and loath to be spurred on by Churchill.

If there was obvious disarray between Britain and America, the lack of trust and derision they accorded the Free French forces was even greater. On that, at least, they were agreed. Churchill suggested to Eden – 'for your information and as background in deep shadow'[10] – that he advise the Americans to encircle the German atomic installations thought to be in the Stuttgart area before the French could get hold of them.

The distrust between the Allied leaders was more than shared by the Allied High Command, and the divisions became worse – even petty – after a timely intervention by Montgomery, the British field marshal in charge of ground forces in the D-Day landings, thwarted a German counter-offensive in the Ardennes in December 1944 – to the embarrassment of General Omar Bradley who commanded the attacked American troops. On 24–5 March British and Canadian troops successfully crossed the Rhine, and it was a peculiarly elated Montgomery who telephoned his three army commanders on 26 March to tell them he was now going to go between Dorsten and Bocholt and head straight for the Elbe. He knew full well that this was in contravention of the order that Eisenhower, as supreme Allied commander, had given only the previous day – an order to clear the whole Rhine area of any remaining pockets of resistance before continuing eastwards.

Eisenhower's order was then, and is now, seemingly totally inexplicable, for Allied intelligence knew full well the German positions, strengths and intentions – its 'Ultra' code-breakers were reading them from German communications. When General Kurt Student tried to launch a counter-attack from Mülhausen towards Eisenach, he was countered in strength thanks to a decrypted Ultra transcript dispatched in plenty of time. It was also known that the Germans had effectively run out of fuel.

On 27 March Montgomery sent Eisenhower a signal which spelt out his intention even more clearly. It ended, 'I have ordered the 2nd and 9th Armies to move their armoured and mobile forces forward at once and get through to the ELBE with the utmost speed and drive. The situation looks good and events should begin to move rapidly in a few days.'[11]

The British War Office was aware of Eisenhower's previous order (SCAF 247), but it was so concerned that opportunities were now going begging that it supported Montgomery: '. . . don't feel obliged to take too much notice of SCAF 247'.[12]

Eisenhower responded by taking away command of the 9th Army from Montgomery and giving it to Bradley, ordering Monty to nursemaid Bradley's flank when eventually Bradley would make the main thrust to Leipzig and Dresden, *after* mopping up in the Rhine area. He wrote in his personal diary the word 'crazy' in relationship to Montgomery's suggestion that he head for Berlin.[13]

The British, in turn, were astounded by the revelation that Eisenhower – not Roosevelt but his Army commander – was in touch with Stalin, and coordinating the war effort: SCAF 247 had read, 'my present plans being co-ordinated with Stalin are as outlined in the following paragraphs'. Nor was Eisenhower joking – he actually had written to Joseph Stalin:

Personal message to Marshal Stalin from General Eisenhower.

My immediate operations are designed to encircle and destroy the enemy forces defending the Ruhr and to isolate that area from the rest of Germany . . .

I estimate that this phase of operations will terminate in late April [i.e. in four weeks time] or even earlier, and my next task will be to divide the enemy's remaining forces by joining hands with your forces.

For my forces, the best axis on which to effect this junction would be Erfurt–Leipzig–Dresden. It is along this axis that I intend to place my main effort. In addition, as soon as the situation allows, to effect a junction with your forces in the Regensburg–Linz area, thereby preventing the consolidation of resistance in a redoubt in Southern Germany.[14]

This communiqué certainly let Stalin know that for one reason or another the Americans didn't want to cross him: it strengthened his hand out of all proportion.

This incredible cable has never been adequately addressed by historians. Was it sent because Eisenhower was acting in a power vacuum caused by there being no effective president? But even if he felt he lacked direction from Roosevelt, Eisenhower had his own chain of command which he hadn't used. He should have reported to his chief of staff General George C. Marshall, as cable W64244, from Marshall himself, was later to emphasise. (Churchill had complained directly to the sick Roosevelt, pre-empting this response.) Marshall's own view (cable W64349 to Eisenhower on 7 April) was that it was 'best to maintain momentum in the North with a view to the capture of Berlin before the Russians get there'. This suggests that Roosevelt and the American High Command were at variance with Eisenhower; however, even Marshall was to be ignored.

It would appear that Eisenhower, under pressure from Montgomery, resented criticism from any source – even from Marshall – and was determined, out of pique, to cut Montgomery down to size. This might go far to explain his decision to effectively limit Montgomery's role to that of a spectator. Eisenhower had, after all, just returned from a round of being fêted by his divisional commanders, each angling for promotion in a cloud of euphoria after their own Rhine crossings, each keen to emphasise his loyalty to Eisenhower and Bradley in the face of Montgomery's continuing criticism.

There was another reason for Eisenhower's dealing with Stalin that seems to have escaped almost all historians, and that was the secret accord reached between the Soviet Union and America as a direct result of a 28 July 1944 report from the American joint chiefs of staff. They had addressed a paper to the secretary of state on the postwar decline of Britain and what it meant for the USA in terms of opportunities to be gained in establishing its own empire. The chief power that they envisaged having to contend with was the Soviet Union, with whom they advocated coming to a pragmatic understanding.[15] What this meant, in essence, was that the American armed forces were planning to sell Britain short and soften up Stalin with enough sweeteners that he would allow US finance to stabilise postwar Europe so that America could concentrate on taking over Britain's dissolving empire.

Such an explanation would explain the almost total silence on the part of the American Foreign Office and State Department in response to Eisenhower's otherwise unexplained quasi-presidential action in contacting Stalin. It could well have been the deafening silence of conspiracy.

But such a theory doesn't explain the American change of direction from Berlin to Leipzig. There were no intelligence data to suggest that there were substantial forces ranged against Eisenhower on his intended axis: he couldn't justifiably claim that his change of direction was to enable him to destroy these forces. He knew the size of the inconsequential pockets of German armour left behind, knew that the main industrial targets and factories of the Reich either had been eliminated or were within his grasp, and knew full well that there was nothing much to be gained in tackling an already destroyed Dresden or Leipzig. Did his peculiar reference to 'a redoubt in Southern Germany' have any bearing?

General Bradley seemed more convinced than anyone that Nazi forces in the German Alps could form the nucleus of a new Fourth Reich. He bought wholesale a myth that even Goebbels couldn't persuade the German Army or people to swallow – a myth which envisaged the 'Werewolves', bands of fanatically determined Nazis, charging down every forest slope, armed to the teeth, bent on destruction, causing mayhem behind the Allied lines. The truth, however, was that Nazi Germany was to become the only occupied European country without a clandestine resistance force. The Poles joked that the Germans couldn't resist because it was against orders! Yet Bradley infected Eisenhower with his childishly engaging naïvety and his comic-cartoon mentality, without there being a shred of evidence for any such German force.

In defence of this awesome gullibility, it has been said that Bradley had misconstrued the withdrawal of the German 6th Army from the Western Front to Budapest as being to cover the eastern entrances to this redoubt – a fanciful and unconvincing explanation. As Eisenhower knew that SS General Wolff was negotiating for the surrender of his forces in northern Italy, it seems no less than absurd.

The result of all this discord was a week wasted in rounding up German stragglers. Everyone had assumed that Bradley would press on to Leipzig almost immediately, as there was nothing much to do in the Ruhr. Montgomery had bounced back and declared that he wouldn't go for Berlin direct but would first aim for Lübeck, to shut off the Schleswig-Holstein peninsula and prevent the Soviets getting Denmark, and *then* head south to Berlin. It was all wishful thinking.

Eisenhower, meanwhile, had realised the gravity of his political mistake, and sent a conciliatory humble letter to Marshall: 'If the combined Chiefs of Staff should decide that the Allied need to take Berlin outweighs purely military considerations in the theater I would cheerfully adjust my plans and my thinking so as to carry out this operation.'[16]

But this volte-face was not how he presented the situation to his subordinate commanders. It was obvious that Bradley was in on the Eisenhower policy of deliberate go-slow, and he knew the reason for it – the fact that Eisenhower himself had decided that, despite Stalin's broken promises, the Yalta agreement on the postwar division of Europe would be honoured. Bradley may not, however, have appreciated that the decision to honour it was apparently that of Eisenhower alone. This is shown by cable FWD 18710, in which Eisenhower coolly informed Marshall that Stalin had 'agreed' to the Leipzig thrust even though it was going to be 'deep within that part of Germany that the Russians are eventually to occupy'.

The US administration and presidential advisers showed staggering ineptitude in allowing Eisenhower to continue taking political decisions of that magnitude – decisions not shared with the British or any other government – effectively making himself president by default.

Despite Bradley's best delaying tactics, the three US armies under his control arrived outside Leipzig on 11 April, within a day of starting off, having met only token opposition. They reached the Elbe within hours of having bypassed Leipzig. Bradley was far from pleased.

He was even more embarrassed when he learned from Commander Bill Simpson of the US 9th Army that in the north there was a chance that the bridge at Magdeburg would fall intact to the 9th Army itself. A few days later he wrote to his ADC, Major Chester Hansen, 'I was afraid that the Ninth Army would get entangled in too large a bridgehead to the North, I almost hoped the other fellow would destroy it.' When he was informed that the Germans *had* destroyed the bridge, his comment was 'Thank God.'[17]

The British High Command and Churchill were now confronted with a situation where the armies of the Western Allies had swept through Germany and were kicking their heels on the Elbe – 'presumably to await the arrival of the Russians, holding a static position'.[18] Their position on the Elbe at Wittenberge was only 135 km from the centre of Berlin. In the long term, during the postwar and Cold War years, the Elbe was to be as far east as the Western Allies would ever get.

On 17 April, 572 American bombers pounded Nuremberg as the Americans turned to go south-east. In Berlin, Hitler was already faced with the beginnings of the Soviet blitzkrieg. He ordered all the autobahn bridges around Berlin destroyed; those bridges were possibly the only obstacle that the Allied armies faced.

Even the American chiefs of staff had begun to backtrack. Commenting on the American public perception of the political rift between Ike and Monty, General 'Simbo' Simpson reported to Monty from the War Office, 'It really is frightful . . . If only the American public knew the truth.'[19] That truth was that Eisenhower was missing the chance to take Berlin and so draw the limit of Soviet influence further east.

The truth continued to be only what was perceived. The *Daily Mirror* of 28 April was reporting the 'fact' that 'seven Allied Armies are closing in on Hitler's last-stand redoubt in the mountains of Austria and Bavaria'. Meanwhile, in the north, only two Allied armies were fighting real, not mythical, forces to clear the cities of Hamburg and Bremen. It took them until 29 April to reach and cross the Elbe and race to Lübeck – a bare half-day before the Soviets. This time they advanced with permission: Eisenhower had belatedly seen the extent of his oversight about Denmark, and with the death of Roosevelt on 12 April the power vacuum at the top of American politics had been filled by Harry Truman.

The Western Allies now sat back, opposite Berlin – spectators, waiting for the Soviets to finish their act. As Montgomery was to comment to

Marshal Brooke, 'The flood of German troops and civilians fleeing from the Russians is one that can seldom have been seen before . . .'[20]

All the way down the Elbe the watching Western Allies witnessed the fear-crazed exodus of a dispirited desperate people; many war-seasoned veterans of the superior race wept openly at the relief of being captured by Western troops. Following a bizarre lapse of security, it transpired that the German High Command had known about Stalin's agreement with the Western Allies at Yalta and had known exactly where the Allies would stop. The Elbe became the river Styx for people wanting to escape from their expected hell. Whispered tales of Soviet wanton destruction, pillage, murder and rape had already swept over the waiting Allies. Protestations that medieval horrors were about to engulf the German population created a general feeling of unease among the troops, but, as many of the Allied personnel had seen Belsen and other camps, sympathy was scant.

The Soviet Approach to Berlin – Rivalry and Distrust

In November 1944 Stalin had summoned his Stavka (High Command) and, in response to a question by General Antonov, had proposed Marshal Georgi Zhukov as the overall commander in the coming invasion of Germany. He had drawn rough guidelines showing that Marshal Ivan Koniev should swing south as part of a large pincer movement towards Berlin, the other jaw being Zhukov's Army Front. Mischievously, Stalin had stopped the drawing 65 km short of Berlin, shrugged, and said 'First come, first served.'

Deputy Supreme Commander Zhukov should never have been placed in such an ignominious position – of jousting with his own junior commanders for a prize such as Berlin itself. He had been one of the few survivors of the pre-war purge of Soviet commanders and officers. A lowly cavalry conscript in 1914, by 1937 he commanded the Cossack Cavalry Corps. He had won his first battle with modern weaponry in 1939, during the Japanese incursion into Mongolia. In 1941 he had really come into prominence when, as a Stavka trouble-shooter, he was sent to organise the defence of Leningrad. He had a reputation as being a man with a violent temper, utterly ruthless with the officers of his own command structure – a man with a seemingly almost total disregard for human life. Despite these less than endearing qualities – which gained him the hatred of many, including his main rival Koniev, who had at one time served under Zhukov's direct command – his success in Leningrad had made him a target for Stalin's envy.

Koniev had come from an entirely different background, having risen from within the political commissar command structure – a fact that Zhukov detested. The military historian Boris Nicolaevsky claimed to have studied Stalin's relations with the two men and to have discerned that Stalin purposely set Koniev against Zhukov – rewarding him preferentially and showering him with scarcely merited awards, so as to set him up as a credible rival.[21]

At the end of March 1945, both Zhukov and Koniev, along with their principal staff officers, were summoned to Moscow to coordinate plans for the seizure of Berlin.[22]

On 1 April Major General S. M. Shtemenko, head of the Operations Planning Department, read out a statement to the Stavka: the Anglo-American forces were planning to take Berlin ahead of the Soviet forces. The details given by Koniev[23] displayed a knowledge of Montgomery's plan – a knowledge that may have originated from the Soviet mission at Eisenhower's HQ.

Much to Koniev's annoyance, the Stavka ruled that Koniev's 1st Ukrainian Front should proceed with all possible haste along the axis to Dresden, to face up to the main thrust of the American drive. Zhukov was to have the prize of Berlin fall to his Byelorussian Front.[24]

At the Yalta conference, Stalin had not pressed for the very necessary proper liaison between the Western Allies and the Soviets. At that time – before the lightning advance of the Americans – he may well have thought that the less communication the better, as the advantage seemed to lie with the Soviets. The rapidity of the American advance had therefore come as a great shock to Stalin and the Stavka. Stalin's reaction when a signal from Eisenhower on 28 March had clearly stated that Eisenhower was going to go for Dresden and would also clear out the mythical Nazi alpine redoubt doesn't have to be imagined. His reply was swift: he too was going to work on the same axis towards Dresden – 'only subsidiary forces would attack Berlin'.[25]

Meanwhile the logistic build-up of Soviet forces, gathering like a Mongol horde on the east side of the Oder, had been continuing. The massive war effort was visible for hundreds of kilometres; troops and equipment were so thick on the ground that there was little attempt at camouflage. The Soviet supply lines, stretching some 3,000 km, were based on the railways – 1,200 trains were used in total. Supplies were then offloaded on to horse-drawn, narrow farm carts, which then became the main means of transport,[26] notwithstanding the fact that 22,000 trucks were also used. The artillery were later estimated to have used 1,236,000 shells in the battle for Berlin – 2,250 wagonloads on the first day alone! Intermingled with these essential war supplies, and stretching far behind the war front, were other carts with livestock in cages or in baskets tied on to the carts themselves. Other animals trudged unwillingly behind. To pass through these lines was to step back into the Middle Ages.

Almost a third of the Soviet Union's entire infantry strength and half of its impressive armour – made up of the feared 60-tonne Stalin tanks, the 36-tonne T-34s and the lighter T-70s – was to confront the German forces – sometimes outnumbering the Germans almost fourfold. The main Soviet weapon, however, was the massive artillery, which was being hauled and dragged over roads that might have existed before but certainly not after its passage. In all, 163 rifle divisions, 32,000 guns and 6,500 tanks were set to roll forward.

Bridges were laid across the Oder at night, their surfaces just under the surface of the water, making them difficult to detect and even more difficult to destroy. The building sometimes went on in the open, in daylight, the scale of the exercise making a mockery of the Luftwaffe's desperate attempts to slow down the inexorable process.

Zhukov had allocated Koniev the 28th and 31st Armies from the Byelorussian Front, along with seven artillery divisions, to enable the 1st Ukrainian Front to cut a swathe through Germany below Berlin, across to the Elbe opposite Dresden. Zhukov, and the panorama of the 2nd Byelorussian Front, now threatened Berlin itself, clearly visible to the disbelieving Germans.

The initial plan had been for a massive frontal assault of the Oder and the capture of the only real geographical obstacle between the Oder and Berlin itself – the Seelow Heights, an escarpment strategically overlooking the river crossings. Berlin was then to be captured in a classical pincer movement using the 1st and 2nd Guards Tank Armies, in thrusts from the south-east and north-east. The 1st Polish Army, the 61st Army and the 7th Guards Cavalry would cross the Oder to the north of the city and provide protection on the north flank, while the garrison town of Frankfurt-on-Oder, which lay on the direct Warsaw–Berlin axis, was to be attacked and neutralised by the 69th and 33rd Armies and the 2nd Guards Cavalry. Zhukov planned to use the 3rd Army as his effective rearguard reserve.[27]

Behind these forces and the 1st Byelorussian Front to the north lay an airborne attack and support system commanded by Air Chief Marshal

Novikov from the 16th Air Army Base. Once again the logistics reflect the scale of the Soviet war machine. A total of 290 new aerodromes or airstrips had to be built as the fronts ploughed forward. Apart from their own army support fighters, the three armies were backed by a total of 7,500 combat aircraft, including 2,267 bombers, 1,709 air-attack aircraft and 3,279 fighters – overwhelming the German opposition sixfold.[28]

Zhukov claimed to have planned the attack on Berlin in some detail, using eight aerial surveys of the city and a large-scale purpose-built model.[29]

These were preparations that anyone would expect in wartime, but the Soviet Army differed in two important respects from the Allied armies it thought it might be racing to Berlin. First they had a unique instrument termed the 'penal' battalion – full of convicts, deserters and murderers released from prison – used to swamp enemy positions and find a way through minefields. They also had so-called 'Seydlitz' troops – German prisoners of war who had been 'volunteered' into uniforms resembling their own German uniforms (minus the Nazi insignia), sometimes additionally wearing the pre-war national colours in the form of armbands. These somewhat disposable unfortunates were used to infiltrate enemy positions and report back to the Soviets.[30] Fear of retribution from the inevitably conquering Soviets prevented them from defecting.

In the army of what they termed the 'Great Patriotic War', a fervour and expectancy had arisen, as the troops realised that victory was within their grasp. Thoughts of revenge and of savouring the spoils of war were just under the surface. The number of Communist Party membership applications shot up as the men suddenly started to believe in the cause that they were supposedly fighting for. The 1st Byelorussian Front registered 5,890 Party applications that March.[31]

With such an immense scale of operations, the Soviet forces were unwieldy, hardly capable of the large-scale, highly mobile warfare at which the Germans excelled. But they didn't generally bother with tactical manoeuvres – they just launched a full-frontal attack on whatever was in their way. Starting with their artillery, they pulverised every metre of territory before they occupied it.

The Germans realised that the ponderousness that they had previously faced with some success and turned to their advantage now had to be countered without the element of surprise, with scarcely any fuel, without fresh troops, and with increasingly suspect discipline. For a couple of years' inexorable suffering in Russia had made the battle to control German discipline just one battle too many – German commanders were fully aware of the devastating effect on morale of constant retreats and reverses.

It was therefore more than fortuitous that, long before these reverses had begun in earnest, Hitler had developed his own 'fortress mentality', the result of which was a string of heavily defended towns stretching from the Baltic to Silesia. Königsberg, Insterburg, Folburg, Stettin, Küstrin and Breslau were prime examples. The German divisions now fell back in haste into these enclaves. The fact that they could no longer readily retreat further, due to lack of resources – most especially fuel – bolstered their willingness to fight, and they were urged on by the hysterical messages from Hitler's command centre. When Königsberg was surrendered by its garrison commander, Otto Lasch, Hitler screamed treason and ordered Lasch's execution – somewhat belatedly, as he was already in captivity. The obvious problem for the Germans was that there were now so many Soviets that they could both attack the fortresses and pour through the gaps between them. The Germans faced a swarm of destroyer ants: their morale cracked.

To the north, 2 million East Prussians fled along the Baltic coast in dire weather, in fear of retribution from General Konstantin Rokossovsky's 2nd White Russian Front. No reason could gainsay their terror: it was based on centuries of history. Some 450,000 were evacuated from Pilau; others fled to Danzig (present-day Gdansk), where 900,000 sought refuge, many of them trudging across the frozen waters of the Frisches-Haff lagoon to reach safety. There were desperate scenes. Estonians and Latvians were among the thousands that perished on the march. The scenes were described by the historian John Erickson:

Columns of refugees combined with groups of Allied prisoners uprooted from their camps . . . they trudged on foot or rode in farm carts, some to be charged down and crushed in a bloody smear of humans and horses by the juggernaut Soviet tank columns racing ahead with the infantry astride their T-34s. Raped women were nailed by their hands to the farmcarts carrying their families . . . families huddled in ditches or by the roadside, fathers intent on shooting their children or waiting whimpering for what seemed the wrath of God to pass.[32]

The Oder was now to become the new 'Eastern Wall' that Hitler promised would see off the Asiatic hordes. Hitler seemed to have forgotten that the Western Wall along the Rhine had gone, and that the Russians had overwhelmed his first 'Eastern Wall' – from the Sea of Azov to the Baltic – while he was still planning it.

However, the Soviets had learnt a bitter lesson about attacking a large city, for in January Hermann Balk's 4th Panzer Corps had created havoc for three weeks while defending Budapest from the Soviets, giving Malinovsky's 2nd Ukrainian Front and Tolbukin's 3rd Ukrainian Front a dreadful warning about the dangers of precipitate, unthinking advance.

The Siege of Berlin

Berlin now housed only about 2.5 million citizens. Apart from the constant bombing, their existence had been made unreal by the bombardment of Nazi propaganda. Amazingly, no thought seemed to have been given to the defence of the city itself until 8 March 1945, when Lieutenant General Helmuth Reymann drew up plans.

These plans envisaged, first, a forward line comprising of the Seelow Heights and the Alte Oder and Dahme rivers, extending about 80 km. Then an obstacle belt, which never became very effective, was to be based on the fortified buildings and road junctions behind this front. An outer defence ring was based on the actual city boundary, and an inner defence ring, based on the S-Bahn or district railway system, formed a far more effective barrier. Lastly would come a defence of the so-called Zitadelle – the centre of Berlin itself – based on the natural boundaries afforded by the island of the River Spree and the Landwehr Canal, which gave protection to most of the ministry buildings.

A labour force of some 70,000 people was organised under labour chief Hans Werner Lobeck and shipped about by the S-Bahn and U-Bahn (Underground) railway systems. In the city itself horse-drawn carts carried the bulk of the building materials. It soon became apparent that there was a shortage of wire and ferro-concrete, a shortage of tools, and a unifying despair among a sometimes unwilling workforce.

The defences for the outer ring were augmented by some twenty or so local artillery batteries. Hardly any of the workers thought much of the obstacles they were building – there were few covered positions in the outer ring, which ended up being for the most part a simple ditch.[33] The Berliner joke was that there was no need to worry – when Ivan saw the Berlin defences he'd die laughing!

The inner ring was much better, as it consisted of steep railway embankments, with taller buildings affording good lines of crossfire.

Tanks and anti-tank guns were dug in strategically at crossroads, and the city's 483 bridges were prepared for demolition. The U-Bahn tunnels were blockaded at critical points.

The Zitadelle was to prove by far the most impressive barrier, with each of its massive buildings fortified against attack. Guns and tanks were also dug in at what were considered its weakest points, both sides of the main east–west axis, especially in the Tiergarten. Communication between unit commanders, however, was via the ordinary city telephone exchange.[34]

Despite the lack of proper communications and the lack of proper planning in its defence, the city itself presented a very formidable physical obstacle – potentially greater than Leningrad. But, however great the potential obstacle, it was defended by what was to prove no more than a dad's army of motley volunteers. First there was the Hitler Youth, made up of boys from twelve to sixteen years old. Then there were the Home Guard equivalents, the Volksturm units – men who were divided into two categories: those with and those without weapons!

The commanding officer of the 42nd Volksturm Battalion had 400 men – 180 of whom had Danish rifles, but no ammunition. They had four machine-guns, but no one knew how to use them. As they had no uniforms, they were ordered to turn out in 'suitable civilian dress'. When they were finally assembled, they decided that without any guns or uniforms it was all too pointless – so they went home.[35]

Young women from the German Girls League were to form so-called 'Mohnke' units, fetching and carrying and sometimes even fighting.[36]

The Soviets had good intelligence about the chaos in Berlin, but their estimates of the forces ranged against them was recorded as 1,000,000 'effectives' (anyone who could hold and fire a gun), 10,000 guns and mortars, 1,500 tanks and some 3,300 aircraft. These figures were to prove somewhat on the high side.[37]

Covering from the junction of the Havel and the Elbe in the north down to the area opposite Leipzig in the south was the German 12th Army, comprised of the 39th Panzer Corps, the 41st Panzer Corps, the 48th Panzer Corps and the 20th Corps. But the 160 km length of the Oder front was held by Army Group Weichsel, under the command of Colonel-General Gotthard Heinrici. He had an outstanding reputation for holding defensive positions, and had General Hasso von Manteuffel's 3rd Panzer Army covering his northern flank as well as General Theodor Busse's 9th Army to his south, covering the direct route into Berlin and linking with the Frankfurt-on-Oder garrison.

However, Heinrici had lost several of his best armoured units when Hitler transferred them to Budapest, believing that for some reason the Soviets would not attack Berlin directly. Heinrici now had only some 850 tanks. His desperate and forceful representations to the Führerbunker resulted in some 30,000 totally untrained men being sent to him with only 1,000 rifles.[38]

Busse's 9th Army was expected to bear the brunt of Zhukov's thrust. He had fifteen weak divisions and the 30,000–40,000 men of the Frankfurt-on-Oder garrison. He had the air support of Colonel-General Robert Ritter von Greim who, contrary to Soviet estimates, only had some 3,000 aircraft over the whole of the Eastern Front and, furthermore, was short of aviation fuel.

Opposite Zhukov, across from the Seelow Heights, the waters of an artificial lake had been released into the Oder Valley bottom, turning it into a nightmarish swamp. The defenders on the Heights themselves were too busy to watch the attempts to cross this – they had run out of barbed wire the day before the assault, and were painfully aware that they had only two and a half days' supply of artillery shells. Behind them they had a fall-back line of fortified defences called the Hardenburg Line. But once that line had gone there was nothing effective to stop the Soviet horde from reaching Berlin.

Zhukov's army now ranged 15 km north and south of Kienitz, itself less than 85 km from Berlin. On 16 April at 04.00 sharp, 140 searchlights lit the Oder Valley and the German-occupied Seelow Heights. The earth reared in an unbroken wall several metres high – thrown up by the massive artillery bombardment that now engulfed the defenders.

As German intelligence had learned of the Soviet intentions in advance, most of the Germans had left the Seelow Heights. They knew from experience how long the bombardment was likely to take, and silently reoccupied their positions as it tailed off. Those who arrived too early had bleeding eardrums by the time their colleagues joined them.

But the searchlights were directed forwards, not upwards at the clouds as in the so-called 'artificial moonlight' technique of the British that Zhukov was trying to copy. For the attackers this meant a nightmarish world of black shadow and light-blindness, a world in which the defenders had a tremendous advantage as the silhouetted units stumbled on towards them. Angrily the forward-unit commanders screamed orders to turn out the lights, and equally angrily the superior officers at the back ordered them back on again. The lights went on and off in a bizarre Morse code; the effect was that the accompanying 730 Soviet ground-attack aircraft – already blinded by the pall of smoke – gave up and returned to their bases, accompanied by some 455 equally frustrated heavy bombers.

Thousands of Soviet troops died trying to storm the now occupied Heights and cross the Hauptgraben and Alte Oder waterways, where the temporary bridges they had set up were sitting targets for German artillery. Seventy German suicide planes also attacked the bridges over the Oder. There was carnage now on the Soviet side.

The increasingly frustrated Zhukov ordered his commanders to lead their men from the front. Eventually General Katukov of the Forward Command was ordered to commit his reserve tanks into the fray. His objections, that this would only add to the congestion without producing much increase in fire-power, were ignored. Wave after wave of tanks and infantry eventually overwhelmed the defenders and also managed to cross the marshland both sides of the Küstrin road, but only after Katukov's objections had been proved tragically correct.

To have used his tanks in that manner across a virtual swamp had proved a huge mistake, but to clog their progress with even more tanks was to prove the biggest disaster of Zhukov's military career. He was by now two days behind schedule, and having to explain his lack of progress to a sceptical Stalin.

The villages around that sector, such as Lietzen, now became strongpoints for the SS Nordland Division as they fell back during the next four days. They were pounded into oblivion. A survivor, a seventeen-year-old guard, Helmuth Altner, said the unforgettable smell of scorched flesh hung heavily over the buildings as he retreated. There was total disorder as the remnants of the Nordland Division made it back to the northeastern Berlin ring road, among them thirty of the Britische Freikorps, including John Amery (to be hanged for treason in December).

Meanwhile General Vasilii Chuikov's 8th Guards Army, part of the 1st Byelorussian Front, breaking free and sweeping in under Colonel Yefin Gritsenko, overcame an 18th Panzer Division counter-attack at Diedersdorf, on the main road to Berlin from the east, but with heavy losses, as the Soviet tanks of the 1st Tank Army were still nose to tail.

The newly created Müncheberg Panzer Division was overwhelmed by the 5th Shock Army in a scene of utter devastation. Journalist Konstantin Simonov relates how Chuikov in his advance came across a forest glade where hundreds of burnt-out tanks, armoured trucks and ambulances had tried to escape, cutting down swathes of trees in their panic: 'a bloody mass of mutilated corpses lay strewn along the clearing as far as the eye could see'.[39]

While Army Group Weichsel fell back into the outer ring of the city itself, a very different situation existed on Koniev's front.

Koniev's troops had crossed the Oder at Steinar, some 85 km from Berlin, on the night of 17 April and he pressed on rapidly to the next obstacle – the Neisse. His commander of the 3rd Guards Tank Army, Colonel-General Rybalko, ordered his tanks to ford the 60 m river without waiting for bridges to be built. It was only a metre deep. By midnight on 18 April they were 45 km beyond the River Spree and level with Lübben. There was effectively no opposition.

Koniev's orders had been to force the Spree and advance rapidly to Potsdam and south-west Berlin – for 'Daring and resolute progress – bypassing towns, with no protracted fighting to be undertaken. This last point to be impressed on Corps and Brigade Commanders.'[40] As soon as the 3rd Guards and 4th Guards Tank Armies were across the upper Spree, Koniev got in touch with Stalin. Stalin suggested, very unpractically, that Zhukov transfer his armour to follow Koniev's route and augment his success. Koniev had other ideas. After prolonged discussion, an impatient Koniev was given the go-ahead to attack Berlin from the south. Stalin significantly failed to tell Zhukov of this change of plan.[41]

While Zhukov was hammering his way through the crumbling defences of the north-west, and while Koniev was racing across to the south of Berlin, having effectively isolated Busse and the 9th Army, the mood in the Berlin Bunker was one of optimism. 'What was needed', said Hitler, 'was a pincer movement to crush Koniev, by the 9th Army.' Field Marshal Wilhelm Keitel, chief of staff of the OKW, the Combined General Staff, now lived up to his two nicknames – the 'nodding ass', and 'Lakaitel' (little flunkey). He matched, if not bettered, this insane appraisal: 'If the German defences can hold out one day more then the Russians will be forced to abandon their offensive.'[42]

A French doctor later recalled that in the streets of Berlin itself there was 'No excitement – no groups talking in the streets – men go about their work and women queue in front of the shops – the squares are full of children at play.'[43]

Heinrici didn't share in the madness: he tried desperately to get Hitler to agree to let the 9th Army, with whom he was in contact, fall back from the Oder and try to effect a breakout, before it became isolated and destroyed.[44] When Hitler refused – thereby sealing the fate of this army – Heinrici himself decided to withdraw, without reference to Hitler, to save the 3rd Panzer Army from a similar fate. By doing so he left the problem of Berlin's defence to General Helmuth Weidling's 56th Panzer Corps.[45]

Koniev now became annoyed at the speed of progress of Rybalko, who had become unnerved at the prospect of possible flank attack. The mettle of the man can be judged by his signal: 'Comrade Rybalko you are moving like a snail – shift.'[46]

Suitably, it was on 20 April – Hitler's birthday – that General August Winter (Jodl's deputy as chief of the OKW operational staff) publicly admitted for the first time that the war might go badly for Germany. Drinking the last of a bottle of champagne, he then left the OKW headquarters at Zossen in a hurry. It was just one hour before the Soviets arrived.[47]

Major Boris Polevoi, political commissar for Koniev's headquarters, recalled the scene when he entered the village of Zossen, 24 km south of Berlin:

> To the casual eye, this village looks no different from many others in the neighbourhood of Berlin; brick cottages, each one a replica of the next; red brick church; sickly trees entwined with wild grape, and the inevitable pigeons nesting in the eaves.
>
> The only thing that might strike one as rather odd is the untidiness of the usual back yard. And there is a curious absence of paraphernalia outside the sheds and barns.
>
> The village stretches into a wood. The trees are densely planted. The ground under them looks as though someone has been over it with a vacuum cleaner. You stroll a few yards – then . . . What in the world is this?
>
> In a clearing stand twenty-four concrete buildings, camouflaged with excessive care and nearly invisible among the young pines. The concrete paths running between the buildings are overhung with netting. The compound is surrounded by a barbed wire fence through which a high-tension current could be run.
>
> By the side of the road are pillboxes splashed with dull yellow paint almost invisible even a few yards away.
>
> Hans Beltau, the German engineer who had charge of the complex electrical installations, willingly showed us over the place. He had been only too glad to remain discreetly behind when his masters were getting out.
>
> The lifts were not working so we had to descend by means of a

spiral staircase. At last we reached the bottom. Corridors branched in every direction. They were lined with numbered doors.

Everything in this devil's kitchen testified that the Red Army's blow had been so staggering and unexpected that it caught even the German General Staff unprepared. The floors were strewn with documents, maps and reference books. In the office of the Chief of Staff a dressing gown lay flung over a writing desk; on the floor lay a pair of bedroom slippers.

The bed in the adjoining room was unmade. On a small table stood a bottle of wine, a couple of glasses half-full, and a dish of apples. Underwear and family photos spilled out of a half-open suitcase.[48]

He forgot to mention that it had been defended by seventy children between twelve and fifteen with three anti-tank guns. They were mown down – the Soviets were now becoming accustomed to having to do this. He did note that 'The last message from the apparatus for running a far-flung Nazi empire ended with the words – "Ivan is literally at the door." '[49]

The Entry into Berlin

On 20 April Koniev ordered his men to 'categorically break into Berlin tonight'. They did: they entered the southern suburbs. Koniev had won the race. But the finishing-tape was to prove more than elastic, in both military and political terms.

On 21 April, the day that Berlin's sewerage, electricity and gas services started to break down, Zhukov's men broke into the northern suburbs. They were divided into street-fighting units, each group consisting of engineer platoons, flame-thrower platoons, six anti-aircraft guns and a company of infantry. Behind came the familiar horse-drawn carts, carrying ammunition and now loot.[50]

To the Germans in the city centre, a greater threat than the Soviet Army now became the SS squads – notices in the centre of the city proclaimed, 'Cooking by electricity is now punishable by DEATH.'[51]

Rumour circulated that Weidling had fled to the west, so Hitler declared him a traitor – until Weidling turned up at the Bunker, furious, to protest his innocence, whereupon he became the honoured defender of the Zitadelle. But he was the exception. It was on 21 April that General

Busse of the 9th Army ran out of artillery shells. Heinrici told him to ignore Hitler and get out to the west to try to link up with General Walther Wenck, who had been held up the other side of Potsdam in his drive to relieve Berlin from the west.

While Heinrici and Busse withdrew their armies, studiously ignoring Hitler, SS general Felix Steiner was now to realise just how much Hitler had lost touch with reality. He was ordered not to fall back but to attack Zhukov and cut off the head of the Soviet attack. 'You, Steiner, are answerable with your head for the execution of this order!'[52] Seventeen thousand completely untrained men were supposed to be sent to assist Steiner in this enterprise, but unfortunately they had no idea where he was. Hitler now ordered the 56th Panzer Corps back into Berlin – not realising that its remnants had been there for some time.

Koniev, having beaten Zhukov to the suburbs, now prepared to attack the last few kilometres directly into the city centre. For the final assault across the Teltow Canal, he massed his artillery at a density of 650 guns per kilometre – almost literally wheel to wheel.

Zhukov was very close behind, attacking from the north, north-east and north-west. Buildings that the Allied bombers had left standing were now to be blown apart. By 26 April 464,000 Soviet troops, 12,700 guns, 21,000 rocket-launchers and 1,500 tanks ringed the inner-city barricades – a mere 16 km long and 5 km wide.

By now, the mood in the city had long since changed. Party members, police cadets and field gendarmes set up roadblocks to prevent people fleeing, and scoured cellars for deserters. Lampposts sprouted with corpses bearing cards roughly written with messages such as 'I hang here because I am a defeatist', 'I hang here because I criticised the Führer' and 'I am a deserter and thus will not see the change in destiny.' Nevertheless several thousand deserters did go into hiding.[53]

Keitel toured the forward areas seemingly oblivious to reality and the evidence of his own eyes.[54]

On 23 April the city became 'pram capital of the world', as 'people moved around the remnants of their possessions in these convenient vehicles'.[55] All traffic through the U-Bahn and the S-Bahn had stopped on the 21st, when a civil engineer who tried to prevent boreholes being dug for explosives – set to destroy the tunnels and possibly drown thousands of people sheltering in relative safety – was shot on the spot.[56]

Facing the Soviets in a Zitadelle divided into segments, each under its own commander, were 9th Parachute Division in sector A, Müncheberg Panzer Division in sector B, the SS Nordland Panzergrenadier Division at Templehof in sector C, and so on – leaving the artillery section in the region of the Tiergarten. Unfortunately some military genius had forgotten that the three huge ammunition dumps on which the defences really relied in any resistance of more than four days lay outside, in the Jungfernheide Volkspark and in the outer reaches of the Tiergarten and Templehof. All of these were quickly overrun.

By now the city centre was littered with craters and dead bodies, soldiers with their weapons lying where they had died. Furtive civilians hugged the contours of the broken buildings. Terrified groups clustered silently in small shelters, contrasting with the noisy hysteria which affected the thousands that packed into shelters made for only several hundred. The stench of fear was everywhere among the near deserted streets as the sound of gunfire increased.[57]

The Soviet armies moved in for the kill. The 7th Corps came down Prenzlauer Allee from the north-east; the 26th Guards Corps and the 32nd Corps came up Frankfurter Allee from the east. The 5th Shock Army's third component, the 9th Corps, came into Treptow Park – pushing back the Nordland Division. Then, in the early hours of the morning Chuikov's troops traversing the Schönefeld airfield came across several tanks from Koniev's 3rd Guards Tank Army. Zhukov didn't learn about this until the evening, at 19.00. He greeted the news of Stalin's betrayal with disbelief, then blinding anger.[58]

That Zhukov hadn't even realised that Koniev was attacking Berlin says much for the standard of the Soviet communication system of those days; but, as Air Chief-Marshal Novikov and his staff and all their co-ordinators supporting both armies knew the situation all too well, it could reasonably be assumed that Stalin had ordered Novikov and Koniev not to reveal the situation to Zhukov himself.

At this late stage (by which time the two armies could well have been engaged in numerous accidental exchanges) exchanges between Zhukov and Stalin then established that new boundary lines were to exist between the two Soviet Fronts, the Byelorussian and the 1st Ukrainian. Within the city the demarcation was along the main railway line leading north from Lichtenrade. This order was made effective from 06.00 Moscow time on 23 April.

This was more provocation from Stalin, for it set Chuikov in direct competition with Koniev's 3rd Guards Tank Army. It could have been at this juncture that Chuikov may have been ordered to block Koniev's path to the Reichstag.[59] A furious Koniev now took over control of the Teltow Canal assault.

On the evening of 24 April, Hitler's orders from the Bunker continued to have their unreal ring: 'The main task of the OKW is to attack from the south-west, north-west and south, in order to bring the battle for Berlin to a victorious conclusion.'

On the morning of 25 April, by which time Alexanderplatz was occupied by the 7th Corps, and Chuikov was threatening Templehof Airport, Heinrici visited von Manteuffel and then went on to the 25th Panzer Division's HQ, where, to his amazement, he found Jodl trying to persuade Steiner to attack. Heinrici subsequently recorded his sentiments:

> To get to the command post from Berlin, Keitel and Jodl had passed interminable columns of fugitives and broken units that had been mixed up with them during the night and again during the morning. They had seen for the first time the true picture known to every combatant, whether at the front or rear. If their eyes had not been completely closed to the truth they would have come to the conclusion that the war had inexorably reached its end.[60]

What Keitel hadn't bothered to tour was any of the many impromptu hospitals now treating the mangled casualties of this unnecessary continuation of the war. At Neukölln the operating theatre was a former cloakroom, where amputations were carried out on a wooden table covered with a mattress. Surgeons operated without gloves or anaesthetic, with instruments only perfunctorily boiled. The operating light was manufactured from two bicycles, the pedals turned by hand.[61] Shortly afterwards the SS graffiti on the wall of the Müncheberg Division's HQ spelt out their perceived truth: 'We withdraw – but we are winning.'[62]

By the night of 26 April Chuikov's 8th Guards and 1st Guards Armies had crossed the official line of demarcation that had been agreed by Stalin, right up to the line of Potsdamer Strasse and beyond. The Byelorussian Front was now well beyond the Templehof–Potsdamer boundary, and this can have been no less than deliberate, for it placed a huge bulge of Soviet-occupied territory across the intended line of march of the 3rd Guards Army of Koniev's Ukrainian Front.

Chuikov, in his memoirs, makes light of this issue,[63] but the advance must have been sanctioned by Zhukov himself. Significantly the recorded signals traffic now in existence gives absolutely no indication that this cynical move was about to, or indeed had, taken place.

Koniev was now poised to attack Badensche Strasse with the 28th Guards Tank Army, on an axis between Kaiser Allee and Postdamer

Strasse. The troops had been hurried into position though the whole of the area from the Havel to the Heerstrasse had been inadequately secured – a deliberate risk taken in order to press home his initiative. The 55th Tank Guards Brigade was on the flank thrusting down Kantstrasse for Charlottenburg station, Savigny Platz and the Zoo. The pall of smoke rose 300 metres above the city as the bombardment began.

It was not until late morning that Koniev's forces realised that virtually the whole of the eastern half of their intended line of advance was already occupied by Chuikov's troops, whom they had been bombarding for hours. Soviet lines had been sacrificed *en masse* for political gain.[64]

There is far more to this episode than the scant memoirs and recorded signals now available. We are asked to believe that Koniev's observers were unable to detect the unmistakable sound and sight of Soviet weaponry, and that Chuikov's units had no occasion to make any contact with Koniev's forces on the ground. A full-scale encounter might have occurred, and indeed cannot be ruled out.

As a consequence of the bitter all-day recriminations that must have followed – recriminations which are now traceable only as a consequence of subsequent actions – at midnight Moscow time the Stavka ordered a new boundary line to be drawn, taking into account the existing situation on the ground. The line – which stretched from Mariendorf to Templehof station to Viktoria und Louise Platz, and along the S-Bahn – effectively spelt out that the prize of the Reichstag was not to be given to Koniev, even though in many ways he was better sited to attack.[65]

In utter disgust, Koniev left the field, transferring his command in Berlin to Colonel-General Rybalko. The whole of the right wing of his attack, including the 9th Motorised Corps and the 1st Guards Division, had to be shifted across to the left, to attack Savigny Platz, causing chaos and even more unnecessary loss of life.

If Koniev had left a deliberately weak left pincer movement in order to attack in strength on the right – straight for the Reichstag – then so had Zhukov, whose weakness in the west was appreciated by both General Wenck, stuck outside Potsdam, and General Busse, trying to save the remnants of his 9th Army. Both started to urge General Weidling to consider breaking out to the west. General Keitel, however, reflecting Hitler's orders, commanded Heinrici to attack the 2nd Byelorussian southern flank – an order which Heinrici just ignored.

In a plethora of pointless toing and froing, Keitel visited Steiner on 28 April and was personally assured that Steiner would attack the whole 2nd Byelorussian Front! It was only on his way back to his own HQ that

Keitel heard that the 3rd Panzer Army was in full retreat. Steiner had been humouring a madman.

Incensed with rage, Keitel summoned von Manteuffel and Heinrici for a meeting at a crossroads. Von Manteuffel's chief of staff, General Müller Hildebrand, was so suspicious of Keitel's intentions that he organised an ambush at the same crossroads, his men being in covering positions before Keitel arrived. When Keitel turned up, he found whatever evil intentions he had harboured had to be tempered by the grim reality of loaded guns being much in evidence. Thwarted, he screamed at Heinrici that what was needed was the shooting of a few thousand deserters, then the problems would melt away. According to Heinrici, he himself turned and pointed at the desperate black-faced soldiers trundling past – a defeated, demoralised army – and asked Keitel to start the execution himself. Faced down, Keitel left in fury.

All units in Berlin were now showing signs of disintegration. The Müncheberg Panzer diarist wrote on 28 April, 'Increasing signs of disintegration and despair, but K [Keitel] brings news that American Armoured Divisions are on their way to Berlin, which makes them in the Reich Chancellery more certain than ever.' Then, as if talking about some parallel world, he continued:

Nervous breakdowns from artillery fire . . . Flying courts martial appear in our sector – General Mumment has requested no further such courts visit our sector – a division that contains the most highly decorated personnel does not deserve to be persecuted by such youngsters . . . blond and fanatical with hardly a decoration between them. He has made up his mind to shoot any court-martial team that he comes across in person.[66]

On 29 April at 22.00, von Manteuffel phoned Heinrici to say that he was witnessing a scene he hadn't envisaged since 1918 – 100,000 of his men, half his divisions and all his supporting flak units were trekking west. There is very little doubt that, as a realist, Heinrici encouraged this trek to save his men further massacre. Shortly afterwards he was relieved of his command.

General Weidling was, as wags in his unit put it, now defending an ever decreasing Bockwurst. The 3rd Tank Guards Army of the Ukrainian Front was now going to the Kurfürstendamm, where the large department stores such as Ka-De-We were more than usually crowded for that time of the year, not with late-night shoppers but with an assortment of men from several German units. This was the heart of the city, but the Ukrainian Front could still have approached the Reichstag had it wished, without the immense barrier of the River Spree and the massivity of the Moltke Bridge that confronted Chuikov. But while the 3rd Army was literally clearing out the shops, Chuikov was directing the attack on the Moltke Bridge, which began at 02.00 on 29 April.

The River Spree formed a seemingly impregnable knuckle near the Lehrter station, pushing northwards, overlooked by the massive Red City Hall and the Ministry of the Interior – the so-called 'Himmler's House'. Chuikov's units had just released some 7,000 prisoners from the Moabit prison, and tired from this conflict, took several hours to storm the massive structure of the Moltke Bridge, spanning the water. It had been incompletely blown by its defenders, otherwise there would have been another few thousand deaths. At 07.00 the 150th Division had stormed the Ministry of the Interior, but it took it all day to quell the defenders, who were eventually cleared with the assistance of the 674th Rifle Regiment. The next obstacle was the Red City Hall, where another epic confrontation took place.

Meanwhile the 32nd Corps and the 9th Corps were pressing units of the SS back towards the Reich Chancellery.

While Soviet gunners were hauling artillery pieces up on to the upper floors and roof of the Red City Hall, and some ninety pieces of heavy weaponry on to the very roof of the Ministry of the Interior, to assist in wiping out resistance in the Kroll Opera House, another massive fortified structure, Weidling was trying to persuade Hitler to surrender the city. Afterwards he wrote, 'Catastrophe was inevitable if the Führer did not revise his decision to defend Berlin to the last man, and if he sacrificed all that were fighting in this city, for the sake of a crazy ideal . . . The struggle was without sense or purpose.'[67]

Shortly before midnight on 29 April Hitler asked the OKW, 'Where is Wenck? Where is the 9th Army.' He received remarkably truthful answers – except that no one really knew the scale of the 9th Army's defeat. In fact Busse was trying to escape with 30,000 of his men, the rest of his original 200,000 men having been lost without firing one effective shot in defence of the city itself. Of these 30,000, only some 3,000–4,000 men were eventually to make it across to join Wenck's army and retreat west to capitulate to the Western Allies.

It was another six hours before Hitler was to ask General Wilhelm Mohnke, now in charge of the Chancellery force, to tell him where the Soviets were at that time. The answer he obtained was that the Soviets

Overture to Götterdämmerung

The Capture of Berlin

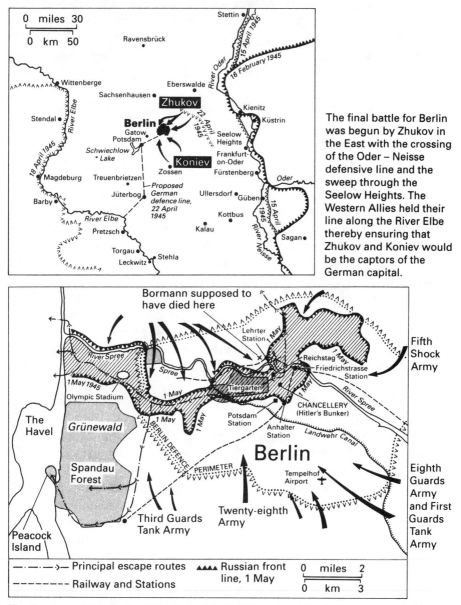

The final battle for Berlin was begun by Zhukov in the East with the crossing of the Oder – Neisse defensive line and the sweep through the Seelow Heights. The Western Allies held their line along the River Elbe thereby ensuring that Zhukov and Koniev would be the captors of the German capital.

— · — ·—>— Principal escape routes   ▲▲▲▲ Russian front line, 1 May
– – – – – – – Railway and Stations

The final assault on Berlin at the end of April 1945 reduced the territory controlled by the Germans to a narrow strip from which various escape routes emerged. The line of the railway to the South was intended to mark the limit of Koniev's forward thrust into Berlin. In fact his troops pressed further – unwittingly engaging Zhukov's troops in the North West of the city and allowing a vital opportunity for the fleeing German officers.

had occupied Friedrichstrasse U-Bahn station and the Adlon Hotel at Wilhelmstrasse. They were, he was told, outside the Chancellery at Voss Strasse. The answer cannot have been anything but designed to persuade Hitler that he had no time left, for it was blatantly untrue. The Soviets at that time were occupying the Anhalter station, but they certainly had not occupied the Friedrichstrasse station, nor were they anywhere near as close to the Chancellery.

On 30 April a massive artillery barrage, starting at 13.00, softened up the Reichstag and the Chancellery. No reply came from the expected anti-tank guns; instead the Soviets came under fire from the giant flak towers that remained unconquered. The Chancellery itself came under infantry attack as soon as darkness fell, but, before that, some soldiers had made the 200 m dash and had blown a hole in the door of the Reichstag with mortars. They poured inside. At 14.30 a rifleman, Sergeant Meliton Kantariya, could be seen waving a red banner from the second floor of the Reichstag itself. At 18.00 the initial troops were strongly reinforced. In total darkness a banner party carrying the especially designed flag of the Military Council of the 3rd Shock Army of the Byelorussian Front found its way to the roof of the building. The banner flew over the Reichstag just seventy minutes before May Day.

As far as most Soviet troops were concerned the battle was over, although the fighting still continued.

It is worth reflecting that the battle for Berlin ought never to have taken place at all – militarily it was totally unnecessary. Had there been trust between the Allies, had there been a proper agreement at Yalta, and had there not been the symbolic need for a May Day victory parade it might never have happened.

The eventual relative sanity of the German generals Heinrici, Busse, Steiner and others indicates that, given longer to contemplate reality, the German Army would have almost certainly chosen to surrender its shambolic, vindictive Charlie Chaplin of a Führer to the victorious powers. Once a nation had itself surrendered such a leader, that act would itself kill any chance of the myth of his leadership being resurrected.

Instead we have the lingering Hitler myth, despite the fact that, in deciding to attack Berlin and pinpoint the Reichstag, Stalin also pinpointed Hitler's weaknesses, cruelly exposing his real status as a military leader.

What the battle of Berlin really proved was man's capacity for wilful self-deception. In particular, it tragically confirmed the extent of one man's personality disorder, and the full cost of its effects.

It will be noticed that, in discussing the Soviet rivalry and revelry, I have not once mentioned the storming of Hitler's Bunker.

By the time that Soviet guns ceased firing at 15.00 on 2 May, 125,000 Berliners had died and the Soviets had lost (at least according to their records) 304,887 men – the heaviest casualties that were sustained in any battle in the Second World War. But not one soldier was killed storming the Bunker.

There was no storming of Hitler's bunker.

History has become somewhat distorted, for a firmly held belief has grown up that before the Führer's death his Bunker had been valiantly defended.

From all available records, it is quite clear that the Soviets didn't even know the location of Hitler's Bunker. It is also evident that not a single Soviet rifleman attacked it. As will be seen, the mood within the Bunker was hardly one of stoical resolve; it was more one of hysteria, venomous recrimination, tearful recall and funk.

4

The Bunker

The legend of the Bunker has loomed large in the mythology of the far right; not just in Germany but elsewhere in Europe too. Very early on in the conflict between the Croats and the Serbs in the former Yugoslavia, Western reporters in Croatia were to hear eulogies of the Bunker's last defence and comparisons with the Croats' own situation.

In the ideology of this newly emerging right wing there now exists a well-defined image of Hitler's Bunker under seige. Desperately determined, grim-faced, valiant SS guards – Sepp Dietrich's élite Leibstandarte, their black uniforms somehow still magically pristine, with the glistening silver 'SS' on the collar – are shooting machine-pistols from the hip, mowing down the Red Army hordes as they fight for the Führer, while the Bunker – a marvel of underground engineering – slowly surrenders its secrets, an underground Valhalla ablaze with glory.

The reality of Hitler's Bunker was that it was part of a complex which was probably more hastily planned and shoddily executed than any of the many other bunkers that the fearful Führer had built to pander to his phobias. This complex of central interlinked bunkers near the Foreign Office, Reich Chancellery and Propaganda Ministry had never been intended to house a command structure, only convenient air-raid shelters. The upper level of Hitler's own bunker had been started in 1936, a modest affair with walls a mere metre thick, at that time designed to serve the old Reich Chancellery alone. The whole complex was, in any case, a quite ridiculous place to choose as a command centre, its only virtue, as a sarcastic Soviet colonel was later to remark, being that it was 'near to the shops'.[1]

As, from mid-1944, the Allied bombing forced an underground existence on the planners of the indestructible Thousand Year Reich, so the complex became progessively enlarged, progressively deeper, and progressively entombed in concrete. The intended temporary air-raid shelters became an enforced permanent feature as the Americans pounded the city by day and the British by night. There was hardly any respite, and in any case there was nowhere else to go in the centre of Berlin itself – the magnificent Reich Chancellery building was unusable, its huge rooms, with their immense slabs of marble, massive desks, ponderous doors and multiple heavy ornamental candelabra, being manned only as a military command post.

With his acolytes in the Bunker, Hitler was some 24 km from the OKW headquarters at Zossen, south of Berlin. It made no sense for Hitler, the ultimate commander-in-chief, to be separated from his General Staff like this – or did it?

Hitler was by now so aware of the dangers of criticism, of the infectious nature of dissent among his Army commanders, that he had resorted to the extraordinary measure of asking them for a written pledge of silence before they were allowed to enter into any 'conference'. The very word 'conference' implies a somewhat different concept, but each military chief was to swallow his pride and agree to be gagged.[2]

Hitler had by now quarrelled with all the commanders-in-chief of the Army, eleven of eighteen field marshals, twenty-one of nearly forty full generals and all commanders of the three sectors of the Eastern Front. Yet they still carried out his orders, putting into practice ideas that they almost all acknowledged, even at the time, to be military madness.

General Walter Warimont's publication[3] of the transcripts of the various 'conferences' gives a remarkable insight into the facile nature of the discussions between Hitler and the General Staff – discussions that often left matters completely unresolved or even made no attempt to address the problem to hand. It gives a haunting picture of unreality: professional field marshals indulging a foot-soldier of another era, allowing him uninterruptedly to give them his homely, irrelevant wartime anecdotes and to answer their worried specific concerns with glib obvious inaccuracies, all against a backdrop of impending disaster. With a mixture of seeming pride and a sense of evident foolishness, Warimont records that the General Staff realised that Hitler was by then totally incapable of carrying out the simplest of military operations, and was held in the utmost contempt by these very same men who hastened, out of habitual subservience and a sense of patriotic duty, to help him destroy their fatherland.

They had at first tolerated his imbecility with varying degrees of reluctance, but as the war became obviously and inexorably lost their hostility towards Hitler boiled under the surface. In pragmatic terms, in the last few months of the war many Army commanders did determine to do the best they could with the resources to hand and to ignore any contrary orders. Many were only too happy not to receive too many orders that flew in the face of reason, and welcomed the respite that Hitler's isolated existence in the Berlin Führerbunker was to give them. In the last two months of the war almost all except Krebs, the chief of the Army General Staff, and Jodl, the chief of the OKW operational staff, considered his orders totally irrelevant. They knew the war was irrevocably lost.

But, despite what he saw as defeatist apathy, Hitler rightly feared that the inclusion of his own little circus of sycophants into a vast Army command bunker would dangerously expose his own physical state to ridicule, and his mental status and his decisions to question. So, along with Bormann, Ley, Lammers and Goebbels, he sought and preferred isolation – even though he must have been aware of the military consequences of this voluntary separation of commander from command structure.

For separation there certainly was: one small switchboard, one radio and one radio-telephone were the sum total of Hitler's links from the Bunker to the outside military reality. By choosing to remain in his Bunker, Hitler was deliberately abdicating responsibility for the conduct of the war – a fact that didn't pass unnoticed by the OKW, although it seems to have escaped historians. It must be assumed that Hitler was overwhelmingly fearful of unseemly retribution from his own people and from the Army High Command, fearful of an Army revolt, humiliation, and of being handed over alive to the Soviets or to the Western Allies.

The Berlin Bunker contrasted dramatically with the OKW headquarters at Zossen, where a bunker complex at least seven times larger than the Berlin system had a central switchboard, possibly the largest in Europe, connecting with all parts of the Nazi empire, directly linked to and servicing the Combined General Staff.

Zossen would have been the obvious place to be if Hitler had really wished to continue the war. But Hitler wished instead to continue the *façade* of war. His Berlin Bunker wasn't even on a direct line to the Zossen headquarters: it was served by a hastily installed switchboard, effectively completed by Siemens in November 1944, which was about the size one would nowadays expect to find in a sleazy hotel. There was room for only one switchboard operator, who, as it turned out, was to be the untrained Sergeant Rochus Misch. To get through to Zossen, Misch had first to reach Central 200, a relay station in the flak tower at the Zoo station, a mile or so from the Bunker. As a result, when the final Soviet assault swept into suburb after suburb, harassed staff officers sat next to Misch while he telephoned old acquaintances in the different sectors of Berlin to ask them if they had seen any Soviet tanks recently. For the whole of the last week of the war the switchboard was effectively dead.

Next to the increasingly desperate Sergeant Misch sat a radio communications officer with only a German Army medium- and long-wave transmitter. He had no short-wave transmitter, and for the radio telephone to be linked up to transmit and receive he was totally reliant on a length of wire dangling from a patched balloon tethered directly above the Bunker. This balloon was effectively destroyed twice by artillery fire, and the land line was also destroyed on 27 April.

To plan grand strategy, Hitler's rump state became dependent on the BBC Overseas World Service broadcasts. Heinz Lorenz, of the Propaganda Ministry, helped in the last few days by Hans Baur, Hitler's pilot, edited transcripts of these broadcasts so that they would be suitable for the Führer's ears, and ironically it was a cleaned-up version of a BBC broadcast on 28 April that enabled Hitler to learn of Himmler's attempt to usurp his authority and bargain with the Allies.

So it was that an air-raid shelter became the nerve centre for the rundown of the war – a nerve centre with derisively few communications facilities. Hitler, now nothing more than an embarrassment to the OKW, was, as far as everyone was concerned, in the best place possible – effectively out of sight and out of mind.

The Layout of the Bunker

The part of the Bunker complex that Hitler was eventually to occupy (the lower level) was 17 m below ground level and covered with 5 m of concrete, itself covered with another 4.5 m of earth. In 1943, as the force of the Allied aerial bombardment increased, a private Berlin construction firm, Hochtief, was called in to reinforce the original, upper, Bunker. But in 1944 this firm was called back to construct the lower Bunker – the Führerbunker proper. Each heavy nearby explosion nevertheless brought down a shower of fine debris inside the Bunker, and the noise rendered conversation inaudible even in the deepest level. The occupants hardly felt as if they were adequately protected, and showed repeated concern that the walls themselves were only a very modest 2 m thick. The construction was both hasty and incomplete. The walls remained unlined in many places, and the painting had never been completed and varied from none at all to patches of grey and an overall dirty red colour. Luxuriant black mould flowered in the corners, on the ceilings and in patches on the walls, where SS officers had scratched lurid graffiti. Water seeped continuously into the room housing the small 60 kW diesel generator, having to be mopped up at least three times a day.

The upper Bunker could be reached from the Chancellery itself, by stairs leading down from the butler's pantry into a narrow space enclosed by three watertight bulkheads. This narrow entrance was called Kannenberg's Alley, since Hitler's cook, Kannenberg, brought all the food, except Hitler's, through it. One bulkhead sealed off the passage to the Foreign Office, another sealed off access to the Foreign Office garden; the third gave guarded access to the upper levels of the Bunker itself. A narrow corridor, which doubled as a general dining-area, ran barely a few metres from this bulkhead before it reached a narrow wrought-iron staircase of twelve steps which curved steeply down to the lower level. Each side of this dining-area were half a dozen rooms which were no bigger than cupboards. Magda Goebbels and her six children would end up crammed in four of these cupboards, while her estranged husband was later to have his own little bedsitting-box in the lower Bunker, in a room previously used by Dr Morell to prepare his quack injections. The other rooms in the upper section served as servants' rooms and lumber rooms, excepting a small kitchen used to prepare Hitler's vegetarian meals.

The lower section, entered through another bulkhead, constantly guarded by two SS men, had fifteen rooms spread both sides of another narrow central passageway divided by a thin partition into a small conference area and a communal sitting-passage through which everyone trundled. Unbelievable as it may seem, this small conference area was where Hitler used to preside over his daily staff meetings. The rump of the Germanic world was being directed by a Führer with horizons of 6 m at most, except when the doors of a small map room were opened to give another few metres of claustrophobic space. There was absolutely no way to avoid face-to-face confrontation in such a corridor. Nor, as many were to complain, was there any way of avoiding face-to-face body odour. The door at the end of the conference room led to another small space, shut off by a steel door from the emergency-exit stairs. Contrary to its function as a secure escape route, this sequence of outside doors was also more often than not opened to assist ventilation, the air pumps in the lower level being quite unable to cope with the number of occupants.

To the intense discomfort of all, Hitler detested the fresh air draught and ordered not only the door shut but all the ventilation pumps to be switched off during his conferences. He claimed that the air passing through the blower system produced too much pressure, affecting his ears and his balance. In consequence it was frequently observed that officers coming out of his two- to three-hour briefing sessions would themselves be staggering, their gait mirroring that of the Führer.[4]

A small space at the end of the conference room had originally been designed as a cloakroom, but had now become a dossing room for the guards – the so-called 'dog-bunker'. Three small camp-beds and numerous boots imparted a choice fragrance to the otherwise welcome incoming draught.

From the security aspect the design was pitiably inadequate, as the ventilation difficulty was so severe that the occupants faced nothing less than suffocation without this through draught.

The situation was to become absolutely unbearable in the last few weeks of the war. For this we have the testimony of Johannes Hentschel, the chief electrician in charge of the damp generator room diagonally opposite Hitler's quarters. The totally inadequate diesel motor powered the air pump, electricity generator and water pump for both levels of the Bunker. As Hentschel put it, 'In that last desperate fortnight, I had to run electric cables strung out on the floor in the corridor. I used fire hoses as an emergency substitute for water piping, and one of these hoses sprang a leak. With all of the comings and goings, these hoses and cables got as tangled as spaghetti.'[5]

Hentschel also described the overload that his solitary generator faced in the last weeks, when the Reich Chancellery basement had become a casualty clearing-station housing some 500 wounded soldiers. This had woefully inadequate ventilation and water supply, and Hentschel switched the generators to pumping out water from the underground artesian well below the Bunker, for use by the surgeons in the first-aid station. The ventilation in the Bunker suffered even more.

To the right of the conference corridor, apart from the generator, were two rooms (approached via a drawing-room) occupied by the SS surgeon Ludwig Stumpfegger, Goebbels's bedsitter, and a single room divided up between the secretaries and guards, the back wall of which was the so-called emergency telephone exchange. To this link with the outside world most of the personnel gravitated, as did most of the daily visitors such as Bormann, the transport officer Erich Kempka and the chief valet Heinz Linge, all of whom lived outside the Bunker itself until the last hectic weeks.

To the left of the conference corridor, approached via an ante-room, were Eva Braun's bedsit and the bathroom she shared with Hitler – each small, spartan, poorly lit room hardly furnished. These were separated by her dressing-room, no bigger than a wardrobe, stuffed full of dresses and furs. The ante-room also led to the Führer's bedroom and living-room. The final door to the left of the corridor led to the map room.

In the last week the through traffic into the Reich Chancellery basement had to negotiate a roof fall, caused by two direct hits by heavy artillery. The exhausted medical staff and SS men trundled through this thick debris – dust filled the upper Bunker. The whole of Kannenberg Alley became a mêlée of soldiers, their packs and their mess-tins. Then, almost as if to order, the toilets all blocked simultaneously as the sewers jammed. The only toilet half-usable was Eva Braun's, which was now shared with her female companions, Magda Goebbels and the secretaries. All complained of the pervading stench of the blocked toilets and the lack of facilities. Blondi, Hitler's favourite Alsatian, delivered pups, which were put in the unusable toilet area. There was scant relief afforded by the opening of the emergency-exit doors, for the outside air itself was now acrid with smoke.

All the communal areas – the general dining-passage, the general sitting-room and the conference passage itself – became strewn with the paraphernalia of chaos. Several testimonies describe the true state of affairs. The whole Bunker was littered with half-eaten sandwiches, empty Shultheis beer bottles, and numerous bottles of Steinhager schnapps, some half-empty, left on the narrow benches – even on the very benches on which Hitler used to pause on his painful journeys around the lower Bunker. Hitler had now to be supported at almost every step he took, not least because of the danger of falling over the cables and rucksacks. In the upper Bunker, heavy drinking sessions had led to the inevitable results – aggravating what was now a decidedly less than desirable residence.

This picture of a badly planned, badly built, poorly ventilated, claustrophobia-inducing hutch of an air-raid shelter – crammed with occupants inured to filth and squalor – hardly accords with the Nazi myth. It hardly suggests the spartan barrack-room cleanliness associated with well-ordered troops. Indeed, it is well worth considering the exact nature and discipline of the troops in the Bunker.

The Occupants of the Bunker

Apart from the twenty or so SS guards who occupied the corridor and slept outside the bulkheads or in the cloakroom, there were other concentrations of guards sharing the nearby Chancellery bunker with Bormann or occupying a third, separate, bunker, which housed General Wilhelm Mohnke, the SS commandant of the Chancellery.

The mood among the SS men incarcerated in the Bunker has been recalled by one of these guards, Captain Helmut Beermann:

> The whole atmosphere down there was debilitating. It was like being stranded in a cement submarine, or buried alive in some abandoned charnel house. People who work in diving bells probably feel less cramped. It was both dank and dusty, for some of the cement was old, some new.
>
> In the long hours of the night, it could be deathly silent, except for the hum of the generator. When you came upon flesh-and-blood people, their faces seemed blanched in the artificial light. The ventilation could be now warm and sultry, now cold and clammy. The walls were sometimes grey, some bleached orange; some were moist and even mouldy. The constant loud hum of the Diesel generator was broken only when it switched over and coughed. Then there was the fetid odour of boots, sweaty woollen uniforms, acrid coal-tar disinfectant. Towards the end, when the drainage packed up, it was as pleasant as working in a public urinal.[6]

The praetorian guard that had been formed under Sepp Dietrich as the LAH – the Leibstandarte Adolf Hitler, or Adolf Hitler Lifeguards – had their barracks at Lichterfelde, a few kilometres north of Berlin, but during the last month had moved to the two Reich Chancellery barracks on Hermann Göring Strasse. The forty members of the FBK, or Führerbegleitkommando, had been recruited from the ranks of the LAH. They were the élite – the men whose devotion and fanaticism were to spark the legend of the heroic defence. They were responsible for Hitler's security, *pari passu* with the RSD (the Reich Security Service), whose detachment served under the command of SS general Johann Rattenhuber.

Several of these men were veterans from the Eastern Front; many had been wounded – the general morale was at rock bottom. Their discipline outside the Bunker in the Reich Chancellery was the subject of adverse criticism, and their behaviour and attitude inside the Bunker was, to say the least, ambivalent. Speer was one who realised that the stale sandwiches strewn about the floor went with unbuttoned tunics. He 'tried to ignore SS men clutching beer mugs', but did realise that 'nowhere was there any pretence at saluting a senior officer; all looked uninterested. The officers that did witness Hitler coming towards them in his quarters either took very little or no notice or pushed the door of the secretaries' room shut so that they wouldn't be disturbed.'[7]

Speer was to discern that:

> There was a general air of resentment and an atmosphere of fear, not least among the young men and hardened veterans of the SS. Guards smoked openly in the upper Bunker, and, despite there being a good communication with the secretaries in the lower Bunker, especially with Gerda Christian, as to when the Führer would surface, they increasingly ignored the warnings, knowing that Hitler was unlikely to come up. Even a few months previously the situation would have been impossible for me to even conceive. It seemed to me that the officers were afraid of even attempting to discipline their men for their slovenliness, almost as if they were reserving their discipline for the battleground.[8]

So this was the real mood and standard of discipline of Hitler's guards. The truly remarkable fact is that, despite this atmosphere of observable military staleness and smouldering soldierly revolt, military 'conferences' still went on – select senior officers, such as the obsequious Field Marshal Keitel, walked past this phenomenon as if it didn't exist, on their way to or from three suffocating hours in a sweat-drenched corridor in all too close proximity to Hitler.

We have a rational general's impression of those meetings, which proved suffocating – but, according to his testimony, not as a result of the ventilation. 'Everyone was physically almost suffocated by the atmosphere of servility, nervousness and prevarication. You felt at the point of physical illness. Nothing was genuine except fear.'[9]

The sense of fear felt by the generals was the very real sense of being acutely aware that, if they failed to go along with the rantings of an obviously irrational, out of touch, decidedly ill and decidedly odd man, they could be denounced and shot as traitors. Yet all the while, as professionals, they knew they had some responsibility for the men they were being asked to sacrifice in absurd military gestures. They also must have felt both impotence at being placed in such a situation and shame – individually and collectively.

Now the Army High Command was to witness the final throes of Hitler's tortured personality. He was to exhibit the irrationality of a vindictive spoilt child and to spend most of his waking hours silent or in a hysterical rage. Hitler was playing soldiers with the names of divisions long since destroyed, an extension of his withdrawal from responsibility. He knew full well that these paper divisions didn't exist, as he had personally given the orders not to destroy the names of any division, even if it contained only one soldier. This order was supposed to be in the interests of general morale: in reality it was in the interests of his morale – his performance as commander-in-chief was now only for his little entourage in the Bunker.

Now he was playing war games without any effective input of advice from the Army, his decisions were exposed as unbelievably vacillating, totally amateur, infantile and even bizarre. He gave an order to send a reserve unit of twenty-two light tanks to the vicinity of Pirmasens, then changed this to the vicinity of Trier, then changed it to the direction of Koblenz, and eventually in so many other directions that the exasperated tank commander decided to become 'lost'. Allowing for Hitler's illness, it must be asked whether this was the true measure of his 'military genius', but history has so far chosen not to contemplate such a proposition. Most if not all of Hitler's actions in the last three weeks were either fatuous or vindictive. As the Allies smashed through the German cities or reduced them to rubble, Hitler's recorded reaction was quite often 'Good'. He gave orders for the destruction of several of those remaining.

When the military situation *had* to be explained to him – and reality forced its way in – it was inevitable that Hitler would reach the zenith of his hysterical capability. This explains the outburst on 22 April when General Staff officers reported widely that Hitler had suffered a nervous breakdown. He had learned not only that a supposed attack by General Steiner (using mythical troops), which Hitler had expected to throw back the Soviets, had not taken place, but that Steiner had put the phone down in the middle of being given his orders.

Hitler's screams and raging alerted the whole Bunker. In a violent demonstration of what rage can do to mitigate the effects of Parkinson's disease, he waved both his fists in front of a purpled face. This was witnessed by all at the conference that day, including, apart from Bormann, Field Marshal Keitel, Generals Jodl and Krebs, Vice-Admiral Voss, two liaison officers, Hewel and Fegelein, and two stenographers,

Herrgesel and Hagen. His raging went on for several hours. Finally, defiant orders were given: Hitler himself would lead the defence of Berlin, even if his military commanders outside the city (like Steiner) wouldn't even answer the phone! All participants left, shaken by Hitler's collapse.

He was to suffer further rages and humiliation when it became obvious that first Göring and then Himmler had taken action on their adjutants' reports about the Bunker scene, believing that Hitler had become totally incapable of command. Himmler let it be known that Hitler had suffered a brain haemorrhage, a rumour picked up by the BBC. Worse was to come. Lorenz, in the Ministry of Propaganda, finally picked up a BBC broadcast quoting a Reuters report to the effect that on 22 April Reichsführer SS Himmler had offered the Western Allies the capitulation of the Third Reich.

Hitler's bouts of anger at this supposed treachery kept the level of tension high until all visitors stopped. Almost all these visitors seemed to have become infected with the blinding, nostalgic hysteria that was being peddled in and around the Bunker. Among the last were Hanna Reitsch and Robert Ritter von Greim. Whereas Reitsch, though a test pilot, was known to be somewhat hysterical and fanatic, von Greim was a field marshal, fully aware of the magnitude of the disaster that faced the German forces. He had just come from Obersalzberg, where the whole of Hitler's redoubt now looked like a lunar landscape. Yet, according to General Koller, who contacted him from Rechlin to find out the situation at the Bunker, von Greim was blandly reassuring on the phone: 'Don't despair! Everything will be well! The presence of the Führer and his confidence have completely inspired me. This place is as good as a fountain of youth for me!'[10]

Koller couldn't believe his ears – 'The whole place is a lunatic-asylum,' he is alleged to have said to himself. A far easier explanation was that von Greim was in the lion's den, confronting the same fears that excluded rational comment.

But, can the fear in the Bunker have only been the result of one man's demoniacal, imbalanced state? Hitler himself was too physically ill and mentally incapable to keep control, as is evidenced by the slack attitude of his own guards towards his presence. But there are multiple testimonies which give a clear indication of the mastermind who was inculcating the atmosphere of fear.

In the Nuremberg Trial, the names of twenty-four defendants were listed without reference to rank or title. There was little point – everyone knew them. Had Martin Bormann been added to that list without his official designation as Reichsleiter (Reich Leader), chief of Party Chancellery, and secretary to the Führer, hardly anyone would have known who he was. Even so, only a handful of Nazi district officials had ever heard of him.

A petty criminal with a police record, Bormann was short, thick-set, revoltingly aggressive and extraordinarily vindictive – both to his wife, whom he used deliberately to humiliate in public, and to his brother. The son of a bricklayer, he displayed little intelligence and even less grasp of reality. In August 1944, while the Reich was imploding, he was still obsessed with trying to obtain the ancestry of his grandparents to try to prove his racial purity, claiming the meanwhile that his father had been a rich quarry-owner!

This peasant with a chip on his shoulder, had, however, by dint of low cunning, wheedled his way into being the Führer's secretary and had taken full advantage of Hitler's personality disorder, feeding Hitler's paranoia and stoking the suffocating pyre of sycophancy. His grasping nature made him so unpopular that Hermann Göring, at the Nuremberg Trial, was to claim that, if Hitler had died earlier and he himself had succeeded him as Führer, he wouldn't have bothered getting rid of Bormann, for without Hitler to protect him Bormann's own staff would have killed him off. At the very same Nuremberg Trial, Bormann's own secretaries refused to defend him when he was tried *in absentia*.

Bormann's domination over the Führer is best indicated by Speer:

> After any conference with Hitler it sometimes happened that the adjutant would announce Bormann, who would come into the room carrying his files. He spoke monotonously and with seeming objectivity and would then advance his own solutions. On the basis of one word 'Agreed', or on the basis of a vague comment from Hitler, Bormann would then draft lengthy instructions. In this way some very important decisions were taken.[11]

Speer was speaking about the late autumn of 1942, but he acknowledged that by the last few months Bormann – called the 'Robespierre of the Bunker' for his ability to change whispers into death sentences by telling tales to Hitler – was totally in control, freely interpreting the Führer's orders and getting these typed up on sheets already bearing Hitler's alleged signature.[12]

Speer was well aware that Himmler was at loggerheads with Bormann, but, with his own vast empire around him, Himmler was fireproof. Goebbels, however, was not. Speer relates how Bormann used to marginalise Goebbels at every step, giving Lammers the tasks that would have normally fallen Goebbels's way. Goebbels was to take Speer into his confidence about his worries in this regard, but no effective alliance was possible against a secretary such as Bormann, in a constant position of influence at Hitler's side.

In the last few weeks of their tawdry existence in the Bunker, Goebbels was to learn from telephone-operator Misch that Bormann had even rerouted all his personal calls, under the guise of a 'Führer's order', and Goebbels found himself totally unable to counter the situation.

Bormann, along with the vulgar alcoholics Ley and Lammers, managed to enmesh Hitler in a cocoon of paperwork, effectively limiting all outside access. Ley's own newspaper, the *Nachtausgabe*, was used to feed Hitler's hatred and confirm his fears. After the July bomb plot it had screamed hatred of the nobility in German society, the Prussians and the high-born generals who lacked the common-sense, earthy values that Ley parroted back at Hitler on every possible occasion.

Everyone in the Bunker was extremely wary of Bormann. The SS guards knew how petty could be his complaints and how vindictive he could prove; the secretaries kept their distance – in short, everyone was on their guard. When not on duty, Bormann spent most of the day drinking with Stumpfegger, who, even in the last two weeks, when casualties were dying in the Reich Chancellery casualty station, operated upon by inexperienced young surgeons and even by physicians who had never had occasion to practise surgery for forty years, stayed firmly behind the partition wall of the corridor opposite Hitler's suite.

Drinking in the Bunker also became a favourite pastime for Ambassador Hewel, the Foreign Office liaison officer and another of the old-time Nazis, whose visits now became as permanent as the sleeping-bag which he'd brought with him.

The incessant drinking was amazingly tolerated by Hitler, and a cloud of nostalgia and self-pity was its inevitable result. From 24 April onwards, as the Soviets smashed forward, genuine, unadulterated fear – not the fear that went with sycophancy – gave everyone due cause either to sober up or to get really plastered. Many did the latter, with inevitable results. While the upper Bunker in particular became even more unbearable as a result, hysteria also hit hard in the lower. Even Bormann started to get eloquent about the role of destiny. And where there was eloquence – where rhetoric was needed – there too was Dr Goebbels.

Goebbels had an intellect far greater than that of his Nazi contemporaries. I say this not as a result of reading his diaries or listening to recordings of his addresses of exhortation and adulation – these were sheer bombastic nonsense and sloppy romanticism. If, however, his Nationalist Socialist letters of the early days are read, they are consistent with the fact that he graduated as a PhD in 1921, for they show an altogether superior intellect, which he had deliberately subjugated for political advance. He had no one but himself to blame for his infamous rise and his presence in the Bunker. 'Beware of intellectualism,' he wrote in these letters; 'the most important thing is politics.'

Careful never to sound too intellectual, his forte was to say nothing in any conference. He never wittingly expressed an opinion that he couldn't plaster in fine-sounding phrases extolling the Führer or his alleged ideals.

Now, in the Bunker, the fastidious little man was trapped in a verbal cage of his own making, in close proximity to a smelly myth that he had helped create. He was in despair – not that it stopped him eulogising. Soon he too was drinking champagne to excess.

The Death of the Goebbels Family

So seemingly attractive is the Nazi myth in some quarters that the eulogies of the past have imperceptibly become the facts of the present, strengthening as each generation fails to challenge them. The squalid fetor in the Bunker is now little in evidence. Instead we have many writers whose style and reminiscences are best exemplified by the description given by young Captain Gerhard Boldt, on service in the Bunker. Of Magda Goebbels, who was sharing two minute, partitioned rooms with her six children, aged from four to twelve, he wrote: 'Waiting for their end, Frau Goebbels gave no sign of fear to the last. Vivacious and elegant, she used to come up the spiral staircase two steps at a time. She had a friendly smile for everybody. Her admirable strength of character was perhaps inspired by her fanatical faith in the Führer.'[13]

Or perhaps not. For Albert Speer was a close friend and confidant of Magda's. In the last few days in the Bunker he saw her in a very different light. First, he was totally convinced that Magda was no less than terrified – very close to total collapse. Moreover, he was equally convinced that she had been caught up in a ghastly set of circumstances out of which she could see no way of escape. In his opinion she, along with her children, had been more or less volunteered for suicide – by her husband. Speer didn't believe for one moment that she would have taken the decision without being bullied into it.[14]

When Speer went to see her on his final visit to the Bunker, on 24 April, Joseph Goebbels took him to her small box of a room and deliberately stayed throughout the visit, limiting their conversation to the topic of her health. Since Joseph and Magda couldn't stand one another, and Speer had previously always seen Magda alone, Speer thought that this meant quite clearly that she was to be given no last-minute avenue of escape.

Nor was Magda in any shape to trip gaily about the Bunker or go up stairs two at a time. She was suffering from paroxysmal tachycardia – sudden attacks of increased heart-rate – part of a very acute anxiety state. Speer's own account reads:

> An SS doctor told me Frau Goebbels was in bed, in a weak state suffering from heart attacks. I asked to be received. I would have preferred to speak to her alone but Dr Goebbels was waiting in the antechamber and led me into the small bunker chamber where she lay in a simple bed. She looked pale and talked in a feeble voice about irrelevant matters; yet one could feel how she suffered at the idea of the inevitably approaching hour when her children would be put to death. Goebbels stayed in the room and this limited our conversation to her state of health. Only towards the end did she indicate what was on her mind. 'How happy I am that Harald [Harald Quandt, her son by another marriage] is still alive.' I too felt rather inhibited and did not know what to say. Her husband had not granted us even a minute in which to say our farewells.[15]

Medically, it is almost certain that Magda Goebbels would remain in a similar state, continuing to have faints and palpitations, probably lying down for most of the few remaining days. The cause of the anxiety would remain, but, as will be seen, it remains to be determined how much of her anxiety was for herself and how much for her children.

The fact that she remained in bad health, having palpitations and faints, is substantiated to some extent by the admission of Hitler's secretary Frau Gertraüd Junge that after 27 April she had to look after all six of the Goebbels children in the Bunker, including attending to their meals, as Magda felt too incapacitated.[16] Considering the circumstances, this itself could be considered a further indictment.

Nor does Magda's statement about being glad that Harald was alive equate with her supposed, often quoted, sentiments that, for her children, 'the world without Hitler was a too too wicked place'. Yet Hanna Reitsch carried out of the Bunker a letter from Magda Goebbels to the very same Harald Quandt which matched even the histrionic Reitsch in rhetoric and posturing. Magda wrote, 'God will forgive me as a mother provided I have courage to carry out this deed myself and do not leave it to others. When the time comes, I shall give my darlings sleeping potions and then poison, a soft and painless death.'[17]

According to Werner Naumann, Goebbels's aide (who claimed he had offered to save the children himself), on 1 May, with Hitler by now dead, he and Goebbels had absented themselves from 5 to 6 p.m. so that Magda could get on with her declared intention. 'I could not talk this wilful woman out of her deed. Her husband was not present nor was I,' Naumann claimed. He said that Magda Goebbels had told him that she had given the children a drug called Finodin in a bar of chocolate – to prevent air sickness on the trip to Berchtesgaden that they had been told would shortly be taking place with 'Uncle Führer'.[18]

This would fit in with the intentions claimed in her letter to Quandt. However, Sergeant Misch and others have testified that the children were frightened and crying and had to be dragged back to their bedrooms – an account far distant from the gay impression given by several writers that at this time the Bunker was 'filled with [the children's] shouts and laughter'.[19]

There are also various testimonies as to the presence of a dentist, Dr Helmut Kunz, an SS major, in the vicinity of the children's bedrooms at about 5 p.m. He ran a small dental laboratory in the basement of the Reich Chancellery, but was not a customary visitor to the Bunker. Several, including Naumann, were to notice him there on 1 May with Dr Stumpfegger. (Later, in the 1960s, Kunz was involved in a libel suit in which he swore that he had not been involved in the death of the Goebbels children.)

Other testimonies note the supportive role of several secretaries clustering around Magda Goebbels just before the children's death, suggesting that she was having hysterics and was in no fit state to carry out any murders. I myself think it highly unlikely that, if she had been involved, she could have herself carried them through successfully. Either way, there is absolutely no proof of who did kill the children.

Almost every later testimony contains indications of the shock, horror and disgust of the Bunker personnel *before* the murders, as they witnessed what they obviously saw as the build-up to the inevitable deed. Sergeant Misch, for instance, testified how he watched Frau Goebbels comb the hair of the crying children in the room opposite his telephone hutch, before they were led – or, in the case of twelve-year-old Helga, dragged – to their death: 'I watched all of this with apprehension; I was appalled.'[20] But no one did anything about it.

The whole of the Bunker mythology is encapsulated in the story of Magda Goebbels. It is the truth of what really happened to Magda and the children that exposes the cold, heartless savagery underneath the rhetoric, and exposes the extent to which Bunker survivors were afterwards unwilling to relate just how inured to bestiality and squalor they had become.

The Soviet post-mortem testimony later showed that there was clear evidence of severe bruising before death – specifically on Helga, the eldest child – indicating that a quite violent struggle had taken place. Even worse, there is Soviet testimony[21] which relates how the children's bodies were found crudely stacked on top of each other in the corridor. If this testimony is true then it must be assumed that sometime after their death at approximately 5 p.m. someone had wanted the children's bunks. By the time of the eventual breakout from the Bunker at 11 p.m., all concerned were walking past the bodies of the little children which were stiffening and curling as they went into rigor mortis. No one seemed to notice: the children were dead; they were irrelevant.

According to several witnesses, most especially Sergeant Misch and the Hitler Youth leader Artur Axmann, the children were seemingly especially irrelevant to Dr Joseph Goebbels himself – the extoller of Germanic superiority; the man with the loudly proclaimed intention of dying as an example of loyalty – and to their doting mother, the beautiful Magda, used so often in Nazi propaganda pictures with her six blond children to show the high point of Germanic family virtues. Axmann testified that:

> I came over from my command post in the Wilhelmstrasse and into the lower Bunker around 6.30 p.m., Tuesday, May 1. I wanted to say goodbye to both the Goebbels. I found the couple sitting at the long conference table with Werner Naumann, Hans Baur, Walter Hewel, General Krebs, three or four others. Dr Goebbels stood up to greet me. He soon launched into lively memories of our old street fighting days in Berlin-Wedding . . . But there was not a word about his family. Magda Goebbels just sat there, saying little, head high. She was chain-smoking and sipping champagne.[22]

The testimony of Frau Junge, Hitler's secretary, falsely implies some semblance of decency in attending to the bodies of the dead children. She claimed to recall 'a nurse and a man in a white uniform . . . dragging a huge wooden chest which seemed very heavy'.[23] She presumed that this chest contained the bodies. The facts were again rather different – there were no such niceties, as she must have known full well.

Magda Goebbels went back to her own bedroom (that of the children) to prepare herself for her own death, and Joseph Goebbels presumably walked past his children's piled-up bodies to collect his wife and make sure she accompanied him on their joint 'suicide'. Once again details are amazingly scant, and because of this it must be emphasised that there is absolutely no circumstantial evidence for the exact details of their death. Hugh Trevor-Roper's imaginative account was that two shots were fired by an SS orderly.[24]

Dr Goebbels's adjutant, SS captain Günther Schwägermann, had orders to cremate the Goebbels's bodies, so that they would not be recognisable to the Soviets. To ensure this last service, Goebbels had given him a silver-framed photograph of the Führer from his writing-desk. Schwägermann repaid this generosity by a token sprinkling of petrol. He left the bodies just outside the Bunker, making no attempt either to bury or to cover them. With escape on his mind, it is clear that the corpses of the Goebbels were even less relevant to Schwägermann than the corpses of the children had been to either Magda or Joseph Goebbels.

The lightly charred bodies of the Goebbels were later found and identified by the Soviets. As will become evident, the post-mortem descriptions of the body of Joseph Goebbels at least allowed very little room for conjecture about his identity. Before he died, he had desperately tried on two occasions to betray Magda, and even to betray the ideal of a noble suicide pact, by attempting to negotiate his own salvation.

For weeks the Bunker personnel had been subjected to the mentally exhausting effect of living a life of fearsome sycophancy, unreality and isolation, in degrading surroundings. Their zombie-like existence had been constrained as much by the mental strait-jacket of subservience and spurious rhetoric as by the concrete walls, squelching floors and sodden toilets. Their numbed state was not normal.

Pyschiatrists have long been aware that when people are thrown into close proximity in such surroundings a condition known as 'prison psychosis' can eventually occur. Little wonder that, as we shall see, the aberrant mood of the Bunker people was to allow them, in May 1945, to commit actions which they would subsequently view with utter disbelief and shame.

5

The Death of Hitler

There are now a considerable number of conflicting testimonies about how Hitler and Eva Braun are supposed to have died. Some of these are confused, some are deliberately duplicitous; very few are unchanged! Before trying to establish what really happened, it will be useful to give a brief explanation of how the presently accepted account(s) came into being, and to comment on the sources upon whose evidence these accounts are based.

'Anyone who undertakes an enquiry of such a kind is soon made aware of one important fact: the worthlessness of mere human testimony.'[1] So wrote Hugh Trevor-Roper, the British intelligence agent chosen to make the first enquiry into the Führer's death, on behalf of the British government, to silence the seemingly paranoid claims of Stalin that the West had somehow colluded with Hitler and allowed him to escape.

Trevor-Roper's comment about the fallibility of human witness is interesting, as it reflects his frustration – frustration that even though the British had scoured the internment camps for witnesses he nevertheless had so little information available, obtained from very few sources.

His subsequent book, *The Last Days of Hitler*, was amazing for the paucity of information that it had uncovered, especially since he had been working with not only the full cooperation of MI6 and MI5 but also the additional resources of Military Intelligence.

It can now be revealed that Trevor-Roper had also had access to a copy of the diary of Hitler's movements kept by his valet, Heinz Linge. This had been obtained surreptitiously by an intelligence officer, Colonel John McCowan, on behalf of Dick White, the then chief of British intelligence in Berlin. Very early on, the possession of this record of exactly who was present in the Bunker towards the end gave Trevor-Roper a tremendous advantage in his questioning of the available witnesses: their stories could be immediately checked for accuracy, and they themselves, as witnesses, could rapidly be given the impression that the British had found out the full story, thus encouraging them to give true testimony.

The actual testimonies that Trevor-Roper did accumulate were not published as such – only his analysis of them. It comes as no surprise, therefore, to study even the most voluminous edition of his book *The Last Days of Hitler* and find that his whole account of Hitler's demise was contained in no more than thirty-six pages, almost all of which was non-specific material. When the padding was removed the total was a mere five pages!

According to this account, there was a farewell ceremony with various members of Hitler's staff:

> Hitler and Eva Braun shook hands with them all, and then returned to their suite. The few others were dismissed, all but the high priests and those few others whose services would be necessary. These waited in the passage. A single shot was heard. After an interval they entered the room. Hitler was lying on the sofa, which was soaked with blood. He had shot himself through the mouth. Eva Braun was also on the sofa, also dead. A revolver was by her side, but she had not used it; she had swallowed poison. The time was half-past three.[2]

Trevor-Roper's book has been extolled as a brilliant investigative work, but the part played by British intelligence and John McCowan has never properly been acknowledged – the only reference being a note in the introduction indicating that a 'stout bound volume 14 inches by 7' had been found by a 'British visitor'.[3]

Nevertheless, the book did contribute to the essential initial destruction of a Hitler myth – that of the survival of a ghostly Führer, waiting in the wings, ready to return. The five pages were the only account initially available of Hitler's end, and they lived up to their remit.

The Bunker was included in the postwar Soviet zone in Berlin, and access to it was now forbidden. The Soviets maintained total secrecy about the finding of corpses and their identification, failing to respond to an American request for information through the General Staff, and, after the British secret service had learned that the Soviets were examining a jawbone that was believed to be Hitler's, failing to rise to the bait when the British military commander in Berlin, Brigadier-General Fort, asked his Soviet opposite number, General Siniev, for details of the resulting dental records.[4] Without any post-mortem findings with which to compare the known facts about Hitler's medical status, no genuine historian could even attempt to enquire further into the real truth.

In the mid-1950s the Soviet Union released several key witnesses to the last days in the Bunker who had been captured and identified soon after the fall of Berlin. This stimulated the enlarged, third edition of Trevor-Roper's book, as these witnesses were made available for him to question shortly after their return to the West.

Even so, the new edition was not able to include the testimony initially given by many of these witnesses to their Soviet captors, for the Soviets remained silent about this. In several instances this initial testimony was thought to differ considerably from the testimony given upon release, but such doubts emanated only from former fellow prisoners in various prisons in Moscow, who had remembered a different tale. Many believed that the changed testimony of the returning witnesses came as a result of their access to the testimony of their colleagues who had earlier escaped to the West, bringing a sudden need for the marrying of minds.

In the absence of any other details from the Soviet side, the Trevor-Roper account remained unchallenged and uncorroborated. That didn't prevent many of the Nazi survivors of the Bunker giving their individual accounts in newspaper articles and in books, and these accounts now started to embellish the details alleged to have been obtained by Trevor-Roper. For the very reason that the British intelligence service never made available the detailed testimonies of these witnesses, in the form of their initial accounts, the stories about the Bunker grew apace, unchecked and seemingly unabashed by fears of rebuttal.

The only real fresh information – information which totally altered the whole situation – came when the Soviets released data about their capture of the Bunker, the finding of burnt and buried corpses, and, at long last, some details of the post-mortem procedures carried out to identify the corpses of the Führer, Eva Braun and others.

These revelations came piecemeal. First, in 1965, Yelena Rzhevskaya published a quixotic, incomplete article entitled '*Berlinskie Stranitsy*', ('Berlin Notes'), in the Russian periodical *Znamya*. The author later enlarged this into a slim book describing how she had been the interpreter attached to the Red Army unit that, at the end of the war, had been given the task of finding Hitler dead or alive. This book made reference to documentation which became available three years later in a book published by Lev Bezymenski, a Soviet journalist who co-edited the Russian journal *Novoe Vremya*. This book was published in West Germany first and then in England under the title *The Death of Adolf Hitler*. It was the first time that the Soviets had seemed officially to accept that Hitler was dead – the reason for their acceptance lying in the all-important post-mortem reports.

All historians waited for Trevor-Roper's response, and in 1971 a new edition of his book indicated his awareness of his position: 'a historian who aims at accuracy must examine the evidence'.[5] But it is somewhat surprising to find that in taking account of the post-mortem reports on Hitler – reports based on scientific evidence and opinion; reports which contradicted his own evidence based on that human testimony he had so despised in his foreword – Trevor-Roper did not consider it necessary to alter the main body of his book. Instead of addressing the challenge to his authorship throughout, he relegated comment on the new findings (indeed the *only* findings as such) to a three-page appendix.

The failure to comment seriously on Bezymenski's evidence was compounded by the fact that Trevor-Roper had by the early 1950s had access to the American archive material resulting from the capture of Dr Morell. This material included Morell's X-rays, among which were a few of Hitler's skull, along with others taken at the request of Dr Giesing and discovered when he was captured. Immediately after the war all these X-rays had been freely available to all and sundry (as had all records of the Americans' questioning of their captives) and they were thought to be the *only* X-rays in existence from which dental comparison could be made with the skulls of the alleged Hitler and Eva, as described in the Soviet forensic data.

Forensic experts, including forensic odontologists such as Professor Reidar F. Sognnaes, had been poring over the results of the comparison of these American X-rays with the newly acquired Soviet post-mortem data. Imagine Sognnaes's surprise when, in the early 1980s, he learned that in 1945 the British had captured Hitler's dentist, Professor Hugo Blaschke, *before* the Americans, and had appropriated the dental records of both Hitler and Eva Braun, among others that Blaschke had been carrying. Furthermore, the X-rays contained in these records had been made available to the British secret service.

Sognnaes would have been even more amazed to learn that, just over a decade later, John McCowan had asked official permission to tell the story of his capture of Blaschke and of his own exploits in the Bunker, intending to have it printed in his local newspaper, the *Hereford Times*. Not only was permission refused but his house, the Walled

Garden at Clyro, was visited by MI5 heavies and all visible data were impounded. He was to be severely cautioned: this, in the late 1950s, was an indication of official British reluctance to have the subject of the Bunker discussed.

Despite Hugh Trevor-Roper's meeting with Professor Sognnaes in the early 1970s, his subsequent editions of *The Last Days of Hitler* also lamentably failed to address the Sognnaes articles, published in forensic dental journals, in which the professor gave his valuable opinion on the Soviet data relating to the supposed corpses of Hitler and Eva Braun. Since this data was at very considerable variance – to say the least! – with the whole argument of Trevor-Roper's book, such an omission is not readily understandable.

Even worse was the fact that in the preface to his fifth edition, in 1978, Trevor-Roper found it necessary to quote Sognnaes's eloquent testimony on the identity of the skeleton found in late 1972 and alleged to be that of Martin Bormann. He actually cited an article by Professor Sognnaes in which Sognnaes also addressed a problem relating to the identification of Hitler and Eva Braun – an article which undermined the whole basis of Trevor-Roper's book, making it certain that the testimonies upon which he had relied, after so much diligent investigation, were totally fraudulent.

It is a sad fact that, unless forced to do so, historians hardly ever read any scientific periodicals or scientific articles concerning matters of historic interest, and they almost never seek professional assistance to further their understanding. And if they do seek such advice they tend to negate its effect by themselves interpreting the advice they have been given so that it fits their own purpose – quite often inadvertently – thus rendering expert, unbiased advice instantly biased and inexpert. But in the case of the forensic data relating to the supposed corpses of Hitler and Eva Braun the carelessness in failing to include Professor Sognnaes's contrary forensic interpretation is inexcusable.

The result is that the supposedly authoritative Western version of Hitler's demise in the Bunker has failed to stand the test of time. It has become twisted into myth, purely because it was based *only* on the suspect testimony of rabid Nazis, who have subsequently garnished their initial testimonies.

Hugh Trevor-Roper's book, excellent though it was, served its momentary political purpose, but writing a book for such a purpose is in itself open to criticism. Without anything more substantial than suspect testimony and careful opinion – without *one* fact – it was bound to be superseded. Western historians have shown themselves reluctant even to *attempt* to establish the truth by considering careful expert forensic comparisons. Their reluctance to establish and include only what is sustainable and probable – not what is politically expedient – is the basis for the failure to provide a half-sensible answer to the mystery of the deaths in the Bunker.

Fortunately there is now available enough expert testimony and enough data to form the basis of a proper investigation. But, before undertaking this, it is necessary to show how the evidence accumulated. Until now the material has never been attributed to its source – a first essential of any proper investigation.

The First Last Witnesses in the Bunker

After the fall of Berlin, British intelligence located about half of the SS guard at Hitler's retreat at Berchtesgaden, in the Bavarian Alps, but these were men who had left the Bunker a few days before the end, on 22 April 1945. From these, a list was drawn up of the people left behind at the Bunker. The Linge diary helped complete the list. Seven witnesses of events in the last few days in the Bunker were found and were interviewed by Trevor-Roper. Three police guards – Hermann Karnau, Erich Mansfeld and Hilco Poppen – Bormann's secretary, Else Krüger, and most importantly Erich Kempka, Hitler's transport officer, were interviewed by both Trevor-Roper and the Americans at Moosburg, near Munich. The American testimony from the cross-questioning of the histrionic Hanna Reitsch was added to the testimony of a casual visitor to the Bunker, Baroness von Varo.

From the testimony of these witnesses and helped by the detailed entries in Linge's diary, Trevor-Roper prepared his initial report. On 1 November 1945 this report was submitted to the British government and to the Four Power Intelligence Committee in Berlin itself.

In fact almost the whole story of the suicide of Hitler and the finding of the bodies given in *The Last Days of Hitler* was based on the testimony of Kempka, as he was the only one of these witnesses who claimed to have been in the Bunker at the time: the others had all allegedly been otherwise engaged.

However, Kempka's testimony had already been revised, for the first person to interview him – a journalist from *Life* magazine – was told that Eva had shot herself through the heart while Hitler had shot himself through the right temple. As Kempka also said that only a small spot of blood had been visible on the Führer's forehead when he was found, this story was considered ridiculous and was promptly altered.

Before the publication of Trevor-Roper's book, however, Artur Axmann, the Hitler Youth leader, was discovered in Austria, and a set of documents purporting to be Hitler's last will and testament surfaced due to the finding of Major Willi Johannmeier, who had buried these documents in a bottle in his garden. Then, in the spring and summer of 1946, two of Hitler's secretaries, Frau Gerda Christian and Frau Gertraüd Junge were found. Frau Junge was later to publish her own extended testimony.[6]

But all this provided very little information about Hitler's supposed death. Frau Christian claimed she had heard the details from Hitler's valet, Linge (at that time in Soviet custody). Frau Junge had got the story second-hand from Major Otto Günsche, Hitler's SS adjutant. Artur Axmann claimed to have arrived *after* the death, just in time to inspect the bodies.[7] The whole of the evidence about the deaths of Hitler and Eva still only came from Kempka. Little wonder that it only took five pages.

It should have taken less, for, as was admitted by Kempka in the early 1970s, his original testimony was not altogether truthful. According to this later admission, he had not heard the shot that was supposed to have killed Hitler and had not in fact known anything first-hand about the deaths, as at the time they took place he had been sent for some petrol by Günsche. He wasn't even there! Instead, he now said, he was above ground, returning to the Bunker with some cans of petrol, when he met the funeral cortège coming to the surface.[8]

Why had he lied? In his own words, 'Back in 1945, to save my own skin, I told the British and American interrogators just about anything or everything I thought they wanted to hear. Since they kept grilling me about "that shot" I finally told them that I had heard it. It seemed to make things easier.'[9]

So, assuming he was not only claiming to have lied, for yet another reason, the whole of the classic *The Last Days of Hitler*, and the British propaganda exercise which accompanied the book to counter what was said to be Soviet propaganda about Hitler having escaped, was based on the false testimony of one man.

This supposedly authoritative version put out by British intelligence was not well received by those who favoured the myth of the Führer's survival – nor by those who realised that there was not a single fact to substantiate its veracity.

Before we look at the later testimony of the Bunker survivors released by the Soviets in the 1950s, it is worth remembering that at this stage:

● No one had witnessed Hitler or Eva Braun die.

● The first report submitted to British intelligence stated that Hitler had shot himself through the mouth and Eva had taken poison.

● Not only did this report not accord with Kempka's first testimony – which was considered too ridiculous – but it was based on further false testimony.

The Pilot's Tale

On 8 October 1955 thousands of people from all over West Germany gathered at Friedland, near the border with East Germany, to welcome home the first big batch of prisoners of war returned from the Soviet Union as a result of an agreement between Soviet premier Nikolai Bulganin and West German chancellor Konrad Adenauer. At 2 p.m. 598 prisoners arrived in Friedland's displaced-persons camp. Later another 192 were brought into the camp, which had seen 2 million prisoners return from Soviet Russia in a decade.

The prisoners, travelling by train, had actually reached the frontier between East and West Germany at 6.30 a.m., at Herleshausen. They had travelled packed into converted cattle-trucks.

In Poland, of all places, where the population had no reason to remember them with affection, they had been brought fresh fruit by the locals as the train wound its laborious way. But in East Germany the reception had been a good deal cooler: no contact had been allowed, and heavily armed East German police had lined the route at every stopping-point from Frankfurt-on-Oder.

Greeted by the welcoming committee of the vice-chancellor, Herr Blücher, the minister for refugees, Professor Oberlander, the prime minister of Lower Saxony, Herr Hellwege, and the chairman of the Free Democratic Party, Dr Dehler, the crowd then dispersed into groups, each looking for their relatives or friends.

The world's press was there in force and tried every trick in the book to be the first to interview two people in particular: Hans Baur, Hitler's pilot, and Heinz Linge, Hitler's valet.

The press did not have long to wait, nor did their quarry show any reticence about being questioned, even though Linge looked tired in his standard-issue peaked cap and dungarees.

The importance of their testimony could hardly have been over-emphasised, and the journalists knew it, for this was the first untutored account that either man was to give to Western sources. Only Soviet inquisitors had had access to either for a decade. Neither man had had the opportunity of reading Western accounts of the events in the Bunker; both had had their pitiable mail allowance heavily censored. As was said to reporters at the meeting, it was as if they were coming out of a vacuum.

To their amazement, the Reuters and West German news reporters were to hear two totally conflicting accounts – conflicting not just with each other but with the account set out in Hugh Trevor-Roper's book, which had not even mentioned Baur as being among those present at the end. At least one of the accounts had to be false, but if one account was true then the accepted version of Hitler's death had to be drastically revised.

The reporters repeatedly asked for, and got, unequivocal answers. Their reports were carried worldwide.

It is worth recording that both men were subsequently made available for questioning by Trevor-Roper, who also managed to question two other people who had been around the Bunker in its last days and had also returned from the Soviet Union to Germany: Harry Mengerhausen, a member of Hitler's bodyguard, and SS general Johann Rattenhuber. Major Günsche, who had been rearrested and held in East Germany in the gaol at the beautiful town of Bautzen, at least escaped this questioning.

In the introduction to his third edition, Trevor-Roper states of his questioning of Linge and Baur, 'The essential fact is that they everywhere confirm the story as already told by me from other sources. At no point do they conflict with it or even modify it.'[10] This statement is accompanied by a footnote in which he explains that Baur was misquoted in several newspapers, including the *Manchester Guardian* and the *Observer*, and had subsequently disowned the account which had been attributed to him as a result of 'a misunderstanding'.

The extent and nature of the 'misunderstanding' which occurred, witnessed by more than forty newspapermen, can be judged from Baur's statement of 8 October 1955, as allegedly taken out of context by the newspaper reporters:

The Führer looked me gravely in the eyes, shook my hand, said goodbye and shot himself. Eva Braun shot herself at the same time.

I did not stay to see the bodies afterwards and do not know what happened to them.[11]

What part of that statement is likely to have been misinterpreted or misunderstood? The phrases are melodramatic (as was Baur). The least that could be said of them is that they were memorable. It is inconceivable that such phrases would have been misheard by so many. This testimony was hardly supportive of Trevor-Roper's book, nor were any of the subsequent statements made by Baur.

Heinz Linge also rushed straight into print: a contract was made there and then, on 8 October at Friedland, with the *News of the World*, which published his unadulterated and, as will be shown, untruthful testimony on 23 October. As we will see, there can be no mistaking his meaning, and his account stands in stark contrast to the Trevor-Roper version – not just in detail but in substance. Trevor-Roper's assessment that Linge and Baur's testimonies correlated well with the account in his own book appears as no less than wishful thinking.

Before the Final Curtain

What, then, *can* be made of the actual happenings at the time of Hitler's death? The discovery of his alleged will and last testament, and reference to his marriage, repay more substantial examination.

There has been surprisingly little argument about Hitler's marriage to Eva Braun, allegedly carried out by Walter Wagner, gauleiter of Berlin, on 29 April, in the map room in the Bunker, in front of Bormann and Goebbels as witnesses. This paucity of argument is despite the claims of several, including Hanna Reitsch and General Robert Ritter von Greim, that the marriage never took place.

Reitsch's action in tearing up Eva's correspondence with which she was entrusted suggests some degree of jealousy and of embarrassment that her hero could be tarnished by association with a simpleton. It must be admitted that this places her testimony in doubt, but nevertheless there remains no real evidence that the marriage happened at all, other than the oral testimony of Hitler's secretaries and reference to the marriage in his 'will'.

The will and testament that has been attributed to Hitler is a typed document allegedly signed by him. The only first-hand testimony we have of its origin is that of Hitler's secretary Frau Junge, a testimony that tends to be melodramatic and which must be treated with extreme scepticism. She relates how Hitler called for her services and dictated to her two documents.[12] Leaning earnestly forward on a table for support, he dictated non-stop! This is a remarkable and highly unlikely performance for a man affected by severe Parkinson's disease. Witnesses to his 'signature' were Goebbels, Bormann, Krebs and Burgdorf (Hitler's chief adjutant).

Most historians have totally accepted the veracity of this will. Trevor-Roper declared, somewhat characteristically, 'The authenticity has been established without the possibility of doubt by a mass of internal and circumstantial evidence, expert scrutiny of the signatures and the testimony of those that knew him including one of the signatories of the Personal Testament, von Below and his secretary Frau Junge who typed both documents.'[13]

Since the fiasco of the Hitler Diaries, the public has become sceptical about the abilities of handwriting experts and historians, but there are pointers which suggest that it was Goebbels who either invented, dictated or altered the final version of the will, as the language was so similar to his own. The signature – no more than a squiggle – could have been genuine, a good forgery or even a bad forgery – there was, and is, no scientific way of telling.

In any case, given the less than memorable content of rhetoric and anti-Jewish diatribes, it hardly matters – except that the will contains a reference to Hitler's intended fate:

> My wife and I choose to die in order to escape the shame of overthrow or capitulation. It is our wish that our bodies be burnt immediately in the place where I have performed the greater part of my daily work during the course of my twelve years' service to my people.[14]

The only real question is whether this was a genuine reflection of what Hitler himself, or others, wished to happen or whether the document was written in order to deceive. As the documents were not made available to the incoming Soviets, which would have helped perpetuate any intended deception, the latter possibility is almost entirely ruled out. It seems that at some time either Hitler himself was genuinely considering suicide or someone else was doing the contemplating for him.

The later testimony of many Bunker witnesses recalled what they call the final 'happy moments in the Bunker', but the happiness seems to have come not from the *gemütlich*, tearful account of the secretaries, who reported how Hitler had called all the women to assemble in the early hours of 30 April and went down the line nodding gravely to each, in a totally silent, solemn but eloquent goodbye, but from an impromptu party of SS men being held in the garage of the Reich Chancellery on receipt of the news that Hitler had called for his secretaries to say goodbye. There are too many witnesses to this event to justify questioning that it occurred. The SS men's happiness stemmed simply from the fact that they had heard that Hitler was going to commit suicide and they could now attend to the serious business of their own survival. Their festivities got so out of hand that calls for them to quieten down were simply ignored. A tailor, Willi Müller, who had become entrapped in the Chancellery described how the mood suddenly lifted. SS chief Rattenhuber himself seemed in a particularly jocular mood.[15]

Allegedly, in order to test the effects of the cyanide capsules, Hitler's Alsatian, Blondi, had been poisoned at about midnight, in one of the non-functioning lavatories, either by Dr Stumpfegger in front of Hitler, or by Professor Werner Haase in conjunction with Sergeant Tornow, the dog-handler, depending on the testimony chosen. Unless the dog obligingly went through the same procedure twice, out of devotion to the Führer, the varied testimonies are further evidence of the fallibility of human testimony. This had also cheered the SS guards, but they were to have a long wait, and the mood began to become irritable as throughout the night no news came that the deed had been carried out. A Bormann communication from the Bunker later that day declared, 'The Führer is not yet dead.'

At lunchtime on 30 April the SS guards were instructed to collect their final rations from the Reich Chancellery. There was nowhere they could safely go other than the upper Bunker, which was now full of guards – the atmosphere absolutely stifling; the mood vitriolic.

Goebbels, however, saw things differently. In his diary, he described what now unfolded as 'the Twilight of the Gods scene'.[16] But it is worth reminding the reader that the whole, heart-rending scenario of the bridal couple's death, which has been promoted since the war only marginally less effectively than if publicised by Joseph Goebbels himself, has absolutely *no* basis in fact.

Behind Closed Doors

Witnesses such as Baur, Axmann, Kempka and Linge – all of whom have altered their testimony substantially at some point or other – have had their testimony compared and discussed in the minutest detail, giving credence to their every utterance. Excuses for their altered recall have been made by the most erudite authorities, who have smoothed over irreconcilable anomalies and inconsistencies in order to achieve historical accord – even while the witnesses themselves were often busily decrying each other's testimonies as utter rubbish. No Molière farce or Brecht production could ever do this justice.

Each historian has chosen a witness who fits his own hypothesis – somewhat akin to choosing a pet poodle to match a particular outfit. Thus Hugh Trevor-Roper chose to back Kempka and then extended his loyalty to Linge, whom he thought a 'first-rate witness'. (Later we shall see what the Soviets thought!) Similarly, the American journalist (and former intelligence officer) James P. O'Donnell chose to believe Axmann's second version.

No one paid much attention to the testimony about Hitler's dog-handler Sergeant Tornow, who was allegedly witnessed by several to have been restrained at just after midnight in the early hours of 30 April as he was running amok and shouting, 'The Führer is dead.'[17] This, of course, would have been before the farewell to the secretaries, which, as we recall, resembled the best and most dignified of the silent movies. To the cynical and facetious, Tornow's version would explain why the Führer had been so uncharacteristically quiet then!

As will be shown later, there is only extremely contradictory circumstantial evidence to show that *any* touching goodbye scene was enacted. There is, however, a pointer which suggests that Tornow might have been premature in his supposition of Hitler's death, and that is that, if Hitler had indeed died at just after midnight, there would seem to have been an inordinate delay before Krebs, Goebbels and Bormann sought surrender terms from the Soviets early on 1 May and before the eventual break-out from the Bunker. For during such delay the Soviets were consolidating their hold over the capital.

Yet another tearful leaving ceremony allegedly took place – this time after lunch on 30 April. It was mainly the men who were present, including Goebbels, Bormann, Burgdorf, Krebs, Hewel, Naumann, Voss, Rattenhuber, Günsche and Linge. Hitler's pilot, Baur, whose testimony upon his release from the Soviet Union had so amazed everyone, also claimed to have been present in the Bunker, rather than being the worse for wear in the Reich Chancellery, as all the other witnesses' initial testimony stated.

This is when Hitler and Eva allegedly shook hands with all present and retired to their own rooms. The others were supposedly dismissed, but Bormann, Goebbels, Linge and Günsche stayed in the passageway. Artur Axmann, who had originally testified to Hugh Trevor-Roper that he had returned to the Bunker just in time to see the dead bodies, was later to change his testimony and claim that he was not only also present in the passageway but 'as close to the door as possible'.[18] His later testimony was supported by Otto Günsche, who, following his release from Bautzen, recorded, 'There were as I recall at least six people almost as near the door as I, I had very good ears and I was listening intently, Goebbels, Bormann, Linge, Krebs, Burgdorf, Axmann and maybe a few others.'[19]

The question must be asked: why did Axmann change his initial testimony, and why did he choose to repeat this revised testimony in support of Günsche, who in turn supported the most suspect part of Linge's testimony? Was it because, just after Günsche's return, the Günsche testimony, despite Trevor-Roper's influence, became the historical flavour of the month, casting grave doubt on the previously accepted testimony of Linge and Axmann? Were they now all trying to create a stable version to replace that discredited? If so, why?

Was it because of vanity, or did these witnesses know what really happened there, and need to protect that truth?

Let us rejoin Goebbels's 'gods' as the heroes waited outside Hitler's quarters in the corridor/conference room – Günsche, Goebbels, Bormann, Krebs, Burgdorf, and presumably most of the others, possibly including Axmann, ears pressed against the door through which they had last witnessed the Führer they had worshipped depart.

While still waiting for destiny, presumably they missed seeing Frau Junge.

Frau Junge, who was to be the beneficiary of a superb silver-fox fur coat that she claimed Eva Braun had given her just before she died ('I've always enjoyed seeing well dressed women around me, and now I want you to wear this and enjoy it'),[20] claimed that she was the last to see Eva and Adolf. Eva had smiled at her and put her arms around Junge's shoulders. In a memorable last remark, Eva – her hair beautifully done, wearing a blue dress with the scooped but decent neckline that Hitler adored – said, 'Give my love to Bavaria.'[21]

Frau Junge, safely in possession of that one-liner, then thought of the poor Goebbels children, 'playing merrily around the bunker, their happy sounds contrasting with the pregnant silence', and realised they hadn't yet been fed.

Suddenly, after the door shut behind the two of them, I was seized by a wild desire to get as far away as possible. I almost flew up the steps that led to the upper part of the Bunker. But halfway up I remembered the six Goebbels children, abandoned down there: nobody had even thought to give them something to eat at lunchtime, and they were wandering about looking for their parents or Aunt Eva. I led them all to the big round table.

'Come on, children, I'll get you some lunch. The grown-ups have all got so much to do today they haven't had time,' I said as calmly as I could.

I found some fruit and ham and made sandwiches for them, and as they ate I chatted and they answered me cheerfully. They were talking about the safety of the Bunker. It was almost as if they were enjoying the constant bombardment and the explosions outside . . . Suddenly a shot rang out, so close that it silenced us all. The sound echoed round the Bunker. 'Right on target,' yelled little Helmut, without any idea of how accurate he was.[22]

This testimony serves as a reminder of the quality of the evidence upon which historical certainty has been based, for the upper Bunker was several closed doors and a considerable distance away from the room in which Hitler and Eva died. Could Junge's testimony have initially been necessary to support Kempka's version of a brave Hitler shooting himself like an officer?

Linge was another who must have absented himself from the queue in the corridor in order to be the last to see the Führer. According to his version, which Hugh Trevor-Roper quite liked, he followed Hitler along the corridor to the map room. Five days earlier Hitler had told him, 'There is no way out any more, Linge. I have decided with Fräulein Braun that we will die together. Your duty – and my order to you – is to see that our bodies are burned. No one must see and recognise me after death.' Now, said Linge:

I asked if there was anything I could do for him.

Moody, glum-looking, he muttered that I was to remember his orders and carry them out; then I was to try to get away from Berlin.

He held out his hand and I shook it. Then old habit took over and I saluted.

He showed no emotion as I turned away and broke into a run. I did not want to hear the fatal, final shot.

I stopped a little way off, regained control of myself and slowly retraced my steps towards the door of the map room. And then I noticed that whiff of smoke. Slowly I pushed the door open . . .[23]

There was 'just that thin wisp of smoke . . . no noise, no crack of a pistol shot reached me'. The time was exactly 3.50 p.m.[24]

Meanwhile Günsche and the others in the conference room cum corridor had obviously been listening at the wrong door, and for several minutes allegedly guarded this door against all comers.

The contradictions don't stop there. Magda Goebbels was now to make a late theatrical entrance. Overcoming her heart condition, she plunged down the wrought-iron steps from the upper Bunker, flung open the intercommunicating heavy bulkhead doors, and threw herself into Günsche's arms, begging to be allowed to see her Führer. Günsche's orders were to let no one else in, but, surprised and perplexed as he flourished his pistol, he relented and entered the room to relay Magda's request. Frantically she burst past him into the study. Hitler gruffly refused to talk to her.[25]

This episode about which we have very significantly no detail whatsoever, supposedly lasted for two minutes.

Eventually a gaggle were to enter the 'Führer room', having failed to hear any shot, partly, said Günsche, because the heavy steel doors were 'fireproof, gasproof, hence soundproof'.[26]

For the lay reader, a summary at this point may prove not just helpful but essential.

- Many people claimed to have been the last to see Hitler alive.

- Baur was in the room with Eva and Hitler and saw both shoot themselves, but no one saw Baur.

- Linge, one of the many who were 'last to see Hitler alive', didn't hear the shot but saw a curl of smoke from under the fire-proof door (except that it was the wrong door).

- Günsche and most others, with their ears against the right door, failed to see any smoke and failed to hear a shot that even the Goebbels children and Frau Junge could hear in the upper Bunker.

Before we view the next scene – where Günsche, Goebbels, Bormann et al., with Axmann allegedly in tow, push open the door to Hitler's living-quarters and find Hitler and Eva on the sofa in the living-room –

spare a thought for poor Linge, who, according to his initial testimony, found his master dead in the map room:

> At the door of the map room now I paused, for I didn't relish the task ahead of me or the sight I knew would greet me . . . I nerved myself to walk quietly into the room.
> There almost upright . . .[27]

Historians helped smooth away all these discrepancies in the testimonies by the simple expedient of ignoring them. By the 1960s the stories had happily merged: both Linge and Günsche were entering the right door together.

Allowing for the artistic licence shown by the historians, let us accept the remoulded version that seems to satisfy almost everyone completely.

First consider the advice that Hitler was allegedly given about how to commit suicide. According to Professor Ernst-Günther Schenk, who was allegedly told this by his colleague Professor Haase, Haase spent some time with Hitler shortly before the end, advising him on how best to proceed in order to be absolutely certain of death. The timing of this suggests that no one ever previously considered suicide as a possible way out for the Führer – a fact hard to equate with his having possessed Zyankali cyanide vials for many months, and so many previous utterances of intent.

Haase, a supposedly competent physician, apparently told a severe sufferer from Parkinson's disease to shoot himself through the mouth with a revolver while at the same time biting on a glass ampoule of cyanide to make certain.

This testimony seems to please historians: they don't even find it funny. Forensic pathologists certainly do!

First, Haase knew full well that the Zyankali vials were more than effective. They had been tested extensively, by many methods, and the scientists had not been squeamish about using volunteers. Haase had also allegedly tested one of them on Blondi, Hitler's Alsatian, with instant effect. A further gunshot would have been more that superfluous.

In any case, to shoot oneself in the mouth with a revolver takes not inconsiderable grip and steadiness – especially since a certain amount of muscle power is instantly lost as the wrist is flexed to position the gun. The exact effects of taking cyanide will be dealt with later, but it ought to be obvious that, if the Zyankali vial were to be bitten first, Hitler, in the throes of agony, would have to be very quick even to find his mouth let alone fire a gun into it, and Parkinson's patients are not exactly noted for their speed. Conversely, if the gun were fired first he might have difficulty in finding the Zyankali vial.

When in the late 1960s the first post-mortem results were published by Bezymenski, the Schenk story changed. Now Haase was supposed to have advised Hitler to bite on a Zyankali vial while shooting himself in the temple – again a not inconsiderable feat for a sufferer of Parkinson's. Even O'Donnell admits as a lay person that it would take 'one last, vehement act of concentrated will power'.[28] Eva was supposed to have been advised to bite on her vial as soon as she heard a shot!

The Finding of the Bodies

The first Western version of Linge's story described how he had steeled himself to go in alone. In the later version recorded by O'Donnell, Linge claimed that:

> As he slowly opened the door, he was taken aback. The strong fumes made his eyes smart. [Presumably acrid cyanide fumes don't escape from smoke-resistant sealed fire doors, whereas thin wisps of smoke do!] Choking, Linge closed and locked the door and turned back to summon Bormann. 'Frankly, I was trembling,' Linge says, 'and I simply did not have the gumption to go in there by myself. It was too eerie.'[29]

According to this new version, Linge then locked the door and went and fetched Bormann. As Bormann, Günsche, Goebbels et al. supposedly had their ears glued to the very same door – the correct one this time – Linge probably didn't have too long a journey. In any case, he duly 'returned', and unlocked the door to allow Bormann, Goebbels, Günsche and apparently Axmann to accompany him into the room. (In Axmann's first testimony he had to be allowed in to see the dead bodies later.)

Linge, Axmann and Günsche all agreed that they found Hitler and Eva dead. Their story, which has never been questioned by essentially romantic historians, who must have secretly wished to believe it, merits further consideration, as it at least matches if not betters the quality of the previous testimony.

The crept into the fume-cupboard of a room, in line behind Bormann (failing to see the stoically heroic, smoke-resistant Baur, who must have by now been skew-eyed as, according to his testimony, he had been in there quite a while).

According to Linge's first testimony:

There, almost upright in a sitting position on a couch, was the body of Adolf Hitler.

A small hole the size of a German silver mark showed on his right temple and a trickle of blood ran slowly down over his cheek.

He was wearing an uniform I had carefully laid out for him a few hours earlier. It was scarcely crumpled.

One pistol, a 7.65 Walther, lay on the floor where it had dropped from his right hand. A yard or so away lay another gun of 6.35 calibre. . .

The body of Eva Braun – she was the only woman who counted in Hitler's life during the years I knew him – was sitting by my master's side. I believe she had died a few minutes before the Führer, whose wish it had been that in death they should be together as they had been for so many years in life.

No mark showed on the face of Eva Braun; it was as though she had fallen asleep. She had swallowed an ampoule of poison, one of a dozen which Hitler had got for just such a circumstance as this, from an Army doctor. They were for the women attached to his staff and for the wife of Dr Goebbels; but above all for Eva.[30]

If that description needed still more sentimentality, Major Günsche later duly obliged, telling O'Donnell how:

A small Dresden vase, which had been filled only that morning with greenhouse tulips and white narcissi, had tipped over spilling water on to Eva Braun's blue chiffon spring dress near the thigh. It had fallen to the carpet, unbroken. Linge, ever the valet with a sense of order, picked it up, examined it for cracks, filled it with the fallen flowers, and set it back on the table. 'At least two minutes – two very long minutes – passed before any of us said or did anything, except watch what Linge did with the white vase,' Günsche related.[31]

And Gertraüd Junge later described what she saw when she entered the room after the bodies had been removed:

On a side table stood Eva's little revolver, beside a square of pink silk chiffon. I saw the cyanide capsule of yellow metal on the floor beside her armchair. It looked like an empty lipstick tube. Spread over the armchair, which was upholstered in a blue and white patterned fabric, was a large bloodstain. It was Hitler's blood.[32]

Later additions to the testimony made it quite clear that Eva and Hitler were as comfortably close to each other in death as they had been in life immediately before, when they were seated next to each other on the sofa and 'Eva had kicked off her buckskin shoes and pulled her feet up snugly underneath her lithe body.'[33] When she was found, her head was snuggled comfortably on to Hitler's shoulder. It can't have been so bad after all! Junge's descriptions of her brightly coloured scarf and the blue and white velvet sofa complete the scene: one of manly love, female devotion, touching togetherness, and that heady mixture of ill-fated destiny and regret at what might have been.

This scene was being reported by hardened, cynical SS men, including Linge and Günsche. By the same devoted servants who had allowed their Führer to become a urine-sodden, soup-stained caricature. By men who had shared in the mood of the jollities of the previous night, induced by the thought of the Führer's death, and had shared in the petulance and disappointment at the increasing delay.

Even allowing for the merging of their testimonies, and taking away the fresh flowers, the white vase and the head-on-shoulder description of the actual death pose – a description surely better suited for shampoo advertisements – there were still glaring discrepancies in the testimonies of the main witnesses. For Axmann and Kempka – who both later allegedly inspected the bodies – still maintained that they found no evidence of any shot through the temple, but found instead that Hitler had shot himself through the mouth.

Allowing for the fact that when several people see an emotional or traumatic incident their testimonies often vary considerably, and that some inconsistencies are the rule rather than the exception, it is still surprising that soldiers would mistake the post-mortem effects of a shot through the mouth and a shot through the temple.

Nor is their description of a shot through the mouth convincing. In most cases if such a wound takes place there is more than just an entry wound – the exit wound is often very, very obvious because of its usual site on the back or top of the head and because of the gore that accompanies it as brain tissue and blood are forced out. The weapon that was allegedly still smoking was a 7.65 Walther. A shot from this weapon would very likely have sufficient muzzle velocity to produce a sizeable exit hole in any skull, normally at least the size of the entrance hole.

Neither was there any adequate description by Linge and Günsche to warrant believing the testimony in this regard. While several testimonies alleged that there was blood on the sofa, and some on the floor, there was no testimony about blood elsewhere, such as on the wall behind the sofa, which according to all accounts wasn't even spotted with gore.

The overall effect of the conjoint testimony is no less than total confusion.

In short, there is no circumstantial evidence that stands up to examination to suggest that Hitler shot himself. Yet almost all historians choose – on the grounds of their considerable forensic ignorance – to believe that facts are not necessary; they have decided, on the confused circumstantial evidence outlined above, that Hitler *did* shoot himself. How and where were really irrelevant.

If Hitler had just blown out his brains, the lay person might think it unlikely that his corpse would be found sitting conveniently bolt upright (in some accounts) with Eva's head on his shoulder. However, whereas this is just within the realms of possibility, far more significant is the story of the Zyankali vials and the cyanide poisoning.

Post-Mortem Influence

Until 1968, when Bezymenski reported that glass fragments which matched the type used in Zyankali vials of cyanide had been found in Hitler's alleged corpse, all historians had settled down nicely with the accepted belief that Hitler had shot himself either in the mouth as Axmann and Kempka observed or through his temple as Linge and Günsche made out. Whereas Eva could swallow poison without dishonour – ' "I want to be a beautiful corpse," she protested'[34] – Hitler, despite his alleged chats with Professor Haase and the test-poisoning of his dog, had taken the officer's way out.

Then came the bombshell – the Bezymenski post-mortem reports – and the story began to change radically. Suddenly attention focused on the need to explain away the glass fragments and to explain why, if Hitler had shot himself through the mouth, the palate was still intact.

It didn't take long for witness testimonies to cater for this unexpected information. Now suddenly there appeared two poison vials for Hitler along with two for Eva – the spares presumably being extra in case they made a mistake![35] According to this testimony, Hitler took one cyanide capsule and carefully placed it in his mouth, and Eva took one cyanide capsule and carefully placed it in her mouth. They left the other two capsules on a convenient small round table. In this version, Eva, who, it is now alleged, had also had some coaching from Professor Haase, was to wait until she heard a shot and then bite into the capsule – in case the sight of her dead lover might break her resolution.[36]

Hitler then bit his capsule and, at the same time, shot himself in the head. Eva bit on her vial simultaneously. They died together on the sofa, freezing into a family-album immobility.

Even though all concerned had to cover their mouths to deal with Eva because of the characteristic bitter almonds stench of the cyanide,[37] no one thought to do so with the Führer. SS general Rattenhuber then allegedly appeared the worse for drink – so shaken by the news that he was 'moaning and groaning'.[38] (This was the same man who had been prematurely celebrating Hitler's death!) Nor did Rattenhuber supposedly have the courage to enter the Führer's room. He hadn't been told of Haase's clever shoot-and-bite technique, and obviously hadn't thought of it himself, so he allegedly jumped to the conclusion that someone had at last killed Hitler, so ending their miserable wait, and had to be reassured that his suspicions were groundless.[39]

Once again it is necessary to digress, this time to deal with the effects of cyanide poisoning, in order to show that, even if Hitler hadn't shot himself, the taking of cyanide by Hitler and Eva would have resulted in a scene scarcely resembling that described.

Zyankali vials were made specifically for the purpose of committing suicide if necessary, to the instructions of Himmler. They had been extensively tested: cyanide being one of the quickest poisons known to man, they worked effectively in seconds (although death could take several minutes in someone who tried to resist ingesting the poison). On taking cyanide, the victim often goes into convulsions, threshing about dramatically, gasping for air. A position known as opisthotonos, where the head and spine are forcibly extended backwards, is not at all uncommon, and quite often the jaw muscles clamp down in what is known as trismus, giving a sick grin which, as we shall see, in this instance would have more than befitted the occasion. However, the patient's collapse is usually profound, and total and gross flaccidity intervenes – a flaccidity totally incompatible with a sitting posture, let alone sitting bolt upright.

Froth around the mouth of the corpse is not only common, but commonly commented upon even by lay persons observing the poisoning.

In the case of the alleged corpses of Hitler and Eva, it is surprising that no one witnessed any single feature that would be in keeping with cyanide poisoning, which once seen is rarely forgotten. No one noticed any froth about their mouths, and no one seemed to recall a stench of bitter almonds, characteristic of cyanide, emanating from Hitler's corpse.

However, the lay person may think these points minor compared with the positioning of the corpses. If two people sitting next to each other on a sofa had each taken an instantly fatal dose of cyanide, the chances of them ending up seated in the alleged *gemütlich* position – blonde head on manly shoulder; one sitting comfortably, toes tucked away under her rump, and the other in a posture of upright, protective defiance – are near to zero. After thrashing around in their death throes in this bizarre game of Nazi Musical Chairs, they would have been extremely unlikely to be still on the sofa at all!

As a pathologist colleague of mine has pointed out, the whole suicide saga is so ludicrous that all we lack is a suitable commemorative photograph signed after the event for the anniversary.

The dismayed reader may by now be thinking that I have treated the subject of the deaths in the Bunker far less seriously than the various testimonies deserve.

I treat the subject lightly simply because to a doctor it is so totally ridiculous as hardly to warrant being taken seriously. To treat such testimonies with anything else than the ridicule they deserve does not serve, and indeed has not served, historical truth. The deference previously given to palpably false testimony by the West was not matched by the Soviets, who were eventually to set some of the witnesses in their custody the task of writing out their copious accounts about Hitler – in an exercise suitably called 'Castles in the Air'.

The whole story of the alleged suicides of Hitler and Eva in the Bunker is totally farcical. The testimony of every single witness is badly tainted; not one witness is credible. There is, moreover, a far greater than normal incidence of changed testimony. This could be partially explained by several factors: the need for conformity, media pressure, or monetary gain.

But, as will be made clear later from the forensic evidence, *none* of the testimonies is honest; and this raises altogether different questions, on an entirely different plane:

- What was the truth? (*One* of them must have known.)

- Why were they telling untruths?

- Was it to hide the truth?

Even at this juncture, before the truth about the deaths is revealed, there are certain other features of the testimony which deserve comment.

First, the initial witnesses in the West seemed distinctly reluctant to address the question of the cyanide poisoning of the Führer. Either they seemed totally unaware of it or they shied away from making any statement. Was this because they wished the Führer to be remembered as having died in the style of an officer, or was there possibly another reason?

Second, those Bunker witnesses who returned a decade later from their sojourn in the Soviet Union had been questioned in detail about the suicide and asked about the cyanide.[40] Yet, upon their return, not one mentioned this fact – even though they had been repeatedly and intensively grilled. Instead, we are led to believe from the testimony of the returning Bunker witnesses that the Soviets thought Hitler had been shot through the temple.

This would suggest that these returning witnesses were covering up the fact that Hitler committed suicide with, or was actually forcibly poisoned by, a cyanide capsule – 'like a dog', as the Soviets were repeatedly to claim in conversations with their Western counterparts. This Soviet claim was, of course, dismissed as nonsensical Soviet propaganda by all the Western historians and media, who at that time firmly believed – with no vestige of proof – that Hitler had shot himself through the mouth.

Following the Bezymenski revelations, the Western historians went to great lengths to emphasise that for Hitler to have committed suicide by using the Zyankali vial bore no particular shame, and that in their opinion not one of the Bunker witnesses they had questioned would have given false testimony about the shot in the mouth to cover up suicide by cyanide.

But 'dying like a dog' – poisoned by someone else – is hardly the same as determinedly taking your own life, and no fanatic Nazi would contemplate such a truth becoming known.

Bormann's telegram 'The Führer is not yet dead', was just minutes before Hitler's death is alleged to have taken place. Should we view it with a little more interest, considering the true mood in the Bunker?

This calls for further conjecture, which fortunately can be answered in a later chapter by reference to Soviet archive material:

- Was Hitler poisoned by forcibly breaking a Zyankali vial in his mouth?

- Was this the secret that couldn't be told?

- Was this the reason for the false testimonies about a gunshot?

- Did guilt at such brutality prompt reports of a beautiful suicide tryst.

Or was there an even more dramatic end?

6

The Funeral and Burial of
Hitler and Eva Braun

When it came to the disposal of Hitler and Eva Braun, first Hugh Trevor-Roper and then subsequent investigators found that the testimonies of the various witnesses available in 1945 were infuriatingly vague, incomplete and unintelligible. Kempka's testimony was the most nonsensical, so investigators tended to rely on that of Artur Axmann.

According to his testimony, as given to Trevor-Roper and others in 1945, Axmann, having along with all the entourage seen the Führer's corpse and that of Eva, stayed behind to help with the dead bodies. At this point Goebbels left. Linge and another SS officer wrapped Hitler's body in a blanket, concealing the head. Hitler was now identifiable only by the black trousers still visible under the blanket.

Unknown to the West, testimony that has recently become available (see the Acknowledgements) reveals that in 1946 Linge was telling his questioners in Moscow that he had prepared *one* blanket – for Hitler alone – and that he duly took the blanket into the room alone, and carefully wrapped the blanket around the Führer so that 'no one could look at the face of the dead Hitler'. According to this testimony Bormann was the only person likely to have seen the Führer's face; the others appeared later.

Linge was to repeat this careful, rehearsed account in his testimony to the *News of the World* upon his release to the West in 1955. On that occasion, however, having had the deficiencies of his initial 1945–6 testimony pointed out to him rather forcibly by the Soviets, the one thin blanket had managed to replicate and prosper – becoming 'thick blankets', one for Hitler and one for Eva.[1]

Later, as it became evident that other officers had claimed to have seen the Führer's face – including Günsche and the stalwart Baur – Linge generously altered his testimony to accommodate their individual accounts, and the blanket no longer covered Hitler's face.

Then, Axmann's testimony continued, two other SS officers carried Hitler's body up the four flights of stairs to the emergency exit.

So much for the corpse of Hitler; but what of Eva? In his questioning by the Soviets, Linge couldn't remember anything at all about what happened to the corpse of Eva! As we shall see, that was perhaps not too surprising.

According to other testimony, Eva – unwrapped – was carried first of all by Bormann, then by Kempka, then passed to Günsche and finally given to another SS man, who carried her up the same stairs into the garden – passing the parcel combined with passing the buck, perhaps. Later testimony made use of that second thick blanket that Linge's initial testimony had forgotten to provide – covering the head, but still allowing the blue dress to identify the corpse.

The first additional witness to the procession was Erich Mansfeld, who left his post in the guard tower to investigate what seemed to be suspicious activity near the Bunker. His 1945 testimony mentioned the black trouser legs sticking out from a blanket and what was described as the 'unmistakable corpse of Eva Braun'.[2] Behind them came the mourners – Bormann, Linge, Burgdorf, Goebbels, Günsche, Kempka and, according to later testimony, Rattenhuber, Stumpfegger, the SS bodyguard commander Franz Schädle and Hewel.[3] (The women had all been banned from the vicinity for a further hour.)

The corpses were placed side by side face upwards in a shallow depression in the sandy soil a few metres from the Bunker entrance, and petrol was poured over them from cans. Günsche dipped a rag in petrol and set it alight, before flinging it on to the ground. The two bodies burst into flames and the mourners stood briefly to attention before hastily retiring. Günsche, in his testimony upon release from Soviet and East German captivity, declared it to have been the worst moment of his life.

Another witness was guard Hermann Karnau, who watched from the garden, by the tower, and saw two bodies lying side by side suddenly burst into flames. Karnau saw that one of them was unmistakably Hitler, except that his head was smashed: 'The sight . . . was "repulsive in the extreme".'[4] This observation contrasted with all others, none of which mentioned a smashed head, which was in any case supposedly covered by a blanket.

Most testimonies put the time as about 4 p.m. on 30 April.

Mansfeld, now back in the observation tower in the unfinished block, kept watching as a pall of black smoke arose and then settled. He could still see the bodies burning. From time to time SS men came out of the Bunker, picked up cans, and poured more petrol over the bodies to keep them alight.

Later Karnau came to relieve him, and both of them went across to have a close look at the bodies. By now the lower parts of both bodies had burned away and the shin-bones of both Hitler's legs were visible. An hour later, at about 6 to 6.30 p.m., Mansfeld noticed them still burning, but the flames were only flickering lowly.[5]

According to Kempka the dousing with petrol used up 180 litres in total,[6] and from about six o'clock the bodies were left to smoulder quietly. There are many reports of comments made by ordinary guards, who were appalled that Hitler's former Nazi comrades didn't seem to give a damn for the bodies. Downstairs in the Bunker there was a general attitude of relief. There are several accounts of exactly how drunk everyone seemed to be getting.

According to Linge, he went up to have a look at the progress of the cremation and saw that 'Eva Braun's once trim figure had jack-knifed, under *rigor mortis* . . . she was now sitting upright as if riding in a saddle. Both arms were outstretched, and her hands seemed to be holding imaginary reins.'[7] His testimony may once again reflect how reliable a witness he was, for the chemical necessary to cause rigor mortis is used up very rapidly after cyanide poisoning, the rigor then being minimal.

The same reliable witness was to tell a secretary that the bodies had been burned until nothing remained. Not to be outdone, Hans Baur's testimony relates how a soldier was sent up who reported, just before midnight, 'both bodies have been so burned that only very small remnants remain. They are unrecognisable.'[8]

Günsche's testimony relates how he too sent up a guard, who at 10.00 p.m. reported that the face and head of Adolf Hitler had been 'consumed by fire beyond recognition'. Eva Braun had 'burned away to fine ash'.[9] (Günsche is also said to have stated that the ashes had been collected into a small box and taken out of the Reich Chancellery.)[10]

General Rattenhuber, just before midnight, ordered a detail of three men to bury the remains. They duly placed the two charred bodies on a tent-shelter canvas and dragged them to an artillery-shell crater a few metres away from the Bunker exit. They tidied up the edges of the crater and tossed the bodies in, then filled the hole with rubble and earth and pounded it firm. The depth was claimed as 'some six feet deeper' than the cremation hollow.[11]

Mansfeld was also a witness to this burial site. He returned to the tower for another period of guard duty just before midnight and noticed that the bodies had gone and that a crater as described near the exit of the Bunker had been converted into a grave – and concealed none too well: the edges were still clearly visible.[12]

The apparent uninterest in the actual burial continued. Axmann, Rattenhuber and Linge all claimed that they hadn't witnessed the burial at all. For a decade the testimonies had been only partly believed, the account obviously incomplete. All attention was focused on the return from the Soviet Union of Harry Mengerhausen – the man whom Rattenhuber had placed in charge of the burial party.

In October 1955 Mengerhausen arrived back in his home town of Bremen to find himself the centre of attention for the world press. His testimony was that he had been captured by the Soviets on the night of 1–2 May, and for ten days in Soviet hands he had steadfastly denied any involvement with Hitler. However, on 13 May he was shown a document (believed to be by Günsche), which purported to be a full account of the death of Hitler and of his burial. Mengerhausen was mentioned as having been in charge of the burial party. Though previously claiming not to know any details of what had gone on, he nevertheless now quickly capitulated and agreed to show the Soviets the burial site.[13]

He took his Soviet inquisitors directly to the grave site on the same day – only to find that it had already been dug up and the bodies had been removed. They had, according to Mengerhausen, been buried on three wooden boards, a metre deep; a man called Glanzer had helped him dig the grave and fill it in.[14]

Finally, according to Mengerhausen, at the end of May 1945 the Soviets took him to a small wood near Finow, about 45 km north-east of Berlin, where he was shown three charred corpses lying in a crate. Two were lightly charred and he had no difficulty in identifying them as those of Joseph and Magda Goebbels; the other he identified as Hitler's. The body was in a bad shape – the feet entirely consumed; the skin and flesh blackened and burned – but the facial structure remained clearly identifiable. There was a bullet hole in one temple, but the upper and lower jaw were both intact.[15]

Even at this juncture there is reason to question some aspects of Mengerhausen's testimony, as there is nothing in Soviet archive material to confirm this confrontation, it being more likely that the bodies of Hitler, Goebbels and Eva were by that time in the vicinity of the headquarters of Smersh – the Soviet Intelligence agency – at Magdeburg, 170 km away.

As we shall see, Joseph and Magda Goebbels had already been identified several times by that stage. Joseph Goebbels had very distinctive physical features. He was no longer a matter of concern for Smersh, in charge of the investigation. The Soviets would have scarcely needed further corroboration from a man such as Mengerhausen, who was in a lowly position and hadn't been involved in disposing of the Goebbels's corpses by burial; he would have had very little to add.

It is also of interest to note that Mengerhausen showed remarkable forensic aptitude in determining the presence of a bullet hole in one temple of a charred corpse which had in fact by then had its brain removed. Such a hole would hardly have been immediately obvious even to a trained pathologist. What would have been far more obvious to a layman was the fact that, by that time, extensive macabre dissection had been carried out on the corpse – a fact that Mengerhausen failed to notice. His comments upon both jaws being intact are also invalid, as by this time the post-mortem had removed the loose lower jaw along with the bridges.

In 1955, however, Mengerhausen was more than aware of the controversy of Linge's testimony about Hitler having shot himself in the temple, and by the time he eventually gave his testimony to Hugh Trevor-Roper the controversy was at its height. His comments about the gunshot wound in the temple have to be viewed in this light, though Trevor-Roper himself still persisted in his belief that Hitler was shot through the mouth, even after hearing Mengerhausen's testimony.[16]

However tempting this new version of events, Mengerhausen's tale of his visit to the Finow woods has to be dismissed. But his testimony about digging a grave for two partly consumed bodies remains convincing enough.

So what can be made of the testimonies about the burial? Before becoming engaged in conjecture, it is essential to emphasise that the discussion that follows does not at this stage relate to the *identity* of the corpses: it only puts into perspective the various testimonies, several of which will be seen to be fatuous.

It is important to recollect that the bodies were laid side by side, face upwards, directly in a shallow sandy trench. There was no attempt to form a proper fire, even though there was plenty of wood available, and other combustible material including tyres from the nearby Chancellery garage. The bodies had no air supply from below, and it could have been forecast that the whole of the back surface of the alleged Führer and his beloved Eva would survive relatively intact for that reason. Indeed, given the SS practice of burning their dead in any retreat, it must have been fairly obvious to those in the Bunker that to use only the 180 litres of petrol that they had collected would merely result in severe charring of the surface parts.

It must have been doubly obvious to those keeping the fire alight that Hitler and Eva were not going to be reduced to ashes, and it is highly likely that, being responsible, they would have reported back on the progress.

Even when their testimony about the burial was first given, there was intense scepticism. Doubts were immediately expressed – but only the doubts that common sense would dictate. No one seemed interested in asking the expert opinion of those in crematoria, engaged professionally in the burning of bodies, or firemen who witness the effects of various forms of conflagration – nor of those forensic scientists who have to pronounce on the end result.

Had anyone bothered to ask, they would have learned that it takes a couple of hours of intense heat at up to 1,200°C to ensure that a body is completely burned – in an oven with controlled conditions. Even then the long bones such as those of the legs are often intact and have to be given a couple of brisk taps with a mallet to make them crumble into smaller debris. In what has now become an exact science, even the size of this debris is predictable.[17]

The temperature that can be obtained by paraffin or petrol fires is by comparison low – only several hundred degrees – and the combustion is inconstant. Although there would certainly be destruction of soft tissues if the fire were prolonged for many hours, there would only be even destruction of what are called the flat bones, such as the shoulder-blades and those bones in the skull which are thin, covered with tissue both sides like a sandwich. Such incomplete combustion would certainly fail to destroy the dentition. It is only at much higher temperatures that some teeth explode or are destroyed. Similarly, major long bones, such as the shin-bones, would remain intact, whereas the smaller, thinner arm-bones and the smaller bones of the wrist and sometimes the ankle might be eaten away.

This realisation makes the testimony of Baur, Linge and Günsche about the bodies being reduced to ashes seem unintelligently untruthful.

In the Bunker Valhalla of Eva and Adolf, only the most perfunctory attempt had been made to get enough petrol, though we know from Kempka's later testimony that there was some 750–1,000 litres of petrol in a half-full underground tank with an outlet in the Chancellery garage. (Later he was to get more petrol for the bodies of Joseph and Magda

Goebbels.) We also know that there was no attempt to get more while the bodies merely smouldered from six o'clock right through to eleven.

To pour 180 litres of petrol over two bodies in sandy soil, which itself mopped up some of the petrol, was almost certain to ensure incomplete combustion. The questions that need to be asked about this incomplete combustion are:

- Was it the result of ignorance?

- Was it possibly the result of indifference, reflecting the mood in the Bunker?

- Was it possibly deliberate?

At present we are led to believe from the testimony of Linge that the Führer's decision to entrust the burial of the bodies to him was made almost at the last minute, giving the impression that no one, including Hitler, had ever planned for his eventual demise – a premiss which cannot be left unchallenged. The roles of Rattenhuber, in charge of the SS guard, and Linge and Günsche, both SS men, have to be considered with a degree of scepticism, for, if there had been previous planning and not the ad-hoc chaos we are supposed to accept happened, they would have been the instruments by which any deceit was carried out.

Before we consider the identity of the corpses of 'Hitler' and 'Eva', as revealed by the post-mortem reports, and come to realise that there is evidence which will radically alter our perception, it may be worth recapping:

- There is no reason to doubt that two bodies, allegedly those of Hitler and Eva, were duly burned.

- There is no reason to doubt that these bodies were very incompletely burned, and that the testimony of Mengerhausen is correct in this regard.

- There *is* reason to question *why* they were incompletely burned, and to question the extent of indifference, apathy, ignorance or wilful deceit.

- There is no reason to suspect that the burned bodies were not those subsequently buried by Mengerhausen and later found by the Soviets.

The end of the Viking funeral was a scene of apathy, indifference, incompetence, mental fatigue, intense latent fear, and the very chaos of war – not a picture befitting a glorious past or reflecting the triumphant

121

moments of certainty that the Nazi clique felt they had shared. Treasured memories are not made of such material. Little wonder, then, that the participants chose to remember it differently. But, as we shall see, this was not the reason for some of the consistent lying.

That reason, cleverly concealed in various ways by the varying testimonies, could be uncovered only by forensic scientists dealing not in opinions but in facts. The crucial data, so in need of expert reappraisal, are the post-mortem reports, viewed clinically and without the distorting lens of political interference.

7

The Discovery of the Corpses –
Forensic Fraud

Instead of conjecture and the fanciful stories of Axmann carrying away Hitler's ashes in a little box to allow future generations to worship the Führer's memory in a Nazi shrine – stories that were repeated and given credence in various forms, by such historians as Hugh Trevor-Roper[1] – we can now rely on the report, dated 5 May 1945, of Soviet guards lieutenant Alexei Panassov for a more accurate account of the finding of the alleged bodies of Hitler and Eva.[2]

We can also rely on other documents concerning the discovery of the Goebbels family.

To appreciate fully the atmosphere present in the mortuary of the Berlin-Buch Hospital, which had been requisitioned by the Soviets and where the forensic examinations of the various corpses took place, it is best to start with the discovery of the Goebbels family and the subsequent post-mortems.

The Corpses of the Goebbels Family

The report on the discovery of the Goebbels' bodies was signed by Lieutenant-General Vadis, the administrative chief of counter-intelligence, Smersh, 1st Byelorussian Front; Major-General Melnikov, the deputy administrative chief of counter-intelligence, Smersh, 1st Byelorussian Front; Colonel Mirozhnichenko, the section chief of counter-intelligence, Smersh, the 3rd Shock Army; Lieutenant-Colonel Barzukov, the administrative section chief of counter-intelligence, Smersh, 1st Byelorussian Front; Leiutenant-Colonel Klimenko, the section chief, counter-intelligence, Smersh, of the 79th Rifle Corps; Colonel Krylov, chief of the political section of the same corps; Lieutenant-Colonel Gvozd, the chief of reconnaissance, 3rd Shock Army; Major Aksyanov, the section chief, counter-intelligence, Smersh, 207th Rifle Division; Major Khasin, deputy section chief, counter-intelligence, Smersh, in the same division; Major Bystrov, the sub-section chief, counter-intelligence, Smersh, 3rd Shock Army; Captain Khelimski, the operations chief, counter-intelligence administration, Smersh, 1st Byelorussian Front; Lieutenant-Colonel Grachov, medical officer of the 79th Rifle Corps Medical Service; and their interpreter, Captain Alperovich, chief of investigating group, reconnaissance, 3rd Shock Army.[3]

To Western eyes there was a quite excessive number of people involved. This, as Soviet Colonel A. Voitov was to point out,[4] was typical of any Soviet document – a sharing of responsibility, for glory and for blame. Their accounts were summarised in a document drawn up by Captain Alperovich, dated 3 May 1945:

On May, 2 1945, in the centre of Berlin, in the bunker of the German Chancellery, Lieutenant Colonel Klimenko and Majors Bystrov and Khasin discovered, in the presence of Berlin citizens – the Germans Lange, Wilhelm, the Chancellery cook, and Schneider, Karl, chief garage mechanic of the Chancellery – a few metres from the entrance door at 17.00 hours the partially charred corpses of a man and a woman; the corpse of the man was smallish, the twisted foot of his right leg (clubfoot) was inside a partially charred metal prosthesis, on the corpse were found the remains of a charred Party uniform of the NSDAP and a scorched gold Party badge; next to the charred body of the woman a partially scorched gold cigarette case was discovered and on the corpse a gold Party badge of the NSDAP and a scorched gold brooch.

At the head of the two corpses lay two Walther pistols No. 1 (damaged by fire).

On May 3 of the same year the platoon leader of Counter Intelligence Section SMERSH, 207th Rifle Division, Senior Lieutenant Ilyin, found in a separate room in the Chancellery bunker the corpses of children [five girls and one boy] aged three through fourteen, lying on their beds. They were dressed in light nightgowns and exhibited symptoms of poisoning. [This differs from the testimony of Voitov,[5] and it is possible that the later testimony alluded to the stacking of the bodies before their removal.]

The above-mentioned corpses having been recognized as those of

Dr Goebbels, his wife, and their children, all corpses were taken, for post-mortem examination and identification by persons who had known them intimately, to the premises of the Counter Intelligence Section SMERSH, 79th Rifle Corps of the 1st Byelorussian front.

For identification of the corpses on the premises, the following prisoners of war – the personal representative of Grand Admiral Dönitz at Führer headquarters, Vice-Admiral Voss, Hans Erich, born 1897; chief garage mechanic of the Chancellery, Schneider, Karl Friedrich Wilhelm; and the Chancellery cook Lange, Wilhelm – were consulted, all of whom knew Goebbels, his wife, and his children well.

Vice-Admiral Voss, Lange, and Schneider identified the corpses unequivocally, during interrogation and in confrontation with the corpses, as Goebbels, his wife and children. Asked on what distinguishing features he based his assertion . . . Vice-Admiral Voss declared that he recognized [Goebbels by] the shape of the skull, the lines of the mouth, the brace which Goebbels wore on the right leg, by the presence of the gold Party badge of the NSDAP [Nazi Party], and the remnants of the charred Party uniform . . .

Voss recognized in the partially charred female corpse the wife of Goebbels and expressed his certainty by the comment that, because of its height (more than medium height) and because of the gold Party badge of the NSDAP this was the body of Goebbels' wife. (She was the only German woman wearing this badge; it had been handed to her by Hitler three days before his suicide.)

Further, on examining the cigarette case near the female body the inscription in German script 'Adolf Hitler – 29.X.34' was discovered on the inside cover. Voss testified that the case had been used by Goebbels' wife during the last three weeks.

On inspecting the children's bodies, Voss identified all of them without exception as Goebbels' children, having seen them all repeatedly; one of the girls, the approximately three-year-old Goebbels daughter Heidi, had visited in Voss's apartment on various occasions.

The above-mentioned persons who had been consulted in the identification of the bodies – the cook Lange and chief garage mechanic Schneider – confirmed emphatically that they both recognized Dr Goebbels in the partially charred male body, basing their assertion on the shape of the face, the stature of the body, the skull formation, and the metal brace of the right leg.

In the presence of the military personnel enumerated in the

present document, the cook Lange also recognized the children's corpses as Goebbels' children; two children he named by their first names, the girl Hilde and the boy Helmut, both of whom he knew personally for some time.

During the external examination of the children's bodies Lieutenant Colonel Grachov, Medical Service, Army Corps, established that the death of the children was caused by introducing the toxic carboxyhaemoglobin into the organism [i.e. carbon-monoxide poisoning].

On the basis of these testimonies we, the undersigned, conclude that the partially charred corpses – of the man, the woman, and the six children – are the corpses of the German Minister of Propaganda Dr Josef Goebbels, his wife, and their children.

Deposition made in the present Document.

The testimonies of Voss, Lange and Schneider, who were consulted for identification, were given by them through the interpreter for German, Chief of Investigating Group, Reconnaissance, 3rd Shock Army, Captain Alperovich.[6]

The thirteen Soviet signatures were followed by those of the three German witnesses.

The first and most obvious possible discrepancy in this document is that it purports to have been signed on 3 May. To achieve this, the bodies – including those of the children allegedly found that very same day – would have had to have been taken to the premises of the 79th Rifle Corps, where the German and Soviet witnesses would all have been present, identification and interrogation carried out, the separate reports coordinated, a decision taken as to the format of the eventual document to be submitted to Stalin, and the whole thing typed, agreed and signed all on the same day. This would be a remarkable accomplishment for any army. There is therefore considerable doubt that this document was either written or signed on 3 May.

There is one pointer, however, which *does* suggest that it was genuinely written *before* the later post-mortems. That pointer was the inclusion of an incorrect surmise from the examining unit medical doctor – himself hardly an expert – that there had been carbon-monoxide poisoning of the six children. This assumption must have been made because of the colour of the corpses, although it is surprising that the tell-tale smell of bitter almonds, typical of cyanide poisoning, was not observed by Lieutenant-Colonel Grachov. Had the post-mortem findings been available, they would surely have been included as a correction for this anomalous finding. This is heartening evidence for this report being a genuine account of what happened.

The next observable discrepancy is that whereas there is seeming total agreement that the corpses were indeed the corpses of Goebbels and his children, neither Lange nor Schneider would go as far as to identify Magda Goebbels with certainty, leaving Voss as the only witness expressing such a certain opinion. But in fact the testimony that Klimenko, the chief investigator, subsequently gave to the Soviet journalist Lev Bezymenski casts doubt on this too:

After the 79th Rifle Corps had occupied the Parliament building, my detachment was billeted in Plötzensee Prison; members of the German armed forces made prisoner in the area of the Parliament and the Chancellery were taken there. Naturally, we questioned them about the fate of the leaders of the Fascist Reich, above all about Hitler and Goebbels. Several among them said that they had heard of Hitler's and Goebbels' suicide in the Chancellery. I therefore decided to take along four witnesses and to drive with them to the Chancellery.

It was afternoon and it rained. I climbed into a jeep, the witnesses and soldiers into an Army truck. We drove up to the Chancellery, went into the garden, and arrived at the emergency exit of the Führerbunker. As we approached this exit, one of the Germans shouted: 'That is Goebbels' corpse! That is the corpse of his wife!'

I decided to take these corpses with us. Since we did not have a stretcher we placed the corpses on an unhinged door, manoeuvred them into the truck (it was a covered vehicle), and returned to Plötzensee.

The day after, May 3, 1945, the corpses of six Goebbels children and the corpse of General Krebs were found in the bunker. They too were taken to Plötzensee.

Later some generals and officers from the staffs of the 3rd Shock Army and the 1st Byelorussian Front came over, and also the Soviet war correspondents Martin Merzhanov and Boris Garbatov. Now the procedure of identification began.

This was done in the following manner: Goebbels' body was laid in a room on a table, the bodies of his wife and children and that of General Krebs, were put on the floor. The witnesses were kept in another room. The first to enter the room was Vice-Admiral Voss, the representative of Grand Admiral Dönitz at Führer headquarters; he had been captured by members of the Counter Intelligence Section of the 3rd Shock Army. Without hesitating he identified Goebbels and his children. The other witnesses did the same.[7]

Despite the official version, the disparity between the certainty of identification of Joseph Goebbels and the disquiet about Magda Goebbels seemed to have extended to Voss as well, and it was to extend further, to the chief of Goebbels's bodyguard, Wilhelm Echold, who, when captured, repeated the pattern.[8]

Before we go on to the actual post-mortem data, it is worth remembering that the non-forensic evidence for the identification of Magda Goebbels was based *entirely* on her height and her gold Party badge. Joseph Goebbels was more distinctive, with his right club-foot and his prosthesis, and the children's bodies were intact – unburned – and therefore easily recognisable, as shown by the photographs of the post-mortems. One of the most poignant reminders of the madness of it all was the photograph of Helga's corpse being held up for photographic identification in the grisly mortuary of the Berlin-Buch Hospital – the white face gripped under the chin by uncompromising leather gloves and held forcibly in position.

The Smersh reports on the Goebbels family demonstrated the application of old-fashioned post-mortem techniques – meticulous in the examination of internal organs, including brains, as well as in the recording of essential external features. Several specimens were excised from specific organs, including the gut, the stomach and its contents, and sections of other tissues such as lung, liver, spleen and kidneys. Lastly, blood samples were taken for biochemical analysis. All specimens were sent on to the Medical-Epidemiological Field Laboratory Number 291, well behind the lines.[9]

In the case of Goebbels's wife and children, there were additional exhibits appended to the post-mortem documents. These were glass splinters found in the mouth of every body.[10]

Document 1 related to Helga. Her mouth had contained splinters of a cyanide-containing ampoule (as did all the others). Her brain matter smelled of cyanide, and chemical analysis of the tissues and blood confirmed cyanide poisoning.

Document 2 related to Heide. Her corpse showed similar findings.

Document 8 related to Hedda. Her tongue on dissection was noted to smell of almonds.

Document 9 related to Holde. Her brain and lungs also smelled of cyanide.

Document 10 related to Helmut. He exhibited identical findings.

Document 11 finally confirmed the cause of death of Hilde, with, yet again, positive evidence of cyanide poisoning.

Two dogs found in the vicinity of the Bunker were also subjected to post-mortem examination on the same day, as they had evidently been poisoned. This Soviet thoroughness was to reveal that a small black dog had first been poisoned with cyanide and then shot in its death throes. The other, an Alsatian bitch with a dark-grey back and light underbelly (Blondi), had been poisoned with a Zyankali cyanide vial.

The later opinion of the Soviet forensic expert Professor Vladimir Smolyaninov was that the two dogs had been used as a toxicological test. One dog had had an ampoule crushed in its mouth; the other dog had had to swallow an ampoule and had then been shot from above.[11]

The story of the use of the dogs to test the Zyankali capsules was now confirmed, and fortuitously there exists a 'Record of Interrogation' – on 7 May 1945, by Lieutenant-Colonel Vasilyev, Chief of Counter Intelligence of the 4th Section of Smersh, 1st Byelorussian Front – of a German prisoner of war named Helmut Kunz, in front of the magistrate Senior Lieutenant Vlassov (who also acted as translator).

Kunz, an SS dentist, related how both Magda and Joseph had on separate occasions asked him to help kill their children. As time ran out he witnessed two young men, one in the uniform of the Hitler Youth, talking earnestly to Joseph Goebbels, who was allegedly refusing their offer of assistance to escape. Kunz then accompanied Magda to the children, where

> I made the injections [of morphine] into the underarm below the elbow, 0.5 c.c. for each, in order to make the children sleepy. The injecting lasted about 8–10 minutes, then I went back into the hall, where I met Frau Goebbels. I told her that we would have to wait about 10 minutes for the children to fall asleep. After 10 minutes Frau Goebbels went with me into the children's bedroom, where she stayed about 5 minutes placing into the mouth of each child a crushed ampoule containing potassium cyanide . . . As we returned to the hall, she said 'This is the end.'
>
> I now went down with her to Goebbels' study, where we found him in a very nervous state, pacing back and forth in the room. As we entered the study Frau Goebbels said: 'It's over with the children, now we have to think of ourselves.' . . .

Question: Were you the only one to participate in the killing of Goebbels' children?
Answer: Yes, I was the only one.[12]

This document answers the question of exactly how the Goebbels children were killed. But the Soviets, having received further testimony from Günsche, were not satisfied with the story that Kunz told, and they were also suspicious of the unlikely scene of children threshing about in their death agonies for perhaps some five minutes while a mother managed to crush more cyanide capsules into her other children's mouths. On 19 May, therefore, Kunz was questioned again. He was now to relate:

She [Magda Goebbels] asked me to help her administer the poison to the children. I refused, telling her that I didn't have the fortitude to do this. Then Frau Goebbels asked me to fetch Dr Stumpfegger, Hitler's first assistant surgeon . . . I found Stumpfegger . . . and said to him: 'Doctor, Frau Goebbels wants you to come to her.' As I returned with Stumpfegger into the hall of the children's bedroom, where I had left Frau Goebbels, she was no longer there, and Stumpfegger immediately went into the bedroom. I waited next door. Four or five minutes later Stumpfegger came back with Frau Goebbels from the children's bedroom; he left immediately without saying a word to me. Frau Goebbels did not speak either, she only wept . . .
Question: Why were you silent about Dr Stumpfegger's participation during the previous interrogations?
Answer: The events of the last days before the surrender of the German garrison in Berlin had shocked me so deeply that I plainly and unintentionally overlooked this circumstance.[13]

We, however, can't overlook the fact that there is now absolute proof of the death of the Goebbels children, and more evidence about the nature of their death.

But what of Magda and Joseph Goebbels, now thinking about themselves – Joseph, as we shall see, to the extent of already having entered into desperate peace negotiations to save at least his own skin?

Was the cold-blooded murder of his children, an act which numbed even SS man Kunz,[14] an act which sealed Goebbels's own fate? Did it make him a leper even in the madhouse of the Bunker – man who would be very unlikely to be allowed to escape his own declared intention to commit suicide? And what of Magda?

The post-mortem on the suspected corpse of Joseph Goebbels began on 9 May. The body had been kept for further identification by anyone else connected with the Bunker who might belatedly fall into Soviet hands. The details of the post-mortem were contained in *Document 5*, 'concerning the forensic-medical examination of the partially burned corpse of an unknown man (presumably the corpse of Goebbels)', dated '9.V.1945, Berlin-Buch, Field Hospital for Surgery No. 496'.[15]

The post-mortem was performed by a commission consisting of chief expert, forensic medicine, 1st Byelorussian Front, Medical Service, Lieutenant-Colonel F. Y. Shkaravski, chief anatomical pathologist, Red Army Medical Service, Lieutenant-Colonel N. A. Krayevski, and Majors A. Y. Marants, Y. I. Boguslavski, and Y. V. Gulkevitch, on orders of Lieutenant-General Telegin of the Military Council of the 1st Byelorussian Front.[16]

In the 1960s, Dr Faust Shkaravski, half Ukrainian and half Polish, was interviewed at his home in Kiev by Bezymenski. One of the first generation of Soviet physicians in the Ukraine, graduating in 1925 in Kiev, he had started his forensic training in 1929. On 4 May 1945 he had been summoned to General Barabanov, chief of medical services with the 1st Byelorussian Front, and told that, as a forensic-medicine expert, he had been requested to serve General Telegin, a high-ranking member of the Military Council, and was to depart immediately for Berlin-Buch, to undertake a very special task.[17]

General Telegin confirmed to Bezymenski that the task of the team that he requested was specifically to examine the corpses of alleged fascist leaders.[18] It was not engaged in any other work which might distract it. Stalin wanted some answers.

Dr Nicolai Krayevski, one of the foremost Soviet pathologists, was also interviewed by Bezymenski, and confirmed that, in addition to Telegin's team, the famous Moscow Professor Grazhchenkov, although not mentioned in the final report, also attended the sessions as an observer.[19]

The dissection was actually carried out by Major Anna Marants, and from the nature of the expertise available the post-mortem was well up to Western standards.

Accompanying the alleged corpse of Goebbels was found a leather and metal prosthesis for a club-foot – a prosthesis which fitted exactly. Along with this were a Walther pistol, the remnants of trouser piping, a white undershirt (the factory markings and laundry marks of which were noted carefully), and the collar of an NSDAP uniform. The man had gone out to meet his death in some style, wearing silk socks and a yellow silk tie which bore a round metal NSDAP badge.[20]

The corpse was of a man of forty-five to fifty years old and of subnormal stature, which was further reduced by the posture of the corpse – the knees slightly flexed and the arms half-extended in front of the body and bent at the elbow joints, into the pose of a boxer, although the lower half of the right arm had been entirely burned away. The face had kept its contours – a fact that had made it still so recognisable – the receding forehead and marked projection of the upper jaw being duly recorded. The genitalia were shrunken and dried.

The face was carefully cut open under the lower left jawbone in order to examine the oral cavity, where one splinter of glass was found between the teeth of the right lower jaw. Not only did the lungs smell of cyanide when dissected, but the toxicological testing also confirmed death as being due to cyanide poisoning.

The teeth were minutely examined. A gold filling was found on the second bicuspid of the left upper jaw, whereas the first and second molars on the left side of the upper jaw had amalgam fillings. There was no fancy bridgework. Unfortunately there were no dental charts or X-rays of Goebbels with which to compare these results.

Even though no definite conclusion about the identity of the corpse was officially reached, the investigators were almost certain that the club-foot and the marked, still preserved, facial features were enough to be confident that they had Goebbels.

I see no reason to think otherwise, but it still needs emphasising that Goebbels died as a result of cyanide poisoning by Zyankali vial, and *not* by shooting himself with a pistol. The 'honourable death' that he espoused didn't take place. There is no evidence as to whether he crushed the vial himself.

In exactly similar fashion, *Document 7* shows how the corpse of General Hans Krebs (wrongly labelled 'Krips') was dissected on the same day. A careless, half-hearted and incomplete attempt had been made to tear off his epaulettes, and the corpse bore evidence of three superficial head and neck wounds that had been sustained before death. Nevertheless there was no gunshot wound, but copious evidence that Krebs had swallowed a cyanide capsule rather than take the military solution and shoot himself.[21]

Then we are confronted with *Document 6*, 'concerning the forensic-medical examination of the partially burned corpse of an unknown woman (presumably the wife of Goebbels)'.[22]

The same team found remnants of a yellow-brown jersey, a snap fastener, a buckle and an NSDAP badge, along with a reddish-coloured hairpiece, which matched the remaining hair on the charred skull. Splinters from a thin-walled ampoule were found in the mouth, and tests confirmed the death as due to cyanide poisoning, there being no evidence of any gunshot wound.

The corpse was that of a thirty- to forty-year-old woman, approximately 156 cm long, and had been so badly charred that very little skin remained that was not blackened. Furthermore, in marked contrast to Joseph Goebbels, the features had been totally obliterated.

There being no easy method of identification, careful attention was given to the jaws. The report reads:

The upper jaw has 14 teeth, of which 4 are natural incisors and 2 canine teeth. The second bicuspid left is artificial, on a gold support with a bridge anchored on the first bicuspid.

The first left molar has a small filling, the second left molar has a gold half crown and a filling, the first right bicuspid has an amalgam filling, the first right molar has a gold filling and the second molar two gold fillings.

Lower jaw – the front part of the mandibula is completely preserved, the right vertical section is also preserved, the left one missing. In the lower jaw are 4 natural incisors, 2 canine teeth, and the first 2 bicuspids . . . the second bicuspid to the left is half-capped in gold, the left molar is fitted with a large filling . . .

The first right molar is missing; a thin gold platelet merging into a gold bridge and crown over the second and third right molars is anchored there.[23]

As they had no comparative data – neither dental records nor dental X-rays – the Soviets had absolutely no proof of identity. The commission thus appended to its report the excised upper and lower jaws, the Party badge, some hair and various other items.

It reached no definite conclusion then, and neither, unfortunately, can we today. Whereas it is highly unlikely that a woman with such evidence of expensive dentistry, lying next to Joseph Goebbels, would have been anyone other than Magda, her identity has never been proved.

So far, then, it can be concluded that forensic examination of the first batch of corpses found relatively easily in the region of the Bunker had yielded Joseph Goebbels and his children, and a woman, wearing a Nazi badge, who could well have been Magda Goebbels.

The only aspect to interest the truly cynical is why the cook and the mechanic didn't readily jump to the conclusion that it must be Magda lying next to her husband – especially after the finding of that well-known badge.

The Corpse of 'Eva Braun'

When we come to the next corpse to be examined by the commission, we may well see a possible reason for that caution.

Ivan Klimenko, section chief, counter-intelligence, Smersh, of the 79th Rifle Corps, was the man actually in charge of the search for Hitler. His postwar testimony to Bezymenski was as follows:

> Naturally we asked Voss where Hitler might be. Voss gave no clear answer and told us only that he had left Berlin together with Hitler's adjutant, who had told him that Hitler had committed suicide and that his corpse had been buried in the Chancellery garden.
> After the questioning I decided to go back to the Chancellery and try to find some clues there.
> We arrived with the jeep carrying me, Voss, a Lieutenant Colonel of the Army Counter Intelligence Service, and an interpreter. At the Chancellery we went down into the bunker. It was dark. We illuminated our way with flashlights. Voss behaved somewhat strangely; he was nervous, mumbling unintelligibly. After that, we climbed up again and found ourselves in the garden, not far from the emergency exit.
> It was close to 9 p.m. [on 3 May]. We stepped up to a big dried-up water tank for fire-fighting. It was filled with many corpses. Here Voss said, pointing to a corpse: 'Oh, this is Hitler's body!'[24]

At this stage Klimenko had his doubts, as the body had darned socks! He left the body where it was, to be picked up the next day. On 4 May the body had disappeared – it had been removed and laid out in one of the halls in the Chancellery.

Five out of six German witnesses picked up in the Reich Chancellery said it was *not* Hitler; the other said it might be. Arrangements had been made for a Soviet diplomat to arrive and confirm identification, but meanwhile the search continued. (Once again a myth has arisen of a Hitler double – this myth being started by journalist James P. O'Donnell's description of the very same incident,[25] in which description he makes out that the body was that of a double – a hearsay claim which cannot be justified. It could well have been no more than a case of mistaken identity.)

Together with platoon leader Panassov and a few soldiers, Klimenko went to the Bunker exit. Private Ivan Churakov climbed into a nearby crater that was strewn with burned paper, and found legs there. Two charred corpses were pulled out, but since they were unrecognisable, and since a Soviet diplomat was supposed to be coming in the early afternoon to identify the supposed corpse of Hitler, Klimenko ordered the corpses reburied.

When the Soviet diplomat arrived, at 2 p.m., he instantly dismissed the possibility of the corpse that had at first been identified by Voss really being that of Hitler. Klimenko then returned to the site outside the Bunker exit, early in the morning of 5 May.[26]

This time he and his men pulled up the two corpses, and also discovered that there were two dogs buried in the same crater. (Details of the post-mortems on these dogs have already been given.)

Another Soviet document – described as a 'Record', dated 13 May 1945 – gives an interesting insight into the original testimony of Harry Mengerhausen. This record of his testimony – given in front of Klimenko, acting as magistrate – was signed by Mengerhausen himself.[27] In it he claimed that, from a Chancellery window, he had observed the bodies burn for only half an hour before being buried in a crater. (This evidence is almost certainly incorrect, given the extent of the incineration of the corpses, but the main issue at stake was the exact site of the burial.) Not only did Mengerhausen identify the crater site on 13 May, he was photographed doing so by a Soviet photographer. According to Klimenko it was the same site where he had found the bodies.

By then the post-mortem on the alleged corpses of Hitler and Eva Braun had already been carried out.

Document 13, 'concerning the forensic-medical examination of the partially burned corpse of an unknown woman (presumably the wife of Hitler)', dated 8 May 1945, described the corpse of a woman approximately 150 cm tall.[28] Her age was difficult to estimate but was gauged at between thirty to forty years old. (Eva Braun was thirty-three in February 1945.) The body had been badly burned – it was by far the most severely burned of the bodies the Soviets examined. Almost the entire top of the head had been burned away, and in the front of the skull this destruction went down to the level of the frontal sinuses (or, in lay terms, almost halfway down the forehead). The temporal and occipital bones (at the sides of the head and at the back, respectively) were thinned, cracked and fragmented by the heat. There was, however, no mention of any evidence of a gunshot wound.

The right side of the face was badly charred, as was especially the right side of the neck, but the left side was better preserved. The corpse had obviously been lying on its left side, the right side being uppermost when burned (somewhat, but not critically, contrary to the testimony on the burning of the bodies). In consequence, the only sections of preserved skin lay from the left shoulder-blade down to the loins and left buttock. The right side of the chest wall and abdomen was so severely burned as to totally destroy the side wall and expose the internal organs to view. The right arm was burned to the extent that the lower third of the humerus (the upper arm-bone) was charred badly and the right forearm and hand were especially mutilated by fire – although still present. The lower limbs had largely escaped the fire, even though the skin was blackened and fissured, and the feet a dirty brown.

To their surprise, the Soviets found two holes in the left side of the chest, not far from the breastbone, which were obviously shrapnel or bullet wounds, each irregular hole measuring a centimetre across. There were also what they described as 'severe injuries to the thorax': in the upper lobe of the left lung were two perforations of 0.4 cm by 0.6 cm, and there was 500 c.c. of blood in the left pleural cavity (the space containing the lung). In the same chest cavity they found six steel fragments measuring up to 0.5 sq. cm. In the upper frontal part of the lining of the heart they found two apertures 0.8 cm by 0.4 cm.: 'They are surrounded by a clearly discernible haemorrhage; similar injuries are present in the direction of the left pleural cavity.'[29]

What these reveal is that the person they were discussing had been severely wounded by shrapnel *during life*, for haemorrhage into the tissues only occurs at such a time; it does not occur after death. Thus, if the cause of death had been cyanide poisoning, and the corpse had been hit by shrapnel as it lay burning, there would *not* have been any such discernible and obvious bruising in the chest wall, the lungs, the pleura or the heart.

Nor would it have been likely that shrapnel wounds would have entered the lower, protected, left side of a corpse lying right side uppermost in a crater! Indeed this *one* piece of evidence discredits the whole saga of this woman ever having gone through with a suicide pact with Hitler.

True, there were indeed glass splinters in the mouth of the corpse, but these were different from the small, thin slivers that had been produced in the other corpses by first the breaking of the ampoule and then the gnashing of the teeth in extremis. 'In the oral cavity, large yellowish glass splinters measuring 1–5 square millimetres of a thin-walled ampoule were found under the tongue and between the teeth'[30] – similar in size to the effect of simply crushing a vial once.

During the autopsy it was noticed that there was a marked smell of bitter almonds (cyanide) about the corpse. But here again the Soviet pathologists seem to have been perplexed. They failed to note any fresh smell of cyanide in dissection of the lungs, brain or intestines, nor indeed on opening the corpse, and indeed none of the organs sent for further forensic and toxicological examination revealed any traces of cyanide.

How then can this be explained? To some extent the smell of almonds can be burned away from exposed organs, but such traces will nevertheless be found on toxicological testing. However, the smell of almonds would envelop any cadaver in which cyanide had been introduced into the corpse's mouth *after* the corpse had been burned – a fact that the Soviets failed to consider.

Their quandary was compounded by it being difficult to envisage a woman committing suicide and then being fatally wounded by shrapnel! Totally bemused, they fudged the issue, choosing to ignore the full significance of pre-mortem haemorrhaging into the tissues and choosing to misrepresent the results of the toxicological testing. In a carefully worded statement of contorted logic, they came to the conclusion that:

In view of the fact that similar ampoules were found in other corpses – [Documents 1–11] – that a smell of bitter almonds developed upon dissection – [Documents 1–11] – and based on the forensic-chemical tests of the internal organs of these bodies in which the presence of cyanide compounds was established – [Documents 1–11] – the Commission reaches the conclusion that notwithstanding the severe injuries to the thorax, the immediate cause of death was poisoning by cyanide compounds.[31]

In other words, faced with a choice between the improbable and what they considered the impossible, and failing to consider the third option of forensic fraud, the Soviet pathologists plumped for the improbable: that a woman fatally injured in both heart and lungs with shrapnel, determinedly chose, even though dying, to commit suicide!

They chose to believe that death had been due to cyanide poisoning because capsules and smells similar to those found in this corpse had resulted in positive toxicological proof in the *other* corpses. They elected to ignore the negative toxicological tests on *this* corpse, even though they knew the extreme sensitivity of the tests for the presence of cyanide traces in the tissues and the almost unheard of failure to detect such traces in cases of cyanide poisoning.

The Soviet pathologists concentrated instead on the dental evidence they possessed – on which they based their whole identification. In keeping with all their reports, they forwarded no official conclusions about this identification.

It is time for us to examine this dental evidence too, and in so doing to reveal the nature of the forensic fraud perpetrated.

It is evident that much of the right side of the upper jaw was destroyed by burning, and that fact alone, makes comparison with other dental records difficult. Even more difficulty was encountered when considering the teeth which were found loose in the mouth. Tooth enamel is very fire-resistant and it is extremely rare for a fire to destroy teeth. Yet during the autopsy only four teeth and one root remnant could be recovered and identified as being from an upper jaw – in itself a very odd finding. These teeth were found lying between the tongue and the palate – an equally curious finding.

The dental diagram meticulously drawn by Hitler and Eva Braun's dentist Professor Hugo Blaschke, captured by the Western Allies, reveals that both of the left bicuspids in the left segment of Eva's upper jaw had large restorations. The autopsy report records wear and decay in the teeth found in the lower jaw but not in those of the upper jaw. In addition, Blaschke's diagram also showed that the upper right molar had a large filling, unlike the upper right molar found on the tongue, which once again was seemingly intact.

On the left side of the lower jaw a total of six teeth were recovered, ranging from the lateral incisors through to the second molar. But whereas *Document 13* from the post-mortem states, 'the second incisor [has] a dark point, the canine tooth, 2 bicuspids, and 2 molars are preserved. All of them are moderately worn, and show visible changes due to dental caries',[32] Blaschke's dental diagram of the mouth of the woman he had treated only a few weeks before – in March 1945 – showed absolutely *no* evidence of dental caries, cavities or other dental defects in the lower jaw. Blaschke's reputation would surely have suffered if Hitler's mistress had been allowed such poor dental care as was implicit in the findings in the

Eva Braun's Dental Diagram

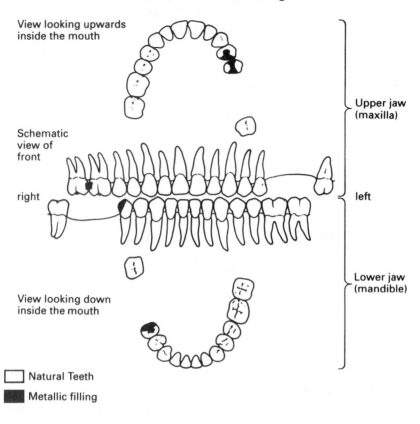

View looking upwards
inside the mouth

Upper jaw
(maxilla)

Schematic
view of
front

right

left

Lower jaw
(mandible)

View looking down
inside the mouth

☐ Natural Teeth

■ Metallic filling

Eva Braun's dental chart was prepared by Professor Sognnaes and based on his interrogation of her dentist, Dr Blaschke, following his capture in May 1945. The chart shows a good set of teeth – even by modern standards – with few fillings and no false teeth. The owner of this set of teeth would not have needed a bridge. The fact that a bridge was prepared for Eva, though never used, and that a bridge was found in the charred female corpse ought to have immediately raised doubts about the corpse's supposed identity as Eva.

corpse of the alleged Eva Braun.

On the right side of the lower jaw no teeth were found – another very surprising finding, considering the resilience of enamel. However, this mystery was initially seemingly solved – though actually compounded – when:

In the oral cavity a bridge of yellow metal (gold) was found under the tongue, unattached, which connects the second right bicuspid and the third right molar by means of a gold crown; on the metal plate of the bridge the first and second artificial white molars are attached in front; their appearance is almost indistinguishable from natural teeth.[33]

In other words, even though the bridge was unattached, it could easily be ascertained that the bridge had been created to replace the lower first right and second molars, anchored by crowns to the second premolar and third molar.

However, Blaschke did *not* indicate any such bridge construction, nor did he show any restoration or any appropriate dental preparation in the adjoining teeth to accommodate any form of bridge, either fixed or removable. Blaschke's diagram did show an inlay of enamel on the tip of the first bicuspid, but nothing else. The tell-tale area under the bridge, where it would have fitted in life, was conveniently missing from the corpse.

Comparison of the autopsy findings with Eva Braun's dental diagram thus proves conclusively that the female corpse found outside the Bunker was *not* that of Eva Braun:

● Eva Braun had twenty-six of her own teeth; the Soviets recovered only eleven. She had all her front teeth; the Soviets found only one – a left lateral incisor.

● Individual comparison of Blaschke's diagram and the few upper-jaw teeth found reveals so many pathological inconsistencies that not even *one* of these teeth was Eva's.

● Blaschke's dental diagram indicates that Eva's left upper-jaw bicuspid had large restorations. No such work had been carried out on the corpse.

● *Document 13* shows that *all* the left lower-jaw teeth of the corpse had severe dental caries, whereas Blaschke's records show that in Eva these were totally intact, a dental check in late March 1945 having proved satisfactory.

● In marked contrast to the caries and wear noted in Soviet *Document 13*, in teeth which were consistently blackened, a gold bridge of the highest standard with white artificial enamel was found – incompatible not just with the teeth colour but with the standard of dental care previously experienced by the unknown woman. There was destruction of the area where this bridge would have fitted, and no teeth where it would have had to have been anchored. Blaschke's records showed no such bridge.

In referring to this gold bridge, the Soviet autopsy report states that it was considered the 'most important anatomical finding for identification of the person'.[34] The question must be asked: what did the Soviets mean by that phrase?

Obviously at the time when the report was made, on 8 May 1945, their opinion was perfectly justifiable. At that time they might well have been thinking that, if they could find dental records or the dentist who could confirm that Eva Braun had indeed been fitted with this bridge, then the identity of the corpse would be proved.

In fact both the dental technician, Fritz Echtmann, and the dental assistant, Käthe Heusermann, who had worked for Blaschke were found on the following day, 9 May 1945. A Dr Arnaudow (a Bulgarian who subsequently took out German citizenship) led the Soviets from the Charité hospital, where they had been searching for Professor Karl von Eicken, an ENT consultant who had treated Hitler, to the ruined Kurfürstendamm, where Blaschke's office was amazingly still intact. The two Soviet Intelligence officers concerned were Andrei Mirozhnichenko, chief of counter-intelligence of the 3rd Shock Army, and his deputy, Vasili Gorbushin. Both had the specific mission of ensuring the true identification of the corpses.

At Blaschke's office they found a Dr Bruck, who quickly told them that Blaschke was not there but directed them to Käthe Heusermann. She in turn directed them to Fritz Echtmann, who was rapidly found at his home. The Kurfürstendamm office itself only yielded old treatment cards.[35] On visiting the Chancellery dental office the Soviets allegedly found some X-rays of Hitler's teeth.[36] They also found a box of gold crowns and duplicate bridges for Hitler and Eva.[37]

Heusermann and Echtmann were first interviewed separately by Gorbushin, assisted by a Major Bystrov. The interview was not a pleasant experience.[38] Gorbushin had been in Leningrad during the worst of the siege, his job having been to seize, question and counter German agents infiltrating the city. His attitude terrified Heusermann. He repeated his questioning of her on several occasions on 10 May, and of Echtmann on 11 May, on which date Heusermann was interviewed for three hours by pathologist Dr Faust Shkaravski, who recorded how intensely nervous and fearful she was.[39] A separate description of her questioning by Gorbushin has since been made by the interpreter at the time, Yeléna Rzhevskaya.[40]

Käthe Heusermann (confirming the testimony of Fritz Echtmann in Soviet archives), revealed that two identical bridges (one being a spare) had been made for Eva Braun, except that 'time to put them into use had run out for dentist and patient'.[41]

When interviewed by myself, and separately on two occasions by Professor Reidar F. Sognnaes, and subsequently in letters to both of us, Heusermann absolutely insisted that *Blaschke had never placed any bridgework in the mouth of Eva Braun*, whose teeth were in relatively good condition – certainly they showed no evidence of the caries found in the corpse. Heusermann disliked Eva Braun, thinking her vain and spoilt, and there is also independent evidence to show that Blaschke himself thought her a difficult person to work on,[42] so neither had any reason to conceal the truth about her dentistry.

There is absolutely no indication that the Soviets fully appreciated the significance of Heusermann's testimony. Her questioner, Gorbushin, was no expert, and might possibly have been entirely out of his depth, confused by all the bridgework, or he might possibly have been overanxious to conclude his investigations quickly. And Dr Shkaravski's testimony suggests that the pathologist's questioning was concentrated on Hitler, not his spouse, and never truly attacked the issue of Eva's bridges.[43]

The blame for the Soviets' failure to appreciate the facts as given to them clearly rests with Gorbushin. For Echtmann certified[44] that the bridge taken from the female corpse was one of his specific construction. Käthe Heusermann certified[45] that the box in the Chancellery had contained only one bridge – one of the two made for Eva, neither of which had ever been fitted. She readily identified the bridge taken from the female corpse as being the second of these, but *again* had insisted it had never been fitted.[46] Gorbushin clearly didn't believe her, preferring the evidence of his own eyes at the autopsy. Instead of ensuring that her testimony went to the pathologists, he ignored it.

Unfortunately the records of the interrogations of both Echtmann and Heusermann were written up 'subsequently'[47] – certainly not in time for perusal by any pathologist. Thus it seems that the Soviet pathologists had no idea of the irony that surrounded their statement that the gold bridgework was the most important finding in the identification of the person! They ought to have concluded that there was no evidence that the female corpse was that of Eva Braun – the minimum scientific statement that could have been made.

If Professor Blaschke's dental diagram and Käthe Heusermann were correct and Eva Braun's bridgework had never been put in place, then the inclusion of this bridgework in the mouth of the female corpse was proof of a carefully conceived forensic fraud.

The ideal forensic fraud is perfected over a long period of time. A look-alike is 'improved' by plastic surgery and expert dental work to become not merely similar but identical to the original. Killing the look-alike would then remove any chance of the fraud being revealed by unconvincing vocal or verbal mannerisms, or by body language. But in the turmoil and chaos of imminent collapse of military and social order, such as happened progressively in 1945, far cruder and more desperate measures had to be adopted, many falling not far short of farce. Professor Keith Mant has described the time when he was a member of the War Crimes Commission forensic pathology service, just after the war, when several bodies buried as genuine Nazis were disinterred and found to bear scant resemblance to the originals.[48] A fraud that remained undetected for longer concerned Gestapo chief Heinrich Müller. His family had pronounced him dead at the end of the war, and the tombstone of Grave 1, Row 1, Division 6, Kreuzberg, bore the touching inscription 'In memory of our dear father Heinrich Müller, who died fighting in Berlin, 17 May 1945.' The family even registered the death in Berlin, on 5 December 1945, and they continued to keep the grave expensively maintained and always befittingly bedecked with flowers – until in 1963 the West German authorities excavated the cherished site and found the composite remains of three corpses.

The inhabitants of the Bunker had as good reasons as any to engage in forensic fraud. All that forensic fakery needed to accomplish was to establish identification. There was no requirement for the corpse to be complete, only that records be available and something be left of the body for comparison with them. What better for this than gold bridgework? This would be easily certifiable as genuine, and easily inserted into a suitable corpse, as long as the underlying teeth were removed along with any other identifying pathology.

In the case of Eva Braun there is strong evidence to suggest that such forensic fakery did take place, for if, as we now know, the corpse was probably *not* Eva's, why did it have Eva's gold bridgework, and why was it lying in what was ostensibly Eva's grave? Obviously such fakery would need prior thought and planning, and probably the assistance of either a dentist, such as SS dentist Helmut Kunz, or a dental assistant.

The intention was obviously that the corpses would be burned out of all recognition. When it came to it, the personnel responsible, dispirited and demoralised, did not attend to their job with diligence, so the whole business was botched and hurried. Thus it was that the corpse of a forty-year-old woman who had died sometime previously from a shrapnel wound to her chest was insufficiently burned to conceal her mode of death. The breaking of a cyanide capsule in her mouth after death had failed to distribute the cyanide through her body. Her lungs could no more inhale the fatal gases than her circulation could spread the evidence of cyanide poisoning to her tissues, for she was already dead.

However, the choice of a poor woman, with imperfect dental health, made it difficult to simulate Eva Braun's dentition, even after the probable removal of many teeth with worse examples of caries than those left.

There is one remaining pointer to exactly how the fraud was carried out which will be essential when we come to consider the alleged corpse of Hitler. In this case, removal of the right lower-jaw teeth beneath the bridge was almost certainly performed before putting the bridge in place, or at least at the same time. From the artificially white nature of the porcelain, it is highly likely that *whoever placed the gold bridge, unattached, under the tongue did so* after *the fire was over – possibly under the misconception that the fire might destroy the essential evidence that was being planted.* This suggests some degree of ignorance, so was unlikely to have been done by a dentist – unless it was done by a dentist under duress. The Zyankali vial was probably crushed into the mouth at the same time.

Not only would such fakery fit with the existing forensic facts, it would also explain the disappearance of the other teeth – especially those on the right, where the bridge ought to have been anchored. It would also explain how the corpse could have sustained fatal shrapnel wounds, and have those large fragments of Zyankali vial present in its mouth, and smell of cyanide.

It seems that the alleged corpse of Eva Braun was a definite example of the use of forensic fakery, but that sadly the Soviets were unaware that they had been duped.

The Corpse of 'Adolf Hitler'

Bearing in mind the nature of this brilliantly simple fakery, which, even though shoddily executed, remained effective for decades, it is time to examine the forensic case of Adolf Hitler. A case described in *Document 12*, 'concerning the forensic examination of a male corpse disfigured by fire (Hitler's body)', also dated 8 May 1945.[49]

This described a corpse, 163 cm long and estimated as being between fifty to sixty years old. It had been wearing a yellow singlet, parts of which remained. Although not as severely charred as the corpse of 'Eva', nevertheless there was considerable damage. The right side of the thorax and abdomen were completely burned, exposing the lung, liver and intestines. A single testicle was found; the left one was missing. The pathologists took the trouble to explore the inguinal canal, where undescended testes sometimes lurk, but without success.

The right arm was present, but severely charred, whereas the left upper arm was charred to a lesser degree. The legs were also charred; the bones had been partially burned, and the right thigh-bone and shin-bone had been fractured (probably after death and during the handling of the corpse). The pathologists noted the left foot was missing. There was no comment as to whether this was due to fire damage or other causes, but a measurement was taken of the right shin-bone – it measured 39 cm – suggesting that the shin-bone on the left side was missing near the foot. For a long bone such as the tibia to be destroyed by fire requires a temperature of over 1,000°C or so – the equivalent of the heat reached in a crematorium, and far beyond the capability of a petrol-induced bonfire. There remains the suspicion that the left foot and lower tibia might have been removed for some reason, the fire masking the removal. According to Voitov,[50] one of the initial suspicions of the investigators was that the loss might have been as a result of a congenital defect, previous amputation or an accident to whomever the corpse had been.

The head of the corpse was missing only part of the occipital bone (at the back of the skull), and at a somewhat later date the claim was made that further bits of occipital bone were found that possibly belonged to the same corpse. Underneath the top of the back of the head, where the occipital bone ought to have been, the intact burned brain and its surrounding membranes were visible. On the right side of the skull the fire damage was more severe, and from the description given it is unclear whether the right temporal (temple) bone was partially destroyed or not; but in any case there was no mention of any evidence of a gunshot wound. Even though the skin of the face and body had mostly been destroyed and the underlying musculature charred,[51] the upper and lower jaws were intact, as were the nasal bones and sinuses.

In the upper jaw was found a bridge connecting nine teeth. The bridge was anchored by pins on the second left and second right incisors. The bridge itself consisted of four upper incisors and both right and left canine teeth, the first left bicuspid, and the first and second right bicuspids. It had been sawn across roughly behind the first left bicuspid – *not* behind the second bicuspid as the several accounts available in both German and English have incorrectly stated.[52]

Before we go any further, it is necessary to add a word of caution. There were noted to be many small cracks in the upper jawbones, almost certainly from the heat. The same small cracks affected the nasal bones. The upper jaw was badly charred, and the upper teeth were locked into position by the tongue, the tip of which was burned and jammed between the upper teeth and the lower jaw, which was later found to be entirely loose in the singed oral cavity. It is not at all clear from the Moscow archives exactly how firmly fixed to the upper jaw the bridge really was. From the charred nature of the jaw it was likely to have been loose even if at some time it had been attached. But how loose?

There is evidence to suggest that the *upper-jaw bridge itself was lying loose in the mouth of the corpse.* Even though the bridge was obviously *intended* to be anchored by pins into the roots of the left lateral incisor and the right central incisor, and by the actual roots of the left central incisor and the right canine tooth, there is no evidence that such fixing ever took place. The photographs of Hitler's teeth that accompanied *Document 12,*[53] show that the posts are indeed in position just below the right central and left lateral incisors. Surrounding these posts seems to be a scant amount of cement. There is no evidence of any root material in either of these two sites – nor, more significantly, in the region of the left central incisor or the right canine tooth – but if the bridge had been forcibly removed from its anchorage it is quite likely that some root material would have been left visible as evidence of such rupture.

Gorbushin's testimony relates how the Soviets asked Heusermann and Echtmann 'to identify the jawbones, which had been taken from the male corpse. Frau Heusermann and Echtmann recognized them unequivocally as those of Adolf Hitler.'[54] However, the upper jawbone is a part of the maxilla, the part of the skull extending up to the eye socket, and would have to be chiselled free – a performance which I very much doubt would have occurred. It would doubtless have been a grisly specimen, which no witness would wittingly forget, but Käthe Heusermann has certified that she was shown no segment of the upper jaw, only a pristine upper-jaw bridge, which she was quite certain she was told was lying loose in the oral cavity. When pressed, she somewhat pedantically explained, 'I am quite certain – absolutely certain in fact – because they argued with me about the way that the upper prosthesis [bridge] would have been fixed. They wouldn't have had to argue if they had found it fitted.'[55]

Support for her account comes from the testimony of Dr Faust Shkarav-

Joseph Goebbels (right), Propaganda Minister and Gauleiter of Berlin, with Robert Ley (centre), Reichsleiter and head of the German Labour Front. Goebbels died in the Bunker, Ley committed suicide prior to trial at Nuremberg. (*Imperial War Museum – IWM*)

The corpse of Joseph Goebbels, found in the Reich Chancellery on 2 May 1945, being identified by Soviet officials. (*Archiv für Kunst und Geschichte, London – AKG*)

Opposite: Helga Goebbels, the eldest daughter of Joseph and Magda Goebbels, poisoned with her brothers and sisters in the Bunker, after the official Soviet autopsy, May 1945. (AKG)

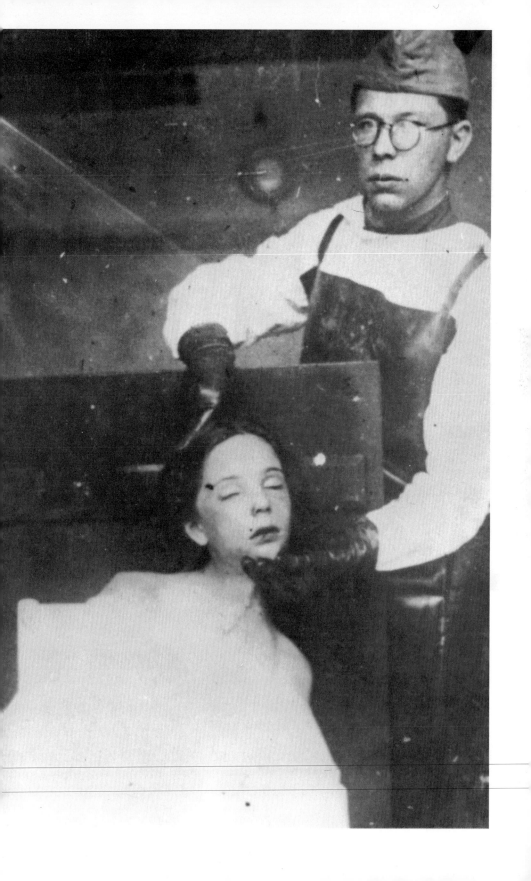

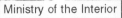

Lehrter Station

Ministry of the Interior

Reich

Tierga

Central Berlin. An aerial view of the Tiergarten, Brandenburg Gate and surrounding districts in March 1945 showing the effects of aerial bombing. The supposed site of Bormann's suicide is just out of view, to the North of the railway on the left-hand edge. The railway embankment briefly provided one possible escape route. By 1 May the Russian front line had captured the Potsdam Station (bottom right) and held the North bank of the river. Above ground, escape routes were virtually closed off. (*AKG*)

Above: Marshal Georgy Konstantinovitch Zhukov (left, 1896–1974). Defender of Leningrad, breaker of the German seige of Moscow, conqueror of the German Sixth Army at Stalingrad and ultimately Hitler's nemesis in Berlin itself. (*AKG*)

Opposite top: One of the last pictures of Adolf Hitler, seen decorating with the Iron Cross a twelve-year-old defender of Berlin against the Russian armies, outside the Reich Chancellery in late April 1945. (*IWM*

Opposite bottom: Reputed to be the last picture of Hitler before his death. Hitler stands at the door of the Reich Chancellery inspecting air-raid damage. (*AKG*

Eva Braun (right) with her sister Gretel. This photograph from Eva's album is undated and was discovered in Frankfurt after the end of the war. (*Hulton-Deutsche Collection*)

Above: The remains of Adolf Hitler, supposedly, after extensive charring. (*AKG*)

Below: Not the remains of Eva Braun, even though they were wrapped in one of her dresses prior to being incinerated. (*AKG*)

Above: The turret of the Bunker. The shallow ditch in the foreground is where the two bodies were burned, drenched in gasoline from the cans in the picture. The soldier peering into the ditch is an American private, those behind him are Soviet troops. This picture must date from at least some days after the Soviet capture of the city, at which point the Western Allies were stationed at the River Elbe, more than fifty miles away. It was probably taken in July 1945. (*IWM*)

Opposite top: The Map Room, where Linge first declared he found Hitler's body before he changed his testimony. The basic wooden bench around the two sides is covererd in brocade as backing; two mattresses covering the seats have been ripped apart. The paintings on the table lie alongside pieces of writing paper, on which are numerous doodles. There is no evidence of blood anywhere in the room. (*IWM*)

Opposite bottom: Eva Braun's bedroom in the Bunker, July 1945. No bloodstains were found in this room. The empty Pommery Champagne bottle seems to serve as a rather pathetic vase, suggesting that talk of the Bunker being filled with fresh flowers is rather fanciful. (*IWM*)

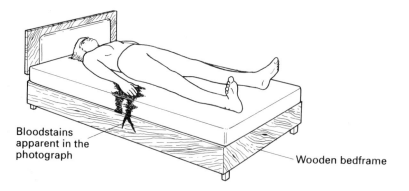

Bloodstains apparent in the photograph

Wooden bedframe

Hitler's bedroom. An Allied soldier points to the bloodstained bed-frame. The bloodstained mattress described by Col. John McCowan is missing, having been removed by Smersh for analysis, but bloodstains can be seen on the upper edge of the wooden base (arrowed). They spill out on to the side of the bed in two rivulets. This dried blood pattern is typical of venous bleeding and the position of the blood is fully in accordance with that of a cut wrist at the side of a recumbent body on the bed (see diagram). Analysis of this blood shows that it was neither Hitler's nor that of the female corpse buried in the garden trench. It could, however have been Eva Braun's – the only person apart from Hitler likely to have dared to share his bedroom. (*IWM*)

picture of the sofa on which Hitler and
Eva were supposed to have calmly and
simultaneously shot themselves and
taken cyanide. Most of the material
on the seat has been ripped away,
leaving the stuffing underneath visible.
The dark discoloration is due to the
ripped material; there is no evidence
of substantial bloodstains.

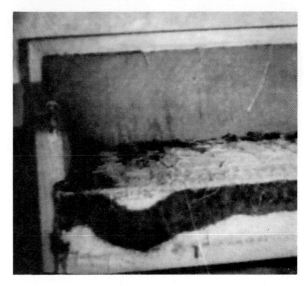

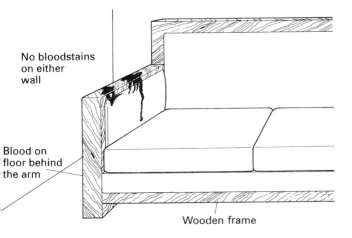

No bloodstains
on either
wall

Blood on
floor behind
the arm

Wooden frame

Wood from a cross-member of the sofa
and the finger of a Russian examiner
indicating the point at which a spot of
blood was found. This corresponds to
the area on the sofa arm where venous
blood flow was seen by *Life Magazine*
photographers and Col. John
McCowan. The diagram shows the
position and nature of the bloodstains
as McCowan and the photographers
recorded them. Remarkably, for a
room in which at least one person was
supposed to have been shot in the
head, there were no traces of
bloodstains on either of the walls
behind the sofa or on the other
armchairs in the room.

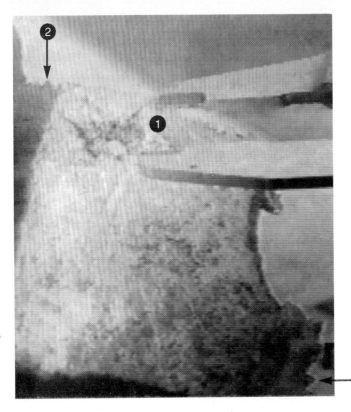

Skull fragment, alleged to be part of the occipital bone, held in Russian archives. The fragment shows a low velocity gun-shot wound (1), which the caliper is measuring. Two features are of additional significance: 2 and 3, arrowed, show the clean separation along suture lines of the bones in the skull of the specimen.

The serrated appearance indicates a non-complete or incomplete lower surface fusion which suggests the skull of a much younger man than the 56-year-old Führer. In a man of 56 the skeletal plates would be expected to have fused, the fusion starting on the undersurface of the bone

3

The skull fragment, alleged to be occipital, and the box in which it was kept in Soviet archives. The underside of an occipital bone should be scored by venous sinuses in a pattern similar to a hot-crossed bun. This pattern is not present in the fragment in Soviet archives, and calls into question whether this is an occipital fragment at all.

Martin Bormann's skull. Whatever else may have happened to it this skull, separated from the rest of the skeleton, was removed from the Ulap Fairground site in 1972. It was covered in a heavy red clay, unlike any found in Berlin or its environs. Despite this fact, it was supposed to indicate that Bormann and Stumpfegger had been killed in their attempted escape from Berlin in 1945. In fact, the skull proves no such thing.

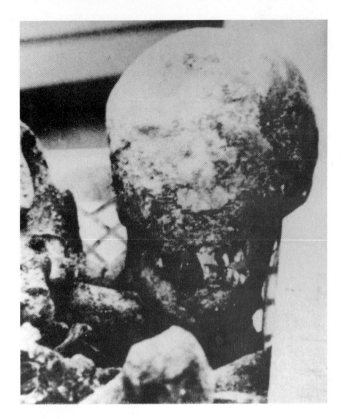

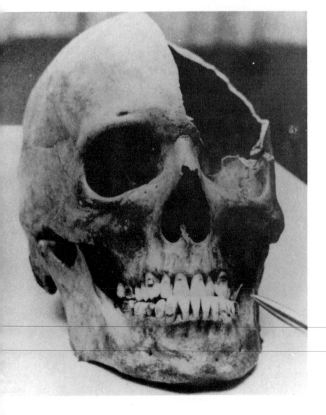

This skull accompanied the one above, said to have belonged to Martin Bormann. It too was uncovered in the Ulap Fairground excavation of 1972, and it was at least accompanied by the skeleton of a large man and showed signs of being buried in nothing more than Berlin's usual soil. It is thought to be the skull of Ludwig Stumpfegger, Hitler's surgeon at the end of the war and poisoner of the Goebbels family. The missing section of skull, intriguingly, has been surgically removed and was not discovered with the rest of the body.

Instant myth-making: this vividly dramatic and wholly imagined version of Hitler's endgame, entitled *The End: The Last Days of Hitler's HQ in the Underground Reich's Office* was the product of the Kukryniski Collective and dates from 1947/8. (*AKG*)

ski to Bezymenski: 'She [Heusermann] described minutely the specific features of Hitler's dental prostheses and drew them with her own hand. I even started to argue with her, because I had overlooked one detail when examining the teeth and had miscounted the steel pins. She turned out to be right.'[56] (Heusermann, referred to as 'Citizen Kate Hozjerman' also added details to the Soviet dental diagrams from the 8 May autopsy.)[57]

We also know that a maxillary bridge of nine teeth and a singed *lower* jaw of fifteen teeth were handed over to the Smersh section of the 3rd Shock Army on 8 May.[58] It is therefore probable that the Soviets found the nine-tooth bridge free in the oral cavity. Yet again, as with 'Eva's' lower-jaw bridge, Soviet archives reveal that the colour of the teeth concerned was surprisingly good for teeth that had withstood a petrol fire. Considering the blackening normally associated with such a fire, this is a gross anomaly which must be addressed. Yet what of the most distinctive feature of the bridge – the fact that it had been sawn through?

According to Heusermann and Echtmann's testimony, when a prosthesis was required for either Hitler or Eva, Echtmann made two such bridges at a time – in case major revision work became necessary due to accident. In fact one bridge had, in October 1944, been sawn off *in situ*, i.e. on Hitler himself, because of problems with an abscess under the remainder of the bridge – it presumably being easier to repair the bridge than to replace it with a duplicate. The question must be asked: why would anyone have gone to the bother of sawing through the duplicate bridge? One reason to do so would have been the fact that X-rays had already been taken showing the cut edge of the first bridge, so anyone professional bothering to make a forensic fake using the second bridge would have been forced to cut the bridge to match.

The lower jaw was found free in the oral cavity – a not entirely unusual occurrence after such a fire, which can destroy the attaching ligaments. No mention is made of any attempt to match the upper and lower jaws, but such a procedure in a burned, contracted oral cavity is no easy task.

The findings that were obvious were duly recorded in *Document 12*: 'The alveolar processes are broken in the back and have ragged edges. The front surface and the lower edge of the mandibula are scorched. On the front surface the charred prongs of dental roots are recognizable.'[59]

In lay terms, the alveolar process is the part of the lower jaw surface containing the tooth sockets. This surface becomes broken when teeth are extracted, but the fractures get smoothed out with time as healing takes place. The fact that the fractures had ragged edges makes it probable that there had been recent tooth extraction, but Blaschke's diagrams for

Hitler's Skull X-ray and Dental Diagram

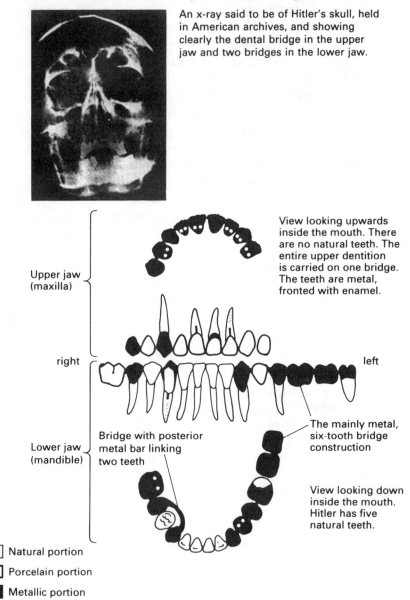

An x-ray said to be of Hitler's skull, held in American archives, and showing clearly the dental bridge in the upper jaw and two bridges in the lower jaw.

Upper jaw (maxilla)

View looking upwards inside the mouth. There are no natural teeth. The entire upper dentition is carried on one bridge. The teeth are metal, fronted with enamel.

right

left

Lower jaw (mandible)

Bridge with posterior metal bar linking two teeth

The mainly metal, six-tooth bridge construction

View looking down inside the mouth. Hitler has five natural teeth.

☐ Natural portion
☐ Porcelain portion
■ Metallic portion

Hitler's dental chart was prepared by Professor Sognnaes and based on his interrogation of Hitler's dentist, Dr Blaschke, following his capture in 1945. The chart shows Hitler had only five natural teeth, all in the lower jaw. His other teeth were metal, fronted with porcelain: the upper jaw is entirely metal and there are two significant and characteristic bridges in the lower jaw.

Hitler indicated no such extractions. The charred prongs of dental roots also meant that extractions had probably taken place at some time (though sometimes teeth can get burned away leaving only such roots). Unfortunately the exact sites of these roots were not noted. In any case there were only five remaining natural teeth found in the lower jaw: the lower central and lateral incisors on both sides and the first right bicuspid.

On the left side of the lower jaw was a bridge construction of six teeth which was supposedly anchored on the roots of the third molar, second bicuspid and canine. The photographs accompanying *Document 12* seemed to show that the curve of the bridge did not quite align with the natural curve of the jaw, and that there were large gaps under the bridged teeth. Unfortunately such photographs can be misleading, and the destruction of the jaw surface by fire could have led to such seeming ill-fitting. On the right-hand side of the lower jaw a very unusual bridge attached the canine with the second bicuspid and molar, by a distinctive connecting bar going behind the intact first premolar. Käthe Heusermann and Fritz Echtmann both readily identified these bridges as being made for Hitler, though the dental cards in Soviet possession showed that this bridgework had been performed before 1934 and not by Blaschke.

At this point it would be fair to contemplate a somewhat macabre forensic fraud, whereby an upper-jaw bridge was inserted into a corpse whose own lower jaw had been surgically removed and replaced with a jaw containing two more of Echtmann's duplicate bridges. This might seem a natural extension of the forensic fraud already seen to have been perpetrated in the case of Eva Braun. The evidence suggesting this possibility was the presence of roots in the lower jaw accompanied by the otherwise unexplained alveolar fractures, normally associated with recent tooth extraction. It was known that Hitler had had no such extractions.

It is extremely unlikely that the same crudity that caused the fractures would be associated with the dentist who would subsequently have had to place the two lower-jaw bridges *in situ* in the prepared mandible that was to be placed in the cadaver. But there was one feature which meant that *had* a forensic fraud been carried out, then it had been done extremely professionally – in stark contrast to the leaving of such tell-tale alveolar fractures. For, according to Blaschke and Heusermann, in the left central incisor of Hitler's upper-jaw bridge a so-called window crown had left an island of enamel severely discoloured – an exceptionally dark brown colour. The Soviet *Document 12* specifically mentions that the same tooth found in the bridge on the *corpse* also contained cracks due to decay and a black spot at the bottom (the incisal edge).

Here, then, we have to choose between two alternatives – and choose against the background of now proven forensic fraud perpetrated upon the corpse of the false Eva:

● The first option: a duplicate upper-jaw bridge, carefully matched even down to the colour of a spot of seeming dental decay, and sawn across to match the original, and a separate previously prepared lower jaw with two duplicate bridges – both inserted into the mouth of the corpse of a bogus Hitler in order to complete forensic fraud.

● The second option: a genuine Hitler, complete with a loose upper-jaw bridge and a loose lower jaw, with inexplicably retained roots and alveolar fractures.

Does the analysis of the comparison of individual teeth in both upper and lower jaws help us to a choice? Bezymenski produced some of the data from *Document 12* in his 1968 book, thus allowing forensic odontologists to make exactly such comparisons.

Several experts compared the reported dentition of the corpse with the data in the diagrams of Blaschke and Käthe Heusermann. Each individual tooth of both the upper-jaw bridge and the two lower-jaw bridges was studiously compared, and the special constructions shown in the bridge-work were also studied in depth. What was forgotten was the very nature of the forensic fraud that may have been perpetrated. Most of the scientists had not questioned Heusermann or Echtmann and thus were unaware of the duplicate bridgework. If the fraud had been perpetrated using the duplicate bridges, then naturally they would match extremely well. Had forensic fraud been perpetrated, it was relying on exactly such profound, learned, but unthinking comparisons!

The only teeth that could be compared to exclude the possibility of such fraud were not the artificial teeth incorporated in the bridgework but the natural teeth left in the corpse: four lower incisors and one right bicuspid – a total of five quite unremarkable teeth that allowed *no* meaningful comparison.

In 1972 five X-ray plates allegedly belonging to Hitler's physicians Dr Theodor Morell and Dr Erwin Giesing were found in the US National Archives. (A word of caution about the authenticity of these X-rays – which nevertheless I personally accept as genuine – is that when the wife of forensic odontologist Dr Lester Luntz examined them she found that the 'original' envelope was marked 'Oct 44', and not 'Okt 44' as would have been the case in Berlin.)[60] These five X-rays when superimposed and matched *do* relate to the same person, presumably Hitler. Furthermore, the detailed examination of the metal bridgework, in both the upper and the lower jaw, *does* compare well with all the bridges described by Blaschke and with those found on the corpse – delighting all investigators, but hardly surprising if the duplicate set of bridges had been placed in the corpse! The delight of the dentists at the University of California at Los Angeles was such that they created computer-assisted models from the X-rays. They found that X-rays of these matched the original X-rays rather well, but then rather spoilt things concluding that, because of the match, the corpse really had been Hitler.

Everyone in the Hitler case has been busy comparing the bridges, the drawings of the bridges, the individual teeth in the bridges, and the X-rays of the bridges without really giving adequate thought to what the bridges really were. What they certainly were not was the man. Even after exhaustive comparison we are still left with the same quandary, the same two options.

A forensic fraud using the same technique as in the case of Eva Braun, but this time including a previously prepared jaw, would undoubtedly have required a surgeon or a dentist for its completion. The fraudulent Eva weighs heavily in the balance when choosing which option, but even so, and despite the anomalies described above, it remains highly unlikely that the corpse was that of anyone other than Hitler, in view of the difficulty that he would have in escaping from the Bunker – especially given his physical state.

The conclusions that can be drawn are that it can no longer be claimed that there is overwhelming proof that the corpse found was that of Hitler. A clever forensic fraud, as described, cannot be ruled out with certainty, and several forensic anomalies still remain to be satisfactorily explained.

There were the remains of a crushed Zyankali vial in the corpse's mouth – splinters and part of the wall and bottom of the vial – and, despite there having been no smell of cyanide when dissecting the brain, the lungs or even the tongue, the members of the post-mortem team confidently expected that the results of the toxicological testing would prove that the male corpse alleged to be Hitler had died as a result of cyanide poisoning. They were shocked to learn from the toxicological tests that *there was no evidence of cyanide residues – or any other poison – in the tissues.*

It is now necessary to join the Soviet forensic pathologists in their dilemma about the cyanide.

8

Poisoning by Cyanide – Forensic Fraud No. 2

Perhaps the most celebrated instance of the use of cyanide was its failure to kill Rasputin, who devoured two cakes laced with a supposedly more than fatal dose, quaffed wine similarly tainted, then survived being shot and bludgeoned, before succumbing to the icy waters of the river outside Prince Yusupov's palace in 1916.

This, however, was a failure more of management than of the principle of cyanide poisoning, for the quality of the cyanide used was extremely suspect. A circus elephant poisoned at the same time, for having been more than amorous with his trainer, consumed over a hundred cream cakes laced in the same way and was looking interestedly for more before he was eventually shot when it became evident that they would have to wait for the cholesterol in the cream to kill him – the 'cyanide' most certainly having little effect.[1]

But real cyanide does have a dramatic effect. The first reported isolation of cyanide was by a Swedish chemist, Carl Wilhelm Scheele, who further distinguished himself by unequivocally demonstrating its lethal effect when he accidentally broke a vial in the laboratory and dutifully died.

Since his convincing demonstration, many have used the poison to similar effect – including the KGB, who in 1959 killed two men by squirting them in the face with cyanide. Earlier, in 1922, two men were charged with attempting to murder a colleague in Leipzig using the same method. But cyanide poisoning never achieved the popularity its effectiveness deserved – possibly because of the give-away all-pervading smell of bitter almonds. It was the smell on his clothing which led to the eventual arrest and conviction of Lieutenant Hofrichter in Austria in 1979. He had had the novel idea of sending gelatine capsules filled with cyanide to several of his superior officers through the post – with literature suggesting that one capsule a month would make them incredibly virile and, furthermore, the first few were *free*. Several of them fell for this sales pitch, thus opening up an instant route for advancement.

Although cyanide was a less than subtle murder weapon, it became far more widely accepted as a means of suicide. In 1925 a man called Feed managed to hide not a capsule but a bottle of cyanide in his wooden leg and committed suicide in prison. Several Nazis, including Göring, managed to secrete Zyankali vials in various orifices before successfully killing themselves. They did so because the use of the Zyankali vial had been refined to the extent that it was claimed that, if the vial were broken into the mouth, death was absolutely guaranteed. In most cases it occurred in seconds.

By the Second World War, a lot was known about the effects of cyanide, its detection by analysis of the level of cyanide residue found in the body tissues, and the dose needed to ensure fatality. This was the reason why specimens of lung, brain, stomach, heart, liver, spleen and blood were sent by the Soviet pathologists for toxicological study.

There were excellent papers produced in that era, which have formed the basis of our present-day knowledge. In 1945 Hallstrøm and Muller[2] had determined that the minimum lethal absorbed dose in cases of fatal oral poisoning was 1.7 milligrams per kilogram of body weight, but that in cases where there was a dose in excess of the minimum required to ensure death the level could rise to almost double that – 3.3 mg/kg. (Zyankali vials contained sufficient to ensure the tissue levels reached the highest levels.)

Modern analytical methods of assessing cyanide traces in the tissues owe much to the methods of the 1940s, but the essential point is that *all* of the methods used – both then and now – have a sensitivity which makes it almost ridiculously easy to detect the presence of cyanide in the tissues in *any* fatality caused by cyanide poisoning.

Some studies – even using the time-honoured analytical methods – have successfully investigated the effect of cyanide on the animal and primate organism at levels of exposure far below the minimum fatal dose – the less than quaintly termed 'primate-incapacitating studies' of Purser and his colleagues.[3] Similar studies have been carried out of extremely low tissue dosage, to try to assess the exact mechanism of the poison and hence to devise possible countermeasures. These again somewhat distasteful studies used what was called the 'guinea-pig swimming-performance method' to correlate the effect of low doses (non-fatal) on the animals' performance and behaviour – the dose being reduced when 'forward motion ceased'.[4]

The result of a myriad of similar studies is that we can now more confidently predict the levels of cyanide that will be found in the tissues of various animals and man in set circumstances, especially significant being the mode of administration.

In animals the cyanide level remains by far the highest in the *blood*, due to the tendency of the cyanide to bind with the red cells. In humans, however, post-mortem examination of the *spleen* shows concentrations which are several times that in the blood in the veins and arteries. This is due to the phenomenon of red-cell sequestration, which occurs only in humans, in which old red cells are trapped in the spleen. Even in blood itself, the levels resulting from a large dose, such as from a Zyankali vial, are up to 10 mg/litre,[5] whereas the minimal level found in any fatality is in the order of 1 mg/litre. According to toxicologist Dr Sheila Dowling, brain and lung tissue levels – while said to be high – are usually only around 15 per cent of the blood level.[6]

In oral poisoning, as in the Goebbels children, the liver and spleen initially contain far higher proportions than are seen in cases of inhalation, for yet another reason – the transport of the substance from the stomach directly to the liver and spleen by a special blood supply, the so-called 'portal system'.

Allowing for all the above considerations, the blood will certainly show evidence of cyanide traces in all fatal cyanide poisoning.

According to the toxicologists Troup and Ballantyne,[7] cyanide poisoning causing death results in a consistent and high concentration of cyanide in all the tissues mentioned above, no matter how the cyanide was taken.

But for how long does the cyanide remain in the body tissues, and for how long is it detectable after death?

The answer is again relatively accurately known. Work done by Ballantyne in 1975[8] showed that concentrations decreased moderately at all temperatures during the first week after death, but that concentrations did not fall below a level easily detectable as compatible with a diagnosis of cyanide-induced fatality. Blood levels dropped the least – still containing well above the level for diagnosing lethal cyanide poisoning after three weeks – but the brain and lungs also kept their measurable levels for at least fourteen days. The liver, kidney and spleen did not retain their cyanide at a detectable level for more than a week.

Since we know that the corpses of 'Hitler' and 'Eva' were dissected on 8 May, and that the blood samples were tested on the same day,[9] we know that there was a delay of a week between death and the toxicological testing. The cyanide levels in the blood, lungs and brain, ought then to have been between three and five times the minimum necessary to establish death from cyanide poisoning – a level in itself incapable of being missed by toxicological analysis. In any case, the corpses of the two dogs, General Krebs and the whole Goebbels family (including the alleged corpse of Magda Goebbels) all acted as excellent controls.

It is certain, therefore, that the alleged corpses of Hitler and Eva Braun would have tested positive had they actually been poisoned with cyanide.

There are no factors such as the effect of burning on the corpses which would have caused any difference in the results of the toxicological testing[10] – as is evidenced by the positive tests on the corpses of Joseph Goebbels and, supposedly, his wife. Much work has been done in this field, for a common cause of cyanide poisoning is the release of cyanide by combustible material.

It is obvious that the Soviet scientists were bemused. They had noted a smell of cyanide about the supposed corpse of Hitler, but had not noticed or recorded any fresh smell on opening the abdominal or chest cavities, nor on dissecting the brain. For a second time they had negative toxicological tests.

Unfortunately they opted for the common-sense approach – there were, after all, remains of a cyanide vial in a corpse that smelled of cyanide among several other corpses that had given positive results to cyanide tests. This could not be a coincidence – whatever the tests said, and whether the brain and lungs smelled normal or not. They concluded, as for 'Eva':

> The presence in the oral cavity of the remains of a crushed glass ampule and of similar ampules in the oral cavity of other bodies (see Document Nos. 1, 2, 3, 5, 6, 8, 9, 10, 11, and 13), the marked smell of bitter almonds emanating from the bodies (Documents Nos. 1, 2, 3, 5, 8, 9, 10, 11), and the forensic-chemical tests of internal organs which established the presence of cyanide compounds (Documents Nos. 1, 2, 3, 4, 5, 6, 7, 8, 9, 10, 11) permit the Commission to arrive at the conclusion that in this instance death was caused by poisoning with cyanide compounds.[11]

Common-sense approaches often hold back progress for centuries. Had the pathologists just reported the anomalous facts, without drawing spurious conclusions which contradicted their own tests, then subsequent investigators would have been able to think of an explanation. And an explanation certainly does exist, which ought to have occurred to the Soviets that May, had they not been under tremendous pressure to draw definitive conclusions.

First it is necessary to point out that the smell of cyanide is detectable by only about half the population, males being less sensitive to its presence than females. However, those who are capable of discerning the smell will quickly realise that it is not only quite characteristic but also pervasive. It can easily be proven that if potassium cyanide is placed in the mouth of a dead animal the scent is sickeningly obvious for weeks. As the eminent forensic scientist Sir Keith Simpson has pointed out,[12] in a closed room the smell can become stale, but a few moments in the fresh air immediately reawaken its recognition.

But in May 1945, in the mortuary of Berlin-Buch Hospital, what the dissectors noticed in the already cyanide-laden presence of the corpses was the fresh scent of cyanide released from the tissues beneath their scalpels as they dissected the lungs and especially the brains of the Goebbels children or, as was separately noted, the tongue of young Hedda.

That they recorded no such smell emanating from the dead tissues of either the alleged Hitler or the alleged Eva was fully in keeping with the failure of the toxicological laboratory to detect even a trace of cyanide in either body.

That should have alerted them to the possibility that, whereas a cyanide capsule had certainly been placed, and crushed, in the mouth of both of these corpses, these must nevertheless have died from other causes. In the case of the female corpse they already had proof of the exact mode of death.

The also ought possibly to have noted the similarity between the remains of the cyanide ampoule in the Alsatian dog Blondi's mouth, in which part of the wall and part of the bottom of the ampoule were preserved, and the remains in the mouths of the alleged corpses of Hitler and Eva. In the 'Hitler' corpse especially, exactly similar remains were noted. It is likely that this fracture pattern was produced by the method by which the ampoule was crushed. From previous testimony it seems likely that Dr Stumpfegger crushed the ampoule between the jaws of a forceps and held the Alsatian's jaw shut. Perhaps this fortuitously produced a pattern typical of not only the initial break but also the lack of grinding, for a grinding spasm of the jaw is absolutely characteristic of cyanide poisoning.

It is also likely that Stumpfegger performed the same exercise for the

Goebbels children, who, however, were allowed to writhe and chomp in their death throes, breaking up the rest of the vial.

Was it Stumpfegger who crushed the vial in the mouth of the forensic fake of a corpse that was to be known as Eva? Did he perform the same last act on the corpse of the alleged Hitler? In either case there would have been no death throes from cyanide, no grinding of the capsule – the pattern found might well have been created in just such a fashion.

Soviet Suspicions

The Soviet forensic pathologists had given their uneasy report, and nearly half a century elapsed before it became clear that they had been working under intense pressure to produce a conclusion that would satisfy Stalin, who was awaiting their discoveries with great attentiveness.

The first piece of evidence to be released, which set in train the subsequent revelations, came in 1993 from Sergei Vladimirovitch Mironenko, the director of the Russian State Archives in Bolshoya Pirogovskaya Street in Moscow. He revealed details of the discovery of what he believed to be part of Hitler's skull, found in an ordinary cardboard box similar to a shoebox, marked 'blue ink for biros', along with photographs of the blood-stained sofa in Hitler's room (at that stage without its fabric covering, which had been sent for forensic analysis) and a blood-stained cross-member of the same sofa after it had been completely dismantled.

Along with the remains were six thick folios of over 2,000 pages – records of the questioning of the Bunker witnesses by the Cheka and its successor the NKVD (the internal secret service) and the deliberations of the experts, both forensic and intelligence, who wrote their final reports for Lavrenti Beria, the notorious head of the secret police, who in turn reported directly to Stalin.[13]

Before the discovery of these folios, rumour more than any evidence suggested that the bodies of 'Hitler' and 'Eva' had been finally destroyed just over twenty years earlier, after several repeated burials. Even after perusing of the folios, Soviet journalists were to repeat the same deeply ingrained story. The exact fate of the bodies will become evident later in the text.

From Käthe Heusermann's testimony, and the testimony of the original May 1945 post-mortem, we know that the lower-jaw bridges with their several crowns and the loose lower jaw shown to Heusermann were taken from Hitler's corpse and used as exhibits to establish identification. These bridges and the lower jaw were allegedly forwarded from Berlin to Moscow, where they became mislaid in the KGB archives; they were not included in the recent findings.

In 1993, intimations about what the Moscow archives might contain suggested that the remains of one skull, minus the lower jaw, might have been sent back separately to Moscow, possibly in keeping with the Russian fascination with phrenology that was prevalent at the time. However, Mironenko would not allow examination of the remnants by Western forensic experts.

The contents of the shoebox may be material testimony to the hunt for one of the world's truly macabre figures. As an *Isvestia* newspaper reporter was to declare as she held the dried-out remains in her hands, 'I do feel rather afraid – not so much about the past, but of my worries for the future: of the ideas and plans that could emanate from within such an ordinary human skull.'

When the discovery of the skull was announced, I immediately suggested verification of its identity by means of a simple test, which it seems the Moscow archivists had not previously considered before I brought it to their attention. I suggested an X-ray be taken of what remained of the sinuses immediately above and below the eye sockets in the newly discovered skull for comparison with Hitler's X-rays in US archives. This would prove whether or not the newly found Soviet skull was Hitler's. My offers of assistance in this were met with silence.

There was also another possibility which I drew to their attention. In the 1970s, Reidar F. Sognnaes, professor of forensic orthodontology at the University of California at Los Angeles, made models of Hitler's bridgework, based on three-dimensional imagery created from the two-dimensional X-rays in US archives, as well as from the diagrams and descriptions that Professor Blaschke left of Hitler's teeth. These bridges could be fitted to the remnant of the newly found skull to see if any match was remotely feasible.

Whereas a positive identification by these methods would help determine whether the Bolshoya-Pirogovskaya skull was that of Hitler, a negative result would mean only that *that* skull wasn't genuine. It was, after all, not even labelled as Hitler's. A negative result would not exclude a correct Soviet identification having *previously* been made from the genuine article in May 1945.

My suspicions about the authenticity of this skull became heightened by another point-blank refusal to allow its examination; indeed, I doubted whether it even existed, for photographs showed that the cardboard box was of such thin material that it had collapsed down on the remains themselves, making it clear that there was no room in the cardboard 'bag' for any intact skull base let alone a skull complete with part of its vault.

One skull fragment (incorrectly designated as occipital) was, however, confidently produced for scrutiny. But examination of this fragment also gave rise to serious doubts about its origin – doubts that will be addressed in full later in this text.

Examination of the six large black folios found with the skull is far more rewarding, for there is little doubt of their authenticity. The story told is fascinating.

In 1945 the Soviets in Berlin were anxious to mollify Stalin's whims and his phobia that somehow Hitler might have succeeded in outwitting him at the last. The forensic uncertainties of the pathologists were smoothed over in a report by the deputy minister of internal affairs, Ivan Serov, to his chief, Beria. He wrote, 'The above listed documents [no longer available] and photographs bear testimony to the correctness of the identity of Hitler. There is no doubt that the corpse of Hitler is identical [i.e. genuine].'

Back in Moscow, Stalin was still extremely suspicious, especially when the British Brigadier-General Fort, fishing for information, tried to convince General Siniev in Berlin that the British had absolutely no doubt that Hitler had died and that the Soviets had his corpse. Having presented this façade of casual certainty, Fort then undermined it by writing to ask Siniev for the results of the dental tests carried out on the corpse's jaw, thus displaying his true ignorance.

In the late summer of 1945 Stalin commissioned a special report on Hitler's death. Responsibility for this report was given to General Kobulov of the NKVD (later to be shot by Beria for his trouble), and the report was finally completed and sent to the then minister of internal affairs, Krugulov, dated 19 January 1946. The chief administrator of POW affairs (GUPVI) of the NKVD gave the operation an extremely evocative name: Operation Myth.

When, in the summer of 1945, the Western Allies were raising their queries about the dental records and the finding of Hitler's corpse, there was a hysterical plea for advice from Serov to Beria:

● What should he do to satisfy Stalin?

● Should he approach the Allies for whatever information they might have?

- Should he re-examine the whole area where the corpses were found in Berlin?

- Should he *lie*, and extricate himself from the whole thing?

No revealing reply is recorded from the wily Beria, but what is subsequently recorded is an opinion that the officers of Smersh who had conducted the first examination of the corpses had acted too precipitously, without enough care or cynicism, and had shown far too much indulgence towards the 'Fritzes'. The mistake would not be repeated. Stalin's displeasure at the Smersh report submitted to him by Abakumov, the deputy commissar of defence, had obviously unnerved Serov, who realised that such displeasure, if repeated, might have serious implications for his future.

The rivalry between Serov and Abakumov became intense, with Abakumov firmly holding to the findings of the first post-mortem that, from the dental evidence alone, it had definitely been the Führer's corpse – even though they hadn't established the mode of death! Serov, on the other hand, was busily decrying the competence of the initial Smersh investigative officers as a way of getting at Abakumov, who had after all stolen a march on him previously by getting a report in first.

A tell-tale phrase attributed to Serov in the folios shows that he interpreted Stalin as believing that the forensic data was almost unequivocal evidence that a forensic fraud had been perpetrated and Hitler had escaped: 'Come what may we will uncover the tracks marking the Imperial Chancellor's escape'.

Serov thus started his Operation Myth in the worst possible fashion. He knew that the forensic experts now advising Stalin, under the Moscow forensic pathologist Professor Semenovsky, had definitely stated that there had been no cyanide poisoning: the Zyankali vials had been forensic fraud. Stalin had interpreted this as proof that the corpse was not Hitler's, but the NKVD were still interested in knowing *how* the corpse had died. Whatever else Serov wrote, his remit was clear: to find concrete evidence of a mode of death. The only evidence that would satisfy Stalin that the corpse was Hitler's was evidence of death by a bullet wound. Serov's reasoning at the time is given away by a multiplicity of phrases in the folios – 'alleged suicide', 'imagined death', etc. – which point to his attitude that any corpse allegedly shot through the head and subsequently faked as having died from suicide using cyanide could not possibly be that of the Führer but must be that of a double.

As part of the vast investigation that was set up by the megalithic

NKVD, operational groups in each major German town under Soviet postwar control began to search for evidence of a double who might previously have been known to the local population.

This seemingly impossible task quickly produced results. The operational group in the town of Bernau obtained information about a certain Gustav Veler who was very similar in appearance to the Führer. Up to 1944 he had lived in Berlin. He had been called in more than once by the Gestapo, who suggested that he change his hair style and shave his moustache. The NKVD then learned that Veler had been sent for by Himmler himself and had been warned, 'If you wear your hair in the same way as the Führer you will disappear for ever.'

The NKVD managed to track Veler down and to interview the Gestapo members concerned. Veler's photograph was included in an NKVD dispatch. It showed a startling resemblance to Hitler.

It was impossible to link a live Veler with a dead Führer, but detailed questioning of Gestapo members confirmed that doubles had existed and that the Gestapo had been aware of them. These reports from Berlin were to alter the Soviet attitude towards their captives from the Bunker.

The briefing papers for Operation Myth, contained in the Moscow archives, included a paragraph emphasising the need for a systematic approach: 'The presence of serious discrepancies in the data concerning the supposed suicide of Hitler necessitates a thorough review. It seems expedient to carry out a careful and comprehensive investigation into the stories of the "suicide" by following a preconceived plan.'

Point 3 of this 'preconceived plan' now became 'To secure every person under investigation by an agent in each cell.'

The NKVD now prepared for 'active interrogations'. The head of the Butyrskaya prison was ordered to allocate individual cells well separated from each other in each of which two prisoners would be held. One would be an NKVD agent. He was also to provide an equal number of rooms for interrogations, and had to ensure 'special measures' for the continuous observation of the prisoners, their special protection and 'speedy escort'.

From the Moscow camps eight POWs were chosen – all of whom had served in the Bunker at the last, including Linge and Baur. The actual reports of the interrogations – some lasting eight or nine hours, and mostly at night – are absent from the folios; instead there are case summaries. It is still possible to ascertain that Baur and Linge were refused permission to sleep in the day and were given rags to wear, all adding to their terror.

It is obvious from the documents that Linge was not trusted. When first captured he had given suspicious testimony that he had previously prepared *one* blanket to wrap around a corpse, and had laid it in the corridor outside Hitler's room, awaiting the suicide. How could this be, asked the Soviets, when there were to be *two* suicides? Surely such commendable forethought would have stretched to two blankets?

Furthermore, even though he went into paroxysms of rage and fear induced by the cold and hunger, Linge kept telling his cell-mate (a Soviet plant – a German called 'Bemen') that he would never crack and therefore could never be convicted of lying, because *only Martin Bormann and he knew the truth*!

His questioners were nevertheless convinced that he *was* lying and that he had deliberately got rid of the second valet by leading him away from Hitler's study at the last minute so that he, Linge, 'could be rid of another witness'. Throughout Linge's testimony to the Soviets he made no reference to the smell of anything like cyanide, only to acrid smoke, which they didn't believe it possible to smell through a closed smoke-proof door.

The Soviets' contemptuous questioning of Linge about the appearance of the alleged gunshot wound on Hitler's temple – according to Linge, a 'small spot of blood' – caused him to confide in Bemen upon his return to his cell. Bemen's report makes interesting reading: the questioning had provoked a response from Linge which would certainly have raised my eyebrows:

> They asked me again about the bullet hole and as to whether there were any traces of blood on the clothes. I replied I had noticed a patch of blood on the right temple – a red dot – not exceeding the size of three stamps. I don't know whether it was in reality a bullet hole – this stain could also have been painted on.

How on earth could Linge, allegedly the last man to see Hitler alive and the first to see his corpse, even remotely conceive that a gunshot wound could have been faked by painting it on? It is a most peculiar statement – and one of many. It is also of interest that the 'small spot of blood' on the temple had grown to the size of three stamps to accommodate the needs of the questioner – and that his initial testimony had been that he had witnessed the blood on the *left* temple.

I have to agree with the views of Linge's questioner that it was inconceivable that, had Linge genuinely witnessed a gunshot wound of the head, he could have failed to have described it more accurately. Instead, Linge had not even come close to reality, despite the alleged wound being the very basis of his testimony. I agree that this was telling proof against the existence of any such gunshot wound.

Linge's testimony also contains a most interesting phrase: Linge claimed he entered Bormann's study to tell him, 'It's done, Minister' – allegedly meaning that Hitler had shot himself. But at that stage Linge had supposedly not opened the door to Hitler's room, which suggests a different meaning which we will consider later.

Linge's testimony relating to Eva was also considered bizarre: apart from recalling that there were no marks on the body, he seemed to have had a total blank as to all other details – even as to who carried Eva's body up out of the Bunker.

It is clear from the testimony that the Soviet inquisitors suspected that if any gunshot had been fired to finish off the Führer it was Linge who had been responsible. (This had also been hinted at by Yeléna Rzhevskaya, one of the interpreters at Linge's questioning, in her book *Hitlers Ende ohne Mythos*.) The final dismissive commentary of the NKVD officer in charge of Linge in the section dealing with Linge's version of the alleged suicide, was 'I personally never heard of a single case when the husband and wife committed suicide using different methods. Neither can one possibly imagine both peacefully seated on a sofa together.'

The questioning of Baur, who was likewise cocooned in cold and hunger, with an agent 'B111' sharing his cell, also produced some interesting observations. Baur was to suffer from weeping fits and depression, but remained 'far too calm' overall. Nevertheless, he related that he 'had learned about Hitler's death from Goebbels and Bormann by which time the corpse was already burning in the garden. He was surprised at nothing except that his leader had shot himself with an ordinary Army pistol and not used his fine personal weapon.' (Readers will remember not just one but two fine personal weapons in the form of the Walther pistols lying on the floor; there had been no previous mention of an Army pistol.)

The Soviet inquisitors were very suspicious about the 'emphasis on trivialities in the story of his farewell and parting from Hitler', especially since Baur had apparently not bothered to go near the body, nor bothered to say farewell to anyone else, nor bothered to ask other witnesses in Berlin or even in the Soviet camps about what had actually happened to Hitler – a fact that they termed 'a strange indifference'. They thought that Baur's answer that he had planned to find out after he had escaped from the Bunker was an obvious lie, in view of what they knew from their agents planted among the prisoners. They were certain that his reaction was due to guilt, and repeatedly asked their NKVD bosses for 'recognition of the fact that Baur is unperturbed because he knows this is all a pretence'.

The countless hours of cross-examination of the witnesses had brought the investigators no nearer the truth than previously. Serov was getting desperate, but he had already set the stage for the beginning of another round of deception.

Forensic Fraud No. 3

Back in Berlin in May 1946 – one year after the event – the discovery of the Bunker was to be re-enacted as if it had only just occurred and there had been no previous investigation whatsoever. A plan of the layout and the positioning of the furniture was undertaken, even including tracing the whereabouts of the furniture that had been removed and restoring it to its original position.

This reconstruction sounds impressive, but by 1946 the Bunker was flooded to a depth of over 30 cm, with dank, blackish water lapping around the rooms concerned, leaving a scum on the floor, and the dank, musty air allowing the proliferation of fungus which blackened the walls. The re-enactment must have been totally farcical. Both Linge and Baur, who were required to re-enact their movements, were noticed to have been more confident after it than before. Little wonder!

On 14 May Linge was taken back to Hitler's room and was asked to verify the position of the desk, the sofa and the cupboard. Allegedly he did so. Only then was everything measured in detail. The Moscow archives record that 'All the stains and splashes on the couch and on the wall were measured and recorded, and pieces of the tacking and of the actual material of the couch and bed were taken for analysis. Scrapings were also taken off the wall.'

The NKVD report claimed that, from examination of the Bunker in 1946, Professor Semenovsky determined that 'the blood on the wall and on the sofa came from a head wound inflicted by a gunshot wound on a subject sitting on the right-hand corner of the couch'. This claim is worth pursuing, because Semenovsky's vital report was signally not included as supportive evidence.

As will be evident later, it is highly unlikely that Semenovsky did comment in such fashion at that stage, before the imminent arrival of the results of the tests of the wall scrapings from Moscow. To do so would have been totally against the basic instincts of a professional. At this stage

Semenovsky was probably waiting to see if the stains were indeed blood and, if so, whether human blood and of what group. Nor would he have been likely to comment without also knowing the results of tests for the blood group of the extensive bloodstains found on the bed in Hitler's bedroom.

The results of this blood analysis are revealing in themselves. They are reported by the NKVD in extremely defensive terms, and it is worth while pursuing the cause for the NKVD's embarrassment.

The Soviet laboratories had easily identified and grouped the blood taken from the two corpses of 'Eva' and 'Hitler' in May 1945. However, the NKVD report suppressed reference to these laboratory-determined blood groups, meanwhile expressing extreme annoyance at the fact that neither Baur nor Linge seemed to recall the Führer's blood group. NKVD reluctance to be caught out is the probable explanation for the failure to specify the blood groups of the two corpses.

The report eventually stated that the blood on the sofa and the blood on the bed were both found to be of group A2 (despite the fact that blood grouping was bemoaned as proving difficult). The NKVD omitted to mention the report on the tests on the scrapings from the wall, which even had there genuinely been blood present would more than likely have proved inconclusive because of the mouldy state of the wall.

The significant fact is that the NKVD were unable to provide Serov with a neat reconciliation of the conflicting evidence, for *the blood groups of the corpses did not match the blood on the sofa and the bed.*

The NKVD must have realised full well that whoever had bled on the sofa had bled on the bed, but that neither the corpse of the alleged Hitler nor the corpse of the alleged Eva had spilt any of this blood.

If the male corpse in Soviet possession was Hitler, then neither the blood on the bed nor the blood on the sofa was Hitler's blood.

If, however, that corpse was not Hitler, then, although neither the blood on the sofa nor the blood on the bed was the blood of the corpse, it might have been Hitler's blood.

Similarly, if the female corpse was not Eva, then the blood on the sofa and bed could have been Eva's.

Confused? The NKVD certainly were. Let us try to put ourselves in their position.

It is now clear why they claimed that the blood on the sofa and wall came from a person sitting on the right side but did not further specify that it had come from their male corpse. They knew it did not!

The NKVD now decided that the bed complicated matters unduly.

They couldn't see why the corpse need have been dragged from the sofa into the bedroom and laid to rest on the bed, and certainly it need not have been dragged from the bed to lie on the sofa. They solved their problem by making no further reference to the bed.

But their overall investigation was desperately close to becoming ludicrous. As we shall now see, not only had they fudged the issue of the non-matching blood groups and deliberately played down the bloodstains on the bed, they had also lied about the bloodstains on the wall and misrepresented both Semenovsky's views and the actual nature of the bloodstains on the sofa.

For we have independent testimony as to the nature of the bloodstains in the Bunker – testimony emanating from Colonel John McCowan, the British intelligence officer, who, after a first illegal, unofficial, trip into the Bunker in 1945, had been officially ordered by Colonel Dick White to go back into the Bunker, in the presence of a Russian-speaking British officer, carrying enough in the way of cigarettes to keep the Soviet guards happily coughing their way to oblivion while McCowan ransacked the Bunker for clues.

Apart from the chance discovery of a bottle of Dewar's whisky under Hitler's bed, McCowan's observations are not only pertinent but are fully backed up by photographs of the inside of the Bunker taken by photographer William Vandivert – photographs which duly appeared in the 23 July 1945 issue of *Life* magazine. For three *Life* employees, dressed in Army fatigues, also managed to get into the Bunker by using the same cancer-inducing bribes as McCowan. Vandivert's photographic record and his companion Percy Knauth's description of his Bunker visit act as our second critical witness.

Vandivert's scene-setting photograph of central Berlin established the mood of the moment – an absolutely mammoth portrait of Comrade Stalin dominated the main street, Unter den Linden, inappropriately housed in what seemed to be a Biedemeier-style frame of light wood. Not so light was the entrance to the Bunker, for his photograph showed that the steel door had been forcibly removed by Soviet Army engineers, using cutting equipment (demolishing the myth that the first to enter the Bunker were a group of Soviet women doctors).[14]

In the ante-room dank water sloshed around their ankles, and carpets squelched soddenly as they walked. Gas masks, unexploded cartridges and mouldering uniforms littered the steps as they descended, while rubbish and paper debris bobbed about in the water. In the entry hall they found evidence of the last-minute fire started by the Germans before they left. Paintings on the wall were burned paper-thin, but chairs and tables were still discernible despite the blackened room.

Hitler's conference room was a complete shambles – with papers strewn over the floor, soiled tables, a reading-lamp, a telephone, a wooden sofa with a fabric back – but there was no evidence of blood.

Moving on, they found a sixteenth-century painting of a Madonna and Child – previously stolen from a museum in Milan – as they entered Hitler's bedroom. His safe had been tackled with acetylene torches, and stood with its door hanging open at the foot of his divan bed, which had by now been stripped of its mattress. A photograph of this room shows a dark stain on the wooden side of the bed where blood had trickled slowly from the mattress above and had collected on the very top edge of the side panel. The blood had not trickled on to the floor, where the Americans found no evidence of blood. (Although the floor was still swimming in water, blood that had coagulated before the flooding would have been unlikely to be washed away.)

Then, excitedly, they entered Hitler's living-room, where the suicides had allegedly happened. Percy Knauth had been one of the very first to interview Kempka, Hitler's transport officer, and had recorded Kempka's first version of events verbatim. Kempka had at that time claimed that Eva, sitting in the right-hand corner of the sofa, which was placed firmly against one wall and was some 45 cm from the corner of the room, had shot herself through the heart. Hitler, sitting next to her, had meanwhile shot himself through the right temple, only a small spot of blood being visible on his head when he was found slumped forward, head on knees.

With this description of the alleged joint suicide in mind, the *Life* men looked closely at the sofa, wall and floor, with torches, in search of any evidence of blood. They searched in vain for any spotting of blood on the wall above the sofa, and failed to find any drips of blood on the floor where the Führer had allegedly slumped forward, nor elsewhere in the room, other than on the floor near the right arm of the sofa itself.

Vandivert's photographs show that Knauth's testimony of 'stagnant water sloshed around our feet' accurately described the rest of the room and the surface of the stone-slabbed floor around the armchair, which stood some 1.5 m away from the sofa, with a wet newspaper half under one of the legs, but that around the sofa itself the floor was at this stage still relatively clear of water and any blood would probably have been readily discernible.

McCowan's testimony is equally certain about the only blood on the floor being near the right arm of the sofa. Nor did he recall blood on the

walls above the sofa. Getting into the Bunker before the *Life* team, however, he had been able to remove bloodstained ticking from the mattress
in Hitler's bedroom, the stain that he had found being centred 'near the
outside edge of the bed, just under halfway down – a pool of blood some
nine inches across which had soaked through the mattress'.[15] Although
failing to find blood on the floor of Hitler's room, he had succeeded in
finding 'a few drops of blood, all close together, some two feet from the
door of the bedroom'. His report and the ticking went straight back to
his boss, Dick White.

The living-room sofa itself was timber-framed and heavily built, with
the timber framing exposed beneath the front of the seat and on the top
of the arms. Heavy velvet material with a white pattern readily showed
up the blood stains, as did the light-coloured wood.

McCowan claimed that 'On the arm of the sofa were two small congealed pools of blood, one larger than the other. The larger one had
trickled straight down on to the floor.'

Vandivert's photographs did not show the top surface of the right arm
but did show that there were half a dozen trickles more or less bunched
into a group towards the back of the arm, one going into a rivulet about
2.5 cm wide as it hit the fabric of the inner surface of the arm and
proceeded further down the arm, not actually soaking the seat itself.

A second solitary trickle, probably emanating from the smaller pool on
the arm, had stained only the adjacent part of the fabric.

The testimony of the *Life* magazine personnel was that on the outer
side of the arm the blood trickled down in exactly similar fashion,
there being enough present to stain the fabric and drip on to the floor
itself.

The newly released Moscow archive data includes Soviet pictures of
the sofa – pictures which match exactly with the American photographs
and McCowan's description of its construction. In the Soviet photographs
the fabric has been stripped from the back of the sofa and from the arms,
revealing the padding that existed underneath. The padding on the back
of the sofa shows no evidence of any bloodstain. Neither does the padding
on the right-side arm show any bloodstaining, except at the junction of
the arm with the seat. The cross-member at this point has been removed,
and a photograph shows that exactly where the broad stream of blood
went down the fabric on the inside of the arm, and met with the seat, it
seeped through to leave a small spot of blood on the underlying padding.
Very obviously the amount of blood was not sufficient to soak through
the fabric at any other point.

The American and Soviet photographs of the sofa and the British testimony all match exactly. They indicate a limited, relatively slow blood loss, dripping to form two separate, congealed pools with clear-cut edges, trickling down as described on to the material and the floor. This is the exact type of blood loss that would be sustained from a cut wrist or wrists. The positioning of the blood on the bed suggests that whoever was bleeding then went to lie down, the spots near the doorway confirming movement between the rooms.

Serov's NKVD report is now exposed as being a total sham, a deliberate fudge of concealment. There had been absolutely no evidence of any gunshot wound, but to find such a wound had been high on Serov's list of priorities.

In fact blood loss of any kind seems to have a dramatic effect on the lay mind. The *Life* team thought that the blood somehow verified that Eva had shot herself in the chest and had doubled over the arm of the sofa, even though the sofa was only 45 cm from the side wall and the amount of blood loss was hardly consistent with such wounding. Even McCowan thought it probable that the Führer had been shot on the bed and someone else had been killed on the sofa.

To return to the NKVD and Serov's quandary, it had now become obvious that Professor Semenovsky's reaction to the re-enactment of the Bunker drama was politically less than helpful. He was not prepared to express any immediate opinion, still less to back Serov's version of events, but instead requested an exhumation of the bodies.

The Moscow archives record that the chief of the Berlin-Buch Hospital received a special instruction from General Siniev, the Soviet military commander in Berlin: 'Taking into consideration the necessity for carrying out special investigative medical examinations I hereby order you to free a post-mortem examination room in the hospital for the examination to be carried out by Professor Semenovsky.' Along with this order, the archives record an NKVD command to allow the enquiry participants to have access to the two crates containing the bodies of 'Hitler' and 'Eva', which had previously been buried in Magdeburg Hospital, in the grounds of the Smersh headquarters.

However, Smersh was in no hurry to hand over the remains, being infuriated at the rubbishing of its 1945 investigative team having attributed death to cyanide poisoning. On 30 May it sent a telegram requesting that General Abakumov himself (by then minister of state security) give permission for the release. The head of counter-intelligence in the Soviet forces in Germany, Lieutenant-General Zelenin, refused categorically to release the corpses to the investigating commission, apparently in revenge for the mistrust and criticism of the 1945 Smersh investigation.

Now a fascinating power struggle took place at the very top of the intelligence world, seriously compromising the effectiveness of Semenovsky's investigation and putting him under even more excruciating pressure than his predecessors.

In the absence of any corpse or skull to examine, Semenovsky wisely refused to resort to conjecture. He couldn't vary in his professional opinion from his predecessors. He had to agree with the now hardened Soviet *medical* opinion that there had been no cyanide poisoning of either corpse but that cyanide ampoules had been placed in the mouths of the corpses, in whom there was no evidence of any gunshot wounds in the skull.

It was stalemate between Abakumov and Serov – a stalemate that resulted in Semenovsky's professional opinion being dispensed with at this point, in favour of its liberal interpretation by the NKVD. Having expressed his opinion, Semenovsky then left the scene to the more innovative amateurs, whose testimony differed from his in its content and value.

The NKVD conclusion was: 'The enigma of the cyanide capsules can be explained by the placement of the cyanide capsules into the mouths of the bodies of two corpses substituted for Hitler and Eva, *after* they were probably shot.'

This meant that the NKVD could envisage only one reason for putting cyanide capsules into the mouths of people already dead: to create the impression of a suicide to cover their true identity. They thought that these two unfortunate corpses had probably been shot, but, as they put it, 'One could ask, Where are the traces of the shot?'

Their dilemma – and Stalin's impatience for an answer – led, I believe, to the completion of the forensic fraud.

In the case of the corpse of 'Hitler', the NKVD were very conveniently to 'solve' the problem they faced by referring to a finding of the 1945 post-mortem: 'The upper part of the skull is partly missing. Only the lower part of the occiput and the left temple is preserved.' (This observation was somewhat contrary to the translation of the findings of *Document 12* in Bezymenski's book, which indicated that only the top part of the occiput was missing in May 1945.)

This gave them the opportunity to conjecture that, after all, the corpse of 'Hitler' might have been shot through the mouth – the bullet exiting through the missing bit of occiput (top of the vault) that they didn't have.

In making this conjecture they ignored the fact that Professor Semenovsky had asked to examine the exhumed corpse specifically to exclude this possibility, by examining the floor of the skull through which any bullet would have had to pass. If, as previously reported, the skull base was normal, such a shot was impossible, however pressing the need for such conjecture.

(It is at this that the contents of the folios cast further doubts on the genuineness of the skull remnants now in the cardboard box in Moscow. For reference is made to an NKVD realisation that the statement in the first report that the occiput was missing meant that it might have been through this bone that a shot through the mouth might have exited: 'Providentially in the 1945 file it is noted that the roof of the skull is absent.' These comments reveal that the NKVD obviously did *not* have access to any previously excised skull, raising the question of whether there was ever any removal of 'Hitler's' skull from his corpse.)

Alternatively, the NKVD thought the shot might have been through the missing part of the right temporal bone (the right temple), high up towards the back, exiting through the same missing occipital bone. This possibility had also been ruled out at the first post-mortem, because the underlying membranes and the right side of the brain (even when excised and sliced) showed no signs of any such gunshot wound.

In the case of 'Eva', the NKVD had an even greater problem to over-come, for if, as was now probably established to Stalin's satisfaction, the corpse had *not* died from cyanide poisoning then it was highly likely that she had died from the shrapnel wounds to the chest – a fate which just couldn't fit with the story of a suicide pact. The NKVD may have thought that the multiple testimony they had been fed by Linge, Baur, Günsche and others was concocted for the sole purpose of getting them to believe that the real Hitler and Eva had committed suicide. What was missing – and very necessary to fit in with this testimony as presented to Stalin – was evidence not only of a gunshot wound to the corpse's head (much of which had been missing) but also that she had after all been hit by shrapnel in the crater *after* she had been buried.

Apparently unaware of the medical significance of the bleeding into the tissues – which occurs only when there is enough pressure in the vessels to drive out the blood, and therefore has to occur before death – the NKVD assumed that to prove the post-burial shrapnel theory all they needed to find was evidence of some more shrapnel in the vicinity of the body. To prove that both corpses had been shot, they needed two burned bits of occiput – his and hers – with neat bullet holes punched in both!

They would then have a complete scenario ready for an epic Soviet film: two corpses had been shot, burned, buried and had cyanide capsules placed in their mouths – and a concocted story had been told by fanatically loyal SS men – all to deceive Stalin that Hitler was dead; but the fraud had been exposed and the truth uncovered by the vigilance of the Soviet citizenry. Stalin would then have had his suspicions appeased. After all, the discovery of the already proven cyanide-capsule fakery had taken him halfway to accepting that the corpses of Hitler and Eva were fakes.

It therefore comes as no great surprise to read that the Moscow commission which had initially undertaken the excavation of the shell crater where the bodies had been found was asked by the NKVD to re-examine the crater itself.

An unattributed statement in the Moscow archives commented, 'It is a real miracle that there in the place where thousands of people had subsequently trodden an answer was found to the question of whether or not the shooting took place.' The statement continues:

> When we investigated the bottom of the crater at a depth of some 50–60 cm we found at a close distance from one another two partially burned parts of skull. On one of them is noticed an open bullet hole. There are foundations to admit that a shot was fired into the mouth or high into the temple at very close distance . . . Examination of the soil around the crater showed fragments of yellowish-brown staining made by fragmented shrapnel.

The investigators, after a half-year investigation, thought that they had produced a presentable case. The two bodies had died of gunshot wounds, and cyanide capsules had been put in their mouths after they had been burned, the female corpse then sustaining shrapnel wounds while lying in the grave. There was serious reason to doubt their identification as Hitler and Eva Braun.

Back in Moscow, Stalin was still dissatisfied. No statement was to be made. There are nowadays very cogent reasons to agree with Stalin's caution.

One of the world's foremost authorities on the forensic study of burned corpses is Professor Tony Busuttil of Edinburgh University, whose expertise was called upon in the Lockerbie and Amsterdam air disasters.

He makes the point that, unless there is a very good reason, the skull usually burns evenly – leaving *no* separate islands of bone such as were reported to have been found in the crater.[16] A low-velocity gunshot wound would not constitute a reason for uneven burning. If the skull had been splintered and shattered by a *high*-velocity gunshot wound, or if there had been extreme force used, sufficient to cave in the back of the skull – such as a violent blow from behind, or dropping the corpse on its head from a height – then unusual effects could be obtained. But the presence of a neat low-velocity gunshot wound in one of the allegedly 'occipital fragments' rules that possibility out.

He stresses that if the skull were lying where the petrol flames could not get to the part of the skull resting against the ground then it would be just possible to conceive of this part coming adrift as the skull around it burned, but in sandy soil petrol invariably soaks into the area behind the corpse and burns it from below.

The admittedly 'miraculous' finding of these two bits of allegedly occipital bone is therefore to be treated with the gravest suspicion.

In fact the Moscow archive material only adequately shows one of these two pieces of bone. It is *not* a piece of occipital bone: it seems to be a piece of the right parietal bone, just where it meets the occipital and temporal bones – from the side of the skull, above and behind the temple. The fact that some of the interlocking bone junctions are seen to be undone but still intact suggests that the bone was artificially removed from a skull and did not come adrift in any fire, as these suture lines are stronger than the bone plate itself, and even more resistant to fire.

The bone in the Moscow archives fits into the palm of the hand, and shows a clearly visible low-velocity gunshot *exit* wound, caused by a bullet passing more or less straight through the skull at that point, and not at any marked angle to the vault at the point of impact.

By far the most likely cause of such a wound would be the direct firing of a revolver through an artificially removed fragment. The alternative – the firing of a revolver into an intact skull – just does not seem feasible, for, from a knowledge of the anatomy of the skull, the likely trajectory can be worked out and can be shown to be inconsistent with the exit angle.

If the bullet travelled without deflection, it could only have been fired from the left fronto-parietal area (the left side of the forehead) – an area found intact on the 'Hitler' skull examined by the Soviet pathologists. It could hardly have been fired into parietal bone on the same side, as this would have created an altogether different type of exit wound, reflecting the acute angle involved.

A bullet can, however, be deflected within the skull by a buttress of bone such as exists in the base of the skull in the so-called sphenoid. A shot into the mouth could thus possibly cause such a wound as in the fragment, but only at the expense of visible evidence of gross destruction of the base of the skull and of the palate – which was not evident in the 1945 post-mortem.

It thus seems almost certain that this piece of parietal bone in the Moscow archives was created to order, and did not come from the skull of either of the corpses found in the shell crater at the Bunker.

When the evidence of burning is further considered, the fraud seems even more obvious and amateur. Other expert witnesses in this field are archaeologists studying the cremation of bone and exactly how it burns under specific circumstances, such as in funeral pyres and in modern crematoria. Jacqueline McKinley in Warminster is studying the variations in fragmentation of long bones and skulls; Michael Wysocki at the University of Wales (Cardiff) is another authority in this field. Both describe how bone cracks and becomes white and mosaic-like on the surface when exposed to intense heat, and how the skull remains intact for a remarkably long period, burning evenly as the fat within the bone gets used up. Female bones typically are consumed faster than male. Michael Wysocki considers the idea that the tops of the skulls somehow came away as complete separate islands of bone to be bizarre. Jacqueline McKinley actually measures bone-fragment size after cremations – estimating the size of such fragments has now been reduced to a science, the story to absurdity.

Examination of photographs of the piece of parietal bone in the Moscow archives reveals that the undersurface is reasonably intact, with very little evidence of conflagration, whereas the outer surface has some blackening around the edges of the gunshot wound – but there are none of the mottled white changes indicative of sustained severe fire damage.

An experienced crematorium manager – a man used to handling corpses – expressed doubt that the two pieces of bone which had allegedly come adrift would have been picked up by the handlers of the corpses when they moved the bodies from the trench where they were burned to the grave site. In his experience men who were not used to such a job would have lifted the corpses roughly by the available arms and legs, and with some distaste, and would hardly bother to engage in the ghoulish task of ferreting for stray bits of bone in the hot, burned gunge underneath. I would agree with his surmise – especially considering the haste with which the bodies were put into the crater and only perfunctorily covered over, as evidenced by the accounts of their discovery. The burial party was, after all, facing possible gunfire. And in that context it is worth recalling that there would hardly be a few square metres of land around the Chancellery where traces of shrapnel were not likely to be found.

Acting on advice from Michael Wysocki I have burned several intact sheep and pig skulls (which contain a lot of fat) with and without suitable gunshot wounds in the posterior vault. Not once was I able to create the effect claimed by the NKVD.

Given the above, there is serious cause to doubt the genuineness of the discovery, referred to in the folios, of the two pieces of 'occipital bone'. These can almost certainly be declared fraudulent.

It seems obvious that the NKVD, now without recourse to Semenovsky's advice, resorted to citing the previous conclusions reached in *Documents 12 and 13* (though not quoted by Bezymenski): that the chest wounds had been created after death and had not been the cause of death. Given their fortunate discovery of shrapnel traces in the surrounding area and the two bits of occiput, they put forward the view – this time medically unsustainable – that the female corpse had been shot through the head, and had not died from her shrapnel wounds.

The *only* reason why the *first* team, in 1945, had with considerable unease put forward the conclusion that she had not died from her wounds was the discovery of the cyanide capsules and the mistaken belief that there had after all been cyanide poisoning. Had there been no such belief then the first set of pathologists would quickly, and I am sure with some relief, have given a diagnosis of death from shrapnel wounds. The NKVD were, probably deliberately, misrepresenting the initial medical viewpoint.

However, in Moscow, we may assume that Stalin had now yet again been assured that the male corpse was almost certainly Hitler's – because of the overwhelming and unchallenged evidence of the dental bridge and Käthe Heusermann's unswerving and impressive testimony.

The archives give no indication of the drama of the conflict of evidence, but drama there must have been, for everyone must have realised that if the corpse were Hitler's there would be no sense in anyone faking a suicide by putting a cyanide capsule in the mouth of a Führer who had already died 'honourably' and heroically from a gunshot wound. The NKVD version looked very shaky.

Stalin's choice was either to believe the miraculously found but shaky new evidence of the two small pieces of skull and accept Hitler's corpse as a fake or to discount the new evidence – in which case there was still *no* evidence to suggest that Hitler had died from a gunshot wound. Little wonder that he chose not to make his deliberations public!

★   ★   ★

The forensic embellishments indulged in by the NKVD were carried out in desperation to appease Stalin. They were made necessary only because of the forensic fraud that they themselves had encountered. The key to the understanding of events in the Bunker lies in the understanding of this Nazi fakery.

I must agree with Professor Semenovsky that forensic fakery had been carried out by the Nazis – for the most obvious of purposes: to deceive.

We now know that in the case of 'Eva Braun' the deception was, as the NKVD correctly surmised, to conceal the identity of the corpse – which certainly was not Eva's.

But what of the corpse alleged to be Hitler's?

It is time we looked more closely at another reason for forensic fraud – the concealment of murder.

9

The Bunker Revisited

According to an article in the magazine *Izkusstoo Kino* ('Cinema Review') 1950 No. 4, by M. Anhaparidtze and V. Tsirgiladze, the Soviets engaged in further re-enactments at the site of the Bunker. A Soviet propaganda film entitled *The Fall of Berlin* was completed in 1948 after reputedly no fewer than eight changes of script. The Führer was shown blowing his brains out by various methods, before the final version plumped for suicide by cyanide.

There are no longer political reasons to falsify the circumstances in the Bunker. Even allowing for the previous confusion, it is possible to reach some rational conclusions about what happened, as long as the limitations of the methodology are appreciated.

In attempting a re-enactment based as far as possible on fact, the investigator is left with only two keys to unlock the mystery of the Bunker:

- First, the implications of the known faking of 'Eva', which, as we shall see, have an indirect bearing on events;

- Second, the critical timing of the events themselves, derived from the testimonies of otherwise duplicitous or suspect subjects, who did not appreciate the significance of their sometimes pedantic utterances.

The forensic data of the post-mortems are the only *facts* that we have relating to the whole of the Bunker saga about Hitler's and Eva's demise. Eva Braun, a quiet, giggling, lisping, thirty-three-year-old Bavarian girl of limited intelligence – a girl who in her last batch of letters, of 18 and 19 April 1945, complained that her dressmaker was charging her 30 marks for her blue dress, and that she couldn't possibly flee Berlin as they weren't allowing cars through[1] – now becomes the key to the unravelling of this mystery, simply because we know that the corpse presented as Eva's was not hers and we know a fraud was perpetrated.

Any case of forensic fraud has to be initiated, then perpetrated and the fraudulent material discovered. Finally, for the fraud to succeed, the false material has to be confirmed as genuine.

Initiation of the Fraud

To state the obvious, it is more than likely that, from the beginning, Eva was a willing party to the fraud, as otherwise there would have been no point in the deception. This alters our perception of the quiet Eva.

The date of the making of duplicate sets of gold bridgework in late 1944 – bridgework never worn by Eva – indicates that by then the deception was well in hand. There is no proof that Eva genuinely required even one of the two gold bridges made for her: they might well have been made *purely* to effect the fraud. Käthe Heusermann herself has hinted that the bridgework was totally unnecessary.[2] The implications are that Eva must at some time have considered that she need not, after all, be pressured into going through with suicide.

It is more than likely that the origins of any such similar forensic arrangements for the Führer went back to mid-1943, for even at that time defeat was looming and contingency plans of various kinds (mainly financial) were being made by the Nazi hierarchy. Final arrangements for both forensic fakes might well have been at a time when escape for the Führer was still a possibility.

But even Hitler himself must eventually have appreciated that his physical state meant that not only could he not envisage his escape, but neither could others.

Himmler's deputy Walter Schellenberg, during questioning by the Western Allies, claimed to be quite convinced that Himmler had ordered the Führer killed.[3] Even if Schellenberg was wrong and such orders had not been given, it is quite inconceivable that the SS would countenance the shame of a degenerate Hitler falling into Soviet clutches, and Hitler's vainglorious pronouncements of suicide had a desperate and unconvincing ring.

Which put Eva in a somewhat difficult position! She had chosen, seemingly of her own free will, to join Hitler in the Bunker in his hour of need, and had allegedly chosen to join him in a suicide pact, conditional on becoming his bride. (Scores of other women in Berlin had supposedly swallowed the Nazi claptrap about devotion unto death and had vowed to die along with their Führer, but the Soviets found only two bodies in the crater, and not half the female population.)

But was Hitler aware that his bride was to be spared? He had already shown his reaction to the alleged treachery of Göring and then of Himmler, and the recollection of the day-long outburst of impotent, vindictive fury on 22 April still lay as an emotional pall in the stifling atmosphere of the Bunker. From analysis of his personality disorder it is evident that he related everything to himself, being incapable of being truly selfless. It is highly unlikely that anyone would have had the temerity to inform Hitler that Eva did not intend to go through with her suicide pact but intended to escape. It would be seen as the final betrayal.

Yet Eva must have had this intention. The eventual implementation of the forensic fraud must have involved Eva herself, as otherwise the deception we know to have occurred would have served no purpose.

If, as is more than likely, Hitler was unaware of the plans to let Eva survive, then Eva had to be more or less dependent on the SS to keep her separate from the Führer (and indeed from the other Bunker occupants) at the very last, for the only staff capable of implementing the forensic fraud were Hitler's own SS guard.

To deceive the Führer when such deception was bound to be discovered by Hitler himself at the last was no less than to defy the Führer. Normally such defiance meant death. But in this instance death would result not for the very same men who had already shown their lack of respect by allowing their soup- and chocolate-coated leader to stumble around the Bunker but for the Führer himself.

To accomplish this, the SS guards would eventually have to release what the Moscow archives called 'the innate hostility of servitude', but it seems that this prospect did not particularly bother them towards the end, when their own survival was at stake.

But *when* would such a plan have finally been put into action?

Perpetration of the Fraud

We know that the corpse identified by the Germans as being that of Eva was that of a woman of roughly thirty to forty years old who had sustained a fatal chest wound from an artillery shell. The archives record that the digestive juices had not started to attack the bowels to any great extent, making her a relatively fresh corpse – within say four days or so of death.

This means that Eva had either decided for herself or had been persuaded not to go through with any suicide pact possibly before but certainly not after the corpse became available. Because of the uncertainty about exactly when the final Soviet assault would take place, it is likely that the corpse had been procured and Eva had agreed to the deception a couple of days beforehand at the latest.

The above assumes that the fraud was perpetrated on a corpse, for it is highly unlikely that a woman fitted with Eva's bridgework during her life, as part of a pre-planned deception, would have been anything other than a valued captive, kept in safety and therefore highly unlikely to sustain a shell wound in her chest during such protective custody.

It is now known that there were scores of female civilian corpses in the vicinity of the Bunker, especially at the entrance to the nearby U-Bahn station. And there was no shortage of the dental expertise needed for the simple forensic fakery that actually occurred – the hurried removal of teeth, and the eventual placing of a bridge in the burned corpse. SS dentist Kunz was at hand in the Reich Chancellery, but even Stumpfegger could have done it. Either could have snapped the cyanide capsule.

If the testimony about the blue dress that was to become 'Eva's corpse's' identity badge, for witness by casual observers, is genuine, this must mean that the corpse was draped in Eva's blue dress *before* being brought out of the Bunker. This itself means that the corpse was at some stage taken into the Bunker, either right inside or just inside the doorway, to be suitably clad and prepared.

Nevertheless, in his initial testimony SS valet Linge was clearly of the impression that he had to provide only one blanket, and was very vague about carrying a second corpse. This points to Linge being well aware of the fact that Eva was to be spared.

A factor complicating any attempt to determine how and when the fraud was perpetrated is the presence of those bloodstains on the bed and sofa. The finding of A2 blood on both, in the manner described, leaves open the possibility that Eva, who by now was recorded as drinking excessively[4] and dining separately, made a futile attention-seeking gesture. This would have been in keeping with a previous incident in which she had melodramatically 'shot herself in the chest', conveniently causing only a flesh wound, before managing to phone her favourite doctor for assistance (despite there being another doctor much closer to hand in her own apartment block).

There is also the possibility that Eva made a fake suicide attempt so as to officially incapacitate herself and so make her unable to go through with any suicide pact.

Had she done this while Hitler was having a final talk with Goebbels, as described by Linge?[5]

Was she found on the bloodstained sofa, or the bloodstained bed?

Was this the reason – genuine or contrived – for the exclusion order which sent most personnel out of the lower Bunker altogether?

The exclusion order involved detailed planning, suggesting an existing arrangement. It is likely that if Eva did try to get attention then she did so at a quite convenient time for events that were already in train.

The clearance from the lower Bunker of virtually all visitors and personnel – the cooks, the secretaries, even the electrician Hentschel – left the emergency exit and the main bulkhead doors sealed by Rattenhuber's SS guards. Rattenhuber himself must have been involved in giving such a strict exclusion order, and this means that he would have known its purpose.

As to what that purpose was, it seems inordinately strange that the SS guard should be so involved if they were just waiting for the Führer finally to commit suicide. They had, after all, been waiting ever since Stumpfegger demonstrated the effectiveness of cyanide poisoning on the dogs. They had even, the night before, been celebrating the old days in the Chancellery basement, in a party which left Baur and Rattenhuber in inordinately good mood – a party in which all seemingly knew that Hitler was going to kill himself. Finally, they had spent the day waiting with increasing irritation for the death of the Führer, so that they could put into action plans for their escape. If the reason for the exclusion ban had been simply to let Hitler get on with it, then the lower Bunker would surely have been cleared far earlier – when the suicide was expected – not at 3.30 p.m.

Discovery of the Fraudulent Evidence

The reason given for the ban was to ensure secrecy when the bodies of the Hitlers were brought up for funeral and burial. Such secrecy is somewhat out of keeping with the burial of the bodies only a couple of metres from the exit door, casually covered with a scant amount of earth and the surrounds treated so roughly as to draw attention to the burial. When considering this aspect of the discovery of the corpses, it must be emphasised that the Soviets were very suspicious about the ease with which the bodies were found and the unusually helpful testimony of Günsche, which had left Mengerhausen with little option other than to show them the exact grave-site.

Günsche's ready unprompted testimony ran counter both to his later accounts and to his oath of loyalty to the Führer. Furthermore, Linge was to state that the Führer's death occurred at precisely 3.50 p.m., invalidating this reason.

The exclusion order was assuredly given to ensure secrecy – but for what purpose?

Confirmation of the Fraudulent Evidence

In the case of 'Eva Braun', initial confirmation of the identity of the corpse resulted from the discovery of the bridge, the records of its construction in Blaschke's Kurfürstendamm office, and the testimony of Fritz Echtmann that he had made it for Eva. That was proof enough for the Soviets.

The fraud would not have been successful if the dental records that Blaschke carried had been available to the Soviets, nor if due credence had been given to Heusermann's testimony about the bridges not having been fitted. This seems to suggest that, when envisaged, the fraud did not depend on the testimony of Blaschke, or Heusermann, and possibly not even on that of Echtmann, but was mostly reliant on the simple presence of a bridge that was ostensibly Eva's. Soviet suspicions would do the rest; contrary testimony would most likely be disbelieved.

In the case of the corpse of 'Hitler', the bridges would once again prove the identity – a positive identification being very necessary to prove it really was Hitler who had died with that cyanide capsule in his mouth.

Where does all this unravelling lead us? To the fact that Eva's escape was pre-planned – probably effected up the stairs of the emergency exit. An escape into certain enforced anonymity and possibly death, just after 3.30 p.m., when the enforcement order began.

It is worth remaining for a moment outside the Bunker, for there can no longer be any legitimate reason to question the exact cremation site, nor the burial site. Nor can there be any doubt that the corpses burned were the corpses buried – the details of the burning with petrol accord reasonably well with the degree of destruction of the corpses, except for the missing lower left shin-bone in the corpse of Hitler.

Gone is the myth of an undiscovered grave. Gone is the myth of the

Führer's ashes being carried into posterity by Axmann. We are now free to indulge in what it must be admitted is relatively uninformed speculation – an alternative scenario for the death of Hitler, inside the Bunker.

I defend this exercise on the grounds that, as it is at least based on a background of forensic data, as an alternative it cannot be less truthful or less accurate than the story that has been accepted to date. However, it has a fatal flaw in that it is based on supposed logic, and it is all too easy to delude oneself that one is being logical and lay oneself open to ridicule. I am nevertheless convinced that even a ridiculed alternative is better than a discredited historical fiction.

Before starting the actual reconstruction, it may be necessary to remind ourselves of the position of the key players, and to clear the stage for their performance.

We are left with several testimonies that at lunchtime on 30 April the Goebbels children were upstairs in the dining-area of the upper Bunker, along with some of the secretaries, who were feeding them and keeping them occupied while their mother, Magda Goebbels, was in her own room – presumably suffering from her palpitations. Since the SS men would probably never have allowed her through the bulkhead door into the lower Bunker in her recorded wild, hysterical attempt to see Hitler, it seems likely that this happened some time before the event of Hitler's death, possibly because she became aware of the change of mood in the Bunker. The secretaries might also have had some inkling of impending events from the talkative Günsche, but, from all accounts, they managed to keep the children from suspecting anything.

We know that Axmann and Baur were almost certainly not in the lower level of the Bunker – both were in the SS quarters, recovering from the Chancellery basement party – so that leaves the lower Bunker occupied by Joseph Goebbels, Martin Bormann and the giant SS surgeon Ludwig Stumpfegger.

It was probably in Martin Bormann's nature both to wish to be dis-associated from guilt and yet to be terrified of not remaining as aware as possible of what was happening. Having played cards and drunk with Stumpfegger in his room for hours on end, he would most likely willingly have remained there while Hitler was persuaded to commit suicide, by Linge or Stumpfegger, with whom the onlookers believed Hitler had struck up a friendship. Given his temperament of impatient aggression, Bormann would probably have wanted to be first to know when Hitler was finally dead. Linge's phrase 'It is done, Minister' – addressed to an eager Bormann – might after all have been significant.

Goebbels's different, more sensitive, character, was equally likely to make *him* wish for total absolution from involvement in Hitler's death, too, combined with a guarantee of safety. He probably remained in his bedsit and not with Bormann in Stumpfegger's room across the corridor from Hitler's.

I place Goebbels and Bormann in the lower Bunker because, as each considered himself to be a figure in charge, it seems inconceivable that they would have meekly gone out of the lower Bunker when ordered to do so by Rattenhuber's SS. The fact that the SS allowed them to indulge in their later peace-making gestures with the Soviets suggests that the SS still wished to go along with the legality of whatever paper state there still existed. It also suggests that both men approved of the hurrying-up process, even if they may not have understood the nature of the SS persuasion.

It is more than likely that Stumpfegger was responsible for breaking the capsule of cyanide into the mouth of the corpse after death.

Hitler was not poisoned, he was not shot, so how *did* he die? We are left to consider only one real practical alternative: the forceful *strangling* of the Führer.

Since the fire consumed all the soft tissues of the neck, the post-mortem would not have been able to detect such violence. The petechiae, or red spots of blood, that strangling produces in the skin, the eyes and other organs would have been burned out of existence. In short, there would have been no forensic method by which the Soviets could have determined whether strangulation took place.

The need to indulge in such devious measures as placing a cyanide capsule in the mouth of Hitler's corpse can now be more readily understood: it was not to conceal his escape but to cover up a murder by faking a suicide that the vacillating Führer did not himself have the courage to commit.

No one in the Führer's exasperated, fearful entourage would readily have accepted responsibility for such a strangulation – not if he had thought that knowledge of his actions could possibly become widespread and lead to his later public shame. The cyanide capsule which Hitler had alleged he was going to use would have been the obvious and perfect cover for such a murder – a murder probably committed in desperation by his entourage, frantic to escape; a final response to Hitler's prevarication and delay in killing himself.

We cannot now appreciate the full extent to which the Soviets were suspicious of the odd or banal comments with which Linge peppered his testimony; however, they may well now fall into place. Linge – the man whom, as Günsche commented, no one, including Hitler, thought overly bright – now becomes the main suspect of having murdered the Führer.

So, although it can not be claimed that Hitler's fate is no longer in dispute, I now choose to use our present knowledge to try to reconstruct the happenings on 30 April 1945, based not on the false testimony of possibly guilty witnesses but still based only on a surmise. But this surmise is backed by hard forensic evidence about the previously claimed methods of death.

The Killing of Adolf Hitler

Outside the Bunker, SS guards slam the heavy steel doors unnecessarily loudly: the mood is sullen, and edgy. Worried reports come in about how far 'Ivan' has progressed: he is in the Stadmitte U-Bahn station, only 200 m away; it is not safe to walk in the Chancellery garden. The reports exacerbate an already unpleasant tension. SS general Rattenhuber has been in constant touch all morning with Bormann and Stumpfegger, with whom he has had a long secret conference. The rest of the time a black-faced Rattenhuber has been angrily confronting some of his staff in the Chancellery bunkers – bemoaning the lack of discipline, yet terrified to try to impose it in case all order then breaks down.

A worried Goebbels, who knows what Rattenhuber and Bormann have been talking about, tries to bury himself in his room, reading one of the only two books now left on his bare table.

We can envisage Hitler shuffling across to speak to Goebbels – eyes water-filled and yet demonic, his face flushed and covered with rivulets of dried tears, with spittle running down from the corner of his mouth. His right arm spasmodically pumps forward his closed fist, with a peculiar lack of synchrony as he beats the stale air to emphasise repeated points – treachery, treachery; a deserving doom for those who betrayed him; devastation for the soft, undeserving German nation that had spurned the chance of greatness he had allowed it to glimpse.

Blank-eyed, dry-mouthed and exhausted Goebbels watches Hitler stumble desperately from wall to wall, agitatedly waving a sheaf of papers, which one by one escape his grasp and flutter on to the table or the floor. He manages to mutter encouragement, his depressed face matching the Führer's for expressionless fear.

Half an hour passes: it seems an eternity.

Bormann is on the phone to Rattenhuber, speaking in hushed tones. His shoulders are tensed as he thrusts his elbows artificially forward to cradle the phone as if to mask the sound further. Stumpfegger, morosely drinking whisky from a cracked urine-sample glass, stares uncomfortably at his short companion, almost glaring across the table.

The call goes out from Rattenhuber: all personnel except those notified have to leave the lower Bunker instantly, and are not to enter until further notice. They are to gather in the upper Bunker or the Chancellery passage until further instructed. The buzz of excited gossip is cut short as, from the upper level, three SS men enter to reinforce the order. The secretaries – some of whom have been drinking, some sleeping, some playing cards – hasten to leave, annoyed at the lack of communication.

In the corridor, Linge has insisted on taking over duties from his deputy, Krüger, whose shift has two hours still to run, and whose protestations are abruptly cut short by Bormann. Sticking his head out of his room, Bormann angrily waves Krüger away and tells Linge to take over and make no noise. Linge, glad of the interjection, sees Krüger out through the bulkhead door and seemingly unnecessarily watches him walk up the steps out of sight.

Returning to the corridor outside Hitler's ante-room he confers briefly with Bormann and pulls a blanket from the floor under the bench, folding it over the chair outside the room. He knocks and enters the living-room – to find Eva, her head thrown back in a seeming dead faint, leaning dramatically against the corner of the sofa, still holding her wrist, dripping blood on to the sofa arm.

Hurriedly gathering up the skirt of her dress, he wraps it around her bleeding wrist and heaves her into his arms. Hitler's bedroom is nearest, and when he stops to push open the door the wrist drips its telltale evidence on to the floor. He then dumps Eva unceremoniously on the bed, where her hand falls limply to her side. He rushes across the corridor to find Stumpfegger and tell him that Eva has attempted suicide.

Stumpfegger curses, puts down his glass, and picks up the bottle of Dewar's instead. Head back, he takes another swig and, carrying the bottle by its neck, accompanies Linge into the bedroom to gaze cynically at the still unconscious Eva, who is engrossed in her hysterical faint. Half-interestedly, he glances at her wrists; then he empties the bottle, drops it on the floor and kicks it under the bed, and kneels to staunch any further flow of blood.

Linge, now moving fast, dashes back to Stumpfegger's office to get dressings and a ball of tape for Stumpfegger, and is collared by Bormann for a report.

Hitler, aware of the activity, has left Goebbels and has angrily shuffled as far as the ante-room to his suite, shouting for an explanation. But the SS guards have now left the lower Bunker – as have most people – and Hitler becomes suspiciously afraid.

He is still shuffling across the ante-room when Linge returns. Asked what is going on, Linge tells Hitler that Eva has cut her wrists, and offers him a cyanide capsule from a small brass case, and the use of the Army pistol that Linge withdraws from the drawer of a table.

Glaring blankly and uncomprehendingly at his manservant, Hitler calls him a 'stupid peasant' and turns his back.

Linge picks up the cyanide capsule and vainly tries to force it into Hitler's mouth from behind – forcing the mouth open by closing his powerful middle finger and thumb across the Führer's mouth, from side to side in the cheek pouch. Despite his feeble state, Hitler manages to turn his head away from the strong grip and lower his head. Linge's increasingly violent efforts can't succeed, even though he is by now half-facing the Führer.

But the affront has been made, the first act of violence committed. Savagely Linge turns the prematurely aged man around and throttles him from behind. Terrified, he holds up the Führer in front of him while the frothing stops and struggles cease.

He is still holding the corpse almost at arm's length when Stumpfegger comes into the room, having left Eva moaning pitiably and suitably loudly in the bedroom. Stumpfegger beckons Linge to lay the corpse down on the floor. Checking that Hitler is dead, he reaches in his pocket and produces an ampoule-crushing forceps. The cyanide capsule is quickly and professionally crushed under Hitler's protruding tongue.

Stumpfegger goes out into the corridor to call the SS guard to bring down the corpse which had been lying outside the Bunker but which had already been brought in and stacked unceremoniously in the guards' cloakroom.

They take the corpse through to Eva's own room, where Eva's favourite blue dress is lying on the bed, the back slit open. The corpse is rolled on to the dress and her head is covered with the same blanket sling that had been used to carry her.

The dummy Eva is placed next to Hitler, now also prepared on his blanket. His face, purpled in the indignation of death, is left partially uncovered as confirmation that the end has finally come.

Eva is brought back from her sobbing hysteria into the real world and is told that Hitler has committed suicide. She doesn't even seem aware of events as she is smuggled up the back stairs.

The sickly smell of cyanide by now pervading the whole room, we can rejoin the disturbed Linge as he opens the door after 'discovering' the 'double suicide' and says the enigmatic words to Bormann – 'It is done, Minister.' He then runs, looking suitably distraught, up the stairs to the upper level and beyond into the Chancellery, shouting the shocking news: 'The Führer is dead.' When he reaches the massive bulkhead door, the tearful face of the once reassuring figure of the cook, Konstanze, appears from within the kitchen. Ever a romantic, she asks, 'What about Eva, Heinz?' Linge stares at her uncomprehendingly for a moment, before pulling open the door and rushing out to the SS bunker, still shouting 'The Führer is dead.'

The talk among those Bunker personnel now present is shattered by Rattenhuber being suitably shocked, even suspicious, at the news. Baur, another pragmatist, avoids all conversation and doesn't want to know the rumours now circulating. Axmann goes to the group in the lower Bunker and joins with Linge in what is to become the loyal chorus: Hitler had died an honourable death; he had died like an officer and a gentleman, shooting himself while taking a suicide vial.

They all have their private thoughts.

The funeral and the funeral pyre go to plan, and the SS dentist Kunz briefly attends to place a gold bridge under the tongue of the fake Eva, completing the forensic fakery, before she is heaved off a canvas sling into the shell crater to be lightly covered with earth, rubble and rubbish.

An SS officer, with his back turned, is seen to be deep in contemplation as the scene fades and Mengerhausen and the burial party disappear into the Bunker. He is freshening up the edges of the crater with the heel of his SS boot.

The rest of the story is known; there is no further need for re-enactment.

Neo-Nazi groups who now revere the story of the Bunker must come to terms with the fact that Hitler was betrayed by all around him – Bormann, Goebbels and finally even Eva. He was even betrayed by his loyal SS guard, despite their loyal ditty: 'When all are disloyal then we remain loyal, so that always on this earth there will remain a banner in front of you.'

One of their number – Linge – probably strangled the fearful vacillating Führer. The SS themselves helped kill the myth.

A verse by the nineteenth-century poet Bogislaw von Selchov might help us realise something that Hitler himself had bemoaned:

> *Ich hasse*
> *die Masse,*
> *die lahme,*
> *die zahme,*
> *die Heut' an mir glaubt,*
> *und die mir Morgen mein Herzblut raubt.*

> I hate the crowd,
> the impotent crowd,
> the pliable crowd,
> which believes in me today,
> and tomorrow will tear my heart out.

10

Break-out

There is multiple postwar testimony, from those who escaped to the West and from those who were captured by the Soviets and subsequently released, to substantiate the fact that a break-out from the Bunker did occur, under the leadership of General Mohnke, who was in direct charge of the Reich Chancellery group of personnel and guards among the entourage at the Bunker.

Much of this testimony is highly contradictory, however, especially when trying to establish the exact whereabouts of individuals at any one time. But it is a characteristic of the questioning of members of a group that discrepancies occur when specific detail is sought. If they did not it would indeed be highly suspicious.

Furthermore, when testimony is questioned too severely it may alter, as the person being questioned tries to meet the seeming requirements of the inquisitor, or genuinely starts to doubt his or her own testimony. Encounters between those questioned quickly compound the innocent alteration of testimonies, which thus become less than original.

All this of course presupposes no intention to deceive – a question which will be separately addressed.

By now – in the 1990s – almost all the survivors of the break-out from the Bunker have learned the exact testimonies of others, and have themselves been questioned on numerous occasions. Several have considerably modified their testimonies as a result of this, and the effect has been to render testimony concerning the whereabouts of any particular individual almost worthless. Even so, there is remarkable agreement on the essential truth, on the main direction of the break-out and how it was organised.

The fact that there undoubtedly was a mass break-out does not rule out entirely separate individual attempts, whether before, after, or indeed during the mass escape. It is now clear that for various reasons many individuals did extricate themselves from the groups that they originally formed part of, to go it alone. Common sense dictated that to be caught as part of a group reduced the chances of being believed an innocent non-combatant.

Historians wanting to make sense of a complex situation have been far too trusting of the majority testimony – sometimes altering the testimonies in their own accounts so as to make them fit. Very little attempt has been made to describe the physical conditions in Berlin at the time of the break-out, nor to ascertain exactly where the escape routes lay.

As the Soviets advanced in Berlin, their soldiers did not just concentrate on the main roads but went through waste ground, gardens and houses to clear snipers from whole blocks of tenements as they moved forward. It proved a costly exercise for the Soviet troops, but the Soviet experience in Berlin, as opposed to in cities such as Warsaw, was that, with few exceptions, an area posed very little further threat once it had been penetrated in this way. Even so, some of the escapees were later to tell of three separate incomplete rings, left behind the advancing ring of steel, set to catch escapees and prevent any organised break-out. These 'rings' were in essence no more than obstructions on the main avenues and Soviet snipers in the buildings on both sides of these streets.

The Berlin civilian population were almost all fearfully confined to basements, U-Bahn stations and shelters, to avoid the shelling. But a few were defiant, so these shelters were approached with caution by the Soviets. The Soviets made very little attempt to use the U-Bahn system to penetrate the centre, fearing that the Berliners, with their superior knowledge of the system, would have mined it effectively. There were also fears that there were plans to divert the River Spree or the Landwehr Canal into the U-Bahn system, to make a watery grave for the attackers – a fear which also managed to deter many would-be escapees.

The Soviet attitude to the U-Bahn was to block obvious exit points, such as stations in their areas of control, where a warm reception would greet any illicit users. However, because of the extensive nature of the system, with its ventilation and access shafts, the U-Bahn remained one of the main avenues of escape. Some twenty thousand refugees now cowered in darkness in the remnant of the system.

The Adlon, Berlin's most fashionable hotel, had relatively luxurious basement shelters well below the city – too well below, as they became flooded in the last few days of the battle for Berlin. Most of the dignitaries staying there spent their time huddled in luxury. It had one of the finest wine cellars in Berlin to fortify their spirits, until the Soviets confiscated the lot. The management, catching the mood correctly, ceased to charge room service when they heard that the Oder defences had fallen. A few of the Bunker entourage found the offer too good to miss and ended their break-out before it had properly begun.

Another consideration for escapees was that they might have to face the hostility of a city population fed on Robert Ley's famous evening editorials exhorting Hitler's Holy Mission in the *Nachtausgabe*, on sale to the very last to a population who had seen, hanging from lampposts the grizzled corpses of men, women and even children, shot by the bizarre emergency courts martial that had been touring Berlin from 17 April to show what happened to defeatists and traitors.

Amazingly, in a similar spirit, the Gestapo were still continuing their phone taps on the citizens of Berlin even up until the night of 23 April. On that night, a young witness, Fritz Leidke, later claimed, several Gestapo men who had taken part in the summary executions took off their uniforms and revealed civilian clothes underneath. When challenged and derided by civilian onlookers, they only laughed.

Outside the centre of Berlin the opposition of the population was more organised. In Wedding – a working-class area, which, when I lived in Berlin in the 1970s, was confidently predicted to become the home of the last communist on earth – the population were openly showing their aggression in more practical ways, such as stoning SS and Army personnel. Similarly Soviet marshal Koniev recalled that in his drive around the south of the city the villagers were physically preventing the Hitler Youth from attacking his troops. Any small military force of Germans hoping to escape would probably find hostility rather than support from the local population, especially once a cease-fire was in effect.

The Main Escape Routes

So what of the escape attempts, of which there is incontrovertible evidence?

On 29 April a Major Arnulf Pritzsch managed to get from the Zoo U-Bahn station to Theodor Heuss Platz and then to Ruhleben station near the Olympic Stadium, passing under Soviet occupied Kaiserdamm and Heerstrasse. On the same day no fewer than seven couriers were sent from about midday onwards. They were, in order of departure, Major Freytag von Loringhoven (an aide to General Krebs); Lieutenant-Colonel

Weiss (aide to Burgdorf); Major Willi Johannmeier (Hitler's adjutant who was accompanied by his own batman, Corporal Hummerich); Cavalry Captain Gerhard Boldt (aide to von Loringhoven); Bormann's aide, SS Colonel Wilhelm Zander; Heinz Lorenz from the Propaganda Ministry; and finally, at about midnight on that Sunday, liaison officer Colonel Nikolaus von Below, who was accompanied by his own batman, Corporal Heinz Matthiesing. All of these nine men eventually got to safety via this direct western route out of the city centre.

All of these couriers were sent when it was deemed officially possible for them to make their escape. Indeed there was still a madness to their missions, for Johannmeier was to carry a copy of Hitler's last testament to try to give it to Field Marshal Ferdinand Schörner, who was still fighting to the west of Berlin; Lorenz was conveying a second copy, and Zander a third, as well as a copy of Hitler and Eva Braun's marriage certificate – which he was under orders to hand to Admiral Dönitz in Flensburg, by the border with Denmark.

Dönitz, a vain, ambitious man suddenly rocketed to fame as Hitler's successor, probably looked forward to receiving confirmation of his official standing. On hearing from Krebs that a courier was on the way bearing this paperwork, he went to the extraordinary length of sending a plane to try to pick up the courier from the River Havel, under the very noses of the enemy. This attempt was doomed to failure – the couriers got to Pfauen Insel (or Peacock Island), on the eastern bank of the Havel, but there was no way in which they could be lifted off in safety. The seaplane, which had miraculously put down on the Havel in the dark, suddenly became the focus of Soviet attention and had to leave; the couriers had to continue their escape by other means.

It is worth remembering that on the night of 25–6 April the famous test pilot Hanna Reitsch and General Robert Ritter von Greim had flown into Berlin's Gatow airport, in a Focke-Wulf 190, on an equally fatuous mission – just to reassure the Führer of their undying loyalty – sacrificing many of their forty-strong fighter escort on the way from Rechlin to thus appease their vanity. When they reached Gatow airport they found that onward progress was already too dangerous by road, but they took a training aircraft and flew the few kilometres into the centre of the city, landing near the Chancellery and losing the bottom of their plane and part of von Greim's foot. Later that day Gatow itself was to fall to the Soviets. Enquiries from Luftwaffe general Koller as to whether flight into Berlin was possible were met with a definite No.

Reitsch and von Greim were to make a similar heroic exit out of Berlin on 29 April, but were extremely fortunate to do so. For all practical purposes, as a means of escape, such flights were out of the question from that time.

The overland attempts were to continue. On the night of 1 May a group of 300 soldiers went up the U-Bahn, from the Zoo station to Adolf Hitler Platz and then up the Heerstrasse. They then turned off for Ruhleben and ended up being caught in Spandau.[1] Before being caught they had proved that there was still an avenue of escape open – directly to the west.

Luftwaffe general Sydow, of the 1st Flak Division, organised a break-out from the Zoo area, up Kantstrasse and then up Reichstrasse to the Olympic Stadium, and then successfully on to Ruhleben. Several hundred infantrymen and several hundred civilians went up 8 km of U-Bahn tunnels to the same stadium, and then 4 km further to the Spandau bridges, yet again proving that there was a negotiable gap present till the last.[2]

There were other gaps, which we now know about from details subsequently given by successful escapees and from Soviet military archives.

In the early morning of 1 May, hundreds got through a gap between the Soviet 12th Guards and 7th Corps, where the U-Bahn tunnels ran straight north from Alexanderplatz. Overland in the same direction, however, the 2nd Guards Army destroyed a tank break-out.[3]

The 3rd Army's three separate corps fought their battles in almost total isolation, leaving large gaps between them, whereas 79th Corps was separated from the rest of the Army by the Schiffert's Canal, and a further gap existed between 7th Corps, as it advanced on Alexanderplatz, and the 12th Guards Corps going in the same direction on the Chaussée Strasse axis.

We thus know with hindsight that there were indeed two main axes of escape still open until the last – directly west or north and then north-west.

The Timing of the Break-out

The most obvious question is surely: why was the break-out so delayed, greatly reducing its chances of success?

The most obvious reason for this delay was that surrender negotiations were in progress. These negotiations were carried out at the instigation of Goebbels, who ordered General Krebs, a fluent Russian speaker, to represent him. The actual story seems little known outside the archives.

Shortly after midnight on 30 April, General Mohnke led Krebs to

Colonel Siebert's sector HQ, from where the latter had arranged safe passage to the Soviet lines. Krebs and one of his aides (Colonel Theodor von Dufwing), the chief of staff to General Weidling (in charge of the defence of Berlin) and an interpreter (Sonderfahrer Neidlands), arrived at 102 Guards Rifle Regiment of the 3rd Guards Division, 4th Guards Corps, and were sent on to Chuikov's HQ, where they arrived at 3.50 a.m. Chuikov was accompanied by a body of officers including three war correspondents – a writer (Vishnevsky), a poet (Dolmatovsky) and a composer (Blantek). It took some considerable time before Krebs discovered who was in charge![4] The documents that Krebs brought with him were sent on to Marshal Zhukov, who in turn telephoned Stalin in Moscow. Von Dufwing was sent back with a Soviet signals major to lay a field cable to the Bunker.

The result was that the Soviet major was shot and von Dufwing was arrested by SS troops, before he was subsequently released – only to find that the cable was, in any case, too short. Somewhat dispirited, von Dufwing reported back to Goebbels and Bormann the fact that the Soviets were demanding unconditional surrender. Goebbels and Bormann then instructed von Dufwing to return and bring back Krebs on any pretext. As von Dufwing set out again at 11 a.m. he managed to telephone Krebs, who instructed him instead to try urgently to relay the cable on a shorter route, because the Soviet HQ was expecting another call from Moscow. Von Dufwing successfully managed to achieve this, but, as soon as the operation was complete, the cable was cut by incoming shell fire. By the time he had returned and again managed to get a call through to the Soviets, von Dufwing learnt that Krebs had been released and was on his way back.

This was not the only attempt that Goebbels and Bormann were to make to save their skins. They had hoped that they would be recognised as official peace envoys and be allowed to fly out to safety to Admiral Dönitz in the Flensburg area under the pretence of inviting Dönitz, as Hitler's successor, to surrender Berlin to the Soviets. The Soviets had already seen through that ploy, yet Colonel V. S. Antonov, commanding the 301st Division of the 8th Corps, 5th Shock Army, received a deputation of four officers, commanded by a colonel, offering surrender terms just as he was attacking Wilhelmsplatz on the morning of 1 May. He duly reported the mission, but was instructed to shell the Reich Chancellery and to engage in no further negotiations. Antonov allowed the German colonel to return with one officer to tell the Reich Chancellery of his progress, but detained both the other two officers. The whole episode had lasted another four hours, by which time all fighting had stopped in his sector.[5]

Antonov was just about to attack the Chancellery at dusk, when an officer with a white flag appeared and declared that Goebbels was now dead and Dönitz had been confirmed as Hitler's successor. This further delay, while Antonov asked for instructions, allowed the break-out to proceed.[6]

Another reason that has been put forward as an explanation for the break-out not happening sooner was the necessity to attend the funeral of Magda and Joseph Goebbels, but concern in this regard was highly unlikely to be the real cause, as examination of the hastily charred corpses of the Goebbels duo was to prove. Furthermore their children lay unburied – somewhat out of keeping with the supposed niceties of the occasion!

In the absence of any other known cause, then, the delay in the break-out must be ascribed to the peace negotiations.

However, one thing can be determined from the story of the 'break-out', for it was later claimed by Mohnke and others that the break-out of the Reich Chancellery group – the entourage of personnel and guards around the Führer – had *originally* been planned for the evening of 30 April. This presupposes that the whole group leadership, including Mohnke, knew beforehand that the Führer was going to commit suicide, or be killed, *before that time*, for a break-out of any group big enough to contain and defend the Führer himself was never considered a possibility.

The limited nature of the break-out was in itself evidence that Hitler was dead. The *initial* intended timing of the break-out suggests that it was expected that he would be, one way or another.

The Organisation of the Break-out

In practical terms, the break-out from the Bunker was hardly a military exercise. There were approximately 700 SS guards and 80 security men defending the Bunker complex; on their own, these had no chance of breaking through the ring of Soviet armour around Berlin. Nor did they have any realistic chance of combining with other scattered German units, which now presented only isolated nuclei of resistance to the Soviet advance. Communication between Mohnke's headquarters and the German Army units, both inside and outside Berlin, was fragmentary, chaotic or non-existent. The only real link of practical use was Mohnke's link with General Weidling, 1½ km away in his Bendlerstrasse HQ.

Mohnke wasn't even aware of the exact Soviet troop dispositions, except in his immediate vicinity; even though he could hear heavy firing on the Unter den Linden close by, he had little idea of the situation further north. General Gustav Krukenberg was later to report, 'If General Mohnke did not have a clue about Russian troop dispositions, I did, for I had been operating out of my command post in the Stadtmitte subway station, having retreated there from my earlier CP in the Staatsoper, on Unter den Linden.'[7]

The myth has arisen that a heroic break-out was intended to link up with General Steiner's Army group to the west. This would envisage a sizeable force – men and tanks – a formation which would have immediately attracted the unwelcome attention of the Soviets. Mohnke knew that there were some armoured units, involving about twenty tanks or so, around the twelve-storey flak tower at Wedding, but little more. It is of interest to note the alleged contents of Mohnke's briefing of his officers:

General Weidling has ordered that active position fighting shall cease at 11.00 p.m., whereupon all German troops must be prepared to try to break through the Red Army iron ring now closing around Berlin. We must attempt this in small battle groups, probing for weak links wherever we can find them. Our general compass direction will be north-west towards Neuruppin [65 km north-northwest of Berlin]. If you get that far, keep moving. This is a general order; there are no more specific details . . . No provision can be made for any rear guard. We *are* the rear guard.[8]

The members of Hitler's court proper had by now dwindled to about twenty. Almost all opted for the break-out.

Mohnke spent the afternoon of 1 May working out details of the break-out with his deputy, Lieutenant-Colonel Klingermeier. They established a march route, organised ten separate groups, and discussed the timing of the escape. Mohnke took command of the first group, and Rattenhuber the second. Werner Naumann, Bormann's personal assistant, took charge of the third, in which group Martin Bormann allegedly started. They decided to start between 10.30 and 11 that night, and to try to get clear of the city barricades by the morning.

By reducing the size of his groups, Mohnke had more or less given free licence to all. It was almost a declaration that the military style of the procedure was of no consequence: escape at all costs was to mean exactly that. I emphasise this because there exist multiple testimonies to the effect that all the group were clad in military uniform – the secretaries wearing helmets and boots, with guns to match. Whereas this adds to the myth, it is at variance with the contrasting testimonies of others, who describe the group as motley – some in civilian clothes, some not; the soldiers themselves still under military command. Testimony of the very same civilians, such as some of the secretaries, who claimed to have changed into civilian clothes at a later stage in the escape, shows that it is likely that they had worn civilian clothes under whatever other clothing they had initially donned.

The testimony of Professor Schenk, who had been running a casualty station in the Reich Chancellery, adds credence to the seemingly obvious fact that it would be a shame for a civilian to be shot through pretending to be a soldier. His testimony covers the time when he was wending his way to the assembly point for the break-out – a corridor leading into the underground garage in the Chancellery:

> I next made my way down the long corridor until I came, for the last time, to the cellar room I had been sharing with at least a dozen Nazi Party bigwigs; most I gathered were from the Berlin *Gauleitung*. They had now abandoned their fancy brown uniforms and belts, the swastika armbands. Several were drunk. Most were still packing miscellaneous bulky loot which they could not possibly carry with them.[9]

Mohnke now asked Weidling to delay any capitulation agreement until daybreak on the morning of 2 May at the earliest, to allow his Reich Chancellery group sufficient chance to get clear of the city – an agreement which he was granted only because he carried the last documents of a fallen state authority. After Krebs returned, Mohnke took twenty minutes to brief his particular group before setting a time for their break-out.

Again Professor Schenk's description rings a note of reality, as opposed to the fanciful tales that have mushroomed to the present. The garage was being lit by the occasional torch, and they waited for the signal to go up into the gaping hole in a side wall into the unknown:

> Now from the dark gangways, they kept arriving, in small groups, both the fighting troops being pulled in from the outside, then the officers and men of the Reich Chancellery Group. The troops, many

of them very young, were already street fighting veterans. Other soldiers had stubble beards and blackened faces; they wore sweaty, torn, field-grey uniforms, which most had worn and slept in, without change, for almost a fortnight. The situation was heroic; the mood was not. The official announcement of Hitler's suicide had not yet reached the lower ranks. But they guessed as much – from the silence of their officers. There was little talk now of 'Führer, Volk and Fatherland'. To a man, each German soldier was silently calculating his own chance of survival. For all the discipline, what was now building up was less a military operation in the classic sense than what I imagine happens at sea when the cry goes out to man the lifeboats.[10]

Mohnke's main problem would be to cross the River Spree, and to head north and then north-west. Before he went anywhere, he had to get his small group from the Bunker to the Kaiserhof U-Bahn station nearby – a mere 100 m dash, but one across an area covered by the Soviets occupying the remnants of the adjacent buildings. It would be a shooting-gallery if the Soviets were to open up in earnest. The path that Mohnke's group had to take through the rubble was lit to some extent by raging fires, but the smoke at least masked them as they ran in groups of four at a time and tumbled down the shell-pocked station entrance.

Mohnke's general plan was then to proceed through the U-Bahn to the next station, Stadtmitte, and turn towards Friedrichstrasse, going north as far as possible towards the borough of Wedding. He presumably hoped to link up with the forces of Major-General Erich Bärenfänger. All the groups were to meet up at the flak tower in Wedding to plan their further route north-west. At this point all the testimonies are as divergent as the separate groups – some seriously so.

Whereas Mohnke was to claim that the above was his overall concept of what was to happen to all the groups, and a plan he instituted as his own, it cannot be said to have received overall acceptance – nor, indeed, to have been implemented by all the other groups. Several, including Axmann, claimed not to have known any details whatsoever about aiming for Wedding, only that they were to head for the Friedrichstrasse station. It could just be that, as with an uncomfortable number of military strategies, this one was written up in triplicate after the event!

What actually happened was that each group held its own discussions both before assembling in the Chancellery garage and after each preceding group had gone. The ten-minute interval between groups was one of the first casualties of their organised planning, as each following group could see the success of the groups before them in making the fateful dash for the Kaiserhof entrance. The interval became shortened to just a couple of minutes, and in less than thirty minutes all ten groups had successfully crossed the first hurdle. Many had determined not to get caught in the U-Bahn tunnels but to exit as soon as possible at Stadtmitte to see for themselves what the conditions were like in the open.

The Progress of Mohnke's Group

I do not intend to follow the progress of all the groups, as my concern is only to highlight the alleged progress of Martin Bormann in Group 3. However, the route of this third group was similar to that of the well-documented first group in the early stages of the escape, and detailed descriptions later made by members of other groups help develop an understanding of the events as they occurred, acting as a check on other testimonies. Following the progress of Mohnke's group also gives us a fair insight into the circumstances they all actually encountered.

In Mohnke's own group were twenty men and four women. Major Günsche, Ambassador Hewel and Vice-Admiral Voss were all members of this group, as were Hitler's cook, two of his secretaries, and Bormann's secretary Else Krüger. The excellent accounts given by all survivors of this group, including Mohnke's own detailed testimony, are both in general agreement and in very great detail – in strange and marked contrast to the accounts later given by the survivors of Group 3, whose accounts are not only scant and vague but worryingly inconsistent.

In Group 3 were Hitler's pilot Baur, his second pilot Beetz, Captain Günther Schwägermann and Goebbels's chauffeur Rach, as well as the giant figure of the surgeon Stumpfegger. Behind them was the one-armed Hitler Youth leader Artur Axmann, who managed to lose Group 4, which he was said to be leading, but allegedly later managed to catch up with Group 3 and was to become one of their spokesmen after the war.

All the first few groups went up towards Stadtmitte station, experiencing roughly the same conditions.

To begin with, an ideal opportunity immediately presented itself to several who wished to remain anonymous. For, as the groups safely crossed over into the mouth of the Kaiserhof station, they found that the platform, 100 m long, was heaving with a mass of frightened humanity. Several took the opportunity to become instantly immobile and watched their comrades push on into the darkness and the unknown. It must have occurred to many that the most obvious danger was in the period before a cease-fire was announced; conversely, the best chance of escape was before the hordes of the Red Army could be organised to seal off the city – in the interval when many of the Soviets would be celebrating their victory. Thus the first group had dwindled to fifteen by the time it reached the next checkpoint, Stadtmitte; and it was much the same with other groups.

Stadtmitte station proved more ordered than Kaiserhof station, and an emergency operating-theatre had been set up in an abandoned yellow U-Bahn car, were several exhausted surgeons were operating by candle and gas light.

The first group was to be forced to surface at Friedrichstrasse station. Mohnke tells a tale which illustrates the teutonic inflexibility that then cost them dear, and made them backtrack to this point.

Less than a hundred yards after we had passed the Friedrichstrasse station platform we came on a huge steel bulkhead. Waterproof, it was designed to seal this tunnel at the point where the subway tube starts to run under the Spree river.

Here – and I could not believe my eyes – we encountered two stalwart BVG [U-Bahn] guards. Both, like nightwatchmen, carried lanterns. They were surrounded by angry civilians imploring them to swing open the bulkhead. They kept refusing. One clutched a giant key. When I saw this ridiculous situation, I ordered them to open the bulkhead forthwith, both for my group and for the civilians. The guards categorically refused. They cited regulation this and paragraph that of their BVG Standing Orders.

Not only were these stubborn fellows going by the book; each had a copy of the book and began reading from it. The regulation, dating from 1923, *did* clearly state that the bulkhead was to be closed every evening after the passage of the last train. It had been their job for years to see that just this happened. I was flabbergasted. No trains had been running here for at least a full week, but these two dutiful characters had their orders, and that was that.

We were armed, of course, and they weren't, and I feel that we might just have been able to escape had we been able to follow my original plan to the letter. I sat for long years in Soviet captivity quietly cursing myself for my strange hesitancy at this critical moment.[11]

(According to Sergeant Misch, the switchboard operator, who went his own way after being 'separated' from his group, this barrier was certainly not present when he went through about an hour later – there being no sign of the two guards, no crowd of demonstrators, and an open bulkhead through which he gratefully passed. This was supposedly after the passage of Group 3.)[12]

All the groups were supposed to try to keep in touch with each other, especially during the trek through the tunnels, but this was easier said than done as the groups were themselves broken up into fours. These were supposed to be spaced at 100 m or so – to avoid all of them being caught in any ambush – but in fact some groups were so scared that they kept only 10 m to 20 m behind those in front. Even so they had little visual or vocal contact, fearing to use their torches.

Forced to surface at Friedrichstrasse station, Group 1 found the nearby Weidendamm Bridge over the River Spree was blocked by a tank trap. Deeming it impossible to proceed through a strongpoint where fighting was continuing, they crossed the River Spree by scampering over on a railway catwalk. The group was now reduced to a mere twelve. They reached the Schiffbauerdamm, where Berlin shipwrights had lived and worked, and there they sheltered in a disued cellar. The time was allegedly about 2.00 a.m.

Going northwards on Friedrichstrasse proved impossible, but they now found a narrow path that led through the rubble which was Albrechtstrasse, through cellars, tenement courts and ruined buildings where engineers had blasted away walls and partitions in recent street fighting. They emerged on to the Invalidenstrasse to the side of the Charité Hospital, which they believed was in Soviet hands; they learned from groups of terrified civilians that the Soviets had swept through the area but that it was now relatively clear.

Proceeding up Invalidenstrasse past the Natural History Museum, they subsequently managed to gain the Chaussée Strasse and continue north, eventually reaching the flak tower in Wedding. There they found Major-General Bärenfänger, among Tiger tanks ringing the flak tower – fresh crews, weapon carriers, and armoured personnel carriers full of soldiers, all bristling with weapons.

On 23 April, on a wild whim of Hitler's, Bärenfänger had been appointed 'Commander of Berlin' – a post which he had proudly held for all of eleven hours. By his haughty refusal to accept any orders that did not come from Hitler direct, he had kept his unit intact while the carnage had gone straight past him. It was, as Mohnke said, 'a fantastic apparition, like a *fata Morgana*'.[13]

Mohnke's resolve to carry the message of the Führer – a message carefully wrapped up in oilskin, along with a small leather sack of diamonds he had '"inherited" from Hitler'[14] and which he had thought it advisable to take along just in case – had disappeared with the early-morning mists. He no longer had any stomach for delivering the Führer's last testament, and he certainly didn't take kindly to being ordered to attend Bärenfänger, his junior, for a conference.

As soon as Weidling's capitulation order was heard at 10 a.m. on 2 May Mohnke, Krukenberg and Bärenfänger ordered the tanks dismantled, all guns spiked, and grenades exploded; then they proceeded to retire, quick march, to the Schultheiss-Patzenhofer brewery some twenty minutes away. It possibly ranked as the most sensible decision of the war, though it was somewhat spoilt by the cloud of nostalgia that rose from the brewery cellar, where Ambassador Hewel regaled them with tales of Hitler – as if they hadn't had enough.

Years later Mohnke confessed that some had not stayed for the party but that he had urged them to slip away to safety (which they did): 'I advised them, now, to try to escape capture when and if the chance should ever come, even by changing into civilian clothes.'[15]

Mohnke didn't even give the order to disperse; instead his party, which had by now picked up some stragglers and amounted to some 150 to 200 strong, sent a Wehrmacht colonel, Colonel Clausen, to try to find the Soviets and arrange a surrender.

Out of the twenty women in the Bunker, only one – Hitler's Austrian cook, Konstanze Manzialy – was not to be recorded as a survivor. She was last seen on Invalidenstrasse, near the Stettiner railway station.[16]

The Progress of Bormann's Group

We learn from the eventual fate of Group 1 that it was possible to escape above ground from Invalidenstrasse to the north of the Soviet ring, and that several did. We know that Misch made it in similar fashion in the U-Bahn itself. It is now time to examine the constraints that faced Group 3, the group that allegedly contained Martin Bormann.

This group allegedly missed a critical left turning in the dark, halfway along to the Friedrichstrasse station. As a result, they decided to surface at the Stadtmitte station. They emerged into Gendarmenmarkt opposite where the Max Reinhardt Theatre faced towards the two cathedrals, but immediately realised that progress was going to be difficult. They therefore ran back into the station and tried to make their way up into Friedrichstrasse itself. Coming to the Weidendamm Bridge, they saw it was blocked by a tank barrier – the same tank barrier previously noted by Group 1.

Here the story given by the survivors of Group 3 begins to be at serious variance with the other testimonies. So serious is the discrepancy that I have used the term 'allegedly' in describing the presumed whereabouts of Martin Bormann up to this point.

When first investigating the events at the Weidendamm Bridge in 1945, Hugh Trevor-Roper found several witnesses who claimed to have been with Bormann at that bridge and to have seen him killed when a German tank in which he had hitched a lift was hit by a bazooka shell. One of these witnesses was Erich Kempka, who was still stoutly maintaining this story when his book *Ich habe Adolf Hitler verbrannt* ('I Burned Adolf Hitler') was published in 1950. He maintained that he had seen Bormann seconds before the blast, riding in the tank that was totally destroyed in the blast. Even though he himself had been momentarily blinded by the explosion, he was – so he claimed – quite sure that Bormann hadn't survived.

Kempka told his Western interrogators in 1945 that he had crossed back over the river and hidden all day with a group of Yugoslavian women before being captured by the Soviets, then escaping and making his way west to the Elbe and being caught by the Americans instead.[17]

Another version that Kempka gave was that Tiger tanks had forced the tank barricade at the north end of the Weidendamm Bridge and had proceeded some 300 m up Friedrichstrasse to reach the Ziegelstrasse when the tank that he was walking alongside had been hit. Eventually Kempka had stumbled into a cellar on Friedrichstrasse, where two women gave him civilian clothes. There he rested, until the following day he got away. (It is, once again, far more likely that Kempka was one of many who took off their military uniform as soon as it had lost its usefulness in subduing their fellow German civilians, and uncovered the civilian suits they were wearing underneath.)[18]

Unfortunately, to complicate matters, Hugh Trevor-Roper had also found three witnesses who subsequently claimed they had been with Bormann *after* the tank explosion on the Weidendamm Bridge. One was Artur Axmann, who himself managed to escape from Berlin to the Bavarian Alps, where for six months he hid with a section of his Hitler Youth followers, before being arrested in December 1945 for trying to form a Nazi underground movement. Axmann's testimony is of critical importance as it differs from all the others. Where it differs it will be dealt with separately, but it is first necessary to deal with the testimony of the tank battle at the bridge.

The testimony given by Harry Mengerhausen was that Bormann was certainly riding in a tank when he saw him at the bridge, but the tank he was riding in was not the one that sustained a direct hit later on.[19]

Kempka's story was to be further put into question, for, according to General Krukenberg's account, five of his Nordland Division tanks had decided to break through the barrier at the Weidendamm Bridge and at 2 a.m. they blasted their way across, engaging in a battle further up the Friedrichstrasse. Bormann was *not* in one of these tanks, and there were no others.[20]

Another alleged witness to this tank battle was Hitler's pilot, Hans Baur. It is worth considering his testimony more carefully. Baur was travelling with Hitler's favourite picture of Frederick the Great, which he claimed the Führer had bequeathed him. The canvas had been cut out of its frame, rolled up, and taped on to the back of his rucksack. Baur claimed to have been dressed quite deliberately in German Army combat fatigues – having allegedly given away his own civilian clothing![21]

This same man also claimed to have been given two direct orders by Hitler on the evening of 29 April 1945. The first of these was:

> You must take the responsibility that the bodies of my wife and myself are burned so that my enemies do not do the same mischief with me as was done with Mussolini.

The second was:

> I have given Bormann several messages for Dönitz. See to it that you get Bormann out of Berlin and to Dönitz by means of your planes at Rechlin.[22]

The first command was remarkable, considering that news of Mussolini's death first reached the Bunker on 30 April!

The second alleged command must also be viewed with scepticism, for, as readers will recall, upon his return from Soviet hands Baur was to give an interview to the newspapers stating that he had actually watched Hitler commit suicide by shooting himself, yet he was later to claim to have been absent entirely from the whole suicide episode, having somehow missed the occasion because he hadn't been 'duly notified until after the event'[23] (a strange oversight if Hitler had made him primarily responsible for the funeral).

Even more suspicious was Baur's subsequent claim to have missed the burning of the bodies of Hitler and Eva – because he felt he didn't have the necessary 'urge or courage' to climb up to the garden to see whether the burning had been properly carried out.[24] Again this contradicts not only his previous claims but also his duty and behaviour as a previously rabid Nazi.

Baur's account of Bormann's break-out has therefore to be treated with the same scepticism.

When he first returned from the Soviet Union, Baur was questioned by Hugh Trevor-Roper at his home in West Germany.[25] He claimed that Bormann had almost certainly been killed in the tank explosion – although matters were confused and he hadn't himself seen the body. His story was confirmed by Linge, also returned from Moscow, in another personal interview with Trevor-Roper.

Soon after there was contact between Axmann (by now working as a sales representative in Berlin) and Baur and others, and Baur's recollection then changed entirely. He now claimed not only that Bormann had not been killed at the tank explosion but that he had personally accompanied him in his further travels. Despite this anomaly and the obvious worry that the new Baur testimony was tailored to fit the Axmann account, it is still worth while examining this new testimony.

Claiming he had failed to keep up with Bormann for some twenty minutes, Baur then saw him 'sitting on the stone steps of a bombed-out house. It was the corner house where the Schiffbauerdamm meets the Friedrichstrasse.'[26] This was on the other side of the Weidendamm Bridge.

According to the testimonies of Axmann, Schwägermann and Baur, what remained of Group 3 went back down the Friedrichstrasse and took a course along the Schiffbauerdamm towards the Lehrter railway station – a course which seems nowadays to be an inexplicably bad choice of route, passing opposite a still burning, still occupied Reichstag building on the other side of the Spree – where the Soviet presence was more than obvious. The Lehrter station itself was a hive of Soviet activity – it had been one of the main focal points of the Soviet attack on Berlin.

Hugh Trevor-Roper claimed[27] that the testimony that they had given led him to believe that they had followed the railway tracks to the Lehrter station, where they divided – Bormann and Stumpfegger walking eastwards along Invalidenstrasse towards the Stettiner station and the others – Rach, Naumann, Schwägermann, Axmann and Baur – going west towards Alt Moabit.

In fact, as we now know from Soviet records, Baur was shot in both legs, chest and arm as he tried to jump down into the roadway after crossing the railway bridge over the Humboldt Harbour, before he got to the Lehrter station, and was found some four hours later by German stretcher-bearers working for the Soviets. He was one who certainly didn't walk down Invalidenstrasse. Schwägermann, Naumann and Rach escaped (Schwägermann into later American custody).

Baur's last alleged recollection of Bormann's whereabouts was that they were opposite the Reichstag on the Lehrter railway tracks, about half a mile from the station. They had left the shelter of the Schiffbauerdamm an hour before daylight and all separately took cover from Soviet sniper fire from the area of the Reichstag.[28]

Baur, on his own on the railway lines, claims then to have seen the first streaks of dawn. It must have been close to four o'clock in the morning – 3.45 at the very earliest. Even if Bormann had continued satisfactorily to the Lehrter station and then into Invalidenstrasse, he would still have had to progress slowly another 800 m further along the same railway track to do so.

The reason why the timing of Baur's alleged last sighting of Bormann is important is its relevance to the testimony of Axmann, who told his Allied inquisitors upon capture that he had come across the dead bodies of Bormann and Stumpfegger. He gave the same testimony to the Nuremberg Trial, where Bormann was sentenced to death *in absentia*, the court choosing to disbelieve Axmann's testimony. The Soviets had the testimony of others – including Major Günther Weltzin, who had accompanied Axmann on his escape but had later fallen into Soviet hands. General Rudenko, the Soviet prosecuting counsel, failed to produce Weltzin's testimony, so we are left to make what we can of Axmann's testimony itself.

Axmann was born on 18 February 1913 in Hagen. A fanatical Nazi, he had succeeded Baldur von Schirach as leader of the Hitler Youth in August 1933, and had lost an arm while serving on the Eastern Front in 1941.

He had been in charge of his own escape group, but had lost several of these men when attempting to go overland to the Friedrichstrasse station. He had caught up with the remnants of Group 3 when the tank exploded at the Weidendamm Bridge, and had dived into a shell hole where he found Bormann, Naumann, Schwägermann, Stumpfegger and the same Baur that, in his repeated testimony to the Soviets over ten years, and in his testimony in 1956 to Hugh Trevor-Roper, had been able to remember nothing detailed about Bormann's escape.

But then in *his* first testimonies, neither could Axmann remember Baur even being in the group, which he carefully specified to contain Naumann, Schwägermann and Rach.

Axmann claimed to have proceeded with this party and Major Weltzin along the same route described by Baur and Schwägermann – along the railway tracks, to the Lehrter station – without encountering the difficulties that Baur experienced.

> We reached the bridge over the Friedrich-List-Ufer just west of the Humboldt Harbour. This bridge leads to the Lehrter Bahnhof S-Bahn station. Several of us jumped down from the bridge and found, to our chagrin, that there was a whole Russian infantry platoon in bivouac under it. They promptly surrounded us. But to our amazement and joy they simply kept announcing in a boisterous chorus *Hitler kaputt, Krieg aus!* [Hitler finished, war over!]
>
> Next, they engaged us in a very pleasant chat in broken German. All seemed to be fascinated by my artificial arm, and I kept showing it to them as if it were the latest product of some Nuremberg toy factory. Then they graciously offered us *papirosi*, cigarettes with paper mouthpieces. Apparently they thought we were simple Volkssturm men returning from a long, hard evening at the front.
>
> What spoiled this bit of fraternization was a psychologically false move by the tipsy Bormann and Dr Stumpfegger. They began to edge away and finally broke out running. This made the Russians suddenly suspicious, but Weltzin and I were able to shuffle off as casually as possible without being noticed.[29]

This alleged episode must have taken some time, after which Axmann went five blocks up Invalidenstrasse before running into heavy Soviet fire. Here, along with Weltzin, he took shelter in rubble until the tanks had passed, before making his way back down the same street. More time had passed.

Now as he came back up Invalidenstrasse, this time going east, he claimed he came across the dead bodies of Bormann and Stumpfegger – behind the bridge where Invalidenstrasse crosses the railway line.[30]

In his first testimonies he claimed that they were both lying out-stretched, the moonlight on their faces. Stopping for a moment he saw they were both dead, but Soviet fire prevented further inspection. Even so there were no obvious wounds, no signs of a shattering explosion. He assumed they had been shot in the back.

In his 1970s testimonies to the journalist James P. O'Donnell, he declared:

> We now came across the bodies of Martin Bormann and Dr Stumpfegger, lying very close together. I leaned over and could see the moonlight playing on their faces. There was no visible sign that they had been shot or struck by shellfire. At first, they looked like men who were unconscious or asleep. But they were not breathing. I assumed then, and am sure today, that both men had taken poison. Weltzin and I did not bother to take pulses. We were in danger and hardly interested in historical moments. We continued eastward. The dawn did not break until about half an hour later, after we had arrived in Berlin-Wedding [a couple of kilometres further on].[31]

O'Donnell claimed that Axmann had said that he had found the bodies before 3 a.m., and this is verified by multiple Axmann accounts that have subsequently surfaced, all placing the event at between 1.30 and 2 a.m.

The tank battle and explosion at the Weidendamm Bridge took place, according to many testimonies, at about 2.30 a.m.!

At the time Axmann claimed to have seen Bormann and Stumpfegger, he ought to have been on the Schiffbauerdamm, making his way on to the railway embankment, so there is an obvious time discrepancy in his overall account. It may be worth examining the relevance of the time discrepancy between Baur's testimony and that of Axmann, which is of the order of some two to three hours. In fact if Baur's testimony is to be credited, then Axmann found the dead bodies of Bormann and Stumpfegger long *before they had been killed*.

So why did Baur change his testimony – after over a decade and after multiple conversations with his Nazi colleagues – and yet change it to such seeming lack of effect?

The answer may be that, by the time that Baur gave his revised version, Axmann had already been disbelieved – partly because of his recall of the timing of events, which everyone acknowledged must be faulty (even though nobody knew why it should be, considering that it had been given so comparatively soon after the event). For Baur's second testimony to be in any way credible – especially since it completely contradicted his first testimony – it could not be seen entirely to corroborate Axmann's already dubious timing.

If believed at all, Baur's new testimony could only hope to add credence to Baur, Axmann and Bormann's journey along the railway having actually taken place. Are we to believe that *this* was the reason for Baur's sudden recall?

The other major difficulty in believing Axmann's testimony to be true was his siting of the bodies of Bormann and Stumpfegger, and, less importantly, why such an ardent Nazi as Axmann, who knew that Bormann was carrying the last testament of the Führer and other important documents that were to go to Dönitz, did not remove these documents rather than let them fall into Soviet hands.

The siting of the bodies, as we shall later see, was to become all-important in the 1970s – more than two decades after Axmann's testimony to Hugh Trevor-Roper – so it is of value at this point to consider a few anomalies about this siting. To do so is rendered more difficult by the determination of historians to claim that they were right all along. This 'rectification by retrospectoscope' applies in its acute form to the Invalidenstrasse railway bridge. Historians and investigative writers had first pointed out that if the bodies of Stumpfegger and Bormann were to have been spread-eagled on their backs by the bridge they would surely have been seen by the other escapees known to have taken that route and passed that point – yet there were no corroborative testimonies.

Several authors have tried to overcome this problem by ingenuously inferring that Axmann meant the subway station 400 m to the north of the main railway station and not the main station itself. Others had tried to make out that Axmann saw the bodies on the railway line *below* the Lehrter Bridge, leaning over the parapet so as to get a better view. This would have made it difficult for him even to contemplate taking their pulses, and doesn't fit with his actual testimony, which has in the main remained exemplary in its consistency.

In evaluating Axmann's testimony I don't find the time discrepancy worrying: individuals vary immensely in their estimation of time. Nor do I find the lack of corroborative testimony worrying, in what was obviously a battle situation. I would accept Axmann's testimony at its face value – the testimony of a dedicated Nazi who might or might not have been telling the truth. Nor do I find the alteration in his testimony relating to the mode of supposed death – a change from a presumption of Bormann and Stumpfegger having been shot in the back, to a presumption of suicide, to a later absolute certainty that they had taken cyanide – to be any more than a natural human tendency to round off the edges of an otherwise good story. What interests me more is the need for a rational, intelligent man such as Baur – a professional pilot – to stick his neck out and face ridicule by changing his story so radically.

There was, however, a *need* to have corroborative testimony backing up Axmann's version. For on 17 February 1953 SS major Joachim Tibertius wrote in the Berne newspaper *Der Bund*:

> After the explosion I lost sight of Bormann, but caught up with him at the Hotel Atlas. He had by then changed into civilian clothes. We pushed on together to the Schiffbauerdamm and Albrechtstrasse. There I finally lost sight of him, but he had as good a chance to escape as I did.

Bormann's dress was an issue which remains a constant problem, for he was variously described by the chief witnesses as wearing a full SS Obergruppenführer uniform, a brown Nazi Party uniform without insignia, or a field-grey uniform. Very obviously Tibertius's testimony casts severe doubt on Axmann's solitary version, for the route that Tibertius and Bormann allegedly took was exactly the same route taken by the majority of escapees – that taken by Mohnke's own party – and from the timing of his description Tibertius and Bormann were only twenty minutes or less behind Mohnke's Group 1.

This leaves us with a quandary, which, as we shall see, increases with the passing of time. For if Tibertius is telling the truth then Baur is lying – a fact entirely in keeping with his change of testimony. More importantly, Tibertius's testimony means that Axmann's testimony is possibly untrue. Axmann had himself allegedly got away and hidden in his girlfriend's house in Wedding; his testimony, true or false, lies like a pall of smoke over the scene now set: the backdrop for the discovery of the alleged bodies of Bormann and Stumpfegger, and one of the most important forensic identifications in history.

11

Aftermath – Intrigue and Disinformation

The world's fascination with the fate of Martin Bormann continued long after the war, fed by public interest in the activities of the Nazi-hunters. The myths of the Bunker trailed across Europe and settled over the New World. A bizarre combination of disinformation and fantasy continued for almost five decades.

The Soviet historian Lev Bezymenski has claimed that a week before Hitler killed himself Bormann sent a cable to Dr Helmut von Hummel, his economic adviser, saying 'I agree to the proposed southward overseas-shipment . . . Bormann.'[1]

The letters that Bormann wrote to his wife on 5 April 1945 confirm that he was using von Hummel, head of Group IIIb of the Department of Economic and Social Affairs, to arrange safe passage for his wife, and a further order on 24 April 1945 finalised preparations for two huts on the east side of the high Goell und Öfneralm, near Berchtesgaden, to be stocked with provisions for those in flight. In a final telephone call to his wife, made on 29 April, Bormann is alleged to have told her to put herself in von Hummel's care: he would contact her as soon as possible.

Bezymenski was quoting from Soviet archive material, photostat copies of which were made available. These gave details of the Soviets' belief that the cable to von Hummel was evidence of Bormann's intent to escape to South America. Bezymenski also gave his opinion that Bormann had crossed into Italy on 16 August 1947, this opinion also being tantalisingly based on Soviet archive material, reflecting the Soviets' continued search for Bormann. No details were given to substantiate these claims.[2]

Bezymenski tried to interview von Hummel, who refused to cooperate, later insisting, however, that the word *Südverlangerung*, or southward-shipment, was often used in reference to shipments of documents

212

transferred to Munich. The term 'overseas' was apparently no more than a reference to Übersee/Straubing, a transit station on the Munich–Salzburg railway line.

The US Army Counter Intelligence Corps was to arrange for Gerda Bormann, Bormann's wife, who was suffering from terminal cancer, to be cocooned by its agents. Living as Frau Bergmann, with full false documentation, she was referred by her Italian doctor to a British Major Adlam, who arranged for her admission for terminal care as a cancer sufferer to a hospital in Merano. The Americans were acting on the mistaken belief that Bormann might return. She died on 22 March 1946. Her husband had not appeared.

First Reports of Bormann

The most important first witness to Bormann's continued existence was a Heinrich Leinau, who insisted that in June 1945 he had travelled with Bormann on a train to Flensburg, by the border with Denmark, having just been released from Sachsenhausen concentration camp. And, according to the author Ladislas Farago, a Danish physician called Preuss claimed that at about that time he was asked for money by a Nazi friend to enable him to help get Bormann out of Denmark.

The Soviets then let it be known that in May 1945 an officer of the 5th Shock Army had found Bormann's diary in the leather coat of a dead German, lying next to a tank that had been disabled. Since neither the coat nor the corpse had been Bormann's, the Soviets had assumed that Bormann had stuffed the diary into a dead man's coat in order to become one of the *Scheintot*, or seeming dead, a fair number of whom existed at the time.

Some thirty years later, to explain away this Soviet claim, *Stern* magazine found two German witnesses who claimed that a French labourer had found a leather coat, and that the diary had not been in the coat at all but was found – in waxed paper! – under the corpse of Martin Bormann on the Lehrter Bridge. The corpse had been attired in woollen pants and vest. They couldn't satisfactorily explain how they knew this interesting, if somewhat belated fact, nor why the French worker, Maurice Lachoux, when eventually tracked down by *Stern*, knew nothing about the alleged incident. Either *Stern* was inadvertently helping in a deliberate disinformation exercise or we must envisage the somewhat ridiculous picture of a corpse in his underpants lying on his waxed-paper-covered diary!

A Frau Thalheimer, the wife of a Munich physician who had regularly treated Bormann in the past, was to claim that in September 1945 she had bumped into him, dressed in leather shorts and shirt, in the Via Leonardo da Vinci in Merano. (This put Bormann in Italy two years before the Soviets subsequently claimed.) Ladislas Farago claimed that Frau Thalheimer was so convincing that Judge Horst von Glassenapp, who was collating data on the Bormann case, received a deposition from Hugh Trevor-Roper stating that he was now disinclined to believe Axmann's story about the death of Bormann at the Lehrter Bridge.

In February 1952 a German journalist Herr Stern, a known neo-Nazi, started a rumour that Bormann was living in Italy. He published a photo of a 'Brother Martino', a thickset individual who looked vaguely similar to Bormann. The story was interesting not in its content – for the fakery was self-evident – but for the reason behind his so-called revelation. Either it was an attempt to gain financial advantage from the gullible – an attempt which failed – or it was the first and most obvious case of disinformation.[3]

In 1960 another 'Bormann' was arrested in Zárate, some 100 km north-west of Buenos Aires, allegedly living under the name of Walter Flegel. A West German Embassy official told Reuters, 'We have Martin Bormann's fingerprints at our office and they are at the disposal of the Argentinian police.'[4] Another newspaper confirmed that there had actually been an urgent request for these fingerprints from the German police headquarters at Wiesbaden, which was allegedly taking the story seriously.[5]

This was to prove yet another fake – yet another deliberate instance of disinformation. The farcical nature of the obviously false revelation and the seriousness with which it had allegedly been taken by the authorities were evidence of both active deception and press promotion. The story arose soon after Adolf Eichmann, the organiser of the Nazi extermination programme, had been abducted from Argentina. Professor Tudaj Friedmann, leader of the organisation that abducted Eichmann, had claimed that he had a long dossier on Bormann and was certain he was alive. Speaking in Haifa while the world awaited the results of the ludicrous identification procedure that was being enacted in Buenos Aires, Friedmann – well aware of the bogus nature of the revelation – determinedly asserted, 'We will eventually get him.'[6]

In May 1961 Dr Gregorio Topolowsky, a former Argentinian ambassador in Israel, held a press conference. In what was to prove a remarkably prescient interview, he told the assembled journalists that Bormann's presence in Argentina was known to the Argentinian police and that they also knew that Josef Mengele, the former SS doctor at Auschwitz, had at one time been in his country.[7]

Then, while he was in gaol in Israel, Eichmann received the brief message 'MUT. MUT. MARTIN' ('Courage. Courage. Martin'). This was immediately assumed to be from Martin Bormann – an assumption that had no substance in reality, despite the fact that the handwriting was immediately declared to be his.[8]

Eichmann himself now told Captain Avner W. Less, a young Berlin-born Israeli police officer, that Bormann was alive.

On 14 August 1961, during the hundred and fourteenth session of the Eichmann trial in Jerusalem, his German defence attorney, Dr Servatius, reiterated that Eichmann thought Bormann was alive. No one really knew whether Eichmann's sons and Adolf Eichmann himself were trying to divert attention and culpability from Eichmann's role in the Holocaust.

Ladislas Farago had claimed that five tapes of interviews with Eichmann in Argentina – the so-called Sassen tapes – contained evidence about Bormann, and had been deliberately withheld from the trial by Willem Sassen, a former Abwehr (Nazi counter-intelligence) officer, who had recorded them. This claim was hardly helped by the refusal of Sassen to become further involved.

The revelations continued. Nicholas Eichmann, the twenty-five-year-old son of Adolf Eichmann, had also said that Bormann was alive and that 'He is not as poor as my father was. Not even the Jews with millions of dollars can get him.'[9]

In an investigative article in the *Daily Sketch*,[10] Comer Clark alleged that the Israeli secret service had told him that Bormann had fled from Spain in 1948 on a Spanish passport in the name of José Possea, and had continued to evade Israeli agents who tracked him from Argentina into Brazil in 1952. He claimed that two Israeli agents had made plans to kidnap Bormann from the east-coast seaport of Salvador, but that Bormann thwarted them in 1958 by entering a clinic and dying of cancer in only a few months. The grave was allegedly to be found near the Andean town of Bariloche, in a suitably quiet spot 10 km outside the town. No proof whatsoever was given for this claim.

Not to be outdone a Spaniard, Angel Alcazar de Velasco, alleged that he had organised Bormann's escape to Switzerland after the war had ended.

Despite all the continued 'revelations', and some ridiculously stage-managed disinformation, the Israeli team led by Tudaj Friedmann continued to hunt Bormann relentlessly.

The discovery of Dr Werner Heyde – an SS doctor wanted for crimes against humanity: the killing of thousands of Jews – led eventually to his trial. Before the trial, Dr Fritz Bauer, the Frankfurt state prosecutor, interviewed Heyde at length. This resulted in an 11 February 1964 Reuters press statement by chief prosecutor Metzner:

> Despite allegations to the contrary, including the testimony of Hans Baur [Hitler's pilot], the office of the Attorney General of the State of Hesse continues to pursue its search for Martin Bormann in the factual belief that the head of the NSDAP survived.
>
> The office of the Attorney General in Frankfurt is satisfied that in the meanwhile it has come into possession of information that tends to prove that Bormann was spared and got away with his life.

Events were to catch up with Heyde: two days later he was found hanging in his cell, while a fellow informant, Friedrich Tillmann, fell to his death from an eighth-floor office.

The story that Heyde and Tillmann had told Bauer turned out to be that Bormann had been hidden by Heyde in the SS hospital at Graasten, not far from the Danish town of Sønderborg. Once again it was impossible to determine whether Heyde and Tillmann were telling a tale to save themselves or were attempting to tell the truth.

Then, later in 1964, the situation was to change dramatically. The East German authorities released statements which revealed that a grave which was claimed to have been that to which Bormann's body had been taken after having been allegedly discovered in Berlin on the Lehrter Bridge had in fact recently been opened as a result of renewed interest in his case. It had been found to be empty, and there was no evidence of any such burial.[11]

On 8 July 1964 Bauer revealed that he had received a statement from an unnamed person in Paraguay to the effect that Bormann was living there. According to the statement, Bormann had been seen on several occasions in Asunción, capital of Paraguay, in the company of Mengele.[12]

By the first week in August the story had firmed up and changed. It was now revealed that in 1959 Bormann had died at the house of a Paraguayan of German origin, a Bernard Jung. He was allegedly buried at Itá, a village some 35 km from Asunción.

A West German journalist, Herbert John, flew to Asunción and motored to Itá to investigate. He found that the only register of burials was kept by the gravedigger himself. John then very unofficially proceeded to dig up grave number G3, identified in the register as belonging to a Juan Hermocilla. He found a toothless skull and some bones lying loosely in wrappings, and decided they probably were Juan Hermocilla's.

Bernard Jung was traced to Spain, where he had surprisingly now suddenly taken residence. He refused either to confirm or to deny that Bormann had died in his house.

The German ambassador belatedly asked for a grave to be reopened. Bauer immediately reacted to this West German government request by claiming that neo-Nazis in South America were deliberately spreading the story of Bormann's death to stop the search for him. A search was nevertheless carried out by his team in conjunction with the magazine *Der Spiegel* and others, who combed the area where Bormann had last been reported seen.[13]

Bauer claimed that a Czech doctor in Paraguay had recently reported treating for cancer a man whom he believed might have been Bormann. West German newspapers reported that another doctor in Asunción had been persuaded to make out a fake death certificate for Bormann, dated two years previously, in order to persuade the authorities to call off the search.[14]

A week later the Paraguayan authorities had shown little enthusiasm for complying with the West German requests. Bauer issued another statement, saying that he thought that the grave that had been 'thought possibly might contain Bormann's remains' was more than likely to contain the bones of some old Indian.[15]

Indeed the Itá grave which had been alleged to have contained the remains of Martin Bormann – who by that time was definitely supposed to have died on 15 February 1959 – was duly found to contain the remains of an Indian, Juan Emillo Hermocilla, as the local villagers had insisted all along!

Bauer now upped the reward on Bormann to the equivalent of £9,000.

In the spring of 1963, Eichmann's son Dieter had been arrested for involvement in a disturbance in Argentina, and the arrest had prompted him to state that Bormann was alive. This gave the police the chance to search Eichmann's house on Calle Garibaldi in Buenos Aires. The search allegedly produced three letters from Bormann to Eichmann dated 7 March 1952, 12 January 1957 and 3 March 1957.[16] On 3 January 1965 another son, Klaus Eichmann, insisted that he too knew Bormann was alive 'for sure'.[17] There remained, however, an unfortunate paucity of facts.

Then, in May 1965, Bormann's sons declared they thought he was dead.[18] This was a strange statement for them to make considering that officially there had been no communication at all between Bormann and his family.

In 1967 the world was shocked to learn that the mass murderer Franz Paul Stangl, responsible for the death of 700,000 Jews, had been arrested in São Paulo ready for extradition. (By this time Brazil was becoming more democratic.) On 17 March the court received a mealy-mouthed half-hearted request for his extradition emanating from the district court in Düsseldorf, phrased as though Stangl had been accused of car theft and failure to pay his TV licence. But now the Poles also demanded his extradition, forcing the German government to act. On 22 June *Der Tagesspiegel*, one of Berlin's daily newspapers, was forced to ask whether Bormann had indeed survived, for Stangl had by now admitted that Bormann had been 'one of us' – meaning one of the South American Nazi survivors.

Determined Bormann-hunters had by this time become interested in sightings in Guatemala. A man was arrested and a set of his fingerprints were sent to the Wiesbaden Crime Bureau to see if they matched those of Bormann – or at least so ran a story carried in the *Guardian* in March 1967.[19] The story got no further; the suspect was duly released.

In October of the same year the Nazi-hunter Simon Wiesenthal said that there was evidence that Bormann was living in Paraguay. It was alleged that he had taken out Paraguayan citizenship.[20]

An Italian physician, Dr Pino Frezza, who had on one occasion accompanied Mussolini to Munich and had met Neville Chamberlain, had also known Bormann. He reported to the Italian ambassador in Argentina that he had met Bormann in Buenos Aires, and in due course a copy of his report was forwarded to the Jewish organisations by the Italian government. Readers have to bear in mind that Frezza was a rabid fascist, and that his testimony was probably motivated by self-interest. Nothing came of his claim.

More significant, however, was the discovery of letters belonging to the Nazi professor von Leers, who for years had headed the Abwehr in South America. In one of these letters von Leers informed a friend that Bormann was in South America, and at that time living in Brazil. Because of the very fact that they had been written so many years previously and that their discovery was accidental, they are more important as evidence than the various completely unsubstantiated sightings and rumours.[21]

Later, and quite independently, an Israeli citizen, Wolfgang Lotz, said that von Leers at one time had lived in Cairo under the name of Omar

Amin. Lotz had known his wife, who claimed that Bormann had at one time visited her husband in Egypt.

In 1968 Michael Bar-Zohar, in his book *The Avengers*, claimed to have interviewed an Asunción physician of Austrian nationality, Dr Otto Biss. Biss's story was that, in the spring of 1959, he had been accompanied by a woman, a widow called Casaccia, to the house of a fascist called Werner Jung, after Josef Mengele had failed to diagnose the condition of a mystery guest who was seriously ill. Jung had been the chief of a local fascist youth group in Paraguay. In conjunction with Hans Ulrich Rudel (the most decorated Nazi Luftwaffe air ace, and a personal friend of the Paraguayan dictator Alfredo Stroessner) he had been involved in hiding Mengele in Asunción at that time. Biss's story therefore carries some weight. His actual account was:

I examined the sick man and spoke to him in German, but he wouldn't answer in that language or in any other of the European languages I know. He insisted on speaking in bad Spanish. So I found it rather difficult to get any help from him to establish the nature of his illness. The [other] doctor realised this, and he bent over the sick man and said, 'You may speak German.' And to my great surprise the men then spoke in fluent German.[22]

Biss, who claimed that the man had a scar on his forehead, as Bormann was known to have, went on:

A few days later a friend of mine came to see me in great excitement. He told me he had met the woman who had come to me and that the man I had seen professionally was Martin Bormann. I got hold of some photographs of Hitler's right-hand man at once. There was no possible doubt. The man I had seen was older than the man in the photos but it was the same man all right. He was certainly Martin Bormann.

Dr Biss stuck rigidly to his account, and interviewed in December 1984 at the age of eighty-five he still stoutly maintained that he was correct.[23]

This account of Biss's was given so consistently that several later authors, writing after the official proclamation of Bormann's death in 1973, have sought to find an alternative explanation. The one that has gained favour relates to the account of Werner Jung himself, who claims that it was he himself who was ill and that there never was any mystery guest.

The Farago Reports

Late on the afternoon of 26 November 1972, word spread that the *Daily Express* was taking delivery of a large amount of newsprint for the night's print run. Shortly before midnight the story broke, and Reuters news agency flashed it across the world: Ladislas Farago, a former American secret agent, had run down to earth Hitler's deputy Martin Bormann in Buenos Aires.

Farago claimed that Bormann had arrived in Argentina on 17 May 1948, travelling tourist class on the steamer *Giovanni C.* from Genoa, Italy. He carried a passport from the Vatican Office of Stateless Persons, dated 16 February 1948, and had been registered (No. 073909) with the apostolic nunciature in Buenos Aires, so qualifying himself for issue with an identity card (No. 1.361.642) by the Argentinian federal authorities. Farago alleged that Bormann had travelled as Eliezer Goldstein – by profession a geologist – allegedly born on 20 August 1901 in the Polish town of Piotrków, son of Abraham Goldstein and Maria Esther Sadrinas. The wife of the Argentine president, Eva Perón, had herself arranged his passage, and on arrival Bormann had been met by General Sosa Molina, minister of war in Juan Perón's cabinet. The documents, carrying official-looking blue stamps, looked decidedly genuine. Farago claimed that Bormann had subsequently been helped by Angelo Borlengi, head of the Ministry of the Interior.

By 17 December 1972 the story had changed considerably, and Farago was facing a hostile New York press audience at an occasion attended by Frank Yablans, the president of Paramount Pictures Corporation, the makers of a film that was due to be produced, based on Farago's book. So hostile was the questioning that Yablans had at one stage to intervene – protesting that 'Mr Farago is not on trial.'[24]

The questions were based on a statement made a week earlier by a certain Juan Jose Velasco, a man deemed by Farago to have been a high-ranking intelligence officer and a personal friend of Juan Perón, but who now called himself only a former employee of Perón's and had gone into hiding.

Before doing so, Velasco had given an impromptu interview to Josef Novitski, the Buenos Aires correspondent of the *New York Times*. He made it clear that the documents that he had supplied for Farago were forgeries, although he gave no indication of why he had been prepared to supply these carefully fabricated documents, nor of who had forged them. He furthermore declared that the photographs which had been described as being of himself and Bormann on the Chilean border were in fact taken outside a Buenos Aires café, the Tortini. They were, said Velasco, of himself and a fifty-four-year-old schoolteacher, Nicolas Siri, who, like Bormann, had a scar on his forehead, the result of a childhood fall. He had allegedly been a friend of the thirty-six-year-old Velasco for some twelve years.

Siri, who was thickset and certainly bore some resemblance to Bormann, was however some 10 cm shorter than the Reichsleiter, and indignantly displaying his Argentinian identification card, No. 1.546.417, he threatened to sue anyone who put his life at risk by saying he was Bormann.

His own story is worth relating. He said that a man who identified himself as Israel Zelman Steinberg

> came up to our table and talked to Mr Velasco and me. He said he had an ultra-modern camera and that he was kindly offering to take a few pictures of us. He did not say what kind of pictures, but I imagined that they would be family snapshots.
>
> Steinberg said we would be doing him a great favour because he was trying out the new camera – with its great capacity to take shots with very little light, without a flash. He gave a whole series of technical reasons – to which I agreed.
>
> He took several pictures of me at the table of the Café Tortini with Mr Velasco and then he asked me if we would please go outside by the door, where there was a light. It was dusk, late afternoon. There he took several pictures of me at the door talking with my friend Juan Jose Velasco.[25]

Farago countered these revelations by insisting that the man in the photograph really was Bormann, and that the documents were genuine. He identified the man with the camera as a certain S. L. Sztemberg, an alleged chief of the Intelligence Division of the Buenos Aires police.

In response to enquiries by the *New York Times* and the *Sunday Times*, the Buenos Aires police claimed to know of no such man. Their denials about Velasco's alleged status were, however, regarded by both sets of reporters as being very vague and defensive. According to the chief spokesman for the Argentinian federal police, 'Mr Velasco is not a commissioner nor a subcommissioner, nor a non-commissioned officer of this police force – that is all I have been authorised to say!'[26]

When the fraud became obvious, the *Daily Express* editor, Ian McColl, demanded that Farago return the $5,000 advance that he had been paid. It then turned out that the publishers of his eventual book, *Aftermath*, had also been led to advance a considerable amount of money. Some of the documents that Farago had relied upon as Argentinian files proved to have been forgeries – some of them based on a previous article in a German periodical which had been roughly translated into a genuine-looking Spanish document.

Despite his denials that the documents were forged, and his insistence that, had he been given time and not rushed by the newspaper to meet a deadline, he would have delivered a genuine Martin Bormann, Farago went on to make some further astonishing claims about having met Bormann in a convent high in the Andes:

> When I was in touch with him [Bormann] in February 1973 he had just moved from Chile to Southern Bolivia. A very sick man, he was being cared for by four German nursing sisters of the Redemptionist Order in their convent near Tupiza, a remote region of Potosí Province in the Andes.[27]

Notwithstanding Farago's extraordinary claims about both Bormann and indeed Mengele, whom he also claimed to have discovered, examination of his voluminous files makes it clear that some of his information was extraordinarily good, especially about some of the financial transactions that had been separately investigated by several intelligence agencies and that he had worked on in conjunction with both the CIA and Israeli intelligence.

Unfortunately Farago's custom of making substantial payments to his informers had attracted to him a few officers in the Argentinian secret service, such as Velasco and the unidentified Sztemberg, who may have seen him as a way to a fortune. Another opportunist who took advantage of the extraordinarily naïve former intelligence officer was the German judge Horst von Glassenapp, who kept trying to sell Farago documents he had kept on euthanasia. Despite being somewhat dubious in his dealings with Farago, von Glassenapp did authorise telephone taps on several families in Germany, including the Mengele family, in order to try to assist Farago make a blockbuster film, on both Bormann and Mengele, from which von Glassenapp himself doubtless hoped to profit. The telephone taps proved fruitless.

Whatever genuine and painstakingly gathered information Farago may have possessed, he had undermined its value by combining it with material of very suspect origins. But there were several investigators who felt that there was a distinct pattern to the continued sightings of Martin Bormann, which, in the late 1960s and early 1970s, seemed to occur whenever the search was on for Josef Mengele. They felt that, allowing for the obvious fact that with such botched investigations and such naïvety there was no need to explain away the failures by inventing any active opposition, there was nevertheless evidence of an orchestrated disinformation campaign launched against their activities. They believed that this was under the direct control of that mastermind of such disinformation Frederick Schwend, who, by arranging for ridicule and scorn to be poured on the unsuspecting amateurs, would put off those more professional investigators.

Schwend, a former SS major, had been the brains behind the forging of British banknotes intended to destabilise the British economy. He was now living in Peru, working as a senior engineer at a Volkswagen plant at Lima. Before he had gone to South America, he had worked for the American Counter Intelligence Corps in tracking fugitive Nazis in order to offer them gainful employment. His job allowed him to travel extensively and develop tremendous influence in all South American countries, and several West German journalists – including Herbert John, who lived in Peru and was investigating the former Nazis – considered him to be the leader of a particularly vicious Nazi group, and more especially one of Mengele's protectors.[28]

In February 1971 Schwend had been arrested for alleged involvement in the murder of a wealthy Peruvian. The investigating judge confiscated papers which were later supposedly examined by Ladislas Farago and allegedly found to contain correspondence between Schwend and Bormann, as well as an address book which listed Bormann's address. However, Farago's account of seeing this evidence is highly dramatic and immediately suspect.

There were undoubtedly present in South America several experts that Schwend could rely on, including Willem Sassen, former head of the Abwehr's disinformation unit 'Skorpion'. Sassen had entered South America in 1948, and had quickly become a disciple of Adolf Eichmann. He recorded some sixty-seven tapes of Eichmann exulting in his extermination programme in gross detail, claiming that he would do the same thing over again.

Even Sassen was to flinch at some of Eichmann's boasts. 'I must say I regret nothing,' Eichmann recorded on one tape. 'It would be too early to pretend that I had turned suddenly from a Saul into a Paul. No, I must say, truthfully, that if we had killed all 10 million Jews that Himmler's statistician [Dr Richard Korherr] had listed in 1933, I would say, "Good, we have destroyed an enemy." '[29]

Sassen was later to sell these Eichmann tapes to the Americans and to become an Israeli intelligence agent, for a fee of $5,000 a month!

However, before Sassen's 1962 conversion – which was based not just on financial gain but equally on fear of assassination – the Israelis were convinced that he had been assisting Mengele and Bormann, though he claimed not to know Bormann's whereabouts. They realised he had been a key figure, giving public-relations advice to Presidents Pinochet of Chile and Stroessner of Paraguay. He was to repay their 'trust' by correctly identifying as Mengele's protector one Wolfgang Gerhard, editor of *Der Reichsbrief*, a fascist newsletter. Bormann's trail had, by comparison, gone totally cold.

Beate Klarsfeld, a Nazi-hunter later famous for her discovery of Klaus Barbie, the 'Butcher of Lyons', was to claim that she knew of a photograph taken of Schwend and Bormann together in South America.[30]

She at least – new in the field – hadn't lost her enthusiasm. But the adverse publicity of attempts such as the Farago fiasco was certain to diminish Israeli interest and to reduce the money available for the quite expensive search, which involved keeping a number of agents permanently based in each South American country. Israeli intelligence investigators today bemoan the opportunities for capturing a live Mengele that were lost purely because the enthusiasm waned. 'It was just a question of time,' said one such agent. 'If we had one more year, we'd have got him. Just one more year and we'd have had him back in Israel, and he would have hanged.'[31]

These same investigators remain convinced that much of the false evidence for Bormann's existence came from an organisation trying at first to rubbish the concept of a live Bormann or a live Mengele or both.

We now know far more about the Mengele family's involvement with Josef Mengele and his exile. Many family and other letters show the extensive but quite expected lengths to which the family covered up their contact with Josef Mengele. These letters, and other evidence discovered later, also reveal the extent of the disinformation orchestrated by his Nazi protectors in South America.

There is now also evidence of the extent to which Nazis within the West German foreign service collaborated with Mengele. For example, the West German embassy in Buenos Aires issued Mengele with a work certificate, enabling him to apply for a passport. Mengele admitted to embassy staff that he had been living under an alias of 'Helmut Gregor' for seven years, but that he was really Josef Mengele. He gave his correct date of birth, the date of his divorce from his first wife, and his addresses in Buenos Aires and in Günzburg in Germany. They duly advised him to apply for an Argentinian identity card and return for his passport. Whereupon he went to the Argentinian federal police, admitted that he had given totally false information upon his entry into Argentina, and was promptly issued with a new identity card – No. 3.940.484. Mengele returned to the West German embassy, where he was ushered into the office and emerged with a brand-new West German passport – No. 3.415.574.[32] All he had forgotten was to get his passport stamped with the words 'War Criminal'!

One explanation of this oversight might be that the West German ambassador at the time was Werner Junkers, a former aide to Ribbentrop and an active Nazi. Even more significantly, he had been Ribbentrop's special envoy to Yugoslavia, where the Ustache forces outdid even the SS in barbarity. Interviewed at the age of eighty-five, Junkers couldn't remember who Mengele was![33]

This should give some idea what the Nazi-hunters were up against in Buenos Aires. In Paraguay and Chile their difficulties were far greater.

We can summarise by stating that there was no factual evidence that Bormann existed after the war. The circumstantial evidence that existed up until 1972 was scant, and mostly of low calibre. The only circumstantial evidence of any measurable value points to Paraguay rather than Argentinia, Chile or Brazil.

Ladislas Farago highlighted some financial transactions which were already known about, and it is these transactions, which had indeed been initiated by Bormann, that now need examination. For they give due cause to suspect that Bormann would have gone to Argentina in the first instance, and also point to very cogent reasons for his leaving the country. Farago's investigation of financial transactions was far more soundly based than other aspects of his claims.

By the start of the war, Nazi feelings had run so high among German immigrants to Argentina that a commission was set up to report on the threat to the Argentine state itself. On 28 November 1941 the Investigating Commission on Anti-Argentine Activities had reported that thousands of German immigrants were 'controlled by the German Reich', and that many received direct financial aid from Nazi Germany.[34] During the early years in power of the fascist supporter Juan Perón, there were over 1,500 Abwehr agents and informers in Argentina.[35]

Perón set aside some 10,000 blank Argentine passports for fugitive Nazis. He also dispatched a personal agent, Carlos Piñeyro, to Copenhagen as a member of the Argentinian Legation, to organise the escape of Nazis to Argentina via the 'Flensburg Escape Hatch'. In November 1945 the Danes expelled him for using his diplomatic status to smuggle Nazis out of Denmark.[36]

Perón helped the Nazis in return for an immense investment in his own country. Reichsbank records showed the extent of only one such transfer. In Aktion Feuerland ('Operation Scorched Earth'), 100 kg of platinum, 16 tonnes of gold, 4,638 carats of diamonds as well as millions of gold marks, dollars, pounds sterling and Swiss francs were sent, along with hundreds of works of art, on six German U-boats to the safe hands of four German trustees in Argentina. These four representatives turned all the booty into currency and gold, then deposited it in vaults in the Banco Germánico and Banco Tonquist. All deposits were made in the name of Perón and his future wife, Eva Duarte. Bormann was said to have been involved in later transfers to Eva's account, via a Ludwig Freude.[37]

It is worth examining the fate of the four trustees who stood between Eva and the money.[38] Ludwig Freude, the first trustee, was a well-known German-Argentinian banker with close Nazi ties. After the money had been deposited, he was investigated on a number of charges, then suddenly, on 6 September 1946, the investigation stopped. It was announced that this had been done by presidential decree.

Although Freude had obviously given in to whatever threat was being instituted, it was not to prove enough. In 1952 he was found slumped over his breakfast table: he had drunk poisoned coffee.

Ricardo Staudt – a prominent businessman, who had ranked second in the Americans' listing of Nazis in South America – was the second trustee. He died in a hit-and-run accident, just after Ricardo von Leute, an officer of Banco Alemán Transatlántico, the third trustee, had been found murdered in Buenos Aires in 1950.

The fourth trustee was Dr Heinrich Dorge, a former aide to Hjalmar Schacht, the Nazis' financial wizard. He had arrived in Argentina in the

1930s, and knew full well the Peróns' ruthlessness, yet he was to die in 1949, his body dumped in a Buenos Aires street.

Had Bormann entered Argentina after the war, then, given his large investment in Eva Perón, he would certainly have realised that the climate was none too healthy, and that there were more bracing financial rewards available elsewhere – in Brazil for example. (When Albert Blume, the alleged treasurer of Odessa, the support organisation for former SS men, died in Brazil in 1983 he left an amassed fortune of £39 million.) Bormann, like Mengele, would probably have found that there was no barrier to moving freely to other states and obtaining citizenship. Especially welcoming was Paraguay. It would most likely have been the influential architect Frederico Haase who would have initiated the arrangements, as he did for several others. His wife was the daughter of Paraguay's finance minister under President Stroessner.

The Argentine Revelations

As far as Argentina was concerned, there had for some time been relative silence about the fate of Martin Bormann when on 2 February 1992 the Buenos Aires newspaper *Clarin* jumped the gun on the Argentine release of state documents relating to several well-known Nazis.

At midday on 1 February 1992, President Carlos Menem and the interior minister J. L. Manzano presided over a meeting which authorised the release for the first time of the Bormann file.

It seemed that the Argentinians considered Bormann to be the most important of all the Nazis. A file had allegedly been opened on him in 1948, and between then and the late 1950s dozens of allegations had been received by the Argentine government concerning his presence in their country. At the request of the USA, a somewhat tongue-in-cheek warrant for his arrest had been put out in 1949.

The files contained details that the Argentine government had received from the West German government and from Interpol. These included Bormann's physical details and copies of his fingerprints. Under continued pressure from the USA, the Argentinians had even bugged the West German embassy.

The files suggest a remarkably lax attitude to following up the various leads, and give an overall impression of either deliberate uninterest or apathy. In folio 28 of the Bormann dossier in the Argentinian archives, reference is made to the fact that 'The secret book of the DAE for 1960 has been destroyed, and for this reason we cannot establish the content of number 3163.'

In folio 49 of the same record we read:

The government office books utilised in this record have been collated, and no file with such a number concerning Bormann has been identified. It seems certain that because the said books were stored in the depository assigned to them, which on several occasions was inundated with water as a result of plumbing breakdowns, the books pertaining to 1957–60 and 1960–67, were destroyed. Thus we do not know whether they contained information on the suspects concerned.

In summary, the files of the 1948–67 period are almost non-existent. The archives have suffered from that scourge of intelligence-file longevity: flooding!

The extent to which the files may have been removed by 'enthusiasts' was acknowledged by President Menem when, his hands resting on a file on Josef Mengele, he declared that Argentina was repaying a debt to humanity by releasing the files. He then signed a decree ordering all agencies to search their files for similar documents, and to return them within thirty days to the national archives (from which they would previously more likely have strayed to the incinerator than the provinces).[39]

The thirty days produced no new revelations about Bormann.

Examination of the archives released in 1992 reveals some interesting facts which reflect on Argentinian uncertainty at the highest level, and throw a new light on the Ladislas Farago affair.

According to the files, in December 1972 the attention of the Foreign Affairs section of the federal government had been drawn to one of its own personnel: the intelligence adviser to the A team, a senior position close to the presidency. He was denoted by a file 707 JJV.

This was none other than the same Juan Jose Velasco whom Farago had at least correctly identified, who had claimed he was retired and of whose identity as a secret agent the Argentine police had officially been entirely unaware.

The reason why Velasco had been investigated also proves interesting reading. It was for 'allegedly passing information on Bormann to a team of journalists from the British *Daily News*'.

Velasco was to remain in position until the last day of Argentina's military regime in 1973, when he was retired by the new president. A hurt Velasco claimed he was never told why.

The Foreign Affairs section was also to try to locate and investigate two others, besides Velasco. Once again these activities are even now of interest. The first man was known as ED, a man who apparently had the identity-card number 1.361.642 – the number that, according to the Farago story, the fake Bormann had carried. The other man they sought was EG, or Eliezer Goldstein, the identity supposedly used by Bormann.

Records of other activities of the Foreign Affairs section that the Farago documents mentioned had apparently disappeared in 1972, forcing the police to admit in 1992 that these particular files were still inexplicably incomplete.

Certain conclusions may reasonably, even if incorrectly, be drawn.

The first must be that in 1972 Velasco had been lying, and that he was being protected at a high level – the protection lasting at least as long as the regime.

We don't know why he was lying, nor for whom he was lying, nor the exact extent of his lies. But we do know that he was involved in giving Ladislas Farago some false documentation that fooled an experienced investigator completely. Velasco was also involved in giving Farago photographs of his Bormann look-alike contact Nicolas Siri, and was thus also instrumental in this deceit. It is unlikely that a high-ranking intelligence officer of thirty-six would have been friends for twelve years with a fifty-four-year-old schoolteacher. It is far more likely that Siri's potential as a Bormann double was recognised and he was then persuaded to participate in the otherwise somewhat unbelievable story of the photographic session at the café.

The second conclusion is that it is quite likely that Farago was taken in by Velasco and 'Sztemberg', working in concert. What we once again don't know is whether the high-level protection afforded certainly Velasco and probably Sztemberg was in spite of or because of their actions. In the case of Velasco, the protection was of sufficient strength to be proof against the findings of the Foreign Affairs section's own later investigation.

The third possibly justified conclusion relates to the concern of this Foreign Affairs section about the sanctity of its own records and the nature of those records. It had established the loss in 1972 of files and documents whose contents and veracity seemed to relate sufficiently accurately to the alleged forgeries as to warrant further investigation of the owners (ED and EG) of the actual identity number and pseudonym referred to by Farago. This loss may have been detected by means of cross-references or by an archivist's or agent's memory. The conclusion that can possibly be drawn is that some of the documentation or information that went missing at that time was indeed pertinent.

We know that some of the documentary evidence produced by Farago was a Spanish translation of a previous *Der Spiegel* article, made to look official by the liberal use of stamps. But the best way to fool an intelligence officer used to looking at Abwehr papers and the like is to include some genuine material with the fake. The end result is the rubbishing not only of the author but of the genuine material itself.

To summarise, the 1992 Buenos Aires revelations show that Ladislas Farago was set up quite deliberately, either as part of a disinformation exercise or purely as part of a clever scam by Argentinian intelligence agents, but that some of the information he was given may indeed have been genuine – as is evidenced by the subsequent actions of the Argentinian Foreign Affairs section.

The files reveal that the last action of the Argentinian police on the Bormann issue came on 28 August 1990, when, in a clean-up operation, they referred the file to Interpol with details of all the previous actions that they had undertaken. The referral was made some seventeen years after the West German government had declared Bormann officially dead – a fact of which the Argentines were fully aware. The question that must therefore be asked is: why did the police in the 1990s bother to forward their files in this manner? This question has still to be resolved.

The Bormann file ends at this point by saying, 'As suggested by all previous proceedings, until this moment there is no information which permits us to establish with any certainty that B [Bormann] has ever entered our country, and/or can be found resident here, nor, likewise that he is even still alive.'

This is an interesting statement, given the 1973 West German proclamation of Bormann's death. It is worth returning to examine the basis for this proclamation – a proclamation based, it was claimed, on clear-cut forensic proof.

12

Digging up the Past

In the whole of the Bormann saga the name of Jochen von Lang looms in the background, for his dedication to proving that Bormann had died in Berlin in 1945 was eventually to pose more questions than it answered.

The Search for Evidence

In 1945 von Lang was a young man of barely twenty, serving with the Hitler Youth in Berlin, subordinate to Axmann, the Hitler Youth leader, himself. His duties placed him in the escape party behind his leader. Axmann's was the sole 'credible' testimony relied upon by historians in the West before the return of the other Bunker personnel from Soviet captivity. Axmann's testimony was that in May 1945 he had seen Bormann's body alongside that of the SS surgeon Dr Ludwig Stumpfegger on the approach to the Lehrter Bridge, while himself attempting to escape.

On 11 September 1962, prompted by von Lang, Axmann gave evidence to Joachim Richter, a young lawyer working in the office of Dr Fritz Bauer, the Frankfurt state prosecutor. This step might have been made necessary because of the evidence of others interviewed by Hugh Trevor-Roper – evidence which at that juncture had caused Trevor-Roper to change his opinion about Bormann's likely demise and which suggested that Axmann had retracted his previous testimony. In his 1971 deposition to Judge Horst von Glassenapp, who was collating accounts of the Bormann affair, a footnote was added to Trevor-Roper's first footnote of 1947: 'I heard that Axmann [later] . . . retracted his testimony. I do not rule out the possibility that he had made up the story in the first place to cover Bormann's tracks.'[1]

But what of the fate of Dr Stumpfegger, the man allegedly found dead next to Bormann? On 14 August 1945 a letter was written to Stumpfegger's wife, Gertrud, at a sanatorium in Hohenlychen. It was signed by a man calling himself Berndt, who identified himself as postmaster at the Lehrter station. It read:

On May 8th this year a soldier was found by employees of this post office on the railroad bridge crossing Invalidenstrasse . . . A military pass in his pocket identified him as Ludwig Stumpfegger. Assuming that the dead man was your husband I am conveying the sad news to you with the expression of my condolence.

Your husband was buried, together with other dead soldiers in the grounds of the Alpendorf in Berlin NW40 at 63 Invalidenstrasse. I am enclosing herewith a number of photographs found on the deceased. His military pass was subsequently destroyed.[2]

This letter was immediately put forward by the Stumpfegger family as proof of his death. A copy was sent to Bauer's office in Frankfurt. It seems that no one ever attempted to trace the mysterious Berndt, even though the records of postmasters in Berlin ought not to have been difficult to find.

This remarkable letter made no mention of Bormann's corpse, which, according to Axmann's testimony, ought to have been lying alongside Stumpfegger's. No equivalent letter was sent to the Bormann family. It must be assumed that, had Bormann's corpse indeed been found alongside Stumpfegger's, then it would have been treated in the same way and buried at the same site.

In 1964 the German magazine *Der Spiegel* made an investigation which resulted in an article on 14 February of that year. 'In actual fact,' went its report, 'the corpse of Stumpfegger *was* found. But of Bormann, who was said to have been lying alongside, there was no trace.'

But then in May 1965, when von Lang was conducting a crusade to prove Bormann's death, a man named Herbert Seidel, a man who is now admitted to have been a member of the Hitler Youth, known to von Lang, told him that in May 1945, at the age of fourteen, when he was foraging for food in the freight yard of the Lehrter station with a friend, he had seen 'two dead bodies' on the left side of the railway bridge. Even though the 'young boy' admitted that there were many dead bodies around in the area and that he had not known Bormann, von Lang thought this was a crucial piece of evidence.[3]

Even before the appearance of Seidel, a Czech named Jaroslav Dedic, who claimed to have been a slave worker in Germany in 1945, wrote a letter to the Prague newspaper *Zemedelske Noviny* claiming that he had directed a burial squad for the Soviets. One of the bodies he had interred was recognised by the foreign workers as being that of Martin Bormann. How they knew it was Bormann when, as Seidel himself pointed out, 'Bormann was totally unknown to the German public' was never explained. Dedic did, however, claim that the body had been found some distance from Invalidenstrasse and had been buried in a cemetery in East Berlin.

The last of von Lang's witnesses was to claim a surprising link with the alleged postmaster Berndt. Albert Krumnov was a fast-talking Berliner of seventy, an invalid with an extraordinary memory. He claimed to have been one of the mailmen in the burial squad that 'Postmaster Berndt' had mentioned in his 1945 letter to Stumpfegger's wife.

He and two of his colleagues, Wagenpfuhl and Loose, had been in the detail ordered to bury the bodies lying around the Lehrter station. Wagenpfuhl buried Stumpfegger and Krumnov buried the other man, whom they had not recognised but – with the benefit of tutored hindsight – now thought 'might have been Bormann'. Amazingly, the taller man (Stumpfegger) was allegedly dressed only in new white underwear, while the shorter (Bormann) was wearing a grey Army uniform without insignia of rank.

Neither Wagenpfuhl or Loose could be found or identified as having been a postworker, but Krumnov was to show even more useful recall. He claimed that these two bodies had been buried well apart from the other dead – failing, however, to explain why this should be so. Furthermore, he was to claim that the burial site of these two bodies had been noted exactly. Krumnov claimed he had buried the shorter corpse (which at that time he had not recognised) beneath a little grove – a square of silver poplars which he chose as a landmark by which to recall the exact spot later!

Von Lang did not think to question the extraordinary prescience shown by this young postman, who would have attended to over twenty corpses that day if part of a burial detachment. Such work, especially dealing with six-day-old corpses, had a numbing effect on even the least impressionable, who quickly became inured to their task, not customarily finding the need for such creative self-expression as the recording of individual grave sites.

Von Lang's enthusiasm for proving Bormann's death infected Richter, who in turn persuaded Bauer to attempt exhumation of Bormann's corpse. There were many difficulties to be overcome before this could be attempted, not the least of which was that in 1961 the Berlin Wall had been built across the very area where Bormann might have been buried.

In May 1945 the area had largely been reduced to rubble, but the essential topography remained. If Bormann had been interred in the cemetery to the east of Invalidenstrasse as Dedic claimed, then the dig needed the agreement of the East German authorities. Meanwhile Bauer's attention focused on that small part of West Berlin in which Axmann, Seidel and Krumnov now showed Bauer the exact points where they claimed that they had last seen the suspected corpses of Stumpfegger and Bormann and where Krumnov claimed the burial had taken place.

The records of the so-called Ulap Fairground, where the bodies had been claimed to have been buried, were carefully examined for any evidence of official burials. This proved negative and seemingly satisfied von Lang, but it is probably unnecessary to remind the reader that not all activities in West Germany were necessarily official!

By this time a certain Horst Schultz from Berlin, who had been contacted by *Stern* magazine, was already on record as having insisted that the corpse of Dr Stumpfegger had indeed been found, but had been buried in the cemetery for military personnel killed in action, at Berlin 21, Wilsnackerstrasse.

Von Lang's reaction to this claim is interesting. Rather than attempting to identify Stumpfegger by exhumation of his alleged grave, he asked for records of *transfer* to this war cemetery from the Ulap Fairground, and also asked a funeral company, Schroedter, for any additional records of transfer. It thus seemed that von Lang had already determined that the vague testimonies of the witness Krumnov were more reliable than the more definite testimony of Horst Schultz. Had he been serious, he would surely have first excluded the records of original burials.

On 19 July 1965, Senior Procurator William Metzner and Procurator Joachim Richter, accompanied by von Lang and Krumnov, looked for Krumnov's silver poplars. Only two poplars still stood in the entire area, but the well-kept park records showed the exact spot where three poplars, as described by Krumnov, had existed. Next morning a spectacular procession was led by a bulldozer and the shirt-clad Richter, who had had archaeological training, with some experience of digging for mummies in

Egypt. As the sultry summer day began, a whole entourage of policemen, reporters and curious Berliners watched as the bulldozers tore a crater in the spot where the bodies had allegedly been buried. The large contingent from *Stern* magazine was led by von Lang, who had reserved pages of the magazine for a sensational spread. Workers went through the loose sand sifting for the merest trace of bone, but the whole day's work yielded nothing.

A *Times* article by Neal Ascherson was scathing:

> On the wasteland beside the railway arches a blue police bulldozer rolls slowly back and forth. It roars and groans, and after each little charge brings up another hundredweight of yellow Prussian sand. Six or seven policemen in overalls shelter from the rain under two trees and lean on shovels. They are looking for the bones of Martin Bormann. Nothing has been found. Under a layer of ash the sand seems firm and undisturbed.[4]

Von Lang now pleaded that he himself be allowed to rent a bulldozer to dig up the whole of the Ulap Fairground site and not just the by now fully excavated sites that had exhausted the stories and recall of his witnesses. He was dispiritedly to claim that 'Even if the bones had been discovered it would have been extremely difficult to identify them.'[5]

Charles Whiting wrote, 'The great *Stern* hunt for the missing Reichsleiter fizzled out ignominiously. Lang's personal hunt for Martin Bormann, which started so long ago in those desperate days in May 1945, is over.'[6]

But Whiting had spoken too soon, for on 7 December 1972, a few days after the publication in the *Daily Express* of Ladislas Farago's report of having found Bormann, the authorities of the state of Hesse announced that they had suddenly found what they suspected to be Bormann's skull and some of his bones, next to those of a larger man presumed to be Stumpfegger. The discovery was said to have been by accident by workmen digging in a spot allegedly only 13 m from where the determined search of the 1960s had yielded nothing. It was, said Procurator Richter, an astounding coincidence.[7]

On 13 December the officer in charge of the case, Inspector Böhme of the West German police, issued a statement confirming that the 'skull was uncovered last week near a spot where some witnesses said that Martin Bormann was last seen'.[8]

The truth about the discovery was that it was hardly accidental. It too can be traced back to the former Hitler Youth member Herbert Seidel.

It is now known that Seidel had contacted von Lang in the summer of 1972, allegedly alerting him to the possibility that excavation was shortly to occur on the Ulap Fairground site. The West German authorities had actually been contacted as far back as 8 September 1972, and been alerted to the needs of *Stern* and von Lang. The construction workers were under the impression that they might earn 100,000 DM if they found the skeleton of Martin Bormann, and the curious West Berlin public were to witness burly construction workers, uncharacteristically playing pat-a-cake with the Berlin sand, until the excited cries of accidental *Eureka!*

Dr Hans Jurgen, medical examiner of the city of West Berlin, identified the shorter skeleton as that of man of between 163 cm and 173 cm tall and between thirty and forty years old. Jurgen had 'practically no doubt' that the skeleton was that of Bormann.[9] Next to it were the remains of a taller man, about 190 cm, who was found lying with his feet next to the shorter man's skull. The Berlin Document Centre held the Race and Resettlement records of Dr Ludwig Stumpfegger, including a rough dental drawing which could be used for comparison with the remains of the taller individual. There were no such records available for comparison with the alleged Martin Bormann, nor were there any X-rays produced for comparison with either corpse.

The main evidence that the examiners had recourse to at that time was a dental chart prepared by Hitler's dentist Professor Hugo Blaschke under interrogation by the Americans after the war. The accuracy of this chart was attested to by Fritz Echtmann, Blaschke's former dental technician, who confirmed in his effective evidence that he had once produced an upper-jaw dental bridge for Bormann to specifications provided by Blaschke. This bridge was missing from the skull, and remained missing despite a painstaking forensic search of the whole area around the body, which was sandy ground and easy to sift.

The find of 'Bormann's skull' interested the forensic odontologist Reidar F. Sognnaes, who, on 9 January 1973, wrote to the German chancellor Willi Brandt asking permission to examine the skull, as he had 'collected extensive data relating to crowns, bridges, fillings and missing teeth in the case of Martin Bormann'.[10] The letter was forwarded to Minister Hemfler of the Hesse Justice Department, who on Friday 2 March sent it over to Procurator Richter, where it arrived just after the office had closed for the weekend. Now an astounding discovery was made: three months after the initial discovery of the two bodies, and exactly ten days after Richter's office had received the letter, a gold bridge was found a metre or so from the grave site.

No one, least of all Richter, has satisfactorily explained how the dental bridge came to be found and how it had been missed by the almost archaeologically thorough search of the grave area.

There was such unseemly haste to declare the bodies forensically those of Bormann and Stumpfegger that the newspapers first carried a chaotic mixture of pictures of the skulls. Examination of these photographs shows that the certainty of the medical examiners displaying these photographs was somewhat misplaced – the skull of the alleged Stumpfegger repeatedly being certified as being that of Bormann!

An anomaly that has not been explained satisfactorily was that dental technician Fritz Echtmann was alleged to have recognised a dental bridge shown him as being of his own handiwork two months before it was actually found![11] Possibly far more important was the statement by Echtmann's former colleague Käthe Heusermann that one of the lower-jaw bridges found with the skull – the bridge on the right, over the lower second bicuspid to the second molar – was *not* one of Professor Blaschke's.

The Berlin forensic expert Dr Matschke concluded on 4 January 1973 that a comparison between the dentition of the skull of the taller skeleton and the 1939 records of Dr Ludwig Stumpfegger showed that, apart from a few fillings and a crown that had been added since the records had been made, there was remarkable similarity between the corpse and the records. He did comment on the fact that there were retained wisdom teeth which had been overlooked in 1939, but he was quite happy that the corpse was indeed Stumpfegger's, especially since evidence of a fracture of the left forearm in accordance with Stumpfegger's known history had also been found.

In examining the remains of the shorter corpse, Matschke sought the assistance of two other experts: Dr Reidel of the Berlin Police Clinic and Dr Muehn, dentist at the Munich Federal Military Hospital. He did so because there were 'fundamental discrepancies' between the records of Professor Blaschke and the findings in the corpse. These discrepancies were neatly resolved by ascribing the discrepancies 'to an error on the part of the attending dentist (Dr Blaschke)'.[12] Would that all anomalies could be explained away so simply! Yet the public and the media accepted such imaginative dismissal of conflicting evidence without demur, and, with no one bothering to contradict Matschke and his colleagues, Bormann was declared officially dead.

By now the ubiquitous von Lang had resurfaced in print, and *Stern*

magazine showed its faith in his opinion by commissioning a facial reconstruction of Bormann for a documentary film which it was ready to peddle
by the time of a final press conference on 11 April. The submission to
the Third Chamber of the Criminal Court in Frankfurt recommended a
Christian burial, and the quite outrageous suggestion that Bormann's
controversial estate – which included criminally acquired wealth – be
legitimised for the benefit of his heirs!

The legalities in the Bormann case were to take many twists and turns
before Procurator Richter offered back the remains to the Bormann family
– on condition that they preserve the bones for any future forensic examination. Advised by Dr Anton Besold – a Munich lawyer and former
member of the Bundestag – the family refused to recognise the bones as
being those of their father. Besold concluded that:

> Since Herr Richter has himself thus indicated that there is doubt
> about the accuracy and finality of the present (forensic) findings, I
> advised members of the family to reject the State Attorney's offer.
> My recommendation was accepted unanimously by my clients. They
> are naturally and understandably reluctant to care for the remains
> of a man who may or may not have been their father.[13]

Before the forensic data is examined, it is worth while emphasising
that the forensic scientists were about to compare Blaschke's sketches of
Bormann's dentition with the forensic exhibits – there being *no* forensic
comparative data such as X-rays. We have to remind ourselves that the
result of such comparison can never lead to a definite statement of identity,
particularly since there was a definite forensic fraud perpetrated on Eva
Braun and we do not know the culprit.

It may be worth taking a closer look at Hugo Blaschke, who died in
1957 still vehemently expressing his Nazi beliefs. He had been born in
Neustadt, West Prussia, in 1887, and had received his pre-professional
education in Berlin, Paris and Geneva.

In 1908 he went to the United States, to the University of Pennsylvania
Dental School, where he entered the course at the age of twenty-one. He
came fourth in his class of 100 students, and his student record showed
him to be well liked – 'fine, friendly, sociable, well dressed and well to
do'.[14] He became a member of the Psi-Omega fraternity, and his student
colleagues called him 'the Count'. According to the graduation record,
'He is a true son of Old Penn, and we have no fear that our Alma Mater

will be well taken care of in the land of the Germans when Hugo returns to his native heath.'

Return he did, to the corner of Kurfürstendamm, where one of his VIP patients was Prince Victor von Wied, who in 1930 brought Hermann Göring to see Blaschke as a private patient. According to Blaschke's own account in US archives, he then himself proceeded to impress SS physician Professor Grawitz with his knowledge of medicines, and became an 'automatically' high-ranking member of the SS – although this 'meant nothing' to him. The nothing turned out to be Hitler, followed by Bormann, Eva Braun and Himmler. The truth was that Blaschke had already joined the Nazi Party in 1931, being an enthusiastic fascist even at that time.

Blaschke impressed his American inquisitors by his affability and easy-going manner, so it is of interest to note that British intelligence officer John McCowan's opinion of him was that he was 'an insignificant-looking man, both nervous and slimy – a man who couldn't be trusted'.[15] Even allowing for the deliberately hostile and cold manner in which the British carried out their interviews, this impression is still worth recording.

Lester Luntz, the Connecticut state forensic odontologist who made a special study of Blaschke and his work, shared McCowan's opinion. He uncovered several photographs of Blaschke in full SS regalia on the terrace at Berchtesgaden with Hitler and Bormann. The relationship with the SS and the honour of SS membership had obviously meant more to Blaschke than he had admitted.

Blaschke seemed to go out of his way to emphasise to his British captors that he had been loathed by Bormann – a fact that McCowan thought worth recalling. The supposed bad relationship between Blaschke and Bormann was also related to the Americans, and was even picked up far later by Professor Sognnaes: when he interviewed Artur Axmann in 1974, he was most surprised to learn that Axmann seemed to know about it.

I was equally surprised to learn from Käthe Heusermann, Blaschke's dental assistant, that Blaschke continued to see the notoriously vindictive Bormann regularly, the last visit being in March 1945, at the specific request of Bormann.[16]

This testimony is corroborated by US National Archives document APO 757, OI-FIR/31, Annex 11, a document containing Blaschke's diagrams and noting his treatments, which had started in 1937. It seems quite remarkable that, over so long a period, Blaschke should have proved, at the same time, so trusted and hated by the Reichsleiter. Rather than a reassuring assertion, the repeatedly emphasised allegations about a bad relationship between Bormann and Blaschke have become a focus of suspicion.

Such suspicion in fact occurred to Sognnaes, but, having determined that the dentists at Nuremberg had thought Blaschke 'a reliable witness', and that the American legal adviser at Nuremberg, Dr Robert Kempner, also thought along the same lines, he sought advice from Blaschke's former dental assistant (who was hardly the most disinterested party) and from one of Blaschke's former patients, Albert Speer. Speer wrote back stating:

I considered Dr Blaschke a reliable person, who appeared to know all the dental conditions of his patients. In any case I can recall that he had a good memory of the prevailing situations regarding my own treatment. I can by no means imagine that he would have knowingly deceived the American interrogators. Furthermore he did not stand in good relationship with Bormann, rather the reverse, so that he could have had no interest in making Bormann's identification difficult.[17]

Speer took the same line in conversation with myself, but when informed of my suspicions about the Eva Braun forensic fraud, and asked to give me details of this bad relationship, he changed his testimony totally – stating that this antagonism was only what he had himself heard in Spandau, from Baldur von Schirach, Axmann's predecessor in charge of the Hitler Youth. He could not remember why they had been discussing such a topic – nor how von Schirach could possibly know about Blaschke's relationship with Bormann, when there was no evidence that von Schirach himself had ever had close contact with Blaschke. Speer, the ultimate pragmatist, had simply suddenly found that his recall was suspect and that he could no longer unequivocally vouch for Blaschke.[18]

By the time that Sognnaes examined the forensic remains, he had been the guest of von Lang and *Stern*, who, in conjunction with Richter, made every attempt to iron out any problems he had with the evidence, and supplied him with the voluminous *Stern* files on Bormann – even arranging photography of the exhibits. Richter had initially cursorily dismissed Sognnaes's offer of assistance, but, once he had realised that Sognnaes was the incumbent president of the International Society for Forensic Odonto-Stomatology the Germans had changed their minds.

So hostile had been their initial reception, and so effusive the subsequent reaction and the hospitality of von Lang and *Stern* magazine, that Sognnaes felt himself obliged to record that the cooperation was 'ultimately productive' and involved some 'difficult and delicate decisions'. He was presented with the opportunity of an interview with the interesting Herbert Seidel, and with the foreman of the construction workers' crew who had found the remains, Wolfgang Zehl, as well as Dr A. Reidel, the Berlin police dentist who was one of the first to examine the skeletons.

Worried about compromising his own high standards, Sognnaes subsequently went out of his way to stress that his strength lay in the fact that he was his 'own man': 'I have neither asked for nor received any national, international, political, moral, religious, let alone commercial backing from any of the interested parties.'[19] He described his research and stay in Berlin as 'largely self-supporting'.

So it was that Professor Sognnaes took the diagrammatic records of Hugo Blaschke more or less at face value, as totally genuine, accepting Käthe Heusermann's supportive testimony without question. He made no reference to the anomalies in the somewhat premature testimony of Fritz Echtmann, the dental technician. As he was to admit to me, 'It was either that or nothing. We had nothing else to compare the forensic dental remains with.'[20]

Nevertheless, allowing for all the excitement which Sognnaes experienced, which was finally to compel him to overlook the dubious provenance of some of the material and come to conclusions about his comparisons which such a provenance rendered unsustainable in absolute scientific terms, it is still fascinating to examine the same forensic data a second time around – with the advantage of being *totally* 'self-supporting', and less involved in the excitement of the chase.

The Dental Evidence

Blaschke's dental diagrams and descriptions of Bormann's teeth directed particular attention to four principal areas.

The first was an incompletely erupted wisdom tooth in the back right portion of Bormann's lower jaw. During Bormann's last visit to Blaschke he was alleged to have complained of a cavity on this incompletely erupted tooth, which was said to have a very dark brown colour. Decay caused by wear against the teeth above had led to exposure of the pulp.

Blaschke's testimony to his American captors had described the problem: 'The lower right third molar [wisdom tooth] has not broken through all the way and therefore occupies a lower position than the second molar.

It has an iodoform filling in the pulp cavity, and a large cavity on its masticating and labial surface is filled with cement.'

The skull that was initially unearthed in 1972 was unrecognisable in any way at all. It was totally encased in reddish-brown clay, but it was claimed that an upper-jaw dental bridge had become somehow dislodged from it – not even being in the near vicinity of the corpse when it had been 'accidentally excavated'. The mask of impacted clay that surrounded the skull was markedly different from the sand surrounding the other, fairly readily cleaned, skull that lay right next to it! The condition of both skulls – one readily cleanable, grinning; the other an amorphous blob – can be seen in the initial photographs released in 1972. This encasement phenomenon, which amazingly did not seem to affect the bones, only the *one* skull, was never properly explained, and analysis of the clay casing was never correctly carried out.

The obvious improbability of finding a solitarily encased skull in sandy soil which had been both disturbed and sifted a few years previously did not escape Professor Sognnaes, who was well aware of the possibility that the skull might have been brought from elsewhere. He himself raised some questions, but failed to obtain any clarification. He accepted that he was unqualified to judge the issue and left it at that – 'since no one really seemed bothered'.[21]

Sognnaes therefore concentrated on the lower right third molar, the first dental evidence he was to examine. He claimed that the skull did indeed have a darkish (yellowish-brown) tooth which had indeed lain slightly lower than the other teeth, thus showing evidence of incomplete eruption. There was, according to Sognnaes, definite evidence of decay, cavities being present in areas of enamel next to the lips and inner cheek, but there was no trace of the iodoform paste and little if any of the cement filling mentioned by Blaschke.

According to Sognnaes's interpretation of these findings, there was 'complete accord' in the findings related to this tooth. However, since there was a high chance of cavities being present in incompletely erupted wisdom teeth, the significance of this on its own was hardly breath-taking. But there was more evidence to follow.

When questioned by the Americans, Blaschke had asserted quite definitely that the lower right wisdom tooth was the only tooth that had given Bormann discomfort. Blaschke's diagrams support this, by not showing any areas of individual teeth with either open decayed cavities or fillings visible from any view.

In the corpse of the alleged Bormann, however, there were several cavities, some as a result of previous fillings coming undone – possibly as a result of cleaning the encased skull itself. The lower left wisdom tooth had a cavity. The upper left bicuspid had an especially obvious cavity where a filling had come away. The lower right first bicuspid had a definite cavity at its end, which would, according to Sognnaes, have been too small to have been seen by the dentist on regular examination, only being found on the tooth after removal from the skull. There were, however, many other smaller amalgam fillings on the biting surfaces of the teeth – especially in the lower jaw – and several minor cavities.

It is obvious that, according to Blaschke's chart illustrating his recall, Bormann himself had not suffered so many dental problems while in Blaschke's hands – a fact supported by Blaschke's testimony. Sognnaes got around this problem by making out that the treatments must have occurred before Blaschke's time. He declared that 'While Dr Blaschke apparently had no other particularly memorable problems with regard to acute pain and decay, there were clearly more chronic problems resulting from episodes of dental caries and trauma arising earlier in the patient's life.'[22]

Sognnaes knew only too well that no dentist could have failed to recall his own treatment only a couple of months after the event, so he assumed that Blaschke had forgotten these multiple problems simply because he himself had not treated them. Even though Sognnaes knew that Blaschke had been considered obsessively meticulous and had been considered to have a good memory for minute detail, he still persisted with this viewpoint rather than consider another alternative.

Apart from the obvious possibility that it was not Bormann's skull, another possibility existed which Sognnaes had not even considered before I questioned him – the possibility that the multiple fillings and cavities that Blaschke had omitted to describe were caused *following* Blaschke's last treatment, and not before it. Sognnaes considered only the two possibilities presented to him by von Lang: a live Bormann in Argentina or a Bormann who had died as described by Axmann's testimony.

Blaschke's memory was to seem even more inaccurate when the two lower central incisors of the corpse were examined. These had been replaced by two plastic posts to support a bridge, and omission of this lower front-tooth bridge completely threw Professor Sognnaes. For on Blaschke's diagram there, startlingly obvious, were two beautifully clean natural teeth without the whisper of a filling.

Sognnaes's quandary was resolved by the following somewhat narrow reasoning:

If Dr Blaschke wanted to conceal specifics of Bormann's dental status he did a poor job, considering the detailed information regarding the rest of his dental treatment data . . . Dr Blaschke did not stand in good relationship with Bormann; rather the opposite; so that he could have had no interest in making his (Bormann's) identification difficult. If on the other hand, the late Dr Blaschke had created a deliberately planted fraud, involving a double of the real Bormann, then it would seem that such a relatively rare type and location of lost teeth, i.e. the central lower incisors, would have been very high on the list of items to include when charting what was meant to be telltale dental evidence. In the final analysis, therefore, I have concluded as a third and more logical alternative that Dr Blaschke simply did not recall any memorable treatment problems in connection with this portion of Bormann's jaw, and that the treatment – whoever's hands were once involved – had probably been rendered by some pre-war dentist – or (by Dr Blaschke) simply too long ago to fortify Dr Blaschke's memory of this particular reconstruction.[23]

What Sognnaes himself seems to fail to recall was an interview he held with Käthe Heusermann where she accurately delineated the exact same dentition as Dr Blaschke – also seemingly having 'forgotten' that there was a lower front incisor bridge. Whereas dentists may remember only the work they do, dental assistants are responsible for keeping accurate records. Heusermann's total disbelief when the incisor bridge was mentioned seemed genuine enough at the time. Indeed Fritz Echtmann, who made Blaschke's bridges, was also questioned by Sognnaes quite some time after he had already certified that the Blaschke diagrams were absolutely accurate. Once again, surely a bridge-maker who actually helped Blaschke fit the bridges on each patient would know whether a bridge had been present on the front teeth, even if it was not of his own making.

When finding such a bridge, dentists would normally look for a clear-cut history of accidental damage. In the case of the pre-war and wartime Bormann there was no such known history. Yet again there was an alternative that had been entirely overlooked. If the skull were Bormann's, then the damage to the front teeth necessitating such a bridge replacement could have been sustained *after* 1945.

The second topic concentrated on by Blaschke had been tooth loss. In the left back areas of both the upper and the lower jaw were spaces, left unfilled by Blaschke, caused by the loss of teeth. These spaces were probably due to the loss of a single tooth, matched in both jaws, although the tendency of the remaining teeth to drift inwards to fill the gap made it impossible to be absolutely definite about this.

The schematic details of this area sketched separately by Blaschke did match well with the photograph of the cleaned skull, indicating that the skull possibly was that of Bormann. In his discussion with American interpreters, Blaschke recognised the difficulty of precise identification of certain teeth, where early extraction had caused drifting to take place in an adult.

Returning to the Berlin skull of 'Bormann', we find the upper-left wisdom tooth totally unerupted. So it was the first upper-left molar that was absent from this skull rather than the third on this side: a fact Blaschke had failed to appreciate. Furthermore, Blaschke denoted the third upper right molar as also being absent, whereas the tooth in the Berlin skull was not only present but had been restored with a gold crown!

The third area of special concern according to Blaschke was the lower right region, where a permanent three-unit bridge construction replaced the first molar by attaching to full crowns on each adjacent tooth. This bridgework, according to Professor Sognnaes, tallied exactly with the findings in the corpse, and indeed Blaschke's diagrams of the lower-jaw bridge do accord remarkably closely with the bridge found in the skull. However, even though there is a certain amount of reabsorption of bone in the lower jaw, there are still visible jagged alveolar spicules (splinters) of bone, suggesting (but not certainly) the possibility that there had been recent tooth extraction even though the bridge had supposedly been fitted long before.

The fourth area of note in Blaschke's diagrams was the presence of a temporary three-unit bridge construction replacing the upper right central incisor, attached by so-called window crowns to the adjacent teeth. Blaschke claimed that this was a temporary construction, because bone loss due to periodontal disease had loosened the surrounding teeth. His testimony was:

The upper right central incisor was missing. It had been lost in 1942. Since the gap had to be closed immediately, temporary window crowns were made for the upper left central incisor and the upper right lateral incisor. The missing tooth was replaced by a porcelain facet on a golden back part. Since all upper incisors were more or less loosened by paradentosis, a bridge support was planned

Martin Bormann's Dental Diagram
in March 1945 and at His Death

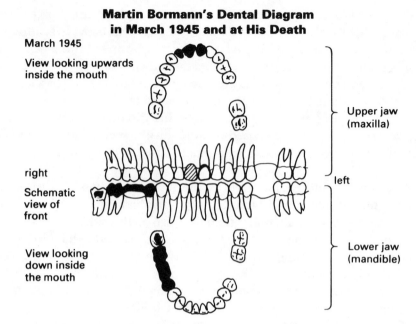

In March 1945 Bormann has a bridge in the upper jaw of three teeth, a bridge in the lower jaw and one filled tooth in the lower jaw.

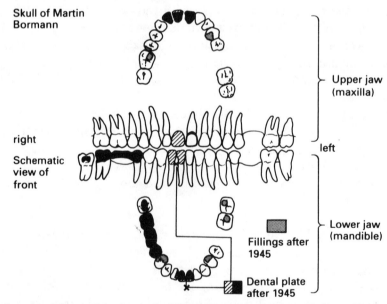

This diagram of the teeth in the skull of Martin Bormann does not show several features, including the oblique fracture in the upper jaw resulting from forcible removal of the maxillary dental plate nor the additional gold-capped molar, nor the 2mm drift to the left of the upper dental plate, all of which occurred after 1945. Even so, the eight additional fillings and the additional plate in the lower jaw are telling evidence of Bormann's postwar existence.

extending from cuspid to cuspid. As however the loosening of the incisors progressed slowly, the temporary arrangement proved satisfactory and the larger bridge was never made.

Examination of the corpse showed that, if the upper-jaw gold bridge that had been found separate from the skull was placed so that it clinically approximated to the one socket area where it would have been fixed, it seemed to approximate 'reasonably' at its other end, where the incisor root would have fitted. The difficulty in estimating the fit was because of the degree of bone absorption in the upper jaw in this area, so Sognnaes took X-rays to confirm this more accurately. The X-rays showed that there was reasonably good accord, but because of the extensive post-mortem destruction of the soft tissue around the already loose incisor root it still was impossible to be exact. Sognnaes was still not wholly satisfied. But clinical examination and X-rays also showed the fact that there was a recent fracture through the jaw running across the jaw surface obliquely, just at the side of the bridge, and this showed no evidence whatsoever of bone remodelling. The fracture had occurred either just before or after death, suggesting *either* the removal of teeth in order to accommodate the bridge at that time *or* that the bridge had been dislodged forcibly.

At this stage Professor Sognnaes started to use the newer scientific methods that had been developed at that time, to double check the authenticity of the mystery upper-jaw bridge, found apart from the body, that he had been trying so hard to match. He first of all used microreplication techniques and scanning electron microscopy, in addition to direct observation and photographs.

The evidence suggested that there was dental wear both on the lower incisor bridge (the bridge that Blaschke had not known about) and on the front edges of the teeth and the porcelain facings of the upper-jaw bridge, suggesting – but not proving – that both bridges had been worn at some time during life. Faking of such wear marks was also possible, so the crux of the matter lay in the *exact* comparison between the upper and lower bridge 'wear' marks. Here the visual anomaly continued, for the upper-jaw bridge seemed to have its central alignment more than 2 mm to the left of the central alignment of the lower-jaw incisor bridge – a difference that no dentist would readily have accepted during life.

For this reason Sognnaes made some models of the upper and lower tooth relationships and then placed them in keeping with the bite marks that he had recorded. Once again it became immediately apparent that the upper midline was displaced at least 2 mm to the left of the lower midline.

Very significantly, Blaschke had not mentioned this problem at all. Nor, in his meticulous drawing of the exact tooth relationships, had he ever indicated such a marked discrepancy. This finding bothered Sognnaes, but he explained it away by suggesting that the periodontal disease in the region of the upper incisors might allow drifting to occur. That accurate recorder Käthe Heusermann, the dental assistant whose job it was to record such data, could recollect no such drift – at least while Bormann had been a patient of Blaschke's.[24] But, yet again, had Bormann survived longer, the drift to the left could have occurred *after* 1945.

Similarly, the wear marks showed that there was an overbite of the upper incisor over the lower, and that this overbite was also asymmetrical – another indication either that there was an inexact fit of this upper-jaw bridge, pointing to possible forensic fraud, or that drifting had occurred. Once again Käthe Heusermann was unable to recollect this asymmetry.

Examination of the teeth of the corpse by scanning electron microscopy showed some slight scratches on the back of the upper incisors which Sognnaes thought in retrospect might possibly be due to the surface's having been damaged by glass splinters – hypothesising that this might be due to the splinters from a Zyankali vial. The reason for his deliberations was that glass splinters had allegedly been found in the mouth of the corpse that eventually had been identified as Bormann. Unfortunately no attempt has been made to try to use the newer techniques of surface analysis, such as EDAX (energy dispersive analysis of X-rays), SIMS (secondary ion mass spectrophotometry) or X-ray probe analysis – extraordinary techniques which could settle this issue once and for all.

But even without the belated use of such measures, the significance of the minute scratches that Sognnaes found is immediately suspect, for very few people would contemplate breaking a glass vial with their front teeth, especially if they were wearing bridgework. The place where such scratches might have been of significance was not at the incisors but at the molars.

The last test that was carried out on the corpse was an attempt to date the teeth by sectioning a loose tooth and using the various techniques of that era, such as estimating the relative degree of transparency of the root apex.

Dental dating tests are remarkably accurate. Recently, Professor

Whittaker from Cardiff University was involved as an expert witness when the vault of a London church was uncovered and found to contain many lead coffins bearing seals which denoted the exact age of the occupant at death. He showed that the dental dating techniques were markedly more accurate than other techniques used in archaeology – results which threw the archaeological world into confusion, to Whittaker's delight.

It is of great interest to learn now that Professor Sognnaes, in the 1970s, estimated that the corpse of the alleged Bormann had been between forty and fifty years old at the time of death. The degree of error that we now know to be probable means that the corpse would have been highly unlikely to have been more than about a decade older (or half a decade younger) than that. His tests therefore leave us with the probability that the Berlin corpse died when almost certainly no older than his early sixties. Bormann was born in 1900.

There were other, non-dental, observations made by the enthusiastic von Lang, who was convinced that the shape of the head and face of the unearthed skull matched the physiognomy of Bormann's face. The same enthusiasm had accompanied the initial incorrect designation of Stumpfegger's skull as Bormann's, and it must be added that Bormann's profile was hardly unique among his contemporary countrymen. Techniques of computer-assisted reconstruction of the face are unfortunately subject to operator error and operator bias, and cannot be taken as anything more than a useful aid to identification.

The only other forensic finding of note among the rest of the skeleton was the presence of a healed collar-bone fracture, in keeping with a known riding accident that Bormann had suffered some years previously. But such an accident was far too common to be a reliable guide to identification.

So the identification of the corpse comes down to the dental evidence. It is once again necessary to remind ourselves that whatever conclusions are prompted by such evidence cannot be absolute, only suggestive, for we are comparing the forensic data with records of dubious veracity. Nevertheless, the comparison may well prove highly informative.

The Possibility of Forensic Fraud

Out of the several combinations of possibilities that a comparison of dental evidence affords us with respect to the alleged remains of Bormann, three basic questions stand out and have to be considered:

- Was there any evidence that it was not Bormann's skull?

- Was there any evidence to suggest that forensic fraud had been carried out in 1945?

- Was there any evidence to suggest that forensic fraud had been perpetrated in 1972?

The answer to the first question becomes obvious in considering the other two possibilities.

So, was there evidence of forensic fraud in 1945?

It could be argued that the following features would support such an analysis:

1. The presence of numerous fillings unidentified by Dr Blaschke in his diagrams.

2. The presence of the lower-jaw incisor bridge – an extraordinary item for Blaschke, Echtmann and Heusermann not to be aware of.

3. The 2 mm or more drift of the upper-jaw bridge, with its asymmetric overbite.

4. The possible evidence of recent extractions under the rear lower-jaw bridge and the oblique fracture in the upper-jaw bridge region.

5. The missing molar which was not missing.

But the very presence of the upper-jaw incisor bridge is an argument against fraud, for what fraud would fail to include such an incredibly obvious feature?

Also against fraud is the extraordinarily accurate match with the drawings of Blaschke not of the bridgework in the upper jaw or the rear lower jaw but of the spacing between the teeth due to tooth loss. The presence of periodontic disease localised in the upper-jaw bridge area is also very conclusive evidence.

In his final analysis, Professor Sognnaes relied upon the methods of forensic odontological comparison – evaluation by means of a scoring system based on the adding-up of so-called 'extraordinary' features (such as the bridges and areas of special interest denoted by Blaschke) and 'ordinary' features such as individual teeth. Such scores are used to guide the clinician in many fields of medicine. Sometimes, however, the scientific value of the scores becomes overemphasised, and the clinician tends to fail to see the wood for the numbered trees.

Sognnaes may have done just that, in that he included as positive evidence features such as the bridges which would of course have been part of any fraud. Nevertheless, there is little doubt that, even subtracting these points, Sognnaes did build up an impressive case against there having been fraud in 1945.

We must conclude, therefore, that in comparing the Blaschke diagrams with the forensic evidence in the case of the corpse suspected to be Bormann's, there is no substantive evidence that a forensic fraud was perpetrated in 1945.

In which case, what explanation is there for the worrying major anomalies of the 2 mm or more shift to the left of the upper-jaw bridge, the inexplicable presence of the lower-jaw incisor bridge and the presence of several fillings which had not been recorded or remembered? It is unreasonable to rely on the astounding accuracy of Käthe Heusermann's recall and on the meticulous diagrams of Hugo Blaschke when they prove useful, but to dismiss their impressive recall as irrelevant when the findings, for just once, do not fit.

The next question therefore must be, was there evidence of forensic fraud in 1972?

All investigators in 1973 had become obsessed with the possibility of a *live* Bormann. The question of forensic fraud was being considered only to permit the continued existence of the same *live* Bormann. It seemingly never occurred to them that the heat of the frenzied search for Nazi war criminals in South America at that time might be dampened considerably by the 'discovery' of *genuine* Bormann remains which would take the heat off others. Yet all the circumstantial evidence would seem to be answered, even if in a facile, non-specific manner, by just such a discovery.

If Bormann's skull and other remains had been placed in the Invalidenstrasse area, along with the remains of Dr Stumpfegger, which might well have been already conveniently available in the military war cemetery, then this might help to explain their accidental discovery in a previously sifted area.

The subsequent finding of the upper-jaw bridge might well indicate that the bridge had, in the first place, been removed from Bormann's skull forcibly, after death (as suggested by Sognnaes, for such removal would almost certainly produce a fracture across the jaw). It might have been removed for its possible solitary use in subsequent forensic fraud, before the decision to use the skull itself. The Bormann skull might justifiably have been considered to contain enough evidence without the addition of the bridge, before the delayed challenge of Professor Sognnaes precipitated the need for the discovery of the bridge as well.

Dental technician Fritz Echtmann's prescient certification of the bridge itself, carelessly included as evidence, was further possible proof both of the separate existence of the bridge and of the intention to use it in forensic fraud.[25]

The very obviously anomalous appearance of the clay-encased skull next to a non-encased skull in the same sandy grave could be explained by their initial burial at different sites, before the disinterment of Bormann's remains and their subsequent reburial in Berlin. The military war cemetery had no such clay deposits – only the same light, sandy soil shared by the rest of Berlin.

The contorted, contradictory, changing, seemingly contrived testimony of Baur, Axmann and others who gave evidence about Bormann's death, and the later evidence of those who claimed to have found his corpse, would now fall into place as at least serving a purpose – that of concealing the truth.

Finally, the forensic data would at last be explained, for the lower-jaw incisor bridge (which, a decade later, Sognnaes himself admitted he suspected from its construction as being of later origin and not Blaschke's)[26] could have resulted from the replacement of lost teeth after a subsequent accident such as a car crash. Similarly, the upper-jaw bridgework, which within a decade would probably have started to drift, might well have proved beyond the capability of a South American dentist to correct, and would have been allowed to continue to drift (resulting in a suitably crooked smile). The multiple fillings could also possibly have been necessitated during Bormann's continued existence.

The *only* forensic data suggesting that the corpse died in 1945 remains the alleged presence of glass splinters in its mouth. If these splinters resulted from a glass vial being crushed, then this could have been a Zyankali cyanide capsule or any other similar capsule. More importantly, it could have been broken at any time, and the presence of the glass splinters proves nothing in this case, especially since subsequent analysis by the forensic scientist Dr Widmann revealed that, although the ampoules in the corpse's mouth were approximately the same size as Zyankali vials, they did not possess the blue lacquered tip characteristic of these vials and so could *not* be verified as having contained cyanide.

Von Lang's need to round off his story brought in another witness, an air-raid warden, Osterhüber, who claimed that he had seen Bormann commit suicide on the Lehrter Bridge in 1945.[27] He had even managed to thwart Bormann's first attempt by dashing a cyanide capsule out of his hand, but was unable to prevent him taking a second. His lively imagination only omits to inform us of how he knew it was Bormann, and whether Bormann was wearing woollen pants and vest at the time!

Von Lang did manage to record for posterity a little-known statement made by Axmann in April 1970, about the exact state of Bormann's corpse when allegedly found on the Lehrter Bridge in 1945. In all his previous statements, as in his questioning at Nuremberg on 10 October 1947, Axmann related how he had been 'standing' in front of an obvious corpse. Now, in the 1970 testimony, however, a more humane, curious and compassionate Axmann appeared. In retrospect, his answers unfortunately suggest earnest coaching:

We knelt down beside both bodies and recognised without question Martin Bormann and Dr Stumpfegger. Both were lying on their backs with their arms and legs stretched out sideways. I spoke to Bormann, ran my hand over him and shook him back and fro somewhat. I noticed no breathing. Both men were wearing the overcoats that they had been wearing previously. They gave an impression of lifelessness, and I could see no wounds or bullet marks. I was also unable to detect any external changes around the mouth that suggested that they had taken poison, at any rate I did not open the mouth. I also observed no striking odour such as prussic acid or strong smell of bitter almonds. The examination and observations I have just described refer to Bormann. I removed no object from their clothing. It was somewhere between 1.30 to 2 a.m. The fires all around illuminated the terrain – that explains why I was able to recognise Bormann's face without doubt. As I recall Bormann's eyes were closed – at any rate not widely open.[28]

If Axmann had knelt next to corpses that had actually committed suicide by cyanide poisoning, had he been *able* to smell such an odour – as from 1946 he had vehemently claimed he could – then he could hardly have failed to recognise the all-pervasive stench.

Bringing attention to Axmann's revised testimony may prove to have been von Lang's most important contribution, for, like much of the evidence he produced, it has a flavour which makes it automatically suspect – as suspect as von Lang's seeming eagerness to promote such material.

Yet, based on the scientific data to hand, we can conclude that there is no contrary forensic data which excludes a forensic fraud having been perpetrated in 1972, using the remains of Martin Bormann. Major anomalies in the forensic data fit far better with the perpetration of such a fraud than with a death sustained in 1945.

There is also evidence that a similar fraud was perpetrated on the corpse of Dr Stumpfegger – evidence which greatly augments the Bormann case. For what I have not so far mentioned is that the left vault of the skull of the Stumpfegger corpse had been surgically excised.

The two photographs of this skull reproduced in the plates section show its state when found. The gaping black hole in the left side of the skull, which demands adequate explanation, was very surprisingly and almost dismissively covered by a half-sentence in the forensic report: 'One skull had been damaged in its parietal area by a steam shovel.'

Further examination of the skull shows this statement to be appallingly inadequate, inaccurate and untruthful. Yet no one has challenged this so-called expert opinion – showing the extent to which both the public and the scientific community can be duped.

A steam shovel has a very considerably greater effect on impact than a shovel wielded by a man. The physical effect of a steam shovel on an intact skull can be likened to the effect of cracking an egg with a knife: the bone caves in and splinters at the edges of the cut, and parallel cracks occur along the main line of impact. In a severe blow the skull can also explode apart due to lateral dissemination of the shovel's force. If the force is masked by the skull's being covered by a layer of sandy earth, the effect is modified somewhat – but only to a limited extent. The impact energy still produces inward implosion of the vault, the weakest part of the skull.

When any vault breaks, it usually does so leaving the same characteristic clear-cut radial fractures (the cracks in the egg). Furthermore, the bony plates of the vault (which can be likened to the panels on a football) are linked by joints which are usually stronger than the surrounding bone, even after death, and so remain intact – unlike the Stumpfegger skull. If the blow caused parallel fractures to the extent that a plateau of bone was driven inwards into the skull, then that bone would still be present and recoverable, and would itself show signs of damage. The edges of any such plateau of bone driven inwards would almost certainly have been very irregular and uneven, especially the lower edge. This effect is a result of the structure of the bone plate, which is composed of two hard outer plates and a softer area of bone in between – rather like a sandwich.

If the blow from the steam shovel were tangential (literally taking the top off the 'egg'), then the edge opposite the initial impact edge would probably show evidence of gross irregularity; and, in any case, since the steam shovel was allegedly being used at the actual time of the 'discovery', once again the pieces would have been readily recoverable.

So, damage to a skull resulting from a steam shovel would be obvious and recognisable.

In the photographs, one can see that the extent of the injury was not properly recorded. The defect is hardly just in the parietal bone (at the top of the side of the head) – it includes the whole of the left frontal (forehead) bone and a good part of the left parietal bone, and includes a part of the left zygomatic bone (the buttress below and alongside the eye socket), which is also missing where it forms the outside border of the eye socket. The inadequacy of the description is quite extraordinary!

Not only that: readers can judge for themselves the extraordinarily clean break, *the vertical cut edge* of the midline where the remaining right side of the frontal bone is visible as it extends backwards and upwards. They can also look at the tell-tale outside edge of the skull – the remaining parts of the left parietal and temporal (temple) bones – which shows it has been broken not in a vertical direction, as would have been expected from this downwards force, but in a *transverse* plane. It is difficult even to envisage a direct blow from a steam shovel causing such a pattern. Had such a blow caused a break, then this break would also have been accompanied by flakes of bone breaking irregularly from the lower part of the skull plates. No such break pattern exists.

In old skulls there is a tendency for the bones to lose their elasticity and become more brittle. With such skulls it is just possible that a concussive effect occurring in very close proximity – as in the case of a steam-shovel blade only just missing the skull – could cause the vault of the skull to crack spontaneously. On these occasions the crack can be vertical, straight through the sandwich of bone that comprises the thin vault – and, furthermore, vertically through the sandwich at the side of the skull, giving a transverse fracture line. Such a crack would possibly give the same appearance in the frontal bone and in the temporal and parietal bone edges as was seen in the cadaver. But it would *not* affect the strong buttress of bone that comprises the orbital zygomatic, the outside margin of the eye socket.

As can be seen from the photograph, there is another oblique fracture, a cut at yet another angle, across this bone. This 25-mm-thick buttress is totally impervious to nearby concussive effects, which can effectively be dismissed as causing such a fracture. Furthermore, even if such a concussion had occurred, it would still have left the fractured piece either *in situ* or immediately adjacent to the skull.

We can conclude that it is almost inconceivable that a direct blow from a steam shovel could have caused the damage to Stumpfegger's skull. We can also conclude that neither could any freak concussive effect have caused this.

In fact the cuts across the skull vault are very similar to the cuts produced by a modern high-speed saw, or even by the cheesecutter-like Gigli saw, used both by neurosurgeons and, sometimes, pathologists.

The overall effect is highly suggestive that someone surgically removed a large part of the vault and the top of the eye socket. The fact that the missing piece of the vault was *not* available, even though the search was archaeological in its thoroughness, supports this contention.

So, faced with the near certainty that the top of the orbit and vault were surgically removed, the question that must be asked is: why?

There can only be one answer: to conceal a defect in the skull – a defect likely to have been a gunshot wound. It is quite possible that a bullet entering the area of the orbit, or more likely the forehead, would have exited through the vault. Axmann's story of there being no mark of any gunshot wound on either corpse would be discredited. And it would be difficult to envisage someone fatally shot bothering to take a Zyankali vial!

The above evidence points to an alternative. Dr Stumpfegger, an unhealthily obvious target of 190 cm tall, was indeed shot and left on the Lehrter Bridge. His body was found, his widow was notified, and the burial was effected in the military cemetery all as previously described.

When, in the early 1970s, it became necessary to create a forensic fraud to divert the anti-Nazi hysteria in South America, Stumpfegger was duly dug up, his skull was refashioned, and the telltale bits were thrown away. His body was laid to rest next to that of Martin Bormann, which itself contained evidence of an existence beyond the Lehrter Bridge and 1945. Two broken capsules – probably not Zyankali vials – were placed in the mouths of the corpses. It only remained to alert the faithful for an accidental discovery which was to convince the world.

But for this alternative theory to be confirmed there has to be more substantive proof than just suspicions about the Argentinian files and the multiple but weak circumstantial evidence that had formed the basis of the previous Israeli conviction that Bormann had escaped retribution.

In 1993 there was to be dramatic confirmation that exactly such a forensic fraud had indeed been perpetrated in 1972.

13

The Paraguay Assumption

No South American state has a more tragic history than Paraguay. Although blessed with exquisite natural beauty and a delightful winter climate, the Riviera of South America, as it has been called, was crushed under the heel of Spanish despotism for two centuries. It gained its independence in 1811, only to fall under the yoke of successive military dictators. One of these, Don Francisco López, plunged it into a war with Brazil, Argentina and Uruguay from 1865 to 1870 which must rank as the bloodiest and most disastrous in history in relation to a country's population. Five-sixths of the entire population perished in that war, leaving only 28,746 men and 106,254 women over fifteen.

Civil wars devastated over 30 per cent of those born to or joining that remainder, aggravating the self-inflicted genocide of Paraguay's own people. Between 1931 and 1935 there was a terrible war between Paraguay and Bolivia over control of an undeveloped area, part of a vast plain known as El Gran Chaco.

Still evident in the countryside are numerous overladen bullock carts straining over wretched trails which, deep with dust in the dry seasons, become impassable in the bog-like conditions of winter. The peasant population are mainly descended from the Guaraní Indians.

Against this background of indigenous poverty, after the Second World War there was obvious potential wealth from the export of abundant oranges, 'Paraguayan Tea' (Yerba maté) and tannin, but the wealth was (and is) distributed mainly among those of European descent. Before the Second World War there were hardly any such Europeans, but then Paraguay became dominated by mainly Italian and German immigrants who settled in protected enclaves, each enclave assuming the national character of the inhabitants. By the 1990s over 100,000 citizens of German nationality had become settled.

This was the backdrop to a state whose people in 1954 had had little choice but to accept President Alfredo Stroessner as yet another in the long line of dictators, and who were eventually to watch in impotence as he was to flee to sanctuary in Brazil, from a long-overdue, successful military coup in February 1989.

Stroessner governed the people by Nazi-like terror methods, assiduously studying and copying Himmler's SS techniques. As a result, each German enclave became an almost impenetrable fortress, impervious to outside enquiries about Nazi war criminals.

Long before Stroessner, the country had effectively become isolated into a hermit nation. From the advent of the first dictator in 1814 until 1852, foreigners had been banned, as was cross-border trade. Paraguay gradually emerged from being the Tibet of the South Americas only in 1879, but by then secrecy was ingrained in the population. In Stroessner's Paraguay of the 1970s it was no different. The borders were effectively screened, the police were present everywhere, a reign of terror existed. All those who chose to talk injudiciously were eliminated, allowing the obvious and flauntingly dismissive arrogance of the Nazi exiles to be displayed in the few decent cafés in Asunción, confident in their presidential protector.

Following the Israeli kidnapping of Eichmann from neighbouring Argentina in 1961, and his successful trial, Paraguay became the haven for all those Nazis nervous about the result of international pressure on the South American republics for their arrest and deportation.

That pressure came most vociferously from the United States of America, anxious to mollify the strong Jewish vote. Israel was the most effective of the states which demanded the return of these criminals, but the Dutch, Polish, Czech and French governments were also vocal, with the West German government itself strongly expressing the very same desires, albeit in a more muted fashion.

It was all a charade.

The CIA, despite advertising the fact that it was sending investigative teams into Paraguay, and starting up a rumour that two of its agents had been found dead in a cinema in Asunción, was actively supporting the Stroessner regime with money and training programmes for Stroessner's secret police. It was even passing on CIA information about Paraguay's neighbouring states.[1] The extraordinary extent of that previous aid and collusion is, in 1994, a political embarrassment to the Clinton administration, which is striving to control the publication of the recently discovered details.[2]

During Stroessner's long dictatorship, successive West German ambassadors dined behind Asunción's splendid Guaraní Hotel in the German restaurant whose Jewish owner was one of the president's chief supporters. They could hardly avoid sharing in the ribald tales of Eduard Roschmann, the SS 'Butcher of Riga', as he boasted of his exploits to his Croat friends. Nor could they have avoided knowing that Josef Mengele and, it was said, Martin Bormann frequently visited the very same restaurant – especially when, as in Argentina, Mengele had applied for and had been granted Paraguayan citizenship in his own name, his application having been backed by none other than the notorious Werner Jung, in conjunction with Stroessner's right-hand man, the so-called 'White Russian' Alejandro von Eckstein.[3]

Another figure was a regular in the same café society. His pragmatic actions reflected a secret deal, done in the era of *realpolitik*, between Israel, the CIA and the Stroessner regime. This figure was the Israeli ambassador to Paraguay, Benjamin Varon. Appointed in 1968, when diplomatic relations had been normalised with Stroessner, he had specific instructions not to raise the issue of Nazi war criminals in Paraguay. These instructions made him the most popular ambassador in the country, and made him confide to a friend, the under-secretary of state Alberto Nogues, that he would have to refuse Mengele a visa to enter Israel if by some perverse chance he were to apply for one.[4] The result of such pragmatism was that under Stroessner in the 1970s and 1980s, Paraguay became Israel's strongest ally in the United Nations – one of only seven countries which never cast a vote against Israel.

Despite the fact that Varon was not pressing for the Nazis' extradition, by 1972 the Nazi-hunters had achieved such support in the United Nations that gestures started to be made by Stroessner himself, offering select investigators the chance to chase after Bormann. This, as we shall see, was an offer he could well afford to make. But at that time it was Mengele that the investigators were after, and the pressure mounted inexorably.

It had started when Esther Abramovici and Sonia Tauber, two Jewish women living in Asunción, complained that the presence of Mengele was becoming so offensive to them that they were prepared to create an international incident. Both were former inmates of Auschwitz, and had little reason not to remember Mengele.

By the summer of 1972 the former CIA man Ladislas Farago had also been tipped off by the Israelis, and, following a remarkably uneventful visit to Asunción, he announced his discovery of Mengele's whereabouts in December 1973. He also put his findings into the hands of the Frankfurt procurator Joachim Richter.

The search for Josef Mengele and the actual discovery of his whereabouts in early 1972 was probably the trigger for the disinformation campaign that was to hit Farago in Argentina; it was very likely the cause of the 'discovery' of the Bormann and Stumpfegger remains.

Even though Farago was discredited by his own misplaced enthusiasm in the search for Bormann, and his reputation was destroyed by the Berlin Ulap Fairground dig, interest in Mengele did not wane. There was just too much hard evidence. It was rumoured at the time that Alfredo Stroessner had enjoyed Mengele's assistance as his own private physician. For whatever reason, Stroessner decided to visit West Germany in the summer of 1973. Coolly received in Bonn, he attended Bavaria and Munich, where his father had been a brewer, and received an ecstatic welcome. In return he invited Alfons Goppel, the Bavarian chief minister, back to Asunción.

Despite all the reassurances subsequently conveyed to Bonn that Mengele was not in Paraguay, the West German government issued a statement through its Justice Department. This was reported in the *New York Times* of 25 October 1973 under the headline 'Auschwitz Doctor said to be in Paraguay':

West German Justice officials said in Bonn yesterday that Dr Josef Mengele, the Nazi physician sought for the last 22 years for alleged mass murders in the Auschwitz concentration camp in World War II, was believed to have been located in a remote village in Paraguay. Mengele, known as the 'Angel of Death', was reported to be in the village of Pedro Juan Caballero, near the Brazilian frontier in the province of Amambay.

Despite the Bormann diversion, the search for Mengele continued. But the search for Bormann stopped stone dead in 1973, faced with the seemingly incontrovertible evidence of the West German pathologists. Little did non-experts appreciate how slovenly and unimpressive had been the expertise on show, or how unwilling the Frankfurt office had been to accept world-class assistance. The case against Bormann's living in Argentina or Paraguay was proved – much to the delight of historians, who had had enough of such 'nonsense'.

The 'nonsense' reappeared around Christmas 1992.

Martin Almada was an educationalist and a self-trained lawyer who represented human-rights movements in Latin America. He had himself suffered at the hands of Stroessner, having been held in captivity from 1974 until his expulsion from Paraguay in 1977. His wife, having been told not of his expulsion but of his supposed death, subsequently suffered a heart attack and died.[5]

When Stroessner fled, in 1989, Almada returned from exile and started to look for the papers relating to his own case. He was given a tip-off that a provincial police station held a stack of documents relating to the Ministry of the Interior Investigating Department, which were shortly to be burned by the police.

On 22 December 1992 the police department in the residential suburb of Solares de Lambaré, near Asunción, was raided by a judicial team headed by the judges José Augustin Fernández and Luis Maria Benítez Riera, accompanied by congressional deputy Francisco José de Vargas. They were acting under the Habeas Data Provisions newly inscribed in the 1992 constitution. The team took into safe custody nearly two tonnes of documents relating to the activities of the Criminal Investigations Department – the DIPC, more commonly known by the dread name of 'Investigaciones' – the former nerve centre for state repression. The documents had been strewn about in a locked room in total chaos, obviously prepared for burning. Witnessed by both press and TV, the judges ordered the immediate transfer of the documentation to the High Court building in Asunción.

Shortly afterwards, on 4 January 1993, another cache of files was discovered in a similar fashion, following another tip-off. This time the files belonged to the judicial section of the secret police themselves. A mountain of information related to the systematic suppression of the Peasant League movement, and specific files relating to the horrendous treatment of individuals, gave the inquisitors the basis of criminal charges against the former president Stroessner.

The search continued. On 8 January a third raid was carried out, on the Ministry of the Interior's Departmento Técnico para la Represión de Comunismo – commonly known as La Técnica. This had been established in the early 1960s with covert US government support. The raid confirmed that La Técnica had continued to operate long after the 1989 putsch which overthrew Stroessner. Following the 22 December raid its senior officers had disappeared, taking with them the most sensitive information. Noemi Yore, coordinator of a district church committee, then received a tip-off that on 11 January an attempt had been made to destroy part of the files seized three days earlier. Following an immediate injunction, these particular files were hurriedly transferred to the national archives.

The cache was complete. Most of the files – labelled the 'Archives of Terror' – were trundled to the huge, square concrete Department of Justice building, where archivists started the laborious task of making sense of the hoard. Initially the documents occupied two rooms on the top floor, spilling out of the cupboards in a chaotic jumble.

Dr Andrew Nickson from Birmingham University was one of the most effective cataloguers, but as soon as news of the files' discovery became known, others with less disinterested motives started to flock around. Unfortunately the security initially proved less than adequate, and one of my informants was able to attend the archives carrying a duffle bag, while noticing others carrying shopping bags and the like. A policeman caught destroying old documents excused himself by saying that the records had at some time previously been computerised! No one now knows exactly what files were destroyed.

Rumour quickly became rampant that the CIA had become involved – being most interested in paying unofficially for retrieval of files concerning its own activities. Officially the US government donated some $40,000 towards the cost of cataloguing – an agreement which ended in September 1993. Although the US ambassador John Glassman had earlier denied US involvement in state repression as evidenced in the archives, he publicly recognised that the CIA had collaborated in the establishment of La Técnica.[6]

In August 1993 a bill presented to Congress in Paraguay proposed that the archive should become a cultural exhibit.

The bulk of the documents came from the first raid. Some 600 bound folios and over 7,000 personal files and transcripts of statements taken under torture reveal that such torture was a common practice against political opponents, and that such opponents were often kidnapped from exile, with the cooperation of the security forces of neighbouring countries. Moreover, the detainees that had disappeared under interrogation had in actual fact been murdered – being filed under a special classification of '*empaquetados*', or 'packaged'. Informants to the security services included a Catholic bishop!

Such information was highly sensitive, but worse was to come. It seemed that Paraguay was a founder member of Operación Condor, an agreement between the military regimes of Argentina, Brazil, Paraguay,

Uruguay and Chile which allowed fugitive Nazis and the like to cross freely from one state's protection into that of the next. It is little wonder that the Nazi-hunters found their job so difficult.

The revelations of some of the contents of the Operación Condor files have already brought interest and confirmation from the other countries involved, most of which have changed their governments to more liberal regimes.

In a denunciation of the activities of Paraguay's ex-president Stroessner, Hugo Coré, vice-president of one of Uruguay's congressional committees on human rights that was searching for missing Uruguayan dissidents, commented that 'There existed a kind of transnational sovereignty among our governments.'[7] He named eight members of Stroessner's government and three members of the Argentine and Uruguayan intelligence services as being responsible for the disappearance of Uruguayan citizens.

Hernan Bordonovitch and Jaime Naranjos, Chilean parliamentary senators, examined the documents and declared that there was irrefutable proof of a military and security terror regime instituted in the 1970s. Chilean president Patricio Aylwin formally requested a document which exposed the activities of a former head of the Chilean intelligence service, Colonel Manuel Contreras.

Such revelations went on and on – the sheer scale is only now being appreciated.

Based on the information being revealed, an extradition order relating to Stroessner was prepared by the Paraguayan courts, for presentation to the Brazilian government. Stroessner's lawyer managed to postpone the forwarding of the request on the grounds that the judge's morality was suspect because he had acted with such speed!

But, for our purposes, what the revelations really mean is that the capture of such a cache of continuingly corroborated material can only point to the genuineness of the revelations about Mengele and Bormann – revelations which produced an immediate and vehement response from a West German government that, as will be seen from the documents themselves, *knew* what I am about to disclose.

Alfred Streim, who has headed Germany's Nazi Record Centre in Ludwigsburg for thirty years, instantly dismissed the 'Archive of Terror' accounts of Bormann's presence in Paraguay as 'absolute nonsense'. For a man in his position, this shows a remarkable lack of knowledge, and a naïvety verging on the obscene. He was quoted in *The Times* of 26 February 1993 as saying of the Bormann revelations, 'It was not only his skull (that had been found and identified in 1973), but the people who tried to break out with him are known and they said that a tank shell exploded near them and he (Bormann) lay there dead.'

Evidently chief recordist Streim's mind stopped recording data immediately after Kempka's initial, subsequently discredited, Nuremberg Trial testimony.

He went on in classic fashion: 'Even if he [Bormann] were only wounded it would have been impossible for him to get out of Berlin – because Berlin was surrounded.'

The Asunción files reveal a somewhat different story.

The pile of police papers from La Técnica contains a note from the Ministry of the Interior's director of foreign affairs, Pedro Propochuk, a Polish-born Argentinian who was later killed by the same regime that he served, allegedly because he knew too much. The note was to his boss, the then La Técnica commissioner Antonio Campus Alum, who now (1994) faces charges of torturing and killing prisoners. It records that West German intelligence knew of Mengele's presence in Paraguay in 1958, and also the purpose of his visit – to treat Bormann.[8] The files also reveal that West German intelligence also knew exactly where Bormann was living.[9] The document was verified as genuine by Judge Benítez Riera.[10]

So what do the documents show?

Martin Bormann arrived in Asunción in 1956, where he stayed before moving to live in the small German town of Colonia Hohenau, 350 km south of Asunción in the Alto Parana zone, along the Parana river that borders Argentina. Despite his reclusive habits, his identity was widely known. For a long time he lived in the house of one Alban Krug.

In 1958 Bormann was treated by a dentist whose office was on the corner of the streets Nuestro Salvador de la Asunción and Fulgencio R. Moreno. In the same year Josef Mengele was admitted to Paraguay for the express purpose of treating Bormann for a stomach ailment – already diagnosed as cancer. During his time in Paraguay, Mengele stayed in the house of Werner Jung.

Mengele's assistance was of little avail, and in 1959 the services of a physician practising in Asunción were requested, again to no great effect. That physician is recorded as none other than Dr Otto Biss (several years before Biss's own revelations). Mengele ceased treating Bormann, and, after a long agonising fight against the cancer, Bormann allegedly died on 15 February 1959 in the house of Werner Jung in Asunción, at Calle General MacArthur.

Two days after his death Bormann was buried in great secrecy in 'the dark of night' in the town of Itá, 35 km south-east of the capital, in a ceremony attended by Werner Jung, the cemetery's caretaker, the driver of the truck that transported the coffin, and a man identified as von Eckstein.

(Readers will recall that in 1964 a West German journalist, Herbert John, had dug up grave G3 in Itá, a grave that John claimed was the grave of Martin Bormann, and the West German embassy in Asunción had also had a grave opened. Grave G3 was the recorded grave of Juan Hermocilla, but a check on the register reveals that Hermocilla's burial was recorded in 1948, and it is unlikely that his grave would have been reused. This is a surprising and unfortunate mistake to have made.)

It is also of no small interest to learn that the documents record that the very same house in which Martin Bormann died was very soon after to be occupied by Dr Peter Benach, West Germany's cultural attaché.

Bormann had entered Paraguay from Argentina under the personal protection of Alfredo Stroessner. Judge Benítez Riera was one of a panel of jurists allowed to see the files. 'Despite the horrendous crimes committed against Jews, Martin Bormann was granted protection by the Paraguayan intelligence service itself and allowed to lead a normal life' was his comment.[11]

So where does that leave us today?

The Paraguayan records are almost certainly genuine. Furthermore there seems to be no reason why the records of Mengele's registration as a Paraguayan national, supported by no other than Werner Jung and Alejandro von Eckstein, should be genuine (as we know) and the records of Martin Bormann false.

Bormann was a registered war criminal, unlike Mengele at that time, so it is not surprising that Paraguayan citizenship was seemingly not granted him – or at least not in his own name – as in the case of Mengele. Nevertheless the records of La Técnica are in fact very unsatisfactory. They contain no fingerprints, no photographs – in fact nothing forensic to back up the police report.

The Propochuk report on Bormann falls very far short of expectations if it is to be quoted as the sole evidence of his existence in Paraguay. Nevertheless, it provides totally unforeseen confirmation of Biss's testimony about being called in by Werner Jung to assist another doctor (Mengele) in treating Bormann. The coincidence continues when the evidence about the Bormann skull found in Berlin is reconsidered. Now at last there is apparently factual evidence to corroborate my hypothesis that the Bormann skull found in Berlin had sustained dental work *after*

Blaschke had recorded the exact status of Bormann's teeth as he had last seen them in March 1945.

This factual evidence, while it seems most likely to be true, is nevertheless infuriatingly difficult to substantiate, because of the delicate situation that exists in Paraguay today, where Stroessner's presence is still felt, even *in absentia*, and where democratic rule is not yet established. Testimony is laced with fear and uncertainty, as in the case of the dentist who allegedly treated Bormann.

Guillermo Heikel was an immigrant from Finland, where he was born on 6 December 1916. He started to practise dentistry in earnest in Asunción in 1942, and retired in 1992. The La Técnica documents refer to Bormann's having received dental treatment in Heikel's office in Asunción. This is hardly surprising when it is realised that Heikel had an extremely close relationship with Stroessner, with the diplomatic community, and with the German community in the exclusively German district of Villa Mora. He also had close connections with Alban Krug, Werner Jung and von Eckstein.

When the Asunción files were released and it was revealed that he had allegedly treated Bormann, Heikel was visited by Israelis anxious to know the truth about this and also about his relationship with the Baker family, who were associated with Mengele. They were also interested in knowing about his West German financial interests.

The Israelis went away empty-handed, and at first, Heikel was very reluctant to talk to anyone about himself, his activities with the ex-Nazis, or his alleged treatment of Bormann and Mengele. Terrified of being involved in the case being launched against former president Stroessner, Heikel fought shy of answering questions that would have implicated him in the treatment of known war criminals, a fact which he continually referred to during the course of the Israeli interview. 'I never knew Bormann. Bormann was a war criminal. I would like to attest that I never knew or treated Martin Bormann or Josef Mengele.'[12]

Later, at a second interview – by now having appreciated that Mengele was not listed as a war criminal at the time that he was supposed to have treated him – Heikel was belatedly quite prepared to speak about Mengele, although still categorically denying that he had treated Bormann.

It seemed that he treated Mengele in Villa Mora – once more he emphasised that he never treated war criminals, nor anyone suspect, at his office at the corner of Nuestro Salvador de la Asunción and Fulgencio R. Moreno in Asunción. He had had no reason to suspect Mengele as 'the Angel of Death', as he gave 'no impression of guilt associated with the killing of Jews in the Second World War'.

Heikel's political pragmatism can be best evaluated from his opinion of Mengele: 'I found Mengele a sympathetic man, cultured and intelligent, with the manners of a real gentleman. He gave the impression of being very affluent, a real man of the world.'[13]

Now in retirement in Asunción, Heikel is unlikely to be more forthcoming, especially with the present political uncertainty. We may never know the truth about Bormann's lower incisor bridge – whether it was Heikel's handiwork, to patch up incisors broken on the steering-wheel of a car juddering over those dusty dirt roads from Asunción to Colonia Hohenau.

It is now worth while recalling the condition of the Ulap Fairground skull of Martin Bormann. It was covered with a gooey reddish-brown clay.

Many people who pay for interment are unaware that a certain amount of recycling of valuable coffins has been traditional not only in underdeveloped countries but in decidedly developed countries too. In 1984 it was revealed that one particular council cemetery in Britain was effectively cutting costs by combining the imaginative use of heavy machinery to level old grave sites with the instant recovery and repeat sale of all coffins, immediately after the funeral – this being discovered only when the local stray-dog population was seen to spurn the village butcher's shop, heading instead for the graveyard and carrying away far more impressive bones. It is more than likely that in a provincial graveyard in Paraguay an expensive coffin was similarly recycled, leaving the mortal remains of Bormann in contact with the ground, while the decidedly more attractive coffin went back to Asunción.

What is known about the soil in Itá? Only that it is in Itá that a very characteristic reddish-brown clay pottery is made, for sale in Asunción and indeed throughout Paraguay.[14]

The weight of forensic evidence that pointed to Bormann's postwar existence is now augmented by the mass of circumstantial evidence that the CIA, Israeli intelligence and the Nazi-hunters had accumulated over the decades – all culminating in the Paraguayan note by Propochuk. Moreover, this suggests that there was another more cynical aspect to the whole saga – the effect of *realpolitik*: the fact that, at the right level, governments knew the truth all along.

It now seems likely that Bormann's skull,[15] could also have been recycled with the aid of Werner Jung and von Eckstein – resurrected to take their place in a successful forensic fake which was designed to dampen down interest in ex-Nazis in Paraguay, a forensic fake which has fooled the world for almost a quarter of a century.

14

Perspectives and Conclusions

Death, especially the death of a tyrant, has a knack of putting life in perspective.

Stalin, the other monstrous historical figure from the first half of the twentieth century, died in circumstances very different from those in the Bunker – surrounded by his own select band of sycophants, in tomb-like silence. The descriptions of his death that we have from this uneasy entourage reveal the extraordinary tensions, emotions and ultimately the overwhelming relief that Stalin's death throes aroused; the mood of numbed and suppressed rage, impotence and impatience was related with the same careful, stilted, reluctant recall that survivors of the Bunker displayed when describing their otherwise imaginative versions of Hitler's death. The tensions of the time still affected those present long after the event.

In the case of the survivors from the Bunker, recall of their own actions at the time of the murder may have influenced the way in which they subsequently related the story almost as much as the need to tell a tale to order. In marked contrast, those surrounding Stalin were probably telling the truth; but, even so, the parallels are curious.

It took two and a half days for Stalin to die from his stroke. During this period, the only person who betrayed his conflict of emotions – of subservience and hate – was Lavrenti Beria, the dreaded head of the secret police. 'As soon as Stalin showed signs of consciousness, Beria threw himself on his knees, seized Stalin's hand and started kissing it. When Stalin lost consciousness again and closed his eyes, Beria stood up and spat.'[1]

Everyone acknowledges that Stalin was hated – Beria's expression of contempt surprises no one – so this story hardly seems to parallel the scenes of loyal, death-defying defence and tragically tearful concern that we have been expected to associate with Hitler's death. Yet now at long last we have the evidence which demonstrates how Hitler did in fact die – brutally, at the hands of loyal followers.

In the scenes around Stalin's deathbed and in the brutality of Hitler's murder and the offhand contempt of his disposal lurked the same base instincts of self-preservation. When Hitler died, the circumstances in the Bunker eventually removed the last vestige of pretence from the actions of his acolytes. Human nature itself is the ultimate dictator.

The Hitler myth ought to have died along with its subject, and might have done so had the truth about the death been made known by the Bunker survivors or, later, by the Soviets. The truth would almost certainly have become immediately apparent had a proper investigation been launched. Instead, the investigations by both the Soviets and the Western Allies were tainted by political expediency.

Had the details of Hitler's demise been made known, and had the burning and disposal of the bodies of Hitler, Goebbels and 'Eva' been described in terms as derisory as their performance, then the sense of national humiliation and shame that the death evoked would have been maximised, and the bubble of mythology would have been pricked at the outset.

Instead, after the war, only extraordinarily half-hearted propaganda was employed by the Allies to try to re-educate a benighted and numbed German nation and oblige it to accept responsibility for the crimes that had been committed by the German state, and this was made ineffective by the lack of clarity and focus about *how* Hitler had died – if he had died at all. While this uncertainty lasted, the legend of the glorious end acted as a last wreath laid on the tomb of Nazism, eagerly grasped at by the still substantial numbers of the old far right who were never to be able to come to terms with their defeat.

That Hitler was murdered by one of his most supposedly loyal subjects is surely the ultimate indictment of the mass national sycophancy which occurred in the German state – a sycophancy which finally snapped with Hitler's murder; a sycophancy which was the real cause of the Germans' later sense of national guilt.

In the immediate aftermath of Nazism, when Europe was a flood of milling, displaced humanity, the subject of Hitler and the Holocaust aroused almost no controversy. Evil was accepted as evil, as the extent of the man-made disaster which had swept Europe like the Black Death came to be fully appreciated. No one was prepared to argue to the contrary in public. Indeed, maybe understandably, no one seemed to want to think about it. Historians of the early 1950s such as Willi Frischauer,[2] disgusted at the lack of interest and the mock surprise they encountered among the postwar Germans they knew so well, who refused to envisage the carnage they had wittingly allowed, summed up their countrymen's attitude in the simple but telling phrase '*Ich habe nichts davon gewüst*', or 'I knew nothing about it' – 'it' being the Holocaust.

It took a further decade to establish the fact that at least half of the 40 to 50 million dead of the Second World War died as a result of deportation, torture, murder in extermination camps and brutal executions.[3]

As the German historian Eberhard Jäckel wrote, 'Never before had a *state* [The Third Reich] . . . decided that a specific human group, including its aged, its women, its children and its infants, would be killed as quickly as possible – and then carried through the regulations using every possible instrument of state power.'[4]

As the fledgling West German state became economically viable, nurtured by the American Marshall Plan, so new generations of German historians began to challenge the views of the old. Three decades later, by the early 1980s, Germany was once again the outstanding economic power in Europe, and with recovery came the now famous *Historikerstreit* – the fight of the historians.

The central issue of the historical divide remained the question of whether the Holocaust of the Jews was a unique event – for which the German nation was uniquely culpable and uniquely to be stigmatised – or whether other examples of 'ethnic cleansing' made the German guilt less than unique. Those who took the view that the Germans were far from unique wished quite understandably to limit the stigma that was being attached to successive generations of Germans. Their antagonists accused them of 'normalising' the Nazi period and 'trivialising' its crimes against humanity.

The academic debate attracted media attention. Several historians – the most notable being David Irving – claimed that the Holocaust had been grossly exaggerated, and in any case had never been intended by Hitler.

I believe that the focus ought to be not on the question of the uniqueness of the crimes against humanity but on the failure, at almost every level in the nation, to counter the staggering, organised sycophancy that surrounded Hitler.

The German people, resentful at their treatment after the First World

War, might have embraced one of several potential 'Hitlers' during the late 1920s and the 1930s. They were a soft target for the pedlars of rhetoric and fervour playing on their sense of frustrated empire.

But there was nothing unique about defeat, nothing unique about resentment, nothing unique about recession. And it was commonplace for all to happen at the same time. There was nothing unique about psychopathia, personality disorders or rabble-rousers. And, dare I say it, nothing unique about Hitler. Continually to claim such a uniqueness is to come dangerously close to providing an excuse for the sycophancy that sustained him, and to encourage an unhealthy mystique about his abilities. Historians may have emphasised what they choose to see as Hitler's uniqueness simply because he has confounded their limited experience of the vagaries of human nature.

What was seemingly unique, and quite outside the understanding of foreigners, was the thirst of the civilised, cultured Germanic people to hear their aspirations voiced and have their future governed by this crude, strange man – the fact that the Germans took Hitler seriously. But once the odd directness of Hitler's rabble-rousing exposition of Germany's plight in Europe had fascinated the working classes, and once they had been provided with ready scapegoats such as the Jews, Hitler's assumption of power was almost cascade-like in its certainty.

There was, however, absolutely no excuse for the educated German populace – politicians, bankers, financiers, lawyers or industrialists – failing to recognise that Hitler was odd: they had access to Hitler's credo, as expressed in his monumentally repetitive book *Mein Kampf*.

From this they knew that Hitler had a truly weird phobia about syphilis, returning again and again to the subject, devoting almost an entire chapter to relating its horrors. They knew that he had an even greater phobia about Jews. And, more important, they knew that he repudiated both conscience and morality – 'I am freeing man from the restraints of an intelligence that has taken charge, from the dirty and depraving modifications of a chimera known as conscience and morality.'[5]

Put simply, Hitler's credo preached hatred:

'All passivity, all inertia, [is] senseless to life.
The Jewish Christ credo – with its effeminate pity ethic . . .
Unless you are prepared to be pitiless you will get nowhere.
If a people is to become free, it needs pride and willpower, defiance, hate, hate, and once again hate.'[6]

The German people should have known full well the consequences of voting for Hitler as Führer. 'Brutality is respected. Brutality and physical strength. The plain man in the street respects nothing but brutal strength and ruthlessness. We want to be the supporters of the dictatorship of National Reason, of National Brutality and Resolution.'[7]

If they failed to appreciate the true nature of Hitler's credo from *Mein Kampf*, they could hardly have missed the barbarity of his sentiments expressed in public, nor the extraordinary crudity of the language he used to express these sentiments and the curses and filth with which he whipped up his audience – Hitler's 'oral enema', as Rauschning was to call it.[8]

Those who surrounded Hitler and sought power in his wake may have paid scant attention to his ideas, other than their vote-catching appeal. Nevertheless, the German people surely realised the direction in which their nation was being launched – the rebirth of nationalism and the vista of conquest. Euphoric at the heady promise of Germanic superiority, they chose to ignore the consequences and the price, and determinedly opted for war by voting for their Führer.

There is nothing unique about that. It's called human nature.

Human nature has also coloured the story of the death of Hitler, both through the deliberately false testimonies of the survivors from the Bunker and through conscious or unconscious intellectual self-interest on the part of historians. It is exactly because of this that it is doubly important to use to its maximum advantage every piece of hard scientific evidence that exists, rather than rely on such tainted testimonies.

In the cases of Hitler and Eva Braun, the views of appropriately qualified scientists were not sought, not recorded, or studiously ignored by politicians and historians alike – especially when these views were inexpedient.

In the case of Martin Bormann's remains, scientific evidence was sought and a summary of the results was disseminated. Unfortunately, however, the full facts were not presented, and scientific debate was discouraged. The quality of the subsequent conclusions suffered in consequence; the fraud that had been perpetrated was missed. Thus political expediency plagued even that investigation too.

Without a systematic approach that avoids undue outside influences and establishes minimal standards, both of investigation and of scientific debate, it is more than likely that historians will be duped by further forensic frauds.

But, given the high political stakes and desperate opportunities that obtained in Berlin at the end of the Second World War, I doubt that there will ever be such a plethora of forensic fraud carried out in more dramatic circumstances, for such pressing, disparate reasons – and with such dramatic success that half a century went by before it was exposed.

Further Reading

The following suggestions are mostly confined to the English language, and are meant to introduce the reader to select texts which amount to only a very small proportion of the immense literature now available.

Even though showing its age, the best overall and easily available biography of Hitler remains Alan Bullock's *Hitler: A Study in Tyranny*, rev. edition, London 1964.

The problems that Germans have faced in coping with their history are best understood by reading Richard Evans's *In Hitler's Shadow*, New York/London 1989; and Charles Maier's *The Unmasterable Past: History, Holocaust and German National Identity*, Cambridge, Mass. 1988.

The difficulties which historians have encountered in researching the mountains of documentary evidence – inadequately, unwillingly catalogued, and sometimes not at all! – are recorded in two works of interest: Ian Kershaw's *The Nazi Dictatorship. Problems and Perspectives of Interpretation*, 2nd edition, London 1989; and John Farquason's *Explaining Hitler's Germany*, London 1983.

Despite an overall reluctance to admit Hitler's direct involvement in any programme envisaged for the future Reich, there remain some works which give such a balance: Klaus Hildebrand's *The Third Reich*, London 1984; and Klaus Dietrich Bracher's 'The Role of Hitler: Perspectives of Interpretation' in Walter Laquer (ed.), *Fascism – A Reader's Guide*, Harmondsworth 1979.

Gerald Fleming's *Hitler and the Final Solution*, Oxford 1986, has finally nailed the myth that the extermination programme itself grew piecemeal without Hitler's full knowledge. Going to many, varied documentary sources for his evidence on Hitler's true role in the Holocaust, his book is a self-evident must.

The overall chaos and lack of governmental and legal structure to the Weimar Republic, which allowed for its ready manipulation, is best covered by Jane Caplan's, *Government without Administration, State and Civil Service in Weimar and Nazi Germany*, Oxford 1988, whereas the corrosive effect of Hitler's misuse of the Weimer system comes out best in Martin Broszat's, *The Hitler State*, London 1981.

Hitler's attraction for the German industrialists and their support for what they saw as a ready charismatic puppet, working to their own self-interests, is brought up to date by Peter Hayes's, *Industry and Ideology, IG Farben in the Nazi Era*, Cambridge 1987.

The belated awareness of the Wermacht and their own sycophantic support for a leader whom they saw as appreciative of their role and importance is best prepared by Wilhelm Diest's, *The Wermacht and German Rearmament*, London 1981; and by Klaus-Jurgen Müller's, *Army, Politics and Society in Germany 1933–45*, Manchester 1984.

Hardly surprisingly there are no effective, really first-rate psychoanalyses of power, although interesting pragmatic analyses are made by Robert Waite in *The Psychopathic God, Adolf Hitler*, New York 1977; Rudolf Binion, *Hitler among the Germans*, New York 1976; and Eberhard Jäckel, *Hitler in History*, Hanover/London 1984.

Perhaps the most pertinent studies are the works on the Germanic public perception of Hitler as a 'representative individual within German Society'. In other words 'one of us', a man of the people. These include J. P. Stern's, *Hitler, The Führer and the People*, London 1975 and Lothar Kettenacker, 'Hitler's Impact on the Middle Class' in David Welch (ed.) *Nazi Propaganda: The Power and the Limitations*, London 1983.

Historians have relatively recently realised the significance of a work which revealed the protective effect of being surrounded by opportunistic sycophants, who then outdid everyone in support of their chosen charismatic leader, encouraging a climate of sycophancy. This was the anatomy of what was called Charismatic Leadership. This viewpoint was originally expressed by Max Weber in *Economy and Society*, ed. Günther Roth and Claus Wittrich, New York 1968, pp. 241–54, 264–71, 1111–57.

It has been applied specifically to Hitler by M. Rainer Lepsius, 'Charismatic Leadership: Max Weber's Model and its Applicability to the Role of Hitler' in Carl Friedrich Graumann and Serge Moscovici (eds.) *Changing Concepts in Leadership*, New York 1986, and further popularised by Ian Kershaw's, *Hitler*, London 1991.

The literature on Eva Braun is virtually non-existent or ought to be. No book can be recommended. In similar fashion the very nature of the extravagant, fanciful claims surrounding Martin Bormann have resulted in a plethora of hardly credible claims and emotional reference. Caution has to be expressed. For those who do read German, I recommend Artur Axmann's own article in *Stern* magazine (1965, No. 19) *'Meine Flucht mit Bormann'* (My Flight with Bormann) and Joachim Fest's, *'Martin Bormann, "Die braune Eminenz"'* in *Das Geschicht des dritten Reiches*, Munich 1963.

References

1: Hitler – the Myth and the Man

1 Trevor-Roper, Hugh, Introduction to the 'Testament of Adolf Hitler', *Hitler/Bormann Documents Feb.–April 1945*, by Francis Jesmond (London: Cassell & Co., 1961)

2 Mann, Golo, *History of Germany since 1789* (London: Chatto, 1968)

3 Hecker, J. F. C., *Die Tanzwut: Eine Krankheit in Mittel Alte* (Berlin, 1832)

4 Speer, Albert, personal communication

5 KTBOKW 1 v 2 p. 170

6 Fest, Joachim, *Hitler* (London: Weidenfeld & Nicolson, 1974 or Harmondsworth: Penguin, 1977), p. 727

7 Irving, David, *Hitler's War 1939–42* (London: Macmillan, 1983), p. 600

8 Ibid., p. 750

9 Speer, Albert, personal conversation

10 Zoller, Albert, *Hitler Privat* (Düsseldorf, 1949), p. 150

11 Irving, op. cit., p. 750

12 Fest, op. cit., p. 727

13 Speer, Albert, personal communication

14 Ibid.

15 O'Donnell, James P., *The Berlin Bunker* (London: Dent, 1979), p. 29

16 Ibid., pp. 136–7

17 Ibid., p. 31

18 Irving, David, *Adolf Hitler: The Medical Diaries: The Private Diaries of Dr Theo Morell* (London: Sidgwick & Jackson, 1983), p. 50

19 Irving, *Hitler's War*, p. 257

20 Speer, Albert, personal communication

21 Irving, *Hitler's War*

22 Irving, *Adolf Hitler: The Medical Diaries*, p. 70

23 Irving, *Hitler's War*, p. 249

24 US National Archives

25 Irving, *Hitler's War*, p. 712

2: The Mind of Adolf Hitler

1 Trevor-Roper, Hugh, *Hitler Directs his War* (New York, 1950), p. 22

2 Trevor-Roper, Hugh, *Hitler's Table Talk* (London, 1953), p. 316

3 Tschuppik, Karl, *Das Tagebuch*, vol. 498 (1927), p. 125

4 Ibid., vol. 526 (1934), p. 15

5 Rötter, Hans Dietrich, *Hitler: The Destruction of the Personality* (Neckergemun, 1965), p. 121

6 Taylor, A. J. P., *The Origins of the Second World War* (London: Hamish Hamilton, 1961), quoted in Langer, Walter, *The Mind of Adolf Hitler* (London: Secker & Warburg, 1973), p. 220

7 Trevor-Roper, Hugh, *The Last Days of Hitler* (London: Macmillan, 1953)

8 Bullock, Alan, foreword to Jetzinger, Franz, *Hitler's Youth* (London, 1958)

9 Langer, Walter, *The Mind of Adolf Hitler* (London: Secker & Warburg, 1973), pp. 221–2

10 Bracher, Karl Dietrich, *Die Aufslözung der Weimarer Republik: Einer*

Studie zum Problem des Machverfalls der Demokratie (Stuttgart, 1957); also Langer, op. cit., p. 222

11 Langer, op. cit., p. 144

12 Ibid.

13 Irving, *Adolf Hitler: The Medical Diaries*, p. 34

14 Langer, op. cit., p. 233

15 Ibid., p. 233

16 Langer, op. cit., p. 223

17 Speer, Albert, personal conversation

18 Speer, Albert, *Spandau: The Secret Diaries* (London: Collins, 1976), p. 346, and personal conversation

19 Langer, op. cit., p. 33

20 Ibid.

21 Ibid., p. 32

22 Tschuppik, Karl, op. cit., p. 15

23 Flanner, Janet, *An American in Paris* (New York: Simon & Schuster, 1940)

24 Rauschning, Hermann, *Gespräche mit Hitler* (New York: Europa Verlag, 1940); quoted by Langer, op. cit., p. 99

25 Boldt, Gerhard, *Die Letzten Tage der Reichskanzlei* (Hamburg: Rowohlt, 1947), p. 15

26 Fest, op. cit., p. 4

27 Speer, personal conversation and op. cit., p. 346

28 Speer, Albert, personal conversation

29 Langer, op. cit., p. 29

30 Ibid., p. 30

31 Ibid., p. 76

32 Ibid.; also von Wiegand, Karl, 'Hitler foresees his end', *The Cosmopolitan*, May 1939

33 Hanisch, Reinhold, 'I was Hitler's buddy', *New Republic*, 1 April 1939, pp. 239–42; 12 April 1939, pp. 270–2; 19 April 1939, pp. 297–300

34 Langer, op. cit., p. 79

35 Olden, Rudolf, *Hitler the Pawn* (London: 1936), pp. 70–1

36 Fest, op. cit., p. 46

37 Speer, Albert, personal communication

38 Langer, op. cit., p. 73

39 Trevor-Roper, Hugh, *The Last Days of Hitler*, p. 274

40 Langer, op. cit., p. 115

41 Kasanin, J. 'The acute schizoaffective psychoses', *American Journal of Psychiatry*, 13 (1933), pp. 97–126

42 Cleckley, Hervey, *The Mask of Sanity* (St Louis: Mosby, 4th edn, 1964)

43 Kendler et al., 1981

44 Otto Strasser, *Aufbau der Deutschen Sozialismus* (Prague: Heinrich Grunow, 1936)

45 Ludecke, Kurt Georg W., *I Knew Hitler* (New York: Scribner's, 1937); also Langer, op. cit., p. 70

46 See, for example, his valet Heinz Linge's testimony in *News of the World*, 23 October 1955

47 Speer, Albert, *Inside the Third Reich* (London: Weidenfeld & Nicolson, 1970 or Sphere, 1971), p. 402

48 Speer, Albert, personal conversation

49 Speer, op. cit., p. 640

50 Langer, op. cit., p. 212

51 Ibid., p. 210

52 Ibid., p. 212

53 Ibid.

54 Ibid., p. 211

55 Ibid., p. 212

56 Ibid.

57 Speer, op. cit., p. 631

3: Overture to Götterdämmerung

 1 Elisabeth Barker, *Churchill and Eden at War* (London: Macmillan, 1978), p. 236

 2 Ibid.

 3 Ibid.

 4 Hull, Cordell, *Memoirs* (London: Hodder & Stoughton, 1948), p. 1451

 5 Hull, op. cit.

 6 Cadogan, Sir Edward, *The Diaries of Sir Edward Cadogan OM, 1938–1945*, ed. David Dilks (London: Cassell, 1971), p. 717

 7 Gilbert, Martin, *The Second World War* (London: Weidenfeld & Nicolson, 1989), p. 657

 8 Ibid., p. 658

 9 Ibid., p. 658

10 Ibid., p. 667

11 Hamilton, Nigel, *Monty: the Field Marshal, 1944–1976* (London: Hamish Hamilton, 1986), p. 441

12 ACICGS(0)/6/9

13 Larabee, Eric, *Commander in Chief* (London: André Deutsch, 1987), p. 476

14 Hamilton, Nigel, *Monty: The Final Years* (London: Hamish Hamilton, 1986), p. 445

15 Matloff, Maurice, *Strategic Planning for Coalition Warfare*, pp. 253–4

16 Cable END 18710 of 7 April 1945

17 Diary of Chester Hansen, entry for 12 April 1945

18 Ibid., entry for 16 April 1945

19 Hamilton, op. cit., p. 247

20 Ibid., p. 500

21 Chaney, Otto P., Jnr, *Zhukov* (Newton Abbot: David & Charles, 1972)

22 Shtemenko, S. M., *Soviet General Staff at War* (Moscow: Progress Publishers, 1970), p. 319

23 Koniev, Ivan S., *Year of Victory* (Moscow: Progress Publishers, 1969), p. 79; Zhukov, Georgi Konstantinovich, *The Memoirs of Marshal Zhukov* (London: Cape, 1971), pp. 587–9

24 Shtemenko, op. cit., pp. 304–5

25 Ziemke, Earl Frederick, *The Battle for Berlin: End of the Third Reich* (London: Macdonald, 1969), p. 64; Seaton, Albert, *The Russo-German War 1941–1945* (London: Barker, 1971), pp. 562–5

26 Zhukov, op. cit., pp. 589–90

27 Erickson, John, *The Road to Berlin* (London: Weidenfeld & Nicolson, 1983), pp. 535–7

28 Novikov, 'The Airforces in the Berlin Operation', *Soviet Military History Journal*, May 1945

29 Zhukov, op. cit., p. 593

30 Tully, A., *Berlin: Story of a Battle* (Simon & Schuster, 1963), p. 102; Tieke, Willhelm, *Das Ende zwischen Oder und Elbe, Der Kampf um Berlin* (Stuttgart: Motorbuch Verlag, 1981), pp. 76–9, 98

31 Zander, op. cit., p. 593

32 Quoted in John Keegan, *The Second World War* (London: Hutchinson, 1989), p. 512

33 Willemer, William, *The German Defence of Berlin* (Berlin: HQ USAR-EUR, 1953), p. 27

34 Ibid., p. 22

35 Ibid., pp. 28–31

36 Tieke, op. cit., p. 192

37 *Great Patriotic War of the Soviet Union, 1941–5* (Moscow: Progress Publishers, 1969), pp. 374–5

38 Heinrici, manuscript quoted in Goszotony, Peter, 'Der Kampf um

Berlin', in *Augenzeugberichten* (Düsseldorf: Deutscher Taschenbuch, 1970), pp. 153–6

39 Peter Slowe and Richard Woods, *Battlefield Berlin: Siege, Surrender, Occupation, 1945* (London: Robert Hale, 1988), p. 512

40 Koniev, op. cit., pp. 105–6

41 Ibid.

42 Ziemke, Earl, *Battle for Berlin* (London: Purnell, 1968), p. 84

43 Rocolle, Pierre, *Götterdämmerung – la prise de Berlin* (Indo-China, 1954)

44 Ziemke, op. cit., p. 84

45 Gosztony, Peter, *Der Kampf um Berlin 1945 in Augenzeugen Berichten* (Düsseldorf, Karl Rauch, 1970), pp. 228–9

46 Zhukov, op. cit.

47 Boldt, op. cit., p. 61

48 Slowe and Woods, op. cit., pp. 72–3

49 Ibid., p. 73

50 Rocolle, op. cit., p. 44

51 Kuby, Erich, *The Russians and Berlin, 1945* (New York: Hell & Wang, 1964 or London: Heinemann, 1968), p. 111

52 Thorwald, Jurgen, *Das Ende an der Elbe* (Stuttgart: Steingruben Verlag, 1950), p. 94

53 Rocolle, op. cit., pp. 34–5

54 Skorodomov, N., 'Manoeuvres of 12th Guards Tank Corps in the Berlin Operation', *Soviet Military History Journal*, March 1978

55 Charles Dahman, personal conversation

56 Le Tissier, Tony, *The Battle of Berlin, 1945* (London: Cape, 1988), p. 112

57 Thorwald, op. cit.

58 Chuikov, Vasilii Ivanovich, *The End of the Third Reich* (Moscow: Progress Publishers, 1969 or London: MacGibbon & Kee 1967 or Panther 1969), p. 184; Voitov personal communication

59 Chuikov, op. cit., p. 269

60 Thorwald, op. cit., p. 165

61 Rocolle, op. cit., p. 47

62 Thorwald, op. cit., p. 179

63 Chuikov, op. cit., p. 184

64 Koniev, op. cit., p. 185

65 Dragunsky, David, *A Soldier's Life* (Moscow: Progress Publishers, 1977), p. 104

66 Thorwald, op. cit., pp. 182–3

67 Weidling, Helmuth, *Der Todeskampf der Faschistischen Clique in Berlin aus der Errinerung des Generals Weidling*, Wehrwissenschaftlische Rundschau, 1962

4: The Bunker

1 Voitov, Colonel A., personal communication

2 Fest, op. cit., p. 730.

3 Warimont, Walter, *Im Hauptquartier der Deutschen Wehrmacht, 1939 bis 1945* (Frankfurt: Grundlagen Formen Gestalten, 1964)

4 O'Donnell, op. cit., p. 46.

5 Ibid., p. 43

6 Ibid., p. 26

7 Speer, Albert, personal communication

8 Ibid.

9 Fest, op. cit., p. 729

10 Trevor-Roper, *Last Days of Hitler* (5th edn), p. 172

11 Speer, 1971 op. cit., pp. 349–50

12 Speer, Albert, personal conversation

13 Boldt, op. cit., p. 61

14 Speer, Albert, personal conversation

15 Reiman, Victor, *The Man who Created Hitler* (William Kimber, 1971), p. 318

16 Galante, Pierre and Silianoff, Eugène, *Last Witnesses in the Bunker* (London: Sidgwick & Jackson, 1989), p. 10

17 O'Donnell, op. cit., p. 206

18 Ibid.

19 Galante and Silianoff, op. cit., p. 5

20 O'Donnell, op. cit., p. 207

21 Voitov, Colonel A., personal communication

22 O'Donnell, op. cit., p. 209

23 Galante and Silianoff, op. cit., p. 26

24 Trevor-Roper, *Last Days of Hitler* (5th edn), pp. 234–5

5: The Death of Hitler

1 Trevor-Roper, Hugh, *The Last Days of Hitler* (London: Macmillan, 3rd edn, 1956), p. xiv

2 Ibid., p. 220

3 Ibid., p. xliii

4 Maximova, Ella, quoting from Operation Myth Soviet Archives

5 Trevor-Roper, Hugh, *The Last Days of Hitler* (London: Macmillan, 4th edn, 1971), p. 277

6 In Galante and Silianoff, op. cit.

7 Trevor-Roper, *Last Days of Hitler* (5th edn), pp. 220–1

8 O'Donnell, op. cit., pp. 181–2

9 Ibid., p. 182

10 Trevor-Roper, Hugh, *The Last Days of Hitler* (London: Macmillan, 3rd edn, 1956), p. xxxii

11 *Observer*, 9 October 1955

12 Galante and Silianoff, op. cit., p. 16

13 Trevor-Roper, Hugh, Introduction to the 'Testament of Adolf Hitler', *Hitler/Bormann Documents Feb.–April 1945* by Francis Jesmond (London: Cassell & Co., 1961)

14 Trevor-Roper, *The Last Days of Hitler* (3rd edn), p. 199

15 Ibid., p. 217

16 Semler, R., *Goebbels: The Man Next to Hitler* (Westhouse, 1947), p. 188

17 O'Donnell, op. cit., pp. 140–1

18 Ibid., p. 180

19 O'Donnell, op. cit., p. 181

20 Galante and Silianoff, op. cit., p. 21

21 Ibid.

22 Ibid.

23 *News of the World*, 23 October 1955

24 Ibid.

25 O'Donnell, op. cit., p. 179

26 Ibid., p. 181

27 *News of the World*, 23 October 1955

28 O'Donnell, op. cit., p. 184

29 Ibid.

30 *News of the World*, 23 October 1955

31 O'Donnell, op. cit., p. 184

32 Galante and Silianoff, op. cit., p. 23

33 O'Donnell, p. 183

34 Galante and Silianoff, op. cit., pp. 4–5

35 O'Donnell, op. cit., p. 183

36 Ibid., p. 183

37 O'Donnell, op. cit., p. 185

38 Günsche, in O'Donnell, op. cit., p. 185

39 O'Donnell, op. cit., p. 185

40 Heusermann, Käthe, personal conversation

6: The Funeral and Burial of Hitler and Eva Braun

1 *News of the World*, 23 October 1955

2 Trevor-Roper, Hugh, *Last Days of Hitler* (5th edn), p. 222

3 O'Donnell, op. cit., p. 187

4 Trevor-Roper, *Last Days of Hitler* (5th edn), p. 223

5 Ibid., p. 224

6 Ibid., p. 219

7 O'Donnell, op. cit., p. 192

8 Ibid.

9 O'Donnell, op. cit., p. 191

10 Trevor-Roper, *Last Days of Hitler* (5th edn), p. 226

11 O'Donnell, op. cit., p. 193

12 Trevor-Roper, *Last Days of Hitler* (5th edn), p. 225

13 Ibid., pp. xxxvii–xxxviii

14 Ibid., p. xxxiii

15 Ibid., p. xli

16 Ibid., p. lvii

17 McKinley, J., 'Bone fragment size and weights of bone in cremations', *International Journal of Osteo Archaeology*, vol. 283–7, 1993

7: The Discovery of the Corpses – Forensic Fraud

1 Bezymenski, Lev, *The Death of Adolf Hitler: Unknown Documents from Soviet Archives* (London: Michael Joseph, 1968), p. 4

2 Report of Lieutenant Alexei Panassov, 5 May 1945, Russian State Archives; also Bezymenski, op. cit., p. 6

3 Reports of Commission, Russian State Archives; also Bezymenski, op. cit., p. 82

4 Voitov, Colonel A., personal communication

5 Ibid.

6 Report of Alperovich, Russian State Archives; also Bezymenski, op. cit., pp. 80–2

7 Bezymenski, op. cit., p. 30

8 Russian State Archives

9 Bezymenski, op. cit., p. 88

10 Ibid.

11 Ibid., p. 42

12 Ibid., pp. 63–4

13 Ibid., pp. 64–5

14 Russian State Archives and Bezymenski, op. cit., p. 65

15 Bezymenski, op. cit., pp. 94–9

16 Ibid., pp. 94–5

17 Ibid., pp. 38–9

18 Ibid., p. 39

19 Ibid., p. 40

20 Ibid., p. 95

21 Ibid., pp. 103–7

22 Ibid., pp. 99–103

23 Ibid., p. 100

24 Ibid., pp. 31–2

25 O'Donnell, op. cit., p. 299

26 Bezymenski, op. cit., p. 33

27 Ibid., pp. 35–7

28 Russian State Archives; also Bezymenski, op. cit., pp. 110–14

29 Bezymenski, op. cit., p. 113

30 Ibid., p. 112

31 Ibid., p. 114

32 Ibid., p. 111

33 Ibid., pp. 111–12

34 Ibid., p. 114

35 Heusermann, Käthe, personal conversation

36 Bezymenski, op. cit., p. 54

37 Heusermann, Käthe, personal conversation

38 Ibid.

39 Bezymenski, op. cit., p. 56

40 Rzhevskaya, Yeléna, *Hitlers Ende ohne Mythos* (Berlin: Deutsche Militar Verlag, 1967), pp. 90ff. (original in Russian, 1965)

41 Ibid.

42 Kempner, R. M. W., *Das Dritte Reich im Kreuzverkehr* (Munich: Beachte Verlag, 1969)

43 Bezymenski, op. cit., p. 56

44 Ibid., p. 55

45 Heusermann, Käthe, personal conversation

46 Ibid.

47 Bezymenski, op. cit., p. 56

48 Mant, Keith, personal conversation

49 Bezymenski, op. cit., pp. 44–51

50 Voitov, Colonel A., personal communication

51 Russian State Archives

52 Sognnaes, op. cit., 1973, p. 48

53 Bezymenski, op. cit., between p. 54 and p. 55

54 Ibid., pp. 54–5

55 Heusermann, Käthe, personal communication

56 Bezymenski, op. cit., pp. 56–7

57 Ibid., illustration facing p. 54, and Russian State Archives

58 Bezymenski, op. cit., p. 47

59 Ibid., pp. 45–6

60 Luntz, Lester, personal communication

8: Poisoning by Cyanide – Forensic Fraud No. 2

1 Troup and Ballantyne, quoted in Bryan Ballantyne and Timothy C. Marrs (eds.), *Clinical and Experimental Toxicology of Cyanides* (Oxford: Butterworth & Heinemann, 1992)

2 Hallstrøm, F. and Muller, K. O., *Acta Pharmacol* 1 (1945), p. 18, p. 282

3 Purser, D. A., Grimshaw, P. and Berill, K. P., *Arch Environ Health*, 39, pp. 396–400

4 Rylands, J. M., *Neuropharmacology*, 21 (1982), pp. 1181–5

5 Troup and Ballantyne, op. cit., p. 230, p. 214 and Curry, *Poison Deletion in the Human Organism* (Springfield, Ill.: 1976), p. 98

6 Dowling, Dr Sheila, personal conversation

7 Troup and Ballantyne, op. cit., p. 23

8 Ballantyne, B., *Journal of the Forensic Science Society*, 15 (1975), pp. 51–6

9 Russian State Archives

10 Mayes, R. W. (toxicologist, RAF Halton), personal conversation

11 Bezymenski, op. cit., p. 49

12 Simpson, Keith, *Taylor's Principles and Practices of Jurisprudence*, (London: Churchill, 1965)

13 For an indication on how access to this material was obtained, see the Acknowledgements

14 O'Donnell, op. cit., p. 286

15 McCowan, John, manuscript in author's possession, and personal conversation

16 Busuttil, Tony, personal conversation

9: The Bunker Revisited

1 Nerinegun, *Eva Braun: Hitler's Mistress* (London: Frewin, 1968)

2 Heusermann, Käthe, personal conversation

3 Trevor-Roper, *Last Days of Hitler* (5th edn), pp. 149–50

4 O'Donnell, op. cit., p. 138

5 *News of the World*, 23 October 1955

10: Break-out

1 Tully, op. cit., pp. 277–80

2 Tieke, op. cit., pp. 415, 419

3 Ibid., p. 386

4 Chuikov, op. cit., pp. 205–37

5 Thorwald, op. cit., p. 190

6 Ibid., p. 205

7 O'Donnell, op. cit., p. 215

8 Ibid., p. 215

9 Ibid., p. 219

10 Ibid., p. 220

11 Ibid., p. 225

12 Ibid., p. 226 fn

13 Ibid., p. 233

14 Ibid., p. 218

15 Ibid., p. 236

16 Ibid., p. 231

17 Trevor-Roper, *Last Days of Hitler* (5th edn), p. 238

18 O'Donnell, op. cit.

19 Ibid.

20 Ibid.

21 Ibid., p. 242

22 Ibid., p. 241

23 *Observer*, 9 October 1955

24 O'Donnell, op. cit., p. 242

25 Trevor-Roper, *Last Days of Hitler* (5th edn), p. xxxii

26 O'Donnell, op. cit., p. 244

27 Trevor-Roper, *Last Days of Hitler* (5th edn), p. 238

28 O'Donnell, op. cit., p. 246

29 Ibid., p. 248

30 Trevor-Roper, *Last Days of Hitler* (5th edn), p. 238

31 O'Donnell, op. cit., p. 249

11: Aftermath – Intrigue and Disinformation

1 Bezymenski, Lev, *Die letzten Notizen von Martin Bormann* (Stuttgart, 1974)

2 *Sunday Times*, 14 May 1967

3 *Daily Express*, 3 February 1952

4 *Evening Standard*, 7 October 1960

5 *Daily Herald*, 30 September 1960

6 *Evening Standard*, 29 September 1960

7 *Daily Telegraph*, 15 May 1961

8 *Morning Star*, 17 February 1966

9 *Daily Mail*, 2 June 1961

10 *Daily Sketch*, 1 October 1961

11 *Daily Telegraph*, 15 July 1964

12 *Guardian*, 14 July 1964

13 *Sunday Times*, 9 August 1964

14 Ibid.

15 *The Times*, 13 August 1964

16 Farago, Ladislas, *Aftermath: Martin Bormann and the Fourth Reich* (London: Hodder & Stoughton, 1974 edn), p. 308

17 Ibid., p. 309–11

18 *The Times*, 13 May 1965

19 *Guardian*, March 1967

20 *Daily Telegraph*, 6 October 1967

21 *Sunday Times*, 6 August 1967

22 Quoted in Posner, Gerald L., and Ware, John, *Mengele: The Complete Story* (London: Queen Anne Press, 1986), p. 128

23 Posner and Ware, op. cit., p. 129

24 *Sunday Times*, 17 December 1972

25 Ibid.

26 Ibid.

27 Farago, op. cit., p. 10

28 Posner and Ware, op. cit., p. 247

29 Ibid., p. 182

30 Ibid., p. 248

31 Ibid., p. 191

32 Ibid., pp. 112–13

33 Ibid., p. 113

34 Ibid., p. 98

35 Ibid.

36 Ibid., p. 99

37 Ibid., pp. 99–100, citing a memorandum from Nicerfero Alcarcon to the Minister of the Navy, 18 April 1946; file no. CF-OP 2315, Federal Coordinancion archives. Buenos Aires

38 Posner and Ware, op. cit., p. 100

39 *Daily Telegraph*, 4 February 1992

12: **Digging up the Past**

 1 Farago, op. cit., p. 356

 2 Ibid., p. 357

 3 Ibid., p. 358

 4 *The Times*, 21 July 1965

 5 Farago, op. cit., p. 365

 6 Ibid., p. 365

 7 Ibid., p. 23

 8 Ibid., p. 28

 9 Ibid., p. 27

10 Ibid., p. 29

11 Ibid., p. 30fn, and personal conversation

12 Exhibit 16, final report on Martin Bormann, 4 April 1973, Frankfurt State Prosecution Office

13 Farago, op. cit., p. 438

14 Sognnaes, Reidar F., *Annals of Legal Medicine*, 1976, pp. 173–201, and 1977, pp. 228–35

15 McCowan, John, manuscript in author's possession

16 Heusermann, Käthe, personal conversation

17 Sognnaes, op. cit.

18 Speer, Albert, personal conversation

19 Sognnaes, op. cit.

20 Sognnaes, Reidar F., personal conversation

21 Ibid.

22 Sognnaes, op. cit.

23 Sognnaes, op. cit. Käthe Heusermann did claim at one time, however, that it was typical of Blaschke's own work. Echtmann became so confused – or so eager to help match the data – that he even suggested that the maxillary bridge described by Sognnaes was in fact probably in the *lower* jaw.

24 Heusermann, Käthe, personal conversation

25 Farago, Ladislas, personal conversation

26 Sognnaes, Reidar F., personal conversation. Käthe Heusermann described this bridge to me as possibly Blaschke's.

27 Von Lang, Joachim, *The Secretary* (Ohio University Press, 1981), p. 351

28 Frankfurt Records of Criminal Action against Martin Bormann, State Prosecution Office. Sheet 745. Documents in Evidence, 1974

13: The Paraguay Assumption

1 Archivos del Terror, Paraguay, c/o Rosa Pilau, director

2 The US government has donated $40,000 for microfiching the records of the Stroessner regime, on the understanding that the USA will provide the equipment and its operators.

3 Archivos del Terror, Paraguay

4 Farago, op. cit., p. 60

5 Personal conversation with Andrea Machain (US-based Paraguayan journalist)

6 Nickson, Andrew, research note, University of New Mexico, in the possession of the author

7 Associated Press report of 19 February 1993 by Pedro Servin, ref. BC Paraguay Police Files No. 0495

8 Report, 24 August 1961, West German intelligence, quoted in report of Propochuk

9 Associated Press, 24 February 1993

10 AFP press-agency report 242246, February 1993

11 *Jewish Chronicle*, 5 March 1993

12 *Diario Noticias*, 28 February 1993

13 Ibid.

14 Andrea Machain, and Mrs Stein, Paraguayan Embassy, London

15 Neither the skeleton of the alleged Ludwig Stumpfegger nor that of the alleged Martin Bormann were complete. Surprisingly, some of the spinal bones were missing. The estimate of the heights of the skeletons was made by an anthropological index using the measurements of the long bones. Surprisingly, no attempt was made to ascertain if the skull of either individual matched the cervical vertebra, especially, of the skeletons concerned. Dr Spengler, the forensic scientist approached to estimate the age of the bones, was given no explanation as to why he had only been given partial skeletons.

14: Perspectives and Conclusions

1 Khrushchev, Nikita, *Khrushchev Remembers* (London: Strobe Talbot, 1971), p. 284

2 Frischauer, Willi, *Himmler* (London: Odhams Press, 1953)

3 Bullock, Alan, *Hitler: A Study in Tyranny* (London: Odhams, 1952), and *Stalin* (London: Harper Collins, 1991)

4 *Die Zeit*, 12 September 1986

5 Langer, op. cit., p. 190

6 Ibid., p. 193

7 Ibid.

8 Ibid., p. 205

Appendix: The Skull – Showing Cranial Bones and Teeth

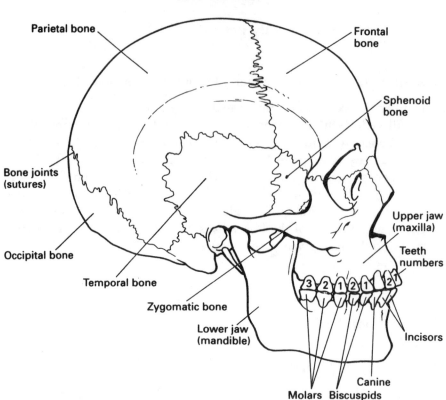

The bones and teeth in the human skull.

Index

Index